French Music and Jazz

French concert music and jazz often enjoyed a special creative exchange across the period 1900–1965. French modernist composers were particularly receptive to early African-American jazz during the interwar years, and American jazz musicians, especially those concerned with modal jazz in the 1950s and early 1960s, exhibited a distinct affinity with French musical impressionism. But despite a general, if contested, interest in the cultural interplay of classical music and jazz, few writers have probed the specific French music–jazz relationship in depth. In this book, Deborah Mawer sets such musical interplay within its historical-cultural and critical-analytical contexts, offering a detailed yet accessible account of both French and American perspectives. Blending intertextuality with more precise borrowing techniques, Mawer presents case studies on the musical interactions of a wide range of composers and performers, including Debussy, Satie, Milhaud, Ravel, Jack Hylton, George Russell, Bill Evans and Dave Brubeck.

DEBORAH MAWER is Research Professor of Music at Birmingham Conservatoire, Birmingham City University. Her books include *The Ballets of Maurice Ravel: Creation and Interpretation* (2006), *Darius Milhaud: Modality and Structure in Music of the 1920s* (1997), *Ravel Studies* (Cambridge, 2010) and *The Cambridge Companion to Ravel* (Cambridge, 2000). Her articles and reviews, also encompassing jazz and dance, have appeared in a variety of books and journals, including the *Journal of the Royal Musical Association*, *Twentieth-Century Music*, *Music & Letters*, *Opera Quarterly*, *Music Theory Online* and *Music Analysis*. In 2008 she was awarded a prestigious National Teaching Fellowship.

Music Since 1900

GENERAL EDITOR Arnold Whittall

This series – formerly Music in the Twentieth Century – offers a wide perspective on music and musical life since the end of the nineteenth century. Books included range from historical and biographical studies concentrating particularly on the context and circumstances in which composers were writing, to analytical and critical studies concerned with the nature of musical language and questions of compositional process. The importance given to context will also be reflected in studies dealing with, for example, the patronage, publishing and promotion of new music, and in accounts of the musical life of particular countries.

Titles in the series

Jonathan Cross
The Stravinsky Legacy

Michael Nyman
Experimental Music: Cage and Beyond

Jennifer Doctor
The BBC and Ultra-Modern Music, 1922–1936

Robert Adlington
The Music of Harrison Birtwistle

Keith Potter
Four Musical Minimalists: La Monte Young, Terry Riley, Steve Reich, Philip Glass

Carlo Caballero
Fauré and French Musical Aesthetics

Peter Burt
The Music of Toru Takemitsu

David Clarke
The Music and Thought of Michael Tippett: Modern Times and Metaphysics

M. J. Grant
Serial Music, Serial Aesthetics: Compositional Theory in Post-War Europe

Philip Rupprecht
Britten's Musical Language

Mark Carroll
Music and Ideology in Cold War Europe

Adrian Thomas
Polish Music since Szymanowski

J. P. E. Harper-Scott
Edward Elgar, Modernist

French Music and Jazz in Conversation

From Debussy to Brubeck

Deborah Mawer

CAMBRIDGE
UNIVERSITY PRESS

CAMBRIDGE
UNIVERSITY PRESS

University Printing House, Cambridge CB2 8BS, United Kingdom

Cambridge University Press is part of the University of Cambridge.

It furthers the University's mission by disseminating knowledge in the pursuit of education, learning and research at the highest international levels of excellence.

www.cambridge.org
Information on this title: www.cambridge.org/9781316633878

© Deborah Mawer 2014

First published 2014
First paperback edition 2016

A catalogue record for this publication is available from the British Library

Library of Congress Cataloguing in Publication data
Mawer, Deborah, 1961– author.
French music and jazz in conversation : from Debussy to Brubeck / Deborah Mawer.
    pages   cm. – (Music since 1900)
ISBN 978-1-107-03753-3 (hardback)
1. Music – France – 20th century – History and criticism.   2. Jazz – History and criticism.   I. Title.
ML270.5.M39   2014
781.68′1650944–dc23

                                                                2014025967

ISBN 978-1-107-03753-3 Hardback
ISBN 978-1-316-63387-8 Paperback

For Ron, Michael and Alex

Contents

Figures

Tables

Acknowledgements

The ideas behind this book have been in gestation across an extended time span and there are many people whom I am very pleased to thank. My interest in the interplay between French music and jazz was first ignited in the late 1970s by Victor Fox, a most enlightened conductor of the Manchester Youth Orchestra, who programmed Milhaud's *La Création du monde*. As the principal viola player, my services were redundant since the viola line is assumed by the alto saxophone. Forced to sit out and listen I was, however, captivated by this music, which later became the focus of my doctorate at King's College London, supervised by Arnold Whittall, and which also led to a fascination with early African-American 'hot' jazz. Some twenty-five years on, it is a real pleasure to be working with Arnold again in his capacity as Series Editor, and I appreciate the insights that he has brought to this project.

I acknowledge the substantial support of the research process provided by various libraries (including the British Library and the Bibliothèque nationale de France), archives (including the Brubeck Collection, University of the Pacific; the Jack Hylton Archive, Lancaster University; and The Finnish Jazz and Pop Archive) and international conferences (held in Dublin, Helsinki, Lancaster, Leeds, London, Montreal and Paris). I am particularly indebted to the many generous-minded colleagues and the anonymous referees, who discussed ideas that are raised in the book, made pertinent suggestions, shared materials, or scrutinized portions of the evolving manuscript. These scholars and friends include Jeremy Barham, Mike Beckerman, Fausto Borém, Darius Brubeck, Chris Collins, Laurent Cugny, Peter Dickinson, Chris Dingle, Michel Duchesneau, Nicholas Gebhardt, Martin Guerpin, Roy Howat, William Hughes, Jack Hylton (Jr), Barbara Kelly, Hans Koller, Richard Langham Smith, Janne Mäkelä, Timothée Picard, Brian Priestley, Michael Puri, Derek Scott, Yannick Seité, John Watson, Tony Whyton, Katherine Williams and Lawrence Woof. Specific acknowledgements are given in footnotes, generally at the start of a chapter. I should also like to thank Vicki Cooper, Fleur Jones and their helpful, accommodating staff at the Press, particularly Pat Harper for her insightful copyediting. For his setting of the music examples with skill and commitment, warm thanks are extended to Steve Bird. I am deeply grateful for the support and patient forbearance of my family: my husband, Ronald Woodley, and my sons, Michael and Alex.

Finally, this project could not have been realized without some financial assistance. I am most appreciative of awards from the *Music & Letters* Trust and the *Music Analysis* Development Fund that have made a sizeable contribution to the costs of setting the music examples. Related production costs, such as those involved in clearing music permissions, have kindly been met by funding from Birmingham Conservatoire, Birmingham City University.

Copyright musical materials are reproduced as follows.

Excerpts from Dave Brubeck, 'The Duke', © 1955, renewed 1983 Derry Music Company. Reprinted by permission. 'The Chickens and the Ducklings', from *Reminiscences of the Cattle Country*, © 1960, renewed 1988 Derry Music Company. Reprinted by permission. 'Three to Get Ready', © 1960, renewed 1988 Derry Music Company. Reprinted by permission. 'Blue Rondo à la Turk', © 1960, renewed 1988 Derry Music Company. Reprinted by permission. 'Unsquare Dance', © 1962, renewed 1990 Derry Music Company. Reprinted by permission. 'Bluette', © 1962, renewed 1990 Derry Music Company. Reprinted by permission. 'Fugue', from *Points on Jazz*, © 1962, renewed 1990 Derry Music Company. Reprinted by permission. I am grateful to Richard S. Jeweler, San Rafael, for his assistance.

Excerpts from Miles Davis, *Kind of Blue* ('All Blues', 'Blue in Green'), with transcribed scores by Rob Du Boff, Mark Vinci, Mark Davis and Josh Davis, © 1959 Jazz Horn Music. Copyright renewed. 'All Blues' (Davis), Universal/MCA Music Limited. 'Blue in Green' (Davis), Universal/MCA Music Limited. All rights reserved. Used by permission.

Excerpts from Bill Evans, *Everybody Digs* ('Peace Piece'), transcribed by Jim Aikin, are reproduced as follows: © 1965 Acorn Music Corp., New York, assigned to Kensington Music Ltd (Suite 2.07, Plaza 535 Kings Road, London SW10 0SZ). International copyright secured. All rights reserved. Used by permission.

The excerpt from George Gershwin, 'Summertime' (*Porgy and Bess* ®), music and lyrics by George Gershwin, Du Bose Heyward, and Dorothy Heyward and Ira Gershwin, © 1935 (renewed 1962) Chappell & Co. Inc., Warner/Chappell North America Ltd, is reproduced by permission of Faber Music Ltd. All rights reserved.

The excerpt from André Jolivet, *Mana* ('La Princesse de Bali'), © 1946 Éditions Costallat, © 2000 Éditions Jobert, is reproduced by permission of Éditions Jobert.

The excerpt from Olivier Messiaen, *Catalogue d'oiseaux* ('Le Chocard des alpes'), © 1959 Universal Edition: UE 13154, is reproduced by kind permission of Universal Edition AG, Wien.

Excerpts from Darius Milhaud, *Caramel mou*, © 1921 Éditions Max Eschig; and *La Création du monde, suite de concert*, Op. 81b, © 1926

Éditions Max Eschig, are reproduced by kind permission of Hal Leonard MGB. Those from the *6ᵉ symphonie* (Sixth Chamber Symphony), © 1929 Universal Edition, renewed 1956 by Darius Milhaud: UE 9629; *Machines agricoles* ('La Lieuse'), © 1926 Universal Edition, renewed 1954 by Darius Milhaud: UE 8142; and *L'Homme et son désir* (Scene V), © 1969 Universal Edition: UE 14285, are reproduced by kind permission of Universal Edition AG, Wien.

Excerpts from Maurice Ravel, *Daphnis et Chloé*, © 1913 Éditions Durand; *Le Tombeau de Couperin* ('Forlane'), © 1918 Éditions Durand; *Sonate pour violon et piano*, © 1927 Éditions Durand; *Concerto pour la main gauche*, © 1931 Éditions Durand; and *Concerto pour piano et orchestre*, © 1932 Éditions Durand, are reproduced by kind permission of Hal Leonard MGB.

George Russell's illustration of the 'Lydian Chromatic Order of Tonal Gravity', together with excerpts from his analyses of Ravel, *Le Tombeau de Couperin* ('Forlane') and (with Bill Geha) Debussy, *Préludes* Book II, No. VIII, 'Ondine', are reproduced by kind permission of Alice Norbury Russell, Concept Publishing Company, Brookline, MA.

Excerpts from Erik Satie, *Parade* ('Rag-time du paquebot'), with reference to the composer's two-piano reduction, ©1917 Rouart Lerolle et Cie/ Salabert, are reproduced by kind permission of Hal Leonard MGB.

Extensive efforts have been made to clarify all copyrights relating to music scores and illustrative materials. In the event that any copyright holder has not been acknowledged, please contact the publisher who will make appropriate amendment in any subsequent edition of this book.

Note on the text

Full references are given at their first citation in the footnotes, with short titles used thereafter. With the exception of specific literary contexts, quotations are presented in English translation within the main text and, where involving previously unpublished translation, in French within the footnotes. Unless otherwise stated, translations have been undertaken by the author. Any text contained within square brackets is editorial.

Music references employ a mixture of bar numbers and rehearsal figures dependent upon the available editions of a score. Generally, bar numbers are found in instrumental music scores, and figures in orchestral or stage works. Scores or jazz transcriptions with rehearsal figures or letters involve a shorthand notation: Fig. 1^{-1} refers to the bar preceding rehearsal figure 1; Fig. 1 denotes the full bar with this label attached; Fig. 1^{+1} refers to the bar following rehearsal figure 1. References to recordings, especially jazz items, include timings in minutes and seconds (0.00), as appropriate.

In musical discussion, separation of pitches by commas indicates a neutral, basic listing, such as for scalic components. The conjoining of pitches by means of '–' denotes a voiceleading progression: a directed linear motion from one pitch to another. More specifically, the sign '/' as in F/F♯, denotes a composite entity and usually serves to highlight modal 'mixture': the presence of alternative pitches used in a flexible, inflected manner, particularly 'blue' and 'real' notes. Where no sharp or flat is indicated, it should be assumed that a given pitch is natural. A minor mode may be shown by lower-case lettering, as in g: I, f: I; or as in the blend: D/d. Similarly, minor chords within a harmonic succession may be indicated in triadic shorthand as: e, d, C, a, G, e, C; or by the qualification 'm', as in the expression: C^9–D♭– E♭$m^{11/7}$–Dm^7. Unless otherwise marked, music examples that involve transposing instruments are presented at sounding pitch. Registral designations (only used sparingly) follow the Helmholtz system, whereby middle C is denoted by c^1.

Introduction – French music and jazz: cultural exchange

Orléans to New Orleans and back again … The lure and influence of jazz upon composers of French modernist music was acknowledged by an article in *The Musical Quarterly*, published as early as 1935.[1] Conversely, as Mervyn Cooke points out, the practice of jazz improvisers 'Jazzing-up classical music is as old as jazz itself,'[2] while for musicians like Dave Brubeck, 'Jazz has always been a hybrid music.'[3] Despite this longstanding double trajectory, there has to date been no dedicated book to test out detailed *musical* interactions in respect of the seeming special affinity between French 'classical' music – predominantly of the early twentieth century – and jazz.

In part, this situation arises as a consequence of certain trends in more recent scholarship, especially, though by no means exclusively, on jazz. It has been crucial to expand the interdisciplinary basis of jazz studies beyond anecdotal biographies, embracing fundamental sociopolitical questions and establishing jazz as an autonomous art.[4] A pertinent summary of this historiographic discourse and its own problematics is offered by Jeremy Barham.[5] In fact, the sheer plurality of disciplines involved and approaches adopted has 'engendered increasingly contentious scholarly traditions'[6] and, among other outcomes, there is a risk that 'jazz as a *musical* phenomenon becomes submerged, concealed or lost'.[7] Thus Barham furthers concerns raised in the 1990s by Gary Tomlinson and Mark Tucker. Furthering Barham, I argue that, while it would rightly be deemed essentialist to

---

[1] M. Robert Rogers, 'Jazz Influence on French Music', *The Musical Quarterly*, 21/1 (January 1935), 53–68. This is by no means the first critique; see Chapter 2. On the complex status of New Orleans, see Chapter 1, n. 38.

[2] Mervyn Cooke, *Jazz* (London: Thames and Hudson, 1998), 112.

[3] Dave Brubeck, 'Jazz Perspective [1951]', *Perspectives U.S.A.*, 15 (Spring 1956), 22–8; reprinted in David Meltzer (ed.), *Reading Jazz* (San Francisco, CA: Mercury House, 1993), 202–7: 203.

[4] For an accessible introduction for non-jazz specialists, including to 'Jazz as "Critical Music"' and 'Jazz and the Academy', see Andrew Bowie, 'Jazz', in J. P. E. Harper-Scott and Jim Samson (eds.), *An Introduction to Music Studies* (Cambridge University Press, 2009), 176–85.

[5] Jeremy Barham, 'Rhizomes and Plateaus: Rethinking Jazz Historiography and the Jazz-"Classical" Relationship', *Jazz Research Journal*, 3/2 (2009), 171–202: 171–4.

[6] *Ibid.*, 172.   [7] *Ibid.*, 173.

offer musical interpretation of jazz without appropriate and sensitive socio-cultural understanding, the opposite is also the case: to ignore the actual musics created would be to grossly undervalue the musicians concerned, performers and composers alike, and simply to lose out. This need to study and celebrate the music (just as true for French music) constitutes an important priority, as does viewing jazz positively rather than defensively across relevant wider arenas, including those of tonality and so-called classical music. Cooke's declaration that 'Currently one of the least fashionable ways of looking at jazz is from the perspective of "classical" music' may be read as a cue for serious reinvestigation since, as he also suggests, 'those who insist on [...] incompatibility [...] cut themselves off from the richness of allusion and crossover'.[8]

This book thus aims to offer a distinctive, in-depth study of this intertextual phenomenon, situated within and being very much of its historical-cultural and critical-analytical contexts. The account is presented from two differentiated perspectives, geographical locations and time frames: 1900–35 and 1925–65.[9] Firstly, it charts the 'conversations' of the title that were initiated by French modernist composers, primarily of the interwar years, with early jazz and its predecessor forms such as ragtime; secondly, it focuses upon those conversations initiated especially by 'modal jazz' musicians of the 1950s and early 1960s with French musical impressionism and trends such as neoclassicism. At one level, there is the sense of a selective French musical reading of early jazz balanced by a jazz history of early twentieth-century French music. Beyond this overview, the book presents a series of case studies, ranging from Debussy to Brubeck.

Immediately, complexities and questions emerge. The first complexity involves matters of definition. As noted perceptively almost eighty years ago: 'Many have attempted to define rag-time, blues and jazz, but most have

---

[8] Mervyn Cooke, 'Jazz among the Classics, and the Case of Duke Ellington', in Mervyn Cooke and David Horn (eds.), *The Cambridge Companion to Jazz* (Cambridge University Press, 2002), 153–73: 153.

[9] Jeffrey H. Jackson's *Making Jazz French: Music and Modern Life in Interwar Paris* (Durham, NC and London: Duke University Press, 2003) offers a valuable cultural history of the phenomenon, which may be seen as complementary to my more musically grounded, interwar enquiries. A more recent sequel, Matthew F. Jordan, *Le Jazz: Jazz and French Cultural Identity* (Urbana, IL: University of Illinois Press, 2010), develops Jackson's cultural territory, adopting a broadly similar structure. Equally, mention should be made of Vincent Cotro, Laurent Cugny and Philippe Gumplowicz (eds.), *La Catastrophe apprivoisée: Regards sur le jazz en France*, Jazz en France (Paris: Outre Mesure, 2013) and, published during the production process for the current book, of Andy Fry, *Paris Blues: African American Music and French Popular Culture 1920–1960* (University of Chicago Press, 2014).

fallen into the error of trying to make too definite distinctions among them.'[10] And, despite all the advances in jazz historiography, there remains much truth in this assertion. Other complexities pertain to the following: theories of relationship; issues of metaphor; the contingency of cultural themes such as national identity, modernism, eclecticism, ethnicity, gender; issues of gaps and overlaps; the establishing of extents and boundaries. Although the French music–jazz theme is interpreted here in a generous fashion, some topics inevitably lie outside its scope: these include interplay between French cinema and jazz, which could be a fascinating separate book,[11] or that between French music and popular culture, more broadly interpreted. While a starting date around 1900 is fairly self-evident though still far from straightforward,[12] a finishing date around 1965 is partly pragmatic, but also a matter of recognition that beyond this time the picture becomes increasingly complex. Peter Dickinson talks similarly of wanting to trace a strand of 'jazz influence' from ragtime through 'to about 1960, after which everything became too confused'.[13] For Darius Brubeck (son of Dave Brubeck) too: 'The evolutionary hypothesis [...] works deceptively well up to this point [1959], but for the longer future and beyond, the organic analogy with its corollary of artistic progress breaks down.'[14] The reader will already have become aware of some 'scare quotes' in the opening paragraphs highlighting terms that are problematic and/or remain to be properly explored beyond the initial statement: clarifications are given at the earliest opportunity in the ensuing chapters.

As for the many questions, those of a detailed nature tend to be contextually derived and are tackled on a case-by-case basis. However, the fundamental large-scale questions that have catalysed and driven this study are along these lines: why is there a particular affinity between the two musics? What does jazz offer to (interwar) French music and its composers; reciprocally, what does French music offer to (modal) jazz and its practitioners? How varied are these musical-cultural relationships between French music

---

[10] Rogers, 'Jazz Influence on French Music', 53.

[11] Excellent sources are found in the writing of Gilles Mouëllic: *Jazz et cinéma* (Paris: Cahiers du cinéma, 2000) and *La Musique de film* (Paris: Cahiers du cinéma/SCEREN-CNDP, 2003).

[12] Chapter 1 begins cultural scene-setting at 1889 and Chapter 6 references much nineteenth-century repertory. Equally, Roy Howat has identified cakewalk-like pieces of Debussy from the 1880s: Roy Howat, *The Art of French Piano Music: Debussy, Ravel, Fauré, Chabrier* (New Haven, CT and London: Yale University Press, 2009), 256; see too Chapter 3 of this current book.

[13] Personal correspondence with the author (31 October 2013).

[14] Darius Brubeck, '1959: The Beginning of Beyond', in Cooke and Horn (eds.), *The Cambridge Companion to Jazz*, 177–201: 200.

and jazz? How might music materials (for example, chordal constructs, genres, forms, timbre) be transformed from one setting to another; conversely, what important constant elements (such as motive, melody, chord, rhythm, or modality) may emerge? How might new musical and cultural meanings be generated through these interactions? Are there potential downsides to cultural exchanges of this kind? Since each case study generates its own discrete conclusion, embracing answers to parts of these questions, there is no separate, overall conclusion, which would give a falsely end-stopped impression. Preliminary responses to these questions are, however, offered at the close of this introduction.

Given the size of the fields involved, a project on French music and jazz could never be comprehensive. Instead, to do justice to the topic, I have sought to balance breadth and depth by adopting a part structure. Part I (chapters 1 and 2) offers extensive coverage of contexts, both historical-cultural and critical-analytical, which are intended to support the composer/topic-based studies that follow, while also being of intrinsic interest. Parts II and III (chapters 3–9) reflect my longstanding curiosity about crossovers between French music and jazz, and aim to provide accessible, further contextualized, music analyses. These essays are broad in scope, but allow for thorough musical treatment of particular 'locations' and their connecting 'relations'. On the one hand, the choice of topics is a personal one, so that another book might offer entirely different, equally valid, subjects. On the other hand, I have included some of the most representative exponents of French music–jazz interplay (Debussy, Milhaud and Brubeck), while not ignoring some who have typically been excluded from the canon (George Russell and Jack Hylton). Although it would have been perfectly justifiable to present case studies on Bix Beiderbecke or Duke Ellington, I have chosen to focus on French and jazz repertories from balancing pre- and post-World War II time frames that share a special interest in modality. The chapters mix predominantly new contributions with two revised republished essays, one of which had become out of print. In particular, 'Crossing Borders II: Ravel's Theory and Practice of Jazz' (*Ravel Studies*, 2010) has acted as a blueprint for this current project.

Chapter 1 presents a wide-ranging historical-cultural survey, charting the main developments chronologically from French and jazz perspectives, as well as across the two domains, with attention paid to gaps: areas that do not receive dedicated treatment in Parts II and III. Implicit are interrelations of historical period and geographical location, plus those that link the French music–jazz dialogue with a range of attendant cultural themes or interwoven 'voices'. Very loosely *poietic* in its emphasis upon creative acts and compositional voices, this chapter complements the second one, which is more *esthesic* – critical, interpretative and analytical – in character.[15] Needless to say, the two are far from mutually exclusive but, in practice, the first concentrates more on 'what?' and the second more on 'how?'

Chapter 2 likewise demonstrates the scope of the topic, this time via critical discourse about relations between matters French and matters jazz-based. It outlines issues in the writings of some French critics and theorists: for instance, Hugues Panassié, who raised the status of 1930s African-American jazz, through to Jacques Derrida's much more recent interview with Ornette Coleman. These critical explorations develop cultural themes from Chapter 1, which are picked up again in individual case studies. Cultural exchange between French music and jazz is viewed in the main as productive and positive, but its contradictory facets and potential negatives are also identified. While no single methodology is advocated, in preparation for Parts II and III the second half of the chapter theorizes 'cultural flow' as an inclusive 'intertextuality' (after Lawrence Kramer, Carolyn Abbate and Michael Klein),[16] which may more occasionally constitute a more precise, historically grounded influence, or individual 'borrowing' (along well-tested lines of T. S. Eliot versus Harold Bloom and, more recently, David Metzer).[17] From an analytical yet hermeneutic stance, Dmitri Tymoczko especially demonstrates fascinating harmonic comparisons across differentiated musical settings;[18] issues of transcription and aural approaches to jazz analysis are also noted. Consideration of the potential effects and meanings created by the interactions raises the crucial matter of extraneous variables; equally, the need for flexibility and an appreciation of plurality is acknowledged.

Part II explores, in a loosely chronological sequence, the impact of early jazz upon French music across 1900–35. Chapter 3 examines the influence

---

[15] This terminology is discussed in Jean-Jacques Nattiez, *Music and Discourse: Toward a Semiology of Music*, Eng. trans. Carolyn Abbate (Princeton University Press, 1990).

[16] Lawrence Kramer, *Classical Music and Postmodern Knowledge* (Berkeley and Los Angeles, CA: University of California Press, 1995); Carolyn Abbate, *Unsung Voices: Opera and Musical Narrative in the Nineteenth Century* (Princeton University Press, 1988); and Michael L. Klein, *Intertextuality in Western Art Music* (Bloomington, IN: Indiana University Press, 2005).

[17] T. S. Eliot, 'Tradition and the Individual Talent [1919]', in *Selected Essays* (London: Faber, 1951), 13–22; reprinted in *Perspecta*, 19 (1982), 36–42; Harold Bloom, *The Anxiety of Influence: A Theory of Poetry* (New York: Oxford University Press, 1973) and *A Map of Misreading*, revised edition (New York: Oxford University Press, 2003; orig. publ. 1975); David Metzer, *Quotation and Cultural Meaning in Twentieth-Century Music* (Cambridge University Press, 2003).

[18] Dmitri Tymoczko, *A Geometry of Music: Harmony and Counterpoint in the Extended Common Practice* (New York: Oxford University Press, 2011).

of predecessor cakewalks, minstrelsy and ragtime on two crucial pioneers, Claude Debussy and his contemporary Erik Satie, during the late years of the Belle Époque (c. 1900–14) and World War I. Contextual coverage of the French and American backgrounds, the composers' experiences of new musics, their related critical writings and our plausible music-interpretative approaches leads to close readings of Debussy's 'Golliwogg's [*sic*] Cake-Walk' and Satie's 'Rag-time du paquebot' from *Parade*, with Stravinsky's music brought in for initial comparison. In addition to first probing the relationship between French music and its cultural other, this case study addresses issues of quotation, paraphrasing and signification, with special reference to Kramer and Metzer. Attention paid to Debussy here balances discussion, in Chapter 7, of Russell's modal jazz rethinking of one of the preludes.

Chapter 4 foregrounds the unique position of Darius Milhaud. A historical introduction to the composer's first-hand experiences in New York (Harlem), via Rio de Janeiro, is followed by a critique of his associated writings and an overview of his jazz-influenced repertory. It is substantiated by a study of the primitivist, balletic *tour de force* of *La Création du monde*, including comparison with popular music and jazz loci. Milhaud's interwar jazzed music is distinguished by its detailed engagement with, and real understanding of, blues scale and timbral issues. This enquiry also supports a later charting, in Chapter 9, of the rapport between Milhaud and one of his most eminent students, Brubeck, and the consequent idea of circularity in classical–jazz relations.

In Chapter 5, Maurice Ravel's engagement, in the later 1920s and early 1930s, with early jazz – especially its precursor-cum-parallel form, the blues – creates a historical successor to Debussy's prewar interest. It offers opportunity to relate the composer's writings on jazz and popular music, as theory, to his compositional practice. Interestingly, Ravel's eclectic theory also holds application beyond his own music (see Chapter 8). His practice generally comprises a mixture of close jazz allusion and some distinct transformation, as jazz both Gallicized and personalized, directed as much by 'unwitting unfaithfulness' to models as by wilful Bloomian 'misreading'. Notably, he is as influenced by other European and American composers, particularly George Gershwin, as by jazz per se. Structurally, this contribution balances a later exploration of Ravel's musical impact upon leading exponents of modal jazz, especially Russell and Bill Evans (chapters 7 and 8). Ravel also provides material, in the shape of *Boléro*, for Jack Hylton's 'jazzing' of French classics.

Part III reverses the formula to investigate, again roughly chronologically, the impact of French music upon jazz across 1925–65. In its concern with interwar 'jazzed' arrangements of light French classics by the popular but under-researched British bandleader Hylton, Chapter 6 mediates Parts II and III. Its inclusion depends on a broad definition of jazz, but also demonstrates that, while Hylton's role was similar to that of Paul Whiteman in the United States, we are not dealing simply with an American–French exchange. Across many French tours, Hylton cautiously endorsed 'hot' jazz and so partially acclimatized a French public to the art of Louis Armstrong and Duke Ellington. This essay presents a jazz history of well-known French pieces recreated across 1925–39 that includes Cécile Chaminade's 'Pas des écharpes', Jules Massenet's 'Méditation' from *Thaïs* and Ravel's *Boléro*. The resultant meanings and relative successes of these arrangements are considered.

Chapter 7 is the first of three to concentrate upon aspects of modal jazz in communication with French music. This most overtly theoretical case study concerns the intriguing Lydian jazz theory of George Russell, a pioneering theorist-composer associated with Gunther Schuller and the Third Stream movement, but generally little-known outside jazz circles. It is Russell's own musical analyses of specific French pieces in his jazz treatise, the *Lydian Chromatic Concept of Tonal Organization* of 1953, which form the focus of enquiry. With reference to Bloomian critical theory, I argue that Russell provides strong (mis)readings of Debussy's 'Ondine' from the second book of *Préludes* and Ravel's 'Forlane' from *Le Tombeau de Couperin* which effectively reverse any acknowledged influence by reframing these pieces within his theory. Despite its provocation and certain technical issues, Russell's example shows the potential for rethinking binaries in terms of a common prominent attribute, such as Lydian modality.

The penultimate Chapter 8 centres on the exquisite creative output of the modal jazz pianist Bill Evans and a range of French music. A valuable opportunity arises to gauge a spectrum of relationships, which extend from neutral intertextual parallels, hermeneutically perceived, through to specific cultural borrowings – some of which then undergo further transformation. Close musical interactions with Ravel (Chopin), Debussy and Messiaen are charted in parts of Miles Davis's album *Kind of Blue*, in which Evans played a crucial role, and in 'Peace Piece' from *Everybody Digs Bill Evans*, both from the late 1950s. Evans's and Davis's affinity with Ravel's Concerto for the Left Hand creates a double relationship since the latter work was likely inflected by the jazz Ravel heard on his 1928 American tour. From a critical stance, Evans's approach reveals congruency with Ravel's flexible eclectic theory and, overall, with Eliot's holistic embrace of cultural heritage.

Finally, the focus shifts for Chapter 9 from the East to the West Coast of America and to a one-on-one teacher–student relationship between

Milhaud and Brubeck, at Mills College in California, that offers an attractive microcosm of the whole French music–jazz debate. Whereas, initially, jazz came to Paris as troop entertainment during the later stages of World War I, Milhaud moved to the United States to escape the Nazism of World War II. This locus points up the circularity and fluidity of French music–jazz interactions since Milhaud, as a classical composer whose own catalyst was early American jazz, inspires and expands the compositional ambitions of Brubeck as jazz pianist. The core matters of polytonality, polyrhythm-cum-metre and complex associated questions of influence are carefully examined. Specific comparison is pursued between Brubeck's 'The Duke' and an early theoretical article on polytonality by Milhaud. More interpretatively, further comparison emerges via Brubeck's albums *Time Out* and *Time Further Out* created either side of 1960, and through later choral settings and ballet writing. This is a close, warm relationship, with the resultant musics too showing a distinct affinity but, while Milhaud undoubtedly helped to develop Brubeck's polytonality, it was predominantly Brubeck's own take on polyrhythm that established him as a mature jazz artist.

As demonstrated across this collection of case studies, and by way of an initial summative response to the questions raised above, the following assertions are offered, which may be borne in mind through the book. As for the reasons that underpin a special affinity between the two musics, I suggest several possibilities: the first, which sounds rather glib, is that of historical circumstance from both perspectives. French interest in jazz does emerge from a *fin-de-siècle* fascination with a much wider exoticism, primitivism and kinds of otherness whose colonial roots cannot be denied. Moving beyond vernacular popular music, such interest is generated by the need for American troops newly arrived in France during World War I to be entertained; early jazz suits the immediate postwar Parisian mood so well in its anti-establishment, rebellious qualities and sheer physical release. Meanwhile, African-American jazz linkage with the classics goes back to the training of stride pianists and to a much more equivocal relationship with European cultural hegemony. There is, however, also a sense that both musics share a minority status: French music in struggling to overthrow German symphonic hegemony and claim its identity; jazz and blues as musics of protest against a far deeper sociopolitical oppression. In terms of interwar French music and modal jazz, I propose that there is, generally, a mutual upholding of the worth of the other's music, and of its potential usefulness as a catalyst for change in the face of respective problems of musical stagnation.

Where the cross-fertilization is concerned, both domains share fundamental concerns with modality, timbre and expressivity, yet each offers the other something slightly different. Positively speaking, this involves new blood to enrich and develop further an established tradition; negatively, one might perceive a threat of dilution or contamination. From both directions, I assert that the resulting musical-cultural interactions are diverse: each spans a spectrum from intertextual parallels through to precise, historically evidenced, eclectic notions of 'source–product' (a transformational process whereby a new product may be created from a given source; specific 'influence'). Within this latter category are several subdomains, including generic allusion, modelling, paraphrase and quotation, with potential emergent meanings ranging, at least theoretically, from homage to mimicry, even theft (see Chapter 2).

From a French interwar perspective, I argue that jazz, at one end of a popular music spectrum, plays a crucial role in catalysing a French-inflected neoclassicism that thrives on a witty lightness of touch, as well as on rethinking an eighteenth-century past. Jeffrey Jackson too refers to the apparent contradiction by which 'American jazz [. . .] became a way of articulating a seemingly lost vitality within the French musical tradition'.[19] Engagement with jazz facilitates an extension of scalic reference, especially the notion of flexible melodic blues collections, and access to closed forms beyond those of the dance suite (twelve-bar blues, thirty-two-bar song form); in the process, blues form and classical sonata may each undergo a measure of transformation. Exchange raises the status of rhythm and timbre, promoting new textural possibilities such as discrete melody and rhythm sections, in an ongoing quest for artistic expressivity. Moreover, I propose that, in turn, this French-inflected dissolution of the old binaries of 'high/low' art plays a significant role in the development of cultural modernism.[20] The potential meanings of such exchange range from positive perceptions of a progressive, adventurous and innovative French music, through to a counterposition where jazz is seen to exacerbate French frivolity, even to fuel cultural degeneration.

From a mid 1950s jazz perspective, I argue that French music, especially of the so-called impressionist school which was successful in its reworking of melodic modes, acts in part as an inspirational catalyst for modal jazz, where improvisation is freed from the constraining formulae of the 'changes'. Dorian and Lydian modes present as notable constants. Together with the possibility of more extended, varied forms for jazz, such French music offers an expressive *sensibilité* founded on a rich textural and harmonic palette. A

---

[19] Jackson, *Making Jazz French*, 118.
[20] For pertinent discussion of this concept of 'high/low' art in an American context, see Lawrence W. Levine, *Highbrow/Lowbrow: The Emergence of Cultural Hierarchy in America* (Cambridge, MA: Harvard University Press, 1988).

special musical meeting-place may be identified in seventh and (dominant) minor ninth chords. Culturally, in this postwar period with America having supported the Anglo-French alliance against Hitler's Nazism, French association arguably conveys a certain cachet, subtlety and sophistication. Conversely, these same qualities (combined with a French negrophilia), viewed stereotypically as rather feminine in contrast to a Germanic or jazz masculinity, may figure in perceptions of some white-American jazz as effeminate, or inauthentic. While modal jazz prepares the way for and works alongside an inclusive jazz–classical Third Stream, some accusations of a continuing 'Eurocentricity', with its associated racist history, linger.

In short, I posit that the relationships revealed between French music and jazz are deeper, more varied and more extensive than has hitherto been realized, and that this special cross-cultural kinship has in the main promoted a mutual artistic enrichment. More widely, it is hoped that the study may act as an exemplar for other cross-cultural explorations.

This book may be read variously: from a full through-reading to a more likely scenario of selecting any one part, or chapter therein. For this reason, each chapter is presented as far as is feasible as a self-standing entity: this sometimes involves an intentional, judicious quantity of overlap and cross-referencing to avoid the problem of missing crucial pieces from any one jigsaw. Conversely, it is possible to trace a range of composers, themes, genres and relations across the volume. For instance, Milhaud appears as a searcher on a quest in Chapter 4 and, to some extent, as a source in Chapter 9. Bloomian misreading may be strongly demonstrated by Russell and arguably by Satie; models are relevant to Evans and Ravel; source fragments (jazz and otherwise) are quoted by Debussy and Milhaud, while larger-scale quotations (French and otherwise) are utilized by Evans and, in transcription or arrangement, by Hylton.

This study aims to interest a diverse scholarly and professional musical readership, classical and jazz-based, as well as final-year undergraduate students, postgraduates, well-informed amateur musicians, concert-goers and jazz enthusiasts. Beyond music per se, it is hoped that the book will appeal to cultural historians and art theorists concerned with probing relations between artistic phenomena, and pursuing ideas of eclecticism, cultural transformation and hybridity.

PART I

Locations and relations

1 A historical-cultural overview

This opening chapter seeks to overview the artistic domain and to emphasize the rich variety of crossovers from French music to jazz and from jazz
to French music through time. From a French orientation, it encompasses
impressionism, neoclassicism and notions of modernism; conversely, it
extends from the very inception of jazz and associations with ragtime and
blues, through swing and bebop, to modal jazz. Upon this basis, the complex
interactions, or dialogues, between a broad canon of twentieth-century
French music and jazz are pursued historically. Particular attention is given
to topics that lie outside the case studies: Auric, Martinů, Beiderbecke's *In
a Mist*, Ellington's explorations, Reinhardt's *Nuages*, Bechet's impact,
Coltrane's 'Impressions', French 'high' modernism (Messiaen, Boulez) and
late Poulenc. While one must be alert to subject positioning and potential
bias, composer-musician testimonies offer a useful, loosely *poietic*, source of
historical evidence. Other interrelations impinge that may embody transition, fusion, or an opposing reaction: these pertain to time (pre-, inter- and
postwar historical periods) and place (geographical-cum-cultural locations
of Europe, especially France but also Britain, and America). Similarly, attention is drawn *en route* to several continuing cultural themes: modernism
(embracing impressionism and neoclassicism); national and individual identity; changing attitudes towards race (including primitivism, *art nègre* and
Parisian negrophilia) and, more indirectly, gender. Modality, too, is a crucial
underlying theme.

It is now necessary to define, at least pragmatically for this book, exactly
what is meant both by French music and jazz. The expression 'French
music' here connotes primarily twentieth-century repertory that might be
termed 'classical', 'art', or 'concert' music.[1] Given the wider classical–jazz
agenda, the adjective 'classical' has something to commend it, but may be
misleading temporally: the music is not Classical in a strict eighteenth-
century sense, though some is neoclassical. 'Art' music is yet more problematic since it tends to convey a value judgement, implying somehow that jazz
is not art music, which is patently not the case. 'Concert' music offers the
most neutral qualification and is largely accurate, at least if one takes the line
that stage music is also encompassed.

---

[1] Cooke, 'Jazz among the Classics', 153.

Moreover, such music may be situated at points along several spectra. On the 'music' side of the agenda, French concert music may constitute a subset of European music. Within Europe there arose, at various historical flash-points, a strong sense of French musical values versus those of an Austro-German hegemony. In turn, European music is part of what might yet be termed 'Western music', which may encompass North American and other repertories, with all its associated cultural baggage, especially in relation to exoticism, or otherness. But Russian and other Eastern European musics are also implicated by virtue of their presence in early twentieth-century France. The sheer fluidity and implications for border-crossing are immediately apparent. Similarly, if we pursue the 'French' dimension, French music may be located within a wider understanding of French culture (including its popular dimensions) and beyond, in more elusive notions of French national identity – Frenchness. In combination, then, French music presents as part of an all-inclusive Western arts culture. Temporally, while the focus is upon the twentieth century, it too is not exclusive: some nineteenth-century repertory is relevant, and strong connections between jazz and neoclassicism do implicate an eighteenth-century past.

The term 'jazz' presents comparable challenges.[2] Jazz is regarded here as an inclusive designation, so subscribing to Brubeck's aspiration of 1951: 'In a little more than a half century the cry of protest has become the voice of liberation, and the musical dialect of an American minority has the possibility of becoming a universal music for all people.'[3] It is viewed as an umbrella term which, in not downplaying distinctive histories and identities, may yet embrace predecessor forms such as cakewalk, minstrelsy and ragtime, together with the predecessor-cum-parallel phenomenon of the blues. Jazz denotes an increasing range of styles that have at least generally accepted historical starting points (if not endings) and geographical-cultural associations: New Orleans (and its revival), Chicago, Harlem, swing or big band, bebop, modal, cool jazz, East and West Coast.

Within this supposedly neutral listing, modal jazz exists as a somewhat disputed term, unrecognized by some scholars and musicians, while others regard it as 'ambiguous'.[4] Nevertheless, Cooke acknowledges the category as one emerging in the later 1950s: 'Take Five' by Paul Desmond (1924–77) is viewed as an early instance, fusing thirty-two-bar song form with 'modal

---

[2] For lengthy discussion of the early meanings of jazz, especially in a French context, see Jackson, 'The Meanings of Jazz: America, *Nègre*, and Civilization', in *Making Jazz French*, 71–103, and analogous chapters in Jordan, *Le Jazz*, including 'Vamp on the Meaning of Jazz: The Cakewalk Comes to Town', 17–38. See, too, 'Meanings, Origins', in Meltzer (ed.), *Reading Jazz*, 37–70.

[3] Brubeck, 'Jazz Perspective', 207.   [4] Tymoczko, *A Geometry of Music*, 376.

techniques',[5] and Davis's *Milestones* (1958) offers a landmark locus in reaction against the harmonic complexities of bebop.[6] Similarly, Alyn Shipton discusses Davis's role in pieces 'built entirely on modes (or scalar patterns) rather than chord sequences',[7] or on a simple chordal alternation, perceiving modal jazz within a transition to free jazz.[8] By contrast, Samuel Barrett emphasizes 'the extent to which modal jazz is rooted in the blues'.[9] For Tymoczko, modal jazz may involve 'highly diatonic pieces with very few chord changes, or relatively chromatic music in which harmonic tension is generated by out-of-key playing', as well as processes of asynchrony.[10] Again, my stance leans towards inclusivity, with modal jazz recognized historically as a tendency of the mid–later 1950s, which yields both East and West Coast proponents. Musically, it emphasizes a restricted scalic and melodic menu, allied to simple chordal support, selected from expanded modal resources; in turn, such modality generates common ground with that of French impressionism.

Outside the temporal confines of this book, the array of jazz styles continues with the emergence of free jazz, jazz-rock fusion and ragtime revival. However, jazz also extends to imported and indigenous practice in Britain, France and beyond, again confounding any ill-guided attempt to create falsely neat separations. Despite its heavy associated baggage, and while fully crediting its African-American origins, jazz is seen as a music that can transcend racial or colour boundaries. It encompasses African-American and white musicians; it exists as a largely non-commercial artistic expression and in commercialized formats, often more musically circum-scribed. Like French music, jazz too features at points along various spectra: from performance to composition; from improvisation to more fixed artis-tic entities, such as in the work of Ellington, or up to a point Brubeck. To recognize such plurality is not to subscribe to some bland homogeneity that fails to respect difference and individuality; rather, difference is part of the interest.[11] On the large scale, we may conceive of a further spectrum with jazz located at one end that extends, arguably via notions of folk art, to popular music at the other. (On this inclusivity stance, see too Chapter 6.)

---

[5] Cooke, *Jazz*, 144.   [6] *Ibid.*, 146.

[7] Alyn Shipton, *A New History of Jazz*, revised and updated edition (New York and London: Continuum, 2007), 482.

[8] *Ibid.*, 483–6.

[9] Samuel Barrett, '*Kind of Blue* and the Economy of Modal Jazz', *Popular Music*, 25/2 (May 2006), 185–200: 186.

[10] Tymoczko, *A Geometry of Music*, 376.

[11] See Ruth A. Solie (ed.), *Musicology and Difference: Gender and Sexuality in Music Scholarship* (Berkeley and Los Angeles, CA: University of California Press, 1993).

In the following survey, the ordering and inclusion of materials have involved academic and subjective judgement. Theoretically, it might have been possible to introduce and cross-relate all relevant genres in a given time span simultaneously, but this would likely have been very messy and confusing for the reader and would not have achieved the objective of a coherent overview. In the absence of a non-linear web structure with hypertext, the guiding principle has been to introduce the main background to a topic or genre before it becomes a potential source, generic or specific, for another music within the process of cultural exchange.

Impressionism, ragtime and early blues (1889–1919)

The so-called Belle Époque ('Good old days'), extending from around 1885 to the outbreak of World War I, felt so more in retrospect than actuality and, even then, only really for those fortunate enough to have been a member of upper-class society.[12] Within this period, the logical starting point for our enquiries from a French perspective is inevitably 1889. This was the year of the very well-documented Paris Exposition or World Fair, itself marking the centenary of the 1789 French Revolution and consequent Republic, with its founding motto of 'Liberté, égalité, fraternité' subsequently reinforced during the Third Republic from 1870. Supposedly upholding an enlightened engagement with, and celebration of, world musics – and indeed where Claude Debussy (1862–1918) first heard the Javanese gamelan – the Exposition was nonetheless a product of colonialism and a promotional opportunity to present a France, specifically Paris, triumphant in its artistic confidence and cultural supremacy. Individual reactions to the Exposition, with its astonishing array of world cultures, ranged from expressions of genuine awe and wonderment, through to the display of outright racial prejudice.

Increasingly, however, there developed a conviction within French cultural attitudes that change was inevitable, imminent and necessary, in tandem with a historical progression through the Dreyfus affair of 1894–99, the need by 1904 for Franco-British 'Entente cordiale', the Sarajevo incident of 1914 and descent into worldwide turmoil. Alongside groundbreaking external and 'internal' discoveries of Albert Einstein and Sigmund Freud, this final decade of the Belle Époque witnessed a cultural radicalism: a challenging of the identity, role and meaning of the arts; a self-consciousness of its place in history; an erosion of notions of objective time; and a need to engage with

---

[12] Charles Sowerwine, *France since 1870: Culture, Society and the Making of the Republic*, second edition (Basingstoke and New York: Palgrave Macmillan, 2009), 89.

emergent modernity itself. This was the beginning of European cultural modernism (our first main theme).[13]

Musically, we encounter landmark works of Debussy, commencing with his *Prélude à l'Après-midi d'un faune* (1892–4), now forever associated with the (im)possibility of defining the start of modern music, cued by its opening solo flute melody.[14] This early composition encapsulates Debussy's ability to mediate between a tonic–dominant functional tonality and a rich, inclusive modality, inspired by oriental practice and generously suffused with a post-Wagnerian chromaticism. It illustrates the allure of exquisite timbral effects and instrumental blendings, including the exotic, timeless ambience created by the restrained use of antique cymbal chimes, towards its close. Another inescapable association in the public imagination for this piece and many later works, including *Nocturnes* (1899), *La Mer* (1903–5), the sets of *Images* and *Préludes* for piano, Ravel's *Jeux d'eau* (1901), *Miroirs* (1904–5) and *Daphnis et Chloé* (1912), is that tag of 'impressionism'. In visual art, some thirty years earlier, Claude Monet (1840–1926) had introduced the term to describe, positively, both the avoidance of hard outlines and the fascination with the play of light found in his *Impressionism, soleil levant* (Impressionism, Sunrise) of 1872. But it is worth recalling that the term was first used in conjunction with Debussy, in a report by the Secretary of the Académie des beaux-arts in 1887, as one of denigration: 'It is very much to be hoped that he will be on his guard against that vague "Impressionism" which is one of the most dangerous enemies of truth in any work of art.'[15] Such 'danger' would, however, later appeal strongly to a range of jazz musicians.

The momentum of the Exposition arguably also helped to fuel a French artistic appetite for so-called primitivism – a further offshoot of modernism – as a return to simplicity and first principles,[16] driven by the likes of Guillaume Apollinaire (1880–1918) and evident in sculptures and paintings by Pablo Picasso (1881–1973), and in the development of cubism itself (see

---

[13] On modernism, see Christopher Butler, *Early Modernism: Literature, Music and Painting in Europe 1900–1916* (Oxford: Clarendon Press, 1994) and Christopher Butler, *Modernism: A Very Short Introduction* (Oxford University Press, 2010). Late in the research process for this book Barbara L. Kelly's *Music and Ultra-Modernism in France: A Fragile Consensus, 1913–1939* (Woodbridge: Boydell & Brewer, 2013) was published.

[14] Paul Griffiths, *Modern Music: A Concise History from Debussy to Boulez* (London: Thames and Hudson, 1986), 7.

[15] Quoted in Stefan Jarocinski, *Debussy: Impressionism and Symbolism*, Eng. trans. Rollo Myers (London: Eulenberg Books, 1976), 11.

[16] See extensive treatment of the topic in Glenn Watkins, *Pyramids at the Louvre: Music, Culture, and Collage from Stravinsky to the Postmodernists* (Cambridge, MA and London: Harvard University Press, 1994).

too Chapter 4). The notion was encapsulated artistically in *Les Demoiselles d'Avignon* (1907) and musically in the rhythmic-timbral icon of *Le Sacre du printemps* (1913), created by Igor Stravinsky (1882–1971) for the Ballets russes. In turn, it connected to the concept of *art nègre*, which was generally met in France, in contrast to America, with a fascination that sometimes bordered on an unconditional negrophilia,[17] even though a then ageing, somewhat baffled, Debussy referred to Stravinsky's *chef d'œuvre* disparagingly in such terms (see Chapter 3).

In America during this same period the African-American form that was ragtime emerged, thriving through the 1890s and the following decade. Although one main reason for discussing the genre lies in its potential for later crossover, it is important to stress as did Edward Berlin at the end of his study that ragtime denotes a successful breakaway from European hegemony, clinched largely before that attempted by American concert composers: 'Ultimately, ragtime is more than a musical style; it is the achievement of cultural independence and identity.'[18]

As a composed, notated music, historical evidence for ragtime has been much better preserved than that for early blues.[19] (For coverage of its related, predecessor form, the cakewalk, see again Chapter 3.) With its inherent emphasis upon a right-hand syncopation set against a regular, march-based left-hand pattern, its name derived from the idea of 'ragged time'. In the words of Terry Waldo: 'as an expression of the loss of innocence, it [ragtime] placed the old manmade folk music in a new mechanized context'.[20] In turn, this tension, precision and studied mechanicity combined to make ragtime, also exploited commercially to great effect, a distinctive product of early modernity. But beyond these more obvious characteristics, writers such as Waldo have sought to emphasize the artistic, expressive legitimacy of classic rags: 'though drawing on folk sources for inspiration, it is art music written for its own sake, primarily as an expression of the artist-composer'.[21] The main thrust and lasting legacy of ragtime has been as an instrumental genre, predominantly for piano, as practised by its

[17] See Petrine Archer-Shaw, *Negrophilia: Avant-Garde Paris and Black Culture in the 1920s* (London: Thames and Hudson, 2000); Jody Blake, *Le Tumulte noir: Modernist Art and Popular Entertainment in Jazz-Age Paris, 1900–1930* (University Park, PA: Pennsylvania University Press, 1999); and Jed Rasula, 'Jazz as Decal for the European Avant Garde', in Heike Raphael-Hernandez, *Blackening Europe: The African American Presence* (New York: Routledge, 2004), 13–34.
[18] Edward A. Berlin, *Ragtime: A Musical and Cultural History* (Berkeley and Los Angeles, CA: University of California Press, 1980), 196.
[19] Cooke, *Jazz*, 27.
[20] Terry Waldo, *This Is Ragtime* (New York: Da Capo Press, 1991; reprinted 2009), 35.
[21] *Ibid.*, 58.

most famous exponent, the African-American musician Scott Joplin (1868–1917).[22] Contemporary with Joplin's death and the closing stages of World War I, American interest in the genre declined just as that in early improvised jazz began to increase (this was also, however, the period of ragtime's being taken up as a resource by modernist composers).

Comparable and broadly contemporaneous with ragtime, yet in many ways more elusive, is the phenomenon of the blues.[23] The blues features both as the other crucial precursor of early jazz, but also as a continuing folk-like practice, which coexists with,[24] and likely impacts upon, jazz itself, as yet another relationship to keep tabs on. (For detailed coverage of the impact of the blues on French composers, see chapters 4 and 5.) While the blues is a major topic in its own right, it makes sense to identify it here as a powerful force and to attempt to establish its essence – more accurately, its complexities. Historically, it emerges as an African-American music within the Southern states in the late nineteenth century, its origins lying in spirituals, work songs and ballads. Sadly though, this turn-of-the-century music, as heard by the likes of Ma Rainey (1886–1939) and William C. Handy (1873–1958)[25] and recorded non-commercially by the farsighted sociologist Howard W. Odum (1884–1954),[26] is now irretrievable. Vital to the identity of the blues are its lyrics that express the melancholy immortalized in its name. The first point of clarification is that the blues references both a genre and its associated twelve-bar blues form,[27] which in turn has much influenced genres of the 1950s such as rhythm and blues, rock 'n' roll and electric blues. Even within the genre are subgenres of country (from its

---

[22] For thorough studies of Joplin, see Edward A. Berlin, *King of Ragtime: Scott Joplin and His Era* (New York: Oxford University Press, 1994) and Susan Curtis, *Dancing to a Black Man's Tune: A Life of Scott Joplin* (Columbia, MO: University of Missouri Press, 1994).

[23] Among a huge literature on the blues, see the many writings of Paul Oliver, including Paul Oliver, Tony Russell, Robert M. W. Dixon, John Goodrich and Howard Rye, *Yonder Come the Blues* (Cambridge University Press, 2001) and coverage in Shipton, *A New History of Jazz*, chapter 1, 'Precursors', 13–53.

[24] See Shipton, *A New History of Jazz*, 31–2.

[25] See, with some justification, his self-appointed role in W. C. Handy, *Father of the Blues: An Autobiography*, ed. Arna Bontemps (New York: Macmillan, 1941). Ma Rainey is often dubbed the 'Mother of the Blues': this first female representation in the French music–jazz story implies the relevance of a gender theme.

[26] See John H. Cowley, 'Don't Leave Me Here: Non-Commercial Blues: The Field Trips, 1924–60', in Lawrence Cohn (ed.), *Nothing But the Blues: The Music and the Musicians* (New York: Abbeville Press, 1993), 265.

[27] Twelve-bar blues form denotes a basic paradigm of a cyclical chordal progression (which may vary between 8 and 16 bars): $I^{(7)}$–; $IV^{(7)}$–I; $V^{(7)}$–I, typically working in conjunction with an AAB melodic/lyric formula, as a development of 'call–response', and the ubiquitous vocal inflections of blues third, seventh (and fifth).

rural origins) and urban blues,[28] which like jazz itself come to prominence at particular times and places, for example, Chicago or Memphis blues. One of the first notated, published examples is *Dallas Blues* (1912) by the white bandleader Hart Wand (contemporary with Handy's *The Memphis Blues*), described by its composer as a 'Southern rag', but the most famous early occurrence is undoubtedly *St. Louis Blues* (1914), with its tango affinity. The blues continues as an influential genre through the interwar years and beyond, with the first blues records appearing in 1920.

Meanwhile, news of these popular musics started to filter back across the Atlantic to enrich an increasingly lively French popular scene, with its café culture, nightclubs, circuses and theatre shows. In 1893, Gabriel Astruc, who would later be associated with Sergei Diaghilev (1872–1929), reported in the Parisian press about experiencing the cakewalk at the Columbian World's Fair in Chicago; he also brought some of the performers back to Paris.[29] The next Paris Exposition of 1900 featured the American band of John Philip Sousa (1854–1932), with its repertory of marches and pseudo-ragtime. Even in a supposedly more tolerant France, the reception of ragtime was, however, very mixed, as would prove the case with jazz too. The composer-cum-jazz historian Gunther Schuller (b. 1925) makes the point that: 'for most Frenchmen, the discovery of Ragtime, as brought to Europe by John Philip Sousa in three successive tours starting in 1900, was a culture shock, seen either as a devastating, barbaric degradation of music created by untutored "black Savages" or, at the other extreme, as a wonderfully new, rhythmically exciting, and energetic export from that unpredictable "New World"'.[30] Contemporary critique bears out this view. For a young Jean Cocteau (1889–1963), observing African-American dancers of the cakewalk at the Nouveau Cirque in 1904, the effect was compelling and made 'everything else turn pale and flee';[31] for some, however, 'the cakewalk is a dance of savages; it is made from a savage music'.[32] In a sense, American

---

[28] A distinction noted and explored some time ago by writers of the calibre of Charles Keil, *Urban Blues* (University of Chicago Press, 1966; reprinted 1991).

[29] Watkins, *Pyramids at the Louvre*, 100–1. For more detail, see Ann McKinley, 'Debussy and American Minstrelsy', *The Black Perspective in Music*, 14/3 (1986), 249–58: 253.

[30] Gunther Schuller, 'Jazz and Musical Exoticism', in Jonathan Bellman (ed.), *The Exotic in Western Music* (Boston, MA: Northeastern University Press, 1998), 283–91: 283. For a detailed contextual and historical study, especially where the latter response is concerned, see Davinia Caddy, 'Parisian Cake Walks', *19th-Century Music*, 30/3 (Spring 2007), 288–317: 295–6.

[31] Quoted in Watkins, *Pyramids at the Louvre*, 101, from Jean Cocteau, *Portraits-souvenir, 1900–1914* (Paris: Grasset, 1935), 89.

[32] Quoted in Jackson, *Making Jazz French*, 83, from *Le Petit Bleu de Paris* (18 December 1908), B pièce 347, Bibliothèque-Musée de l'Opéra.

ragtime in tandem with the whole concept of *art nègre* offered France yet
another new exotic, while also tapping into what Cocteau would later define
in *Le Coq et l'arlequin* (1918) as 'a music for everyday'.[33]

The earliest known products of crossover between French and raglike
musics include innovative short pieces by Erik Satie (1866–1925) such as
La Diva de l'Empire of 1904, followed later in the decade by Debussy's *Le
Petit Nègre* and 'Golliwogg's Cake-Walk'. Other cakewalk, ragtime and
vaudeville associations are found in '... Minstrels' and '... Général
Lavine – Eccentric' from Debussy's two volumes of *Préludes* (1910, 1913),
while continuing the theme of *art nègre* we may note the lighthearted
Rapsodie nègre of 1917 by Francis Poulenc (1899–1963). Around this
time, ironically concurrent with its decline as a popular form, there occurred
a brief flurry of interest among modernist composers in the creative potential of ragtime: there is of course always a time lag in artistic fashions
travelling from one domain to another. Inspired by notated sheet music,
Stravinsky led the way with the 'Ragtime' from *L'Histoire du soldat* (1917–18),
Ragtime for eleven instruments (1917–18), *Three Pieces for Clarinet Solo*
(1918) and *Piano-Rag-Music* (1919) for solo piano. Among works by indigenous French composers should be mentioned *Trois rag-caprices* (1922) by
Darius Milhaud (1892–1974) and the ragtime-cum-foxtrot in *L'Enfant et les
sortilèges* created across 1920–5 by Maurice Ravel (1875–1937). Reciprocally,
many rag-related creations from around this period and a little later contained
references, both playful and satirical, to classical repertory. Some loci received
rather more than their fair share of attention. These included Edvard Grieg's
Peer Gynt suite and Sergei Rachmaninoff's C♯ minor Prelude (referred to
as *Russian Rag*), both reworked by the Harlem-style stride pianist-composer
James P. Johnson (1894–1955).[34] As a loosely French music, Frédéric
Chopin's 'Funeral March' from the Piano Sonata in B♭ minor was frequently
alluded to in New Orleans funerals and reworked – that is, ragged – by the
Baltimore-style musician Eubie Blake (1887–1983), among others.[35]

[33] Jean Cocteau, *Le Coq et l'arlequin* (Paris: Éditions de la Sirène, 1918); reprinted in *Œuvres
complètes de Jean Cocteau*, 11 vols. (Paris: Marguerat, 1946–51), vol. IX (*Le Rappel à l'ordre*),
13–69: 26: 'une musique de tous les jours'; Eng. trans. as 'The Cock and the Harlequin', in *A
Call to Order*, trans. Rollo H. Myers (New York: Haskell House, 1974), 3–77.

[34] Some of Johnson's rags, such as the influential rag-jazz hybrid *Steeplechase Rag*, were
transferred to piano roll as early as 1917; see Shipton, *A New History of Jazz*, 77–8. This was
contemporary with Stravinsky's enthusiasm for the pianola and for the recording medium
of the piano roll.

[35] For a very readable account of such cultural exchange, see again Cooke, 'Jazz among the
Classics', especially 162ff. On Chopin, see Maurice Peress, *Dvořák to Duke Ellington: A
Conductor Explores America's Music and its African American Roots* (New York: Oxford
University Press, 2004), 38. On Chopin's French connection, see too Chapter 6.

Early jazz, swing/big bands and neoclassicism (1919–45)

From a historical stance, this period runs essentially from the Treaty of Versailles and American Prohibition (1919–20), via the Wall Street Crash (1929) and ensuing Great Depression, to World War II (1939–45). For the sake of clarity and balance, the American jazz perspective is presented first – including its engagement with impressionism – as, to some extent, a source for French neoclassicism. Contemporary with the latter part of World War I, the first jazz records were produced in the United States from 1917 onwards. This was early classic jazz in the style of New Orleans – La Nouvelle-Orléans,[36] with its French (and Spanish) colonial history and lively melting-pot culture, featuring African-American and Creole elements. Many a jazz musician started out, typically on melody instruments such as trumpet, clarinet or trombone, in the well-established marching bands of New Orleans. From this background, small-scale syncopated jazz music, such as that of Charles 'Buddy' Bolden (1877–1931),[37] emerged and flourished in the city's legalized prostitution district, Storyville. Characteristic of Bolden's style and that of his contemporaries, and important for its crossover potential, such as in Ravel's *Boléro*, was the distinction between a polyphonic 'front line' of three or four melody band instruments and a rhythm section of double bass, possible drums, guitar/banjo or piano. After Storyville was closed down in 1917, the sound of New Orleans jazz transferred to Chicago and later New York.[38] Ironically, commercial success with a simulated New Orleans style, obtained 'by unashamedly borrowing a black musical genre',[39] came first to a white band led by Nick LaRocca: the Original Dixieland Jazz Band (ODJB). Their first phonograph recordings made in New York included the novelty-based *Livery Stable Blues* and the original number *Dixie Jazz Band One-Step*. Shipton refers to the troubling comedic aspect of their act which resembled a caricatured minstrelsy,[40] though he concedes that they still made a huge impact on the American public.[41]

Of far greater musical potential were the explorations of Joe 'King' Oliver (1885–1938). Oliver's seven-piece Creole Jazz Band in Chicago of

---

[36] On the early eighteenth-century French founding of New Orleans as the colonial capital of Louisiana, see, despite some shortcomings, Shannon Lee Dawdy, *Building the Devil's Empire: French Colonial New Orleans* (University of Chicago Press, 2008).

[37] Cooke, *Jazz*, 49.

[38] Shipton (*A New History of Jazz*, 4–7: 6) makes the point that New Orleans did not have a monopoly on jazz, whose origins are unlikely to have emerged exclusively from that one city, referring to it as 'the supposed birthplace of jazz'.

[39] Cooke, *Jazz*, 51.   [40] Shipton, *A New History of Jazz*, 75.   [41] *Ibid.*, 78.

1923 included one young Louis Armstrong on cornet, and the Creole pianist Ferdinand 'Jelly Roll' Morton (1890–1941), who did much to develop jazz structure and was also an impressive entrepreneur and self-publicist. Morton had written his own *'Jelly Roll' Blues* by 1905, published in 1915 as the first printed jazz piece.[42] Another distinctive player, who worked briefly with Oliver and Armstrong, also joining Will Marion Cook's Southern Syncopated Orchestra on its European tour in 1919 and becoming a catalyst in the later development of jazz in France, was the clarinettist and soprano saxophonist of French descent, Sidney Bechet (1897–1959).[43]

In highlighting the key elements on either side of the Atlantic, proper attention must be given to the brilliant trumpeter-cum-vocalist Louis Armstrong (1901–71).[44] Beyond his stark, impoverished beginnings and his break via Oliver's band, Armstrong's artistic independence was established through his Hot Five and Hot Seven ensembles in Chicago of the mid 1920s, whose performances included highly successful versions of Handy's *St. Louis Blues* – a piece with much transatlantic currency that would be quoted compositionally by Milhaud. Among his salient characteristics may be identified: a virtuosic trumpet technique (high tessitura playing and registral leaps, fluid triplet arpeggiation); unique instrumental and vocal timbres, including the nasal and growly; scat singing; showmanship; and a highly influential approach to swing.[45] Having first appeared in Paris in 1934, Armstrong 'practically became a national hero to Parisians' during the 1930s.[46]

Equally, Fletcher Henderson (1897–1952) and Don Redman (1900–64) should be credited with their perceptive anticipation during the mid 1920s

---

[42] Cooke, *Jazz*, 56.

[43] See Andy Fry, 'Remembrance of Jazz Past: Sidney Bechet in France', in Jane F. Fulcher (ed.), *The Oxford Handbook of the New Cultural History of Music* (New York: Oxford University Press, 2011), 307–31.

[44] Among a huge bibliography on Armstrong, a few texts may be selected: James Lincoln Collier, *Louis Armstrong: An American Genius* (New York: Oxford University Press, 1983); Louis Armstrong, *Satchmo: My Life in New Orleans* (New York: Prentice-Hall, 1954); Robert Goffin, *Horn of Plenty: The Story of Louis Armstrong*, Eng. trans. James F. Bezou (New York: Allen, Towne & Heath, 1947); and Thomas Brothers (ed.), *Louis Armstrong in His Own Words: Selected Writings* (New York: Oxford University Press, 2001), which includes Armstrong's letters to the Belgian jazz critic Robert Goffin and the 'Goffin notebooks' of 1944.

[45] See Louis Armstrong, 'What Is Swing?', in Robert Walser (ed.), *Keeping Time: Readings in Jazz History* (New York: Oxford University Press, 1999), 73–6. A classic history on the period of swing is presented by Gunther Schuller, *The Swing Era, The Development of Jazz, 1930–1945* (New York: Oxford University Press, 2001).

[46] See the popular guide to France today: Danforth Prince and Darwin Porter, *Frommer's France 2011* (Hoboken, NJ: Wiley Publishing, 2010), 37.

of a wind-based big band style, which synthesized lively 'hot' jazz-style solos and aspects of classical harmony;[47] Benny Goodman (1909–86) created a similar ensemble in the mid 1930s. Formally, as well as the ubiquitous call–response exchanges that may be traced back to African vocal origins, this music makes substantial use of the 'riff':[48] a repeated melodic-harmonic patterning, which enjoyed a cross-cultural currency as ostinato. A further feature of emergent big band style with crossover potential is that of 'walking bass': a linear presentation of seventh harmonies played by pizzicato double bass, popularized by Walter Page, who became best known in association with the Count Basie Orchestra. The other crucial figure to introduce here is Edward Kennedy 'Duke' Ellington (1899–1974). From 1927 to 1931 Ellington was resident at the Cotton Club jazz venue in New York's Harlem district, which in 1928 was likely visited by Ravel. Through the 1930s Ellington emerged as the most significant jazz composer and one whose music exemplifies a reaching across jazz–classical boundaries, recognized early on by the likes of the British composer-critic Constant Lambert.[49] Ellington was first heard in Paris in 1933, a year before Armstrong.

It makes sense to contextualize a specific American jazz–French musical interplay via collaboration between the white bandleader Paul Whiteman (1890–1967),[50] active in Paris in 1926, and the American-Jewish composer George Gershwin (1898–1937), who would influence, and be influenced by, Ravel. The product of this now (in)famous interaction, promoted as an 'Experiment in Modern Music', was *Rhapsody in Blue*, premiered in New York's Aeolian Hall in February 1924.[51] Apart from – though partly because of – its cultural crossover, the venture was probably most influential in promoting the notion of a large-scale symphonic jazz: the main thrust of the 1930s swing era. Given that Gershwin's impact also derives from his popular commercial work, creating jazz standards via Tin Pan Alley, we should mention his aptly entitled orchestral piece of 1928 *An American in Paris*. Much later, in 1962, Milhaud would reciprocate with his large orchestral work *A Frenchman in New York*, Op. 399.

---

[47] Cooke, *Jazz*, 82–4.

[48] See J. Bradford Robinson, 'Riff', in Barry Kernfeld (ed.), *The New Grove Dictionary of Jazz*, second edition, 3 vols. (New York: Oxford University Press, 2002), vol. III, 415–16.

[49] See Constant Lambert, *Music Ho!: A Study of Music in Decline* (London: Faber and Faber, 1934).

[50] Paul Whiteman's inclusion within jazz is dependent upon a definition that acknowledges, historically, the broad 1920s usage of the term. But it was also in part from the genre of dance band that the whole era of Swing emerged.

[51] For in-depth discussion, including of the structural challenges and fluidities, see David Schiff, *Gershwin: Rhapsody in Blue* (Cambridge University Press, 1997).

Two particular jazz works stand out in respect of their strong affinities with an earlier French musical impressionism: Beiderbecke's *In a Mist* (1927) and Ellington's *Mood Indigo* (1930, revised 1955). The sadly short-lived Bix Beiderbecke (1903–31) was a superb solo cornet player, whose tone was distinguished by its purity, subtlety and mellow quality: he was one of The Wolverines in 1924 and joined the Paul Whiteman Orchestra in 1927. In addition to his prowess on cornet, he was a pianist and composer, with a wide-ranging and intellectual interest in musical repertory: from Armstrong, Oliver and Dixieland through to Debussy and Ravel, as remarked on by his French biographer, Jean-Pierre Lion.[52] Beiderbecke was known to have listened frequently to works such as Debussy's *Ibéria* and *Prélude à l'Après-midi*, and then to have ruminated upon the sounds at the piano, exploring closer and more distant relationships in his own improvisational processes.[53] One of the few piano compositions that he actually recorded, *In a Mist*,[54] immediately invites association via its title with the first of Debussy's *Préludes* from Book II (1910–13): the exquisitely veiled and smooth, rippling colour-washes of 'Brouillards' (Mists). While Beiderbecke's piece is superficially much more extrovert at *forte* dynamic with accented articulation and dotted rhythms, there is nonetheless a shared usage of parallel fifths/triads, bitonal constructs, unresolved seventh and ninth harmonies, and repeated patterings. Both brief portraits operate in an extended tonality on C, with the temporal indication 'Modéré' (Moderately). On the larger purpose of such interplay, Ed Byrne suggests convincingly that 'these Impressionist mannerisms supplied a new sound to jazz of the 1920s. They added a sense of melodic and harmonic surprise and sophistication to an already vibrant rhythmic jazz piano genre.'[55]

As for *Mood Indigo*, one should note Ellington's later reservations about his work being compared with classical music and unpick some of the attendant issues. In his article, 'Certainly It's Music!', he admits to puzzlement that his music has been shown to 'bear some resemblance to

---

[52] Jean-Pierre Lion, *Bix: The Definitive Biography of a Jazz Legend* (New York: Continuum, 2005), 78–9. See, too, Philip R. Evans and Linda K. Evans, *Bix: The Leon Bix Beiderbecke Story* (Bakersfield, CA: Prelike Press, 1998).

[53] Ralph Berton, *Remembering Bix: A Memoir of the Jazz Age* (New York: W. H. Allen Press, 1974; reprinted Da Capo Press, 2000), 156–9.

[54] For a transcription of Beiderbecke's piece and detailed harmonic analysis, see Ed Byrne, *Beiderbecke's In a Mist* (2008): http//:freejazzinstitute.com.

[55] Byrne, *Beiderbecke's In a Mist*. See too Geoffrey Jennings Haydon, 'A Study of the Exchange of Influences between the Music of Early Twentieth-Century Parisian Composers and Ragtime, Blues, and Early Jazz', DMA dissertation (University of Texas at Austin, 1992), which includes analysis of Beiderbecke's piece.

the compositions of such masters as Bach, Ravel and Stravinsky'.[56] Perfectly reasonably, he makes the point that he is not trying to sound like anyone else and that any similarity results from 'subconscious activity'.[57] He acknowledges that 'no composer can help but repeat to some extent some things from the subconscious accumulation of years of listening to the music of others'.[58] In certain ways, however, his reaction is a little contradictory: on the one hand, he claims to 'appreciate the compliment'; on the other, he denigrates such observation, with reference to *Mood Indigo*, by declaring that: 'in all probability they [classical allusions] do not exist anywhere but in the minds of self-important, over-sophisticated musicologists who like to make an occasional comparison'. This is quite hard to resist! While it is inappropriate and foolish for any scholar to impute compositional intentionality without robust evidence, it would be equally futile for any composer to dictate future modes of listening to their music, once released into the public domain. Earlier in Lambert's *Music Ho!*, to which Ellington had responded,[59] his music had been compared to that of modernist composers in his surpassing of their achievement: 'I know of nothing in Ravel so dextrous in treatment as the varied solos in [...] Ellington's ebullient *Hot and Bothered* and nothing in Stravinsky more dynamic than the final section.'[60] Ellington had naturally been flattered and admitted to being 'wild about some of it [...] What's that bird ... [Stravinsky] "Firebird" – that's it. Great stuff!'[61] Later on, he provided a list of his classical music preferences to *Down Beat* which included Ravel's *Daphnis*, Debussy's *Prélude à l'Après-midi* and *La Mer*, together with Delius's *In a Summer Garden* (1908) and Holst's *The Planets* (1914–16).[62]

[56] Edward Kennedy Ellington, 'Certainly It's Music!', *Listen*, IV/12 (October 1944), 5–6; reprinted in Mark Tucker (ed.), *The Duke Ellington Reader* (New York: Oxford University Press, 1993), 246–8: 246.

[57] *Ibid.*, 247.   [58] *Ibid.*, 246.

[59] Gama Gilbert, '"Hot Damn!" Says Ellington When Ranked with Bach', *Philadelphia Record* (17 May 1935); reprinted in Tucker (ed.), *The Duke Ellington Reader*, 112–14.

[60] Lambert, 'The Spirit of Jazz', from *Music Ho!*, 186–8; reprinted in Tucker (ed.), *The Duke Ellington Reader*, 111.

[61] Gilbert, '"Hot Damn!"', 114.

[62] 'Lists of Favorites', *Down Beat* (5 November 1952), 2–4, reprinted in Tucker (ed.), *The Duke Ellington Reader*, 268–9. Ulanov suggested that Ellington's interest in this repertory was catalysed by his meeting with Will Vodery, musical director of Ziegfeld's *Show Girl*: Barry Ulanov, *Duke Ellington* (New York: Creative Age Press, 1946). Some years later, the influence of European technique on Ellington was discussed by Burnett James, 'The Impressionism of Duke Ellington', *Jazz Monthly*, 3/8 (October 1957), 5–7.

In this spirit, we may suggest at least an affinity between, in Lambert's words, 'the exquisitely tired and four-in-the-morning *Mood Indigo*'[63] and Debussy's sultry and languorous, four-in-the-afternoon *Prélude à l'Après-midi*, with its melodic turn-taking by a woodwind trio of clarinet, oboe and, especially, solo flute. Skilful orchestration-cum-timbre[64] also lies at the heart of the various versions and recordings of *Mood Indigo*,[65] with Ellington's registral rethinking and blending of a New Orleans front line of muted trumpet, trombone (highest) and clarinet/saxophone (lowest), which frames a central clarinet solo. The effect is to create subdued acoustical overtones, not so dissimilar to the unworldly sotto voce stacking of fifths over the bass that opens Ravel's *Daphnis*. The idea of indigo also creates an attractive association of languid, melancholic mood with the blue-violet-mauve, water lily impressionist canvases of late Monet, though the piece was originally called 'Dreamy Blues', until Irving Mills added lyrics after the first radio broadcast in October 1930. A crucial point to emphasize in all of this, however, is Ellington's highly innovative, creative status as a jazz composer-arranger-bandleader who melded styles, as denoted by this first major hit which became a jazz standard.

Beyond *Mood Indigo*, we find further significant classical affinities among a large, varied output of compositions and arrangements created across some fifty years that also explored the blues, popular repertory (for instance, Duke Ellington and His Orchestra in concert with Maurice Chevalier in 1930), gospel and film music (including for the short films *Black and Tan Fantasy*, 1929, and *Symphony in Black*, 1935).[66] As hinted earlier, the whole idea of symphonic jazz, achieved through the hugely popular and commercialized big band medium during the 1930s, involved developing jazz by applying and reformulating aspects of classical orchestral heritage, French or otherwise. Brubeck identified swing's clever balancing act in working with romantic-impressionist harmonic processes but keeping 'enough of the hot core of jazz through its soloists'.[67] Timbral blending of chosen instrumental sonorities was a central concern, as it was to Stravinsky or Ravel, or to dance bandleaders such as Jack Hylton (1892–1965). Especially

---

[63] Tucker (ed.), *The Duke Ellington Reader*, 111.

[64] In turn, this is inseparable from the impressionistic harmonies created – those opening 'evocative chords': Cooke, 'Jazz among the Classics', 159–60.

[65] The version studied here is the 1930 recording (*c*.3.03 duration) made by Ellington with Barney Bigard, who supplied the clarinet theme. See, for instance, on the five-CD collection *Duke Ellington* ('Dejavu Gold Collection', Recording Arts AG: 5X042, 2007).

[66] For more on the composer in his own words, see Edward Kennedy Ellington, *Music Is My Mistress* (New York: Doubleday, 1973; reprinted Da Capo Press, 1976).

[67] Brubeck, 'Jazz Perspective', 204.

notable are Ellington's big band compositions such as the paired *Diminuendo and Crescendo in Blue* (1937),[68] applauded by Cooke as 'arguably the most avant-garde product of the Swing Era',[69] and which might conceivably be viewed as an equivalent of Ravel's experimentation with volume, terracing and tension in *Boléro*.

Ellington's highly successful collaboration with the lyricist-cum-composer Billy Strayhorn (1915–67), creator of the signature tune 'Take the "A" Train' (1939), may be attributed in part to the latter's classical training, which enabled him to polish quite a few of the Duke's compositions. Overshadowed by Ellington, we should credit Strayhorn for his pensive and fluid 'Chelsea Bridge' (1941; recorded for Capitol/EMI on *The Peaceful Side* [1961]: solo piano, duration *c*.3.18), supposedly inspired by a Whistler painting. In its unified melodic-harmonic approach, the piece has been assessed by Strayhorn's biographer as 'an impressionistic miniature [...] more Debussy than Ellington',[70] and was similarly rated by Francis Davis in its version with Webster as soloist: 'as a successful jazz appropriation of Ravel and Debussy, this remains unsurpassed even by Ellington'.[71]

The second half of this survey of interwar activity is founded on French soil, but the American jazz activities already described exert a powerful influence – as part of a wider Americanization, welcomed and rejected – upon French concert and popular music, which helps to foster an incipient French jazz culture. Towards the end of World War I, the band of the African-American bandleader James Reese Europe appeared in France, as entertainment for the American troops. Europe's band intrigued its French listeners not so much by its music, which was largely familiar, but by the sonic, timbral qualities it created.[72] Similarly, the public heard Louis Mitchell's Jazz Kings, which was resident at the Casino de Paris in 1918. Unsurprisingly, the early French taking up of jazz was very much bound up with a pro-American stance, representative of freedom, in light of the

[68] On crossover in Ellington's compositions and elsewhere, see the fascinating study by Katherine Williams, 'Valuing Jazz: Cross-Cultural Comparisons of the Classical Influence in Jazz', PhD dissertation (University of Nottingham, 2012). A later live recording of *Diminuendo in Blue/Blow by Blow* was made by Ellington with Ella Fitzgerald at Juan-les-Pins in June–July 1966: *Ella and Duke at the Côte d'Azur* (Verve: V6 4072-2, 1967; reissued Verve 539 030-2, 1997).
[69] Cooke, *Jazz*, 104.
[70] David Hajdu, *Lush Life: A Biography of Billy Strayhorn* (New York: Farrar, Straus & Giroux, 1997), 85–6. I am grateful to Lawrence Woof for reminding me of this piece.
[71] Francis Davis, *Jazz and Its Discontents: A Francis Davis Reader* (New York: Da Capo Press, 2004), 70.
[72] Jackson, *Making Jazz French*, 18.

outcome of the war; as Maurice Sachs later put it: 'It was the war and the victory which made us so malleable to Americanization.'[73]

Such bands enlivened a pre-existent, continually evolving, European-French popular music scene. Revues included *Pa-ri-ki danse* (1919), *Paris qui jazz* (1920–1) and *Laisse-les tomber!* (1917, starring Gaby Deslys and her Hungarian-American husband Harry Pilcer), which were experienced by the likes of Cocteau and Milhaud. The mid 1920s first witnessed the remarkable phenomenon that was Josephine Baker, starring in the sexually explicit *Revue nègre* (1925) and accompanied by Bechet amongst others. Whiteman's first French tour in 1926 was closely followed by that of Hylton, whose frequent concertizing, myriad recordings and broadcasts came to dominate the French popular scene for several years; it was also Hylton who helped to organize and promote Ellington's Parisian début in summer 1933. Meanwhile, more spontaneous jazz permeated the nightclubs of Montmartre: Bricktop's (where, in 1928, Bechet led a small band before being imprisoned a second time for assault and subsequently deported),[74] Chez Florence, and the Grand Duc; and those of Montparnasse: The Jockey.

In the wake of World War I there emerged, too, the notion of a European, particularly a French, neoclassicism: a reinvocation of values of craftsmanship and tonal/modal order exemplified by a much earlier eighteenth-century era, born out of recent chaos, atrocity and loss of national identity. Such stripping to essentials ('le dépouillement'), including recourse to much smaller ensembles, was consistent too with economic exigency. Stravinsky, while long decrying the problematic neoclassical label,[75] was a vital prime mover with the stage works *L'Histoire* and *Pulcinella* (1920) and Satie, too, innovated with *Parade* (1916–17); see Chapter 3. The work that perhaps best symbolizes 'le néoclassicisme', as an upholding of all that was best within French cultural heritage yet cognisant of its turbulent present, was, however, Ravel's *Le Tombeau de Couperin*, begun in 1914 (predating Debussy's projected set of six sonatas, of which he completed three,

---

[73] Maurice Sachs, *Au temps du bœuf sur le toit* (Paris: Éditions de la Nouvelle Revue critique, 1948), 148: 'C'est la guerre et la victoire qui nous ont rendus si malléables à l'américanisme.'

[74] For an excellent account of the activities at Bricktop's, see Martin Guerpin, 'Bricktop, le jazz et la mondanité (1926–1936)', in Cotro, Cugny and Gumplowicz (eds.), *La Catastrophe apprivoisée*, 33–55; 'catastrophe apprivoisée' is quoted from Cocteau, *Le Coq et l'arlequin.*

[75] There is no place here for extended discussion of neoclassicism; it is rather its role in French music–jazz interplay that matters. For the classic text, still relevant today, see Scott Messing, *Neoclassicism in Music from the Genesis of the Concept through the Stravinsky/Schoenberg Polemic*, Studies in Musicology 101 (Ann Arbor, MI: UMI Research Press, 1988).

1915–17). Its sophisticated modality, rhythmic vitality and structural confidence, its later exquisite orchestration and balleticization, served to make it an archetype of modelling,[76] itself subject to further modelling as in George Russell's reinterpretation (Chapter 7).

Such neoclassicism, especially its anti-Germanic-Wagnerian and anti-Romantic-impressionist sentiments, was the mainstay of the cause that Cocteau promoted in his enigmatic, partisan manifesto *Le Coq*. This text symbolized matters French (the cockerel) in relation to their 'other': multicultural influences (the harlequin). One of its main tenets was the espousal of an everyday art and, by extension, music.[77] Turning its back on impressionism and prewar exoticism, this down-to-earth aesthetic still implicitly endorsed new forms of eclecticism in portraying and responding to the sounds of quotidian French street life: the fairground, barrel organ and music hall. Catalysed by the timely appearance and promotion of Les Six by Henri Collet in 1920, French neoclassicism came to stand, not only for a reassertion of the centrality of melody, tonality (sometimes bi-, poly-) and closed forms of eighteenth-century high art, but also for a lively engagement with the popular present.

This was a present in which everyday lives were being rapidly transformed by the technology of machines, a present epitomized by the new jazz music. Indeed jazz, with its own mechanisms, was often perceived as a metaphor for modernity, as in Robert Mendl's early text.[78] More recently, Jed Rasula has emphasized the extent to which jazz served as a 'generic signifier of modernism', though it is highly disputable that America should receive sole credit for delivering modernity.[79] Despite the tensions with a French nationalist agenda, jazz constituted an ideal vehicle for putting aside the blues of the war years and their enduring economic hardship, for asserting a *joie de vivre*, a legitimizing of the erotic and removal of social inhibition. As Brubeck, who would serve in World War II, aptly remarked: 'jazz became the cultural safety valve for the sexual and aggressive emotions

[76] See Barbara L. Kelly, 'History and Homage', in Deborah Mawer (ed.), *The Cambridge Companion to Ravel* (Cambridge University Press, 2000), 7–26: 19–22; Howat, *The Art of French Piano Music*, 176–86; and Deborah Mawer, *The Ballets of Maurice Ravel: Creation and Interpretation* (Aldershot: Ashgate, 2006), 183–207.

[77] See Nancy Perloff, *Art and the Everyday: Popular Entertainment and the Circle of Erik Satie* (Oxford: Clarendon Press, 1993).

[78] Robert W. S. Mendl, *The Appeal of Jazz* (London: P. Allen & Co, 1927). See Chapter 5, n. 28.

[79] Rasula, 'Jazz as Decal for the European Avant Garde', 14. Rasula usefully considers the role of jazz in modernism, primitivism and so on; however, his dismissive mention of French music influenced by jazz seems rather deprecating and simplistic: 20.

which had become intensified by wartime hysteria'.[80] It was a vital ingredient of the so-called 'crazy years', described so captivatingly by Roger Nichols: 'The gay Twenties, the silly Twenties, the roaring Twenties, when Paris echoed to the sounds of jazz [. . .] The resonance of the "années folles" is long and loud, of a magical time when all things were possible, some of them were still illegal and most of them were fun.'[81]

Typical products of this French music–jazz relationship include Milhaud's *Caramel mou* (1920), *La Création du monde* (1923), the Sixth Chamber Symphony (1923), Ravel's Sonata for Violin and Piano (1923–7), aspects of *Boléro* (1928) and the two piano concertos (1929–31). Also relevant is Poulenc's *Les Biches* (1923), with its 'Rag-Mazurka' that caused the composer some compositional struggle and the 'Adagietto' with its concealed blues plus syncopation. An isolated jazzlike sonority ends his Sonata for Piano Four Hands (1918): Cm^{b9}, with modal mixture at the third and fifth: C, Eb/E, Gb/G, Bb, Db.

The main sources of jazz inspiration comprised a generic mixture of the blues (*La Création*, 'Blues' from Ravel's Violin Sonata) and early jazz in a New Orleans vein (*La Création*, *Boléro*), with occasional allusion to Harlem. As with most cultural exchange, there was an inevitable time lag, so that the cross-references were not generally with Armstrong or Ellington. Excitement and novelty apart, the appeal concerned emotional expressivity, timbre, rhythmic invention and the sense of spontaneity engendered by improvisation. Interestingly, such pursuit of the foreign often served to enhance a certain intrinsic Frenchness (see Chapter 5 on Ravel), although less commonly it resulted in an international fusion (Chapter 4 on Milhaud).

Among East European émigrés resident in Paris, we should credit Bohuslav Martinů (1890–1959) with a wealth of jazz-inspired works, including the wonderful jazz suite-cum-ballet *La Revue de cuisine* (1927), the irreverent *Le Jazz* and another Jazz Suite for small orchestra, both of 1928. Other composers working in and out of Paris included George Antheil, with his *A Jazz Symphony* (1925, revised 1955), which was later conducted by Handy. Beyond France, inspiration from jazz was evident in contemporaneous works of Ernst Křenek (notably his opera *Jonny spielt auf* of 1925–7, later banned by the Nazis), Paul Hindemith and Kurt Weill.

At the more obscure end of Les Six, Georges Auric's *Adieu New York!* (1919) has been regarded as missing a trick since Harlem jazz had hardly arrived on the scene; conversely, it may have been quite canny or prophetic in perceiving that (neo)classical gains from jazz would be relatively short-

[80] Brubeck, 'Jazz Perspective', 202.
[81] Roger Nichols, 'Cock and Harlequin', *The Listener* (30 January 1986), 30.

lived. Having said this, once jazz had entered the subconscious of an artist such as Milhaud, despite his formal renouncing of interest in the genre around 1926, its imprint in blue notes and syncopation had become an integral part of the composer's vocabulary, resurfacing within an eclectic mix, for instance, in *Scaramouche* (1937). This trait is also evident in Stravinsky's return to crossover in the *Ebony Concerto* (1945), created for the jazz clarinettist Woody Herman and his orchestra, upon which Poulenc muses: 'How interesting it is to compare the *Ebony Concerto* with the *Ragtime for 11 instruments* of 1918. The latter [...] is a portrait of jazz. The *Ebony Concerto* is the lesson learnt from jazz by an artist of genius.'[82] Notwithstanding Auric's reservations, a neoclassicism that had lacked the energizing impact of jazz would surely have been a pale, insipid reflection of the vibrant and blended high/low French cultural modernism that emerged in the 1920s to challenge the supremacy of the Second Viennese School, and which has since enjoyed a long legacy.

As an extension of our main agenda, we witness an amplification of activity: to interaction between French concert music and American jazz may be added that of jazz as French popular music. The Frenchification of jazz is a topic documented by Jeffrey Jackson and others,[83] primarily in terms of French musicians, if not strictly new styles. A progression began with largely indigenous bands of the late 1920s, such as those of Grégor et ses grégoriens, Ray Ventura et ses collégiens and Léo Vauchant (formerly of Hylton's band), and led through to the setting up in 1934 of the Quintette du Hot Club de France by the jazz violinist Stéphane Grappelli (1908–97), in partnership with the extraordinary Belgian Romani guitarist Django Reinhardt (1910–53).[84] This process involved a lively critical perspective, a substantial part of which strongly endorsed African-American jazz and presented an idealized blackness (see Chapter 2); it centred around figures such as Hugues Panassié (1912–74) with his *Le Jazz hot* (1934), Charles

---

[82] Sidney Buckland and Myriam Chimènes (eds.), *Francis Poulenc: Music, Art and Literature* (Aldershot: Ashgate, 1999), 369.

[83] See especially Jackson, 'Making Jazz French: Parisian Musicians and Jazz Fans', in *Making Jazz French*, 123–35. Earlier histories include Tyler Stovall, *Paris noir: African Americans in the City of Light* (Boston, MA: Houghton Mifflin, 1996); and Ludovic Tournès, *New Orleans sur Seine: Histoire du jazz en France* (Paris: Librairie Arthème Fayard, 1999). More recently, see Barbara Meister, *Music Musique: French and American Piano Composition in the Jazz Age* (Bloomington, IN: Indiana University Press, 2006) and Roscoe Seldon Suddarth, 'French Stewardship of Jazz: The Case of France Musique and France Culture', MA dissertation (University of Maryland, College Park, 2008). This topic is also being pursued by British scholars such as Tom Perchard and Andy Fry.

[84] See Michael Dregni, *Gypsy Jazz: In Search of Django Reinhardt and the Soul of Gypsy Swing* (New York: Oxford University Press, 2008).

Delaunay (1911–88) and the perspicacious Belgian critic Robert Goffin (1898–1984), author of *Aux frontières du jazz* (1932).

Although bands such as Grégor's were not stylistically innovative, they presented themselves as distinct from American jazz in adopting a certain Latin inflection: this was the infamous age of the tango, as evidenced by the contemporary magazine *Jazz-Tango(-Dancing)*. Equally, following Hylton's example, Ventura incorporated chansons into his jazz repertory while, from an opposite perspective, Charles Trenet experimented with jazz-inspired chansons. The Hot Club de France, active from 1932 until about 1948, upheld, at least for a minority French audience, the importance of dynamic, spontaneous credentials of African-American origin, especially blue notes and syncopation. Its Quintette espoused these values, coupled with an incisive, punctuated Romani style, one of its most celebrated products being Reinhardt's blues-related swing composition *Nuages* (1940).

French identification with, even ownership of, a brand of jazz developed in tandem with the unwelcome consequences of the New York stock market crash: the Great Depression and widespread unemployment in America and Europe. While these circumstances invariably bred xenophobia, such sentiments were directed more towards foreign, including American and British, performers seemingly taking French jobs by playing gigs in France, than to American music per se. As Jackson points out, one of the distinctive objectives of the Hot Club's approach was to promote an international jazz community by establishing 'Foreign Hot Clubs' linked by an International Federation, under the presidency of Panassié. Jazz also featured widely at the 1937 Exposition internationale in Paris.[85] (This exhibition had progressed some way from its 1931 precursor, which, despite a supposedly greater anthropological seriousness, had still been entitled the Exposition coloniale.)

Nonetheless, by the start of World War II, jazz was once more being disparaged as a decadent foreign music, by both the Nazi and the Vichy regimes, though it was not actually banned in France and continued in a clandestine fashion.[86] In Germany, the situation was much more acute, with styles as diverse as jazz and serialism being banned for their perceived dangerous black and Jewish racial associations, and in turn being upheld by their advocates as emblematic of artistic freedom. The Nazi regime failed to silence jazz, however, and thus there even emerged a type of Nazi propaganda swing, which sought to capitalize on its popularity. Again,

---

[85] Jackson, *Making Jazz French*, 188–9. On 'The Jazz Hot Years', see too the extensive coverage in Jordan, *Le Jazz*, 141–84.

[86] Jackson, *Making Jazz French*, 190–1.

Brubeck had his finger on the pulse, in acknowledging 'the powerful symbol of freedom jazz had become in Nazi Germany – and the role it had played toward liberation in the French Underground, Sweden, and England.'[87] As a codicil on issues of national identity, we might add that in London on 31 January 1946, the Quintette du Hot Club de France recorded 'Echoes of France (La Marseillaise)', celebrating Reinhardt's reunion with Grappelli.[88] This was, though, a decidedly ambivalent and quirky remaking of the anthem, which serves to remind us of the complex French establishment–manouche (French gypsy jazz) dynamics of supposed integration and yet lingering segregation.

Bebop, modal jazz, Third Stream and postwar modernism (1945–65)

During World War II the bebop (bop) style emerged, championed by John 'Dizzy' Gillespie (1917–93) and Thelonious Monk (1917–82), in conjunction with the drummer Kenny Clarke (1914–85) and the legendary alto saxophonist Charlie 'Bird' Parker (1920–55). As a response to the increasingly predictable, populist big band scene and in the face of war/postwar economic austerity, there are distinct parallels between bop and the French neoclassicism that had reacted against overblown Romanticism towards the end of World War I. Bop returned to compact ensembles that comprised a front line plus rhythm section, but it retained walking-bass patterns and basic principles of riffs from the swing era. As an abstract music rather than a dance-based genre, it employed underlying harmonies from twelve-bar blues, but with 'flatted 5' substitutions, and increased dissonance via blue notes and bitonal effects, so exhibiting commonality with earlier French and Russian techniques, as used by Milhaud and Stravinsky. The aim was to foreground a virtuosic instrumental improvisation – sometimes almost robotic at frenetic tempo – and to encourage invention, complexity and spontaneity, especially of rhythm and accentuation.

In terms of French connections, Bechet returned to France in 1950 and settled there for his remaining years. Meanwhile, Gillespie performed at the first international jazz festival in Nice in 1948 and at the Parisian Salle Pleyel in 1949;[89] he played widely in Paris during the early 1950s

---

[87] Brubeck, 'Jazz Perspective', 205.

[88] I am grateful to Siv Lie and Mike Beckerman, New York University, for drawing my attention to this recording in summer 2013.

[89] A further French initiative was the setting up of the Jazz groupe de Paris by the musician-cum-critic André Hodeir in 1954; see also chapters 2, 4 and 5 of this book.

disseminating the bop style. Both Parker and Miles Davis (1926–91) also appeared at the Salle Pleyel event, the young Davis having first assisted 'Bird's' innovative bop recordings in the late 1940s. Parker was seriously interested in European modernist composition, particularly that of Béla Bartók, Stravinsky, Debussy and Ravel.[90] He really rated Debussy's *Children's Corner* suite, enthusing to Leonard Feather in an article for *Metronome* magazine entitled 'Yardbird Flies Home (1947)': 'Oh, that's so much music!', and his improvisation on *Merry Go Round* involved paraphrasing *Boléro*.[91] He contemplated formal musical study with Nadia Boulanger (as Quincy Jones had done) and, near the end of his all-too-brief life, with Edgard Varèse.[92]

Around the mid 1950s, we encounter two other associated phenomena: modal jazz and a larger-scale, overarching idea of Third Stream. While it was more of a contemporaneous happening than any strict cause responsible for a consequent effect, the emergence of Third Stream sets an important cultural context for examining more specific relationships between French music and modal jazz. As Harvey Pekar observed in *Jazz Monthly*, relatively close to the time of its inception, 'The term "third stream" was originated several years ago to label jazz that was influenced to varying degrees by western "classical" music. However, there had been quite a bit of this kind of music written and played during the middle-fifties.'[93] Arguably, the trend was begun by Ellington, and was one to which the influential composer-cum-bandleader and bassist Charles Mingus (1922–79) contributed, for instance with his *Jazzical Moods* (1955).[94] In a rather different vein, the pianist Art Tatum (1909–56) was noted for his imaginative jazz versions and reinterpretations of works such as the *Élégie* of Jules Massenet (1842–1912), or Dvořák's *Humoresque* No. 7.

Significantly, in 1955, Schuller and the jazz pianist John Lewis (1920–2001) founded the Modern Jazz Society, later renamed the Jazz and Classical Music Society. And it was while teaching at Brandeis University, Massachusetts, in 1957, and supplemented by intensive summer meetings

---

[90] Robert G. Reisner (ed.), *Bird: The Legend of Charlie Parker* (New York: Da Capo Press, 1975), 203.

[91] James Patrick, liner notes for *Charlie Parker: The Complete Savoy and Dial Studio Recordings (1944–1948)* (Savoy 92911-2, 2000), 58.

[92] Carl Woideck (ed.), *Charlie Parker: Six Decades of Commentary* (New York: Schirmer Books, 1998), 41, 129, 249. See too Brian Priestley, *Chasin' The Bird: The Life and Legacy of Charlie Parker* (Oxford and New York: Oxford University Press, 2007), 127.

[93] Harvey Pekar, 'Third Stream Jazz', *Jazz Monthly*, 8/10 (December 1962), 7–9: 7.

[94] See Priestley's appreciation of Mingus which has stood the test of time: Brian Priestley, *Mingus: A Critical Biography* (New York: Da Capo Press, 1984) and Todd S. Jenkins, *I Know What I Know: The Music of Charles Mingus* (Westport, CT and London: Praeger, 2006).

of the Lenox School of Jazz,[95] that Schuller coined and developed the concept of Third Stream. His intention was to define and promote music that deliberately mediated aspects of classical and jazz techniques, while maintaining the crucial element of improvisation.[96] As Darius Brubeck points out in grappling with the contradictory views of the jazz pianist-academic John Mehegan,[97] this equal partnering of musics also had a distinct intellectual component.[98] Indeed Schuller perceived an equivalent *mélange* in Bartók's modernism coupled with folksong. His subsequent compositions practised this musical philosophy extensively, including *Transformation* (1957), for jazz ensemble, and *Concertino* (1959), for a jazz quartet plus orchestra. Pekar singles out *Transformation* as a substantive early instance of Third Stream, commenting that it 'evolves from "straight classical" writing to a jazz influenced portion'. In particular, he draws attention to the contribution of Bill Evans (1929–80) who offers a special point of connection between Third Stream and modal jazz: 'Bridging these sections is Bill Evans's beautifully subtle improvisation. Evans's [piano] solo eventually disintegrates into a dissonant ensemble passage and on that note the record ends.'[99]

The later 1950s through to the early 1960s was the fairly circumscribed period during which the notion of modal jazz came to fruition: both in New York, centred around Davis, his exact contemporary John Coltrane (1926–67), Evans and others such as Herbie Hancock (b. 1940), and on the West Coast, involving personnel such as Dave Brubeck (1920–2012). The role of a founding father of modal jazz, most especially in his theorizing of the Lydian variety, must surely go to George Russell (1923–2009), also an exponent of Third Stream. The essential principle of modal jazz was one of back to basics. It was sometimes equated with 'cool jazz', though not by

---

[95] Darius Brubeck, '1959: The Beginning of Beyond', 188–9.

[96] For a composite manifesto, listen to Gunther Schuller, *The Birth of the Third Stream* (Columbia/Legacy CK 64929, 1996). An extensive 700-page, autobiographical account of his activities until around 1960 is presented in *Gunther Schuller: A Life in Pursuit of Music and Beauty* (Rochester, NY: University of Rochester Press, 2011). I am grateful to Martyn Harry for alerting me to this magnum opus, following his meeting with the composer.

[97] Notwithstanding, Mehegan produced useful transcriptions of Bill Evans's music, including of 'Peri's Scope' from *Portrait in Jazz* (New York: Riverside RLP 12 315, 1960): see John Mehegan, *Contemporary Piano Styles*, Jazz Improvisation IV (New York: Watson-Guptill Publications/Simon and Schuster, 1965).

[98] Darius Brubeck, '1959: The Beginning of Beyond', 180–1.

[99] Pekar, 'Third Stream Jazz', 9. Gunther Schuller, *Transformation* may be heard on *Brandeis Jazz Festival: Modern Jazz Concert* (Columbia WL 127, 1957; reissued on *The Birth of the Third Stream*).

the likes of Brubeck who criticized 'cool' for alienating its public.[100] Modal jazz involved a stepping back from the increasingly complex, restrictive harmonic changes of highly developed 'hot' jazz to a position from which to celebrate the relative melodic freedom of improvising on a simple scalic basis. It was like choosing to paint with a restricted palette of colours in order to explore subtle new tones.

French music – amid other classical repertory including that with a Russian flavour – constituted a significant inspiration for this genre. There is at least hermeneutic association between the role of Russell and that of Olivier Messiaen (1908–92) as the exceptional French modal innovator, who first publicly set out his ideas in *Technique de mon langage musical* (1944).[101] Modal jazz musicians of the 1950s were seemingly most taken by the prewar impressionist writing of Debussy and Ravel, for its exploration of colour and texture and its fondness for lush dominant ninths. A complexity and richness of interplay is well illustrated by Coltrane's own 'Impressions',[102] the extended title track of his 1963 album (first recorded in 1961), which utilizes melodically two possible sources of pavane. According to Lewis Porter, the first part of Coltrane's theme quotes Morton Gould's *Pavan(n)e* (1938) – with its own affinity to Gabriel Fauré; the second theme may have been elaborately derived from Ravel's early *Pavane pour une infante défunte* (1899),[103] which had been adapted in the interim as a popular song: 'The Lamp is Low' (1939). Harmonically, 'Impressions' models its restricted modal changes upon those in Davis's 'So What' from the album *Kind of Blue* of 1959.

In turn, we learn from Davis's autobiography of the impact of Ravel's Concerto for the Left Hand as an inspirational source for 'All Blues', also from *Kind of Blue*.[104] The particular draw was Ravel's use of white-note modality, especially the Dorian. A rather different relationship – at least a surprising parallel in intricate polymodal evocation of birdsong – is noted by Peter Pettinger between Messiaen's *Catalogue d'oiseaux* and Evans's

---

[100] Brubeck, 'Jazz Perspective', 205.

[101] Olivier Messiaen, *Technique de mon langage musical*, 2 vols. (Paris: Alphonse Leduc, 1944), written during 1942–3.

[102] I appreciate Tony Whyton's offering of this suggestion. See John Coltrane, *Impressions* (New York and Englewood Cliffs, NJ: Impulse! Records A-42, 1963).

[103] Porter now believes these Ravelian similarities emerge from improvisation across 'the bridge'; however, courtesy of two Italian colleagues, he proposes Poulenc's Impromptu No. 3 as a direct melodic source (the same key; eight identical pitches) for the opening of Coltrane's 'Big Nick', as recorded with Ellington in 1962: www.wbgo.org/blog/dr-lewis-porter-on-john-coltrane-more-inspirations.

[104] Miles Davis with Quincy Troupe, *Miles: The Autobiography* (London: Macmillan, 1989), 224–5.

improvisation 'Peace Piece' from *Everybody Digs Bill Evans* of 1958 (see Chapter 8).[105] An intercultural collaboration is denoted by Davis's evocative soundtrack for Louis Malle's innovative film noir *L'Ascenseur pour l'échafaud* (Lift to the Scaffold), starring Jeanne Moreau and Maurice Ronet, recorded in December 1957 and released in 1958. A further extension sees the collaborative jazz-classical album *Legrand Jazz*,[106] created on an American visit, also of 1958, by the Franco-Armenian composer and jazz pianist Michel Legrand (b. 1932), working with Davis, Coltrane and Evans.

We may add into the mix the experience of Brubeck, for whom, rather like Evans, music connoted a fascinating kaleidoscope of styles and genres: jazz, classical, religious and folk sources. Brubeck referred to the notion of a 'mixed musical heritage' that encompassed a huge spectrum 'from African drum batteries to Couperin'.[107] At the centre of this varied context was his long-term relationship with his mentor Milhaud and their shared principles of polytonality and polyrhythm (see Chapter 9).

So, especially in light of the Third Stream cultural background, a case for notable meeting points between French music and modal jazz is not difficult to make. Similarly, we find an ongoing interplay with classical music on the part of swing clarinettist Goodman, who as early as 1938 had commissioned Bartók's *Contrasts*, and later catalysed works by Aaron Copland, Hindemith and others. On 10 April 1963, accompanied by Leonard Bernstein in New York's Carnegie Hall, Goodman premiered the Sonata for Clarinet and Piano by Poulenc. Poulenc had dedicated the sonata to the memory of his good friend Arthur Honegger; however, its performance soon after Poulenc's own death in January 1963 became a double French tribute at the Composers' Showcase event.

Conversely, there are, admittedly more isolated, instances of postwar French modernists continuing to derive inspiration from jazz, as well as those whose music may be illuminated by comparison with jazz as a hermeneutic tool. Indeed Poulenc's poignant central 'Romanza' in G minor may be interpreted as consonant with certain jazz qualities: its quasi-improvisatory opening flourish, embodying modal mixture at the seventh and third: F♯/F, B♭/B; the piano part 'laissez vibrer', with its suspended chord of Gm$^{♯11/♯7}$: G, B♭, F♯, C♯, mingling with B above. In its rhapsodic reprise, the final bars confirm a blues-like flexibility, also sharing seventh and ninth jazz-type

---

[105] Peter Pettinger, *Bill Evans: How My Heart Sings* (New Haven, CT and London: Yale University Press, 1998), 69, 70.

[106] *Legrand Jazz*, including 'Wild Man Blues', ''Round Midnight', 'The Jitterbug Waltz', 'Django', 'Nuages', 'In a Mist'; performers: Miles Davis, Bill Evans, John Coltrane, Michel Legrand and others (New York: Columbia CL 1250, 1958).

[107] Brubeck, 'Jazz Perspective', 206.

harmonies. The clarinet's sustained ascent: E, F, A♭/A, leads via a demi-semiquaver flourish down to the low D. Meanwhile, the piano searches for the dominant via a flattened (Neapolitan), tritonal decoration: C^9–$D♭$–$E♭m^{11/7}$–Dm^7, cadencing onto the G modal tonic and lingering on a hollow fifth. In this introspective, mournful cantilena to Honegger, we might sense a spiritual commonality with the expressivity of the blues.

Late Milhaud manifests vestiges of his earlier love affair with jazz, albeit fully absorbed within his mature style. *Carnaval à la Nouvelle-Orléans*, Op. 275 (1947), for two pianos makes lighthearted reference to his original source of inspiration, and *Le Globe-Trotter*, Op. 358 (1956), suggests a wry allusion to Harlem amidst Milhaud's own nonstop itinerary. More speculatively, one may propose parallels in nonteleological approaches to structuring musical time and narrative that connect modal musics such as Messiaen's *Quatuor pour la fin du Temps* (1941) with those of the African-American avant-garde, and with wholly non-Western traditions, even though Messiaen would not tend to concur. Modality is well-placed to promote temporal stasis. Where Boulez's *Le Marteau sans maître* (1953–4) is concerned, the use of a xylorimba, coupled by the high profile of percussion including bongos, may create association with the African *balafon*, though again the composer would resist perceiving deeper intercultural or stylistic links.[108] Nonetheless, the British writer Paul Griffiths has long asserted the relevance of an African-cum-jazz agenda ('the ensemble, like that of [Stockhausen's] *Kreuzspiel*, is flavoured with the modern jazz of the period')[109] in interpretation of this most sophisticated, synthesized icon of modernism. This is the appropriate point at which to adopt a critical perspective.

---

[108] Pierre Boulez, 'Speaking, Playing, Singing', in *Orientations: Collected Writings*, ed. Jean-Jacques Nattiez and Eng. trans. Martin Cooper (Cambridge, MA: Harvard University Press, 1986), 330–43.

[109] Paul Griffiths, *Modern Music and After*, third edition (New York: Oxford University Press, 2010), 92.

2 Critical-analytical perspectives: intertextuality and borrowing

Relations between the French music and jazz loci established in Chapter 1 are developed here from a critical-cum-analytical (broadly *esthesic*) stance. Essentially, this chapter has a two-part design. To demonstrate the scope and complexity of the topic with its French–American (and British) relations in combination with the classical music–jazz interplay, it commences with a short, selective survey of French-based critical discourse and its attendant ideas apropos jazz, furthering connection with national identities, race, ethnicity and aspects of gender. The focus then shifts to consider wider critical-analytical approaches, pertaining to intertextuality and borrowing, which are relevant to the main case studies, as well as being of interest in themselves.

French critical discourse and jazz

It is well documented that early jazz had a much better initial reception in France than in the United States, which was characterized during the interwar period as essentially conservative, espousing white racial superiority, favouring earlier European culture, but suspicious, even intolerant, of primitivism. We may relate again to Brubeck's testimony from 1951: 'this music, indigenous to America's strange national and racial mixtures, and embodying in its very form the democratic idea of unity through diversity, found more serious consideration in France, in particular, and Europe, in general, than it did at home'.[1]

Some of the earliest critical upholding of early jazz and blues comes not from French critics per se, but from composers such as Milhaud and Ravel, together with Stravinsky, Hindemith and others. As early as 1919, Ernest Ansermet (1883–1969), the Swiss conductor and friend of Stravinsky, had published on African-American jazz in the Francophone Lausanne-based periodical *La Revue romande*, recognizing and validating Claude Hopkins's band, while singling out his clarinettist Sidney Bechet as a superb and memorable jazz artist.[2] In late spring 1923, in his first of various writings

---

[1] Brubeck, 'Jazz Perspective', 202.

[2] Ernest Ansermet, 'Sur un orchestre nègre', *La Revue romande*, no. 10 (15 October 1919), 10–13. We should also note an exceptionally early critical contribution: Jules Huret, *En*

on jazz that balanced the jazz-band and African-American musics, the precocious Milhaud was promoting its creative potential.[3] Even composers who today have been relegated to obscurity such as Maurice Delage (1879–1961), a one-time student of Ravel, were making known their views on jazz in the later 1920s.[4] Likewise, the tragically short-lived and over-looked composer Pierre-Octave Ferroud produced a series of four articles on 'L'Évolution du jazz', in issues of *L'Édition musicale vivante*, spanning February–May 1929. Ravel, assuming a certain superiority as a revered European on his North American tour, urged his hosts to 'Take Jazz Seriously!': 'You Americans take jazz too lightly. You seem to feel that it is cheap, vulgar, momentary. In my opinion it is bound to lead to the national music of the United States. Aside from it you have no veritable idiom as yet.'[5] In a similar vein, he asserted: 'To my mind, the blues is one of your greatest musical assets' (for detail, see pages 139–45).[6]

Alongside these composerly accounts – and that of the pioneering British critic Robert Mendl whose *The Appeal of Jazz* was published in 1927 – we encounter a substantial body of French language-based criticism. This is not to ignore Alfred Baresel's *Das Jazzbuch* (1925), or the intensely negative, idiosyncratic perceptions contained in Theodor Adorno's essays, based largely on popular, commercial German culture,[7] and on his engagement with Walter Benjamin's essay 'The Work of Art in the Age of Mechanical

---

Amérique – De New-York à la Nouvelle-Orléans (Paris: Fasquelle, 1904). I am grateful to Laurent Cugny for this reference.

[3] Darius Milhaud, 'L'Évolution du jazz-band et la musique des nègres d'Amérique du nord', *Le Courrier musical*, 25/9 (1 May 1923), 163ff.; Eng. trans. as 'The Jazz Band and Negro Music', *Living Age*, 323 (October 1924), 169–73. In this same year, we find Émile Vuillermoz, *Musiques d'aujourd'hui* (Paris: Crès et cie, 1923): chapter 17, 'Rag-time et Jazz-Band', 207–15.

[4] Maurice Delage, 'La Musique du jazz', *Revue Pleyel* (April 1926), 18–20.

[5] Maurice Ravel, 'Take Jazz Seriously!', *Musical Digest*, 13/3 (March 1928), 49, 51: 49.

[6] Maurice Ravel, *Contemporary Music*, Rice Institute Pamphlet 15/2 (April 1928), 131–45: 140. On the reasons for such composerly interest, see a contribution in an impressive collection: Martin Guerpin, 'Why Did Art Music Composers Pay Attention to "Jazz"? The Impact of "Jazz" on the French Musical Field, 1908–24', in Luca Cerchiari, Laurent Cugny and Franz Kerschbaumer (eds.), *Eurojazzland: Jazz and European Sources, Dynamics, and Contexts* (Boston, MA: Northeastern University Press, 2012), 47–80.

[7] See Theodor W. Adorno, 'On Jazz [1936]', in *Essays on Music*, ed. Richard Leppert and Eng. trans. Susan H. Gillespie (Berkeley and Los Angeles, CA: University of California Press, 2002), 470–95; and J. Bradford Robinson, 'The Jazz Essays of Theodor Adorno: Some Thoughts on Jazz Reception in Weimar Germany', *Popular Music*, 13/1 (January 1994), 1–25. A thorough introduction to Adorno's ideas is offered by Wayne D. Bowman, 'Music as Social and Political Force', in *Philosophical Perspectives on Music* (Oxford and New York: Oxford University Press, 1998), 304–55.

Reproduction' (1936), first published in French.[8] The first book-length French study, authored by André Cœuroy and André Schaeffner, was simply called *Le Jazz* (1926).[9] It was followed by Goffin's *Aux frontières du jazz*,[10] which, unusually for its time, focused on the performers and their techniques, probing notions of 'hot' and explaining ideas such as 'chorus' and 'break'. From it, we learn of other, more obscure, early commentators such as Pierre MacOrlan.[11] Next came Panassié's *Le Jazz hot*[12] and Delaunay's innovative *Hot Discography*,[13] since republished in at least four editions and still retaining status as a reference work. Interestingly, by 1938, we do find an equivalent American contribution in *Jazz: Hot and Hybrid*,[14] written by the critic-cum-violinist Winthrop Sargeant (1903–86). Through this interwar period, French periodicals such as *La Revue musicale*,[15] under its founding editor Henry Prunières, provided a supportive basis for a diverse collection of article-length critiques of an emerging jazz. Such criticism included a piece on the jazz band and its impact dating from the mid 1920s, echoing part of Milhaud's earlier article, and several during 1927, including that by the Belgian composer-critic Arthur Hoerée.[16] From around 1930, *La Revue musicale* was supplemented by more specialist publications such as *Jazz-Tango*, *La Revue du jazz* and, from 1935–40, by *Jazz-Hot*.

[8] Walter Benjamin, 'L'Œuvre d'art à l'époque de sa reproduction mécanisée', French trans. Pierre Klossowski, in *Zeitschrift für Sozialforschung* (Paris: Félix Alcan, 1936), vol. V, 40–68.
[9] André Cœuroy and André Schaeffner, *Le Jazz* (Paris: Éditions Claude Aveline, 1926), a text exactly contemporary with Paul Whiteman and Mary Margaret McBride, *Jazz* (New York: J. H. Sears, 1926).
[10] Robert Goffin, *Aux frontières du jazz*, second edition (Paris: Éditions du Sagittaire, 1932).
[11] See Yannick Séité, 'MacOrlan jazz writer', in Cotro, Cugny and Gumplowicz (eds.), *La Catastrophe apprivoisée*, 57–66.
[12] Hugues Panassié, *Le Jazz hot* (Paris: Éditions R.-A. Corrêa, 1934). His material had earlier appeared as: 'Le Jazz "hot"', *L'Édition musicale vivante* (February 1930), 9–11, and 'Le Jazz "hot"', *La Revue musicale*, 11 (June 1930), 481–94. For an assessment of the critic's early writings, see Philippe Gumplowicz, 'Hugues Panassié 1930–1934: une cause et un système', in Cotro, Cugny and Gumplowicz (eds.), *La Catastrophe apprivoisée*, 113–19.
[13] Charles Delaunay, *Hot Discography* (Paris: Hot Jazz, 1936).
[14] Winthrop Sargeant, *Jazz: Hot and Hybrid* (New York and London: Jazz Book Club Edition, 1938, enlarged edition 1959); revised and enlarged as *Jazz: A History* (New York: McGraw-Hill, 1964).
[15] See Michel Duchesneau, '*La Revue musicale* (1920–40) and the Founding of a Modern Music', in Zdravko Blažekovic and Barbara Dobbs Mackenzie (eds.), *Music's Intellectual History*, RILM Perspectives I (New York: Répertoire International de Littérature Musicale, 2009), 743–50.
[16] Marion Bauer, 'L'Influence du jazz-band', *La Revue musicale*, 5 (1 April 1924), 31–6; Albert Jeanneret, 'Le Nègre et le jazz', *La Revue musicale*, 8 (1 July 1927), 24–7; Arthur Hoerée, 'Le Jazz', *La Revue musicale*, 8 (1 October 1927), 213–41; and André Schaeffner, 'Le Jazz', *La Revue musicale*, 9 (1 November 1927), 72–6.

During World War II, Panassié wrote a volume in support of swing and another entitled, revealingly, *La Véritable Musique de jazz*, with explicit designations of his 'true' and 'false' jazz.[17] Soon afterwards, Goffin produced his landmark biography of Armstrong, *Horn of Plenty* (1947),[18] with Panassié's equivalent appearing in the same year.[19] This French critical phenomenon was also illustrated in the postwar era by André Hodeir (1921–2011), with his *Hommes et problèmes du jazz* (1954), well-known in Anglophone circles in its Jazz Book Club translation.[20]

Although Hodeir is typically rather dismissive – uncomprehending even – of modernist composers' interactions with and borrowings from jazz, he acknowledges the contributions of Ellington, Parker and bop, Davis and the notion of 'cool', concluding with his perception of the 'Situation of Modern Jazz at the Death of Parker'.[21] He problematizes aspects of improvisation, creativity, melody, swing/rhythm and sound, and attempts analytical engagement with musical practice, including that of Armstrong, his white Jewish contemporary Milton Mezzrow (1899–1972), 'Fats' Waller (1904–43), Coleman Hawkins (1904–69) and Lester Young (1909–59). Hodeir compares jazz and French artistic culture on a modernist theme of change that risks leaving behind its main audience: 'Carried along by the prodigious cadence of constant renewal, jazz dies almost as quickly as it is created [. . .] This phenomenon has been observed in European art [when] Cézanne and Debussy unveiled the beginnings of a "modern art" that is in no way of popular origin.'[22] (For application and evaluation of Hodeir's criticism, see chapters 4 and 5.)

---

[17] Hugues Panassié, *La Musique de jazz et le swing* (Paris: Éditions R.-A. Corrêa, 1943) and *La Véritable Musique de jazz* (Paris: Robert Laffont, 1946); Eng. trans. as *The Real Jazz*, trans. Anne Sorelle Williams (New York: Smith & Durrell, 1942). Written during the Occupation, the manuscript of *La Véritable Musique* was smuggled to America and first published in translation: Daniel Hardie, *Jazz Historiography: The Story of Jazz History Writing* (Bloomington, IN: iUniverse, 2013), 81.

[18] Robert Goffin, *Louis Armstrong, le roi du jazz* (Paris: Pierre Seghers, 1947); Eng. trans. as *Horn of Plenty: The Story of Louis Armstrong*, trans. James F. Bezou (New York: Allen, Towne & Heath, 1947). On Armstrong's collaborative role in Goffin's biography, see Daniel Stein, 'Negotiating Primitivist Modernisms: Louis Armstrong, Robert Goffin, and the Transatlantic Jazz Debate', *European Journal of American Studies* [online], 2 (2011), n.p.: http://ejas.revues.org/9395.

[19] Hugues Panassié, *Louis Armstrong*, Les Maîtres du jazz (Paris, 1947; Nouvelles Éditions Latines, 1969; Eng. trans. New York: Charles Scribner's Sons, 1971), vol. I.

[20] André Hodeir, *Hommes et problèmes du jazz* (Paris: Portulan, 1954); Eng. trans. as *Jazz: Its Evolution and Essence*, trans. David Noakes (London: Jazz Book Club, 1958).

[21] Hodeir, *Jazz*, 267–80.

[22] André Hodeir, 'Perspective of Modern Jazz: Popularity or Recognition?', *Down Beat*, 26/17 (20 August 1959), 40–2; quoted in Darius Brubeck, '1959: The Beginning of Beyond', 182.

Across a substantial postwar period, French radio, assisted by govern-
ment funding, also developed a significant critical role in the continued
upholding of jazz as serious art. Crucial figures included Alain Gerber, who
worked for France Musique, and who would later act as one of Evans's
main biographers.[23] Much more recently, criticism written by the legendary
French philosopher Michel Foucault (1926–84) has been employed by
Tracey Nicholls to elucidate subtle power relations, involving performer,
audience and critic, within the reception of Coltrane's 'free jazz' improvisations from the 1960s.[24] Similarly, critical approaches of Gilles Deleuze
(1925–95) and Félix Guattari (1930–92) that focus on the 'rhizomatic'
mapping concept have been proposed as a means of exploring the historiography of jazz–classical relations without issues of hierarchy or linear
genealogy;[25] on intertextual approaches, see below. As an extension, we
may identify a detailed interview between another outstanding French
philosopher, Jacques Derrida (1930–2004), and the saxophonist-cum-
composer Ornette Coleman (b. 1930), a pupil of Schuller, on the occasion
of Coleman's concerts at La Villette in Paris in late June to early July 1997.[26]

This burgeoning criticism, often propounded by Francophone writers
who were not primarily musicians – Goffin was a poet and lawyer, while
another writer, Michel Leiris (1901–90) was an anthropologist – connects
strongly to a longstanding French intellectual identity. In discussing his own
complex French-Algerian-Jewish identity with Coleman, Derrida states
simply: 'I am of course a French intellectual.'[27] In turn, such intellectual
weight served to effect a change in American societal attitudes towards jazz.

French criticism, jazz and national-political identities

In their mirroring of a wider French national identity, especially through
the later 1920s and 1930s, critical writings on jazz may be seen to trace a
left–right political spectrum that swiftly encompasses issues of race and

[23] See Suddarth, 'French Stewardship of Jazz'; Alain Gerber, *Bill Evans* (Paris: Librairie Arthème Fayard, 2001).
[24] Tracey Nicholls, 'Dominant Positions: John Coltrane, Michel Foucault, and the Politics of Representation', *Critical Studies in Improvisation/Études critiques en improvisation*, 2/1 (2006), 1–13.
[25] Barham, 'Rhizomes and Plateaus', 171. See Gilles Deleuze and Félix Guattari, *A Thousand Plateaus*, Eng. trans. Brian Massumi (London and New York: Continuum, 2004).
[26] Jacques Derrida, 'The Other's Language: Jacques Derrida Interviews Ornette Coleman, 23 June 1997', Eng. trans. Timothy S. Murphy, *Genre*, 36 (Summer 2004), 319–29; originally published in *Les Inrockuptibles*, 115 (20 August–2 September 1997), 37–40, 43; reproduced at *Jazz Studies Online*: http://jazzstudiesonline.org/.
[27] Derrida, 'The Other's Language', 326.

ethnicity. This spectrum reflects, on the one hand, left-wing intellectual values that had emerged earlier in the Third Republic from social movements including anarchism and feminism, and via the 'Dreyfus Revolution'. On the other hand, right-wing colonial values persist and intensify: a new nationalism and anti-Semitism also forged through the Boulanger and Dreyfus affairs later in the Belle Époque.[28] Sometimes, distinctions were more blurred.

A position that deeply endorsed the African-American blackness of jazz as a repressed art, privileging 'hot' jazz, was taken up by Panassié, together with Goffin, Delaunay, Leiris and later, up to a point though not exclusively, by Hodeir. Beyond this privileging, Leiris, like Milhaud, acknowledged a diversity of jazz and that there was both good and bad, though innate quality was not necessarily the final arbiter.[29] We might add the name of Raoul Laparra, a composer-commentator who perceived a trajectory from African roots, through African-American and then white American practice, to French and Spanish perspectives.[30]

Such a positioning was congruent with the broader background of Parisian negrophilia evidenced by those highly enthusiastic responses to an *art/musique nègre* epitomized by *La Revue nègre* (1925). Surprisingly, even the conservative critic André Levinson offered supportive critique of the show's star Josephine Baker in *Comœdia* of 12 October 1925.[31] This positioning was also consonant with an upholding of primitivism, either side of World War I, espoused by avant-garde artists including Stravinsky, Picasso and Blaise Cendrars (1887–1961), which was seen as a vital source for artistic regeneration in its confronting of the European mainstream. Milhaud, with his own Jewish background, was very sensitive to the emotional expressivity of African-American jazz, with its ultimately African roots, as witnessed in the New York of the early 1920s:

> Harlem had not yet been discovered by the snobs and aesthetes: we were the only white folk there. The music [...] was a revelation to me. Against the beat of the drums, the melodic lines criss-crossed in a breathless pattern of broken and twisted rhythms. A Negress whose grating voice seemed to come from the depths of the centuries sang [...] With despairing pathos and dramatic feeling,

[28] For historical discussion of these political perspectives, see Sowerwine, *France since 1870*, chapter 5, 'Challenges to the Republic (1): Constructing the Modern Right', and chapter 6, 'Challenges to the Republic (2): Constructing the Modern Left', 53–88.

[29] Michel Leiris, *Journal 1922–1989* (Paris: Gallimard, 1992), 35: 'partout des jazz, bons ou mauvais'; Darius Milhaud, *Études* (Paris: Éditions Claude Aveline, 1927), 52.

[30] Jackson, *Making Jazz French*, 95.

[31] For an extended quotation, see Carine Perret, 'L'Adoption du jazz par Darius Milhaud et Maurice Ravel: l'esprit plus que la lettre', *Revue de musicologie*, 89/2 (2003), 311–47: 315.

she sang over and over again [...] Its effect on me was so overwhelming that I could not tear myself away.[32]

A mid-point on this critical spectrum is manifested by the likes of Prunières, supported by some of Goffin's comments, which do admit a limited usefulness of more sanitized white arrangements of jazz as a means of popular access. Further along may be located critics such as Cœuroy and Schaeffner, the journalist and theatre impresario Astruc and the composer André Messager (1853–1929). Essentially, Cœuroy and Schaeffner traced the background of jazz from *musique nègre* through to its inception, where their study stopped. While fully cognisant of the predominant African-American origins of jazz, amid Creole, Native American and other elements, they saw little distinction between African and African-American identities, and still harboured preferences for the ordered, filtered and professionally slick white dance bands of Whiteman and Hylton, whose jazz was typically tempered as 'sweet'. Milhaud too had initially been excited by the likes of Billy Arnold's American Band that had given him an early taster of jazz in London,[33] though he later summed up Whiteman's commercial outfit as a 'Rolls-Royce of dance music, but whose atmosphere remained entirely of this world and without inspiration' (on Milhaud's evolving critical response, see Chapter 4).[34] Other French criticism developed a much more acute anti-American reaction: around 1930, Georges Duhamel of the Académie française produced his vitriolic, uncompromising text *America the Menace*.[35]

French criticism, jazz and racism

Towards the farther extreme of this critical-political spectrum, the popular songwriter Vincent Scotto remained a staunch supporter of French music hall, Gustave Fréjaville claimed the 'maddening' degenerative effects of jazz midst an 'invasion of black music and barbaric dances', while Hoerée and André Suarès disputed and denied the essential African-American origins of jazz.[36] Suarès, in particular, resorted to offensive, racist terminology, including 'brutes'.[37] Critics such as René Bizet responded to *La Revue*

---

[32] Darius Milhaud, *My Happy Life: An Autobiography*, Eng. trans. Donald Evans, George Hall and Christopher Palmer (London and New York: Marion Boyars, 1995), 110.
[33] *Ibid.*, 97.   [34] *Ibid.*, 109.
[35] Georges Duhamel, *America the Menace: Scenes from the Life of the Future*, Eng. trans. Charles Miner Thompson (London: George Allen and Unwin, 1931).
[36] Gustave Fréjaville, 'L'Orchestre du Dr Moreau', *Débats* (9 June 1927), n.p. (archived within 'Le Jazz et les spectacles nègres', Ro 585, Collection Rondel, Bibliothèque nationale de France), and his *Au music-hall* (Paris: Aux éditions du monde nouveau, 1923); Hoerée, 'Le Jazz', 221.
[37] Suarès quoted in Jackson, *Making Jazz French*, 96.

nègre in racial terms, claiming that this 'kinetic music was directly related to racial physiognomy: the jazz was in their "legs" and their "skin"'.[38] By extension, and as part of his aim to expose a historiographical underplaying of early French critical ambivalence to jazz, Matthew Jordan points out that for Bizet: 'jazz and the jungle-like moral world associated with it was wholly un-French and totally inappropriate for French culture'.[39]

On the receiving end of such ongoing bigotry and prejudice, Derrida discussed with Coleman his personal experience of racism as a Jewish child in Algeria, coupled by his acute discomfort at witnessing racial segregation on an early visit to America: 'The first time I went to the United States, in 1956, there were "Reserved for Whites" signs everywhere, and I remember how brutal that was. You experienced all that?'[40] Coleman responded that he did, but felt that he found things better in Paris, noting the intellectualism and that racism was at least concealed from one's presence: 'what I like about Paris is the fact that you can't be a snob and a racist at the same time here, because that won't do. Paris is the only city I know where racism never exists in your presence, it's something you hear spoken of [at second-hand]'.[41] Derrida's own stance was, nonetheless: 'That doesn't mean there is no racism, but one is obliged to conceal it to the [greatest] extent possible.'[42]

The problem with the attitudes of Suarès and Bizet is glaringly obvious in its unacceptable racism, but is much more difficult to tackle when subtly concealed, as Derrida intimates. There are, however, also problems with the line taken by Panassié. On the one hand, his was a very positive, seemingly farsighted and enlightened stance; on the other hand, the almost exclusive extolling of African-American early 'hot' jazz meant that effectively it came to represent the only authentic jazz locus, fixed in time and place.[43] Moreover, a recent detailed study by Tom Perchard has even viewed

---

[38] René Bizet, 'Le Music-hall: *La Revue nègre*', *Candide* (8 October 1925), 8; quoted in Jordan's chapter on '*La Revue nègre*, Ethnography and Cultural Hybridity', *Le Jazz*, 102–40: 106.

[39] Jordan, *Le Jazz*, 106. Such complexities are viewed against a wider political (imperial, anti-imperial), racial, technological and intellectual backdrop in Jeremy F. Lane, *Jazz and Machine-Age Imperialism: Music, 'Race,' and Intellectuals in France, 1918–45* (Ann Arbor, MI: University of Michigan Press, 2013).

[40] Derrida, 'The Other's Language', 327. Interracial marriage was only fully legal in the United States from 1967, when anti-miscegenation laws were finally repealed by a Supreme Court decision. This colonial fear of interbreeding – as a supposed tainting of pure, superior racial identity – was subsequently confronted and developed in postcolonial discourse as cultural hybridity by the French philosopher Roland Barthes (resulting in a 'third language') and by the Indian scholar Homi K. Bhabha, *The Location of Culture* (London: Routledge, 1994).

[41] Derrida, 'The Other's Language', 327.   [42] *Ibid.*

[43] On the problematics of this stance, see Gumplowicz, 'Hugues Panassié', 119.

Panassié's stance as 'ultra-conservative' and 'reactionary'.[44] Certainly, the situation regarding primitivism remains one of huge complexity and ambivalence, which historians and critics will continue to debate. But, as critical voices, we should be careful not to assume an implicit superiority from our comfortable, time-sifted position in a wholly different cultural milieu. While those who discredited African-American music and harboured racist attitudes should be denounced, there is a sense of 'no win' when others who adopted pro-African-American stances are also damned. Nevertheless for Panassié, ironically, even postwar African-American bebop was deemed not really to be jazz,[45] so what hope would remain for figures like Hylton, denigrated by the former through the 1930s for his corruption of jazz,[46] together with later musicians such as Evans and Brubeck?

Although Hylton was initially conservative about 'hot' jazz and undoubtedly naïve about Fascist power in the later 1930s, there is no evidence that he held racist views; indeed, in one French critique, he was labelled disparagingly as 'Le petit nègre'.[47] Albeit as astute business moves, he employed the excellent African-American concert bass Paul Robeson in 1931, the tenor sax player Hawkins and, briefly, the incomparable arranger Henderson. Brubeck, too, identified with the limiting problem created by Panassié's perspective: 'The dangerous tendency has been, especially in France, to restrict jazz to the primitive [sic] New Orleans music and to consider any development after that an unwelcome deviation from the African core.'[48] (While the expression 'primitive' is ambiguous, context suggests that Brubeck is expressing frustration at jazz potentially being constrained within its prototype style.) Such a stance effectively created an own-goal for wider, multiracial French involvement and experimentation, though broadly indigenous groups such as those of Grégor or Vauchant, followed by the likes of Grappelli and Reinhardt, maintained a particular foothold, especially before World War II.

Thus Brubeck and others would argue that, whilst jazz is indisputably a genre of African-American origin with many superlative African-American

---

[44] Tom Perchard, 'Tradition, Modernity and the Supernatural Swing: Re-reading "Primitivism" in Hugues Panassié's Writing on Jazz', *Popular Music*, 30/1 (2011), 25–45.

[45] See Panassié, 'The Unreal Jazz', from *The Real Jazz*; reprinted in Robert Gottlieb (ed.), *Reading Jazz: A Gathering of Autobiography, Reportage, and Criticism from 1919 to Now* (London: Bloomsbury, 1997), 792–7.

[46] See Andy M. Fry, 'Jack à l'Opéra', in '"De la musique nègre au jazz français": African-American Music and Musicians in Interwar France' (D.Phil. dissertation, University of Oxford, 2003).

[47] [Writer unknown], 'La Rentrée de Jack Hylton et ses boys à Paris', *Volonté* (14 October 1929).

[48] Brubeck, 'Jazz Perspective', 203.

exponents, it does not have to be solely a black music. By extension, 'The addition of European [predominantly white] elements does not arbitrarily mean bad jazz. Duke Ellington proved this by handling the classical elements in jazz with such originality'.[49] Brubeck is upfront and perhaps a touch provocative, as a result of his experiences, in declaring that 'the harmonic conception of jazz has paralleled that of composed music, except that jazz has lagged about twenty years in its exploitation of harmonic ideas discovered by Europeans'.[50] Surely the way forward, as urged on a large societal scale some fifty years ago by Martin Luther King Jr (1929–68), has to be a balanced, inclusive critical stance that acknowledges the huge role played by African-American musicians in the artistic success of jazz, without simultaneously creating new racial prejudice in denigrating or precluding the contributions of other musicians who may be white.

Matters French, jazz and gender

Implicit, though again often obscured, are issues of gender. With the exception of a handful of extraordinary, strong African-American women, predominantly solo vocalists such as Ma Rainey ('Mother of the Blues'), Bessie Smith (1894–1937), Billie Holiday (1915–59), Ella Fitzgerald (1917–96; 'Queen of Jazz') and Sarah Vaughan (1924–90), followed by the Civil Rights activist Nina Simone (1933–2003),[51] the genre of jazz, and its attendant forms, has thus far remained largely a male-dominated preserve. In fact, not only male-dominated, but one that has sought to perpetuate traditional gender stereotypes, especially where what might be deemed 'macho' credentials are concerned.

One strong historical trait within American jazz that complicates and compromises association with any classical music – let alone a specifically French music – was a homophobic one.[52] Homophobia was prevalent during the 1950s in the United States since homosexuality was a criminal offence (and would remain so for many years); by contrast, same-sex relations had effectively been decriminalized in France after the French Revolution of 1789. Thus Brubeck's classically inspired (white) music, together with that of Chet Baker, came to be disparaged by some as

---

[49] *Ibid.*   [50] *Ibid.*

[51] For a five-CD compilation, see *The Jazz Ladies* (Vintage Jazz Greats, Prestige Records CDSGPBJZ-08, -09, -10, -29, -30, 1996.)

[52] See James Gavin, 'Homophobia in Jazz', *JazzTimes* (December 2001): http://jazztimes. com/articles/20073-homophobia-in-jazz.

homosexual 'faggot jazz'. Francis Davis portrays well the ambience of the times with reference to Baker's admittedly androgynous persona:

> No one thought he was gay, but he sounded effeminate to some – an equally grave offense in the 1950s, a testosterone-counting decade in which the pianist *Horace Silver's* denigration of West Coast cool as *'fag' jazz* was widely and approvingly quoted, and in which two men meeting for the first time each felt obliged, as Norman Mailer once put it, to prove he was 'less queer' than the other.[53]

As one of the most vociferous detractors of 'cool' modal jazz, Silver, an African-American jazz pianist and proponent of hard bop, declared in *Down Beat* magazine of 1956: 'I can't stand the faggot-type jazz, the jazz with no guts. And the discouraging part is that the faggot-type jazz is getting more popularity than the jazz with real soul. The groups that play with a lot of guts are not making as much loot.' Another undercurrent here is an understandable resentment at seemingly greater white commercial success. Alan Kurtz has commented that 'Homophobic Horace didn't mention any names, but to informed readers he was obviously referring to Brubeck, Chet Baker, et al.'[54] (Conversely, others have expressed the view that the problem with Brubeck's European classical inclinations was that they did not go far enough: 'Merely referencing Mozart's "Rondo alla turca" didn't make Dave Brubeck's "Blue Rondo à la Turk" (1959) Third Stream. Instead of combining jazz and classical elements, "Blue Rondo" simply wedged 4/4 blues solos between [*sic*] a bravura 9/8 enclosure.')[55]

Even within this supposedly emasculated classical music context, there is a perceived hierarchy of masculinity: Austro-German symphonic tonal music has traditionally been portrayed as more masculine in character, set in relief against lighter, non-symphonic tonal-cum-modal French music as (even more) feminine. It is the stark situation epitomized by stereotypical comparisons of Beethoven and the French-naturalized Chopin. Inevitable shades still persisted of strong perfect cadences and Susan McClary's

---

[53] Davis, *Jazz and Its Discontents*, 279.

[54] Alan Kurtz's comments upon Marc Myers, 'What Killed Jazz? The Plot Thickens' (11 June 2008): www.jazzwax.com/2008/06/what-killed-jaz.html. For more on these complex connections, see Ingrid Monson, 'The Problem with White Hipness: Race, Gender, and Cultural Conceptions in Jazz Historical Discourse', *Journal of the American Musicological Society*, 48/3 (1995), 396–422.

[55] The performers propose that 'when played by string quartet instead of jazz quartet, time-signature shifts are less abrupt, more organic. Third Stream boosters have long dreamt that string players would someday learn to swing.' 'Turtle Island String Quartet: Blue Rondo à la Turk' (30 November 2007): www.jazz.com/music/archives/2007/11.

imperfect 'feminine endings'.[56] Thus, it could be argued that the particular quality of Frenchness on top of classicism may have contributed to Evans's jazz being regarded by some as inauthentic: his whiteness compounded by accusations of effeminacy, his inherent physical frailty supporting comparisons with Chopin or Ravel (see pages 222–4).

Other critical downsides to the association of French music and jazz

Cultural exchange between French music and jazz is generally viewed (and represented here) as desirable and fruitful, but its contradictory aspects and potential downsides should be identified, from both perspectives. Some equivocations have already been aired under the headings of race and gender. Although a good many French composers were inspired by jazz, others were notably ambivalent in their critical response: we witness, for example, the diverse testimony concerning Poulenc. In 1948, Poulenc's visit to New York on his first North American tour with Pierre Bernac was described in upbeat fashion by his hosts Arthur Gold and Robert Fizdale. The friends went 'up to the Savoy Ballroom in Harlem to watch the jitterbugging and listen to the jazz. "La trompette est parfaite!" Poulenc shouted in approval.'[57] In response to whether he liked and rated jazz, however, the composer had in 1935 declared vehemently: 'Certainly not! I do not like it and I especially don't want to hear about its influence on contemporary music. Born in New York [sic] [...] this substitute amuses me when I listen to it on records while bathing, but it is frankly odious to me in the concert hall.'[58] We might consider that he perhaps protests a little too vigorously, but the inference is that even if jazz is acceptable in itself, perceived essentially as entertainment, it has no place in the compositional development of French classical music.

Even if we look to Milhaud as among the most enthusiastic and knowledgeable composer-aficionados of jazz, his experience embodies conflicting aspects which may have conspired to shape Poulenc's perspective. Reflecting some time later in his autobiography, Milhaud recounts how his ultimate compositional manifesto in favour of jazz, *La Création*, was initially misunderstood: 'The critics decreed that my music was frivolous and more

---

[56] Susan McClary, *Feminine Endings: Music, Gender, and Sexuality* (Minnesota, MN: University of Minnesota Press, 1991).

[57] Gold quoted in Carl B. Schmidt, *Entrancing Muse, A Documented Biography of Francis Poulenc* (Hillsdale, NY: Pendragon Press, 2001), 345.

[58] Poulenc quoted in Schmidt, *Entrancing Muse*, 88. See too Dominique Arbey, 'Poulenc et le jazz', *Les Cahiers de Francis Poulenc*, 3 (2011), 129–33.

suitable for a restaurant or a dance-hall than for the concert-hall.'[59] There is, however, an undeniable triumph in his wry observation of the subsequent hypocrisy and volte-face of the press: 'Ten years later the self-same critics were discussing the philosophy of jazz and learnedly demonstrating that *La Création* was the best of my works.'[60] (For more on the work's mixed reception, see pages 132–3.)

As for Messiaen, hermeneutic studies can reveal fascinating harmonic, textural and motivic commonalities of practice between his pre- and postwar music – especially that inspired by birdsong – and jazz. Barham has identified striking jazz-type voicings, including the signature big-band sonority of the added-sixth chord, amidst quasi-improvisatory gestures and syncopation in 'Joie et clarté des corps glorieux', from the organ work *Les Corps glorieux* (1939),[61] which result from Messiaen's independent theoretical enquiries into modes and non-retrogradable rhythms. Nevertheless, we have to balance this against Messiaen's own distinctly negative take on the genre, aptly summarized as: 'a composer who professed to have little or no feeling for jazz, deplored its adherence to a continuous beat, and strove to distance himself from the jazz-related aesthetic of his immediate predecessors, the group of French composers known as Les Six'.[62]

Conversely, from a jazz-based position, there is evidence that French classical credentials might not always be to an artist's reputational benefit. Among a group of artists interested in jazz–classical exchange through the 1960s and beyond, which includes Cecil Taylor (b. 1929), Chick Corea (b. 1941) and Keith Jarrett (b. 1945), we may consider the case of Anthony Braxton (b. 1945). Braxton is a much-respected African-American saxophonist, composer-theorist and philosopher, who intriguingly defies easy classification: 'I'm not a jazz musician. I'm not a classical musician, either. My music is like my life: it's in between these areas.'[63] On the one hand, his music draws heavily on improvisation, swing and bebop – particularly Parker – and as a saxophonist he has recorded many jazz standards. On the other hand, he studied and has been influenced compositionally by modernism: European (Arnold Schoenberg, Iannis Xenakis, Stockhausen) and American (Charles Ives, John Cage), as well as by electronic music and philosophical mysticism.[64] And thus his music has not been fully

---

[59] Milhaud, *My Happy Life*, 120.   [60] *Ibid.*

[61] Barham, 'Rhizomes and Plateaus', 190–1.   [62] *Ibid.*, 187.

[63] Anthony Braxton, quoted from the composer's website: http://tricentricfoundation.org/anthony-braxton/bio/.

[64] On this blend, see Barham's case study on 'Cecil Taylor, Anthony Braxton and the Confluence of Jazz and "Classical" Avant Garde', in his 'Rhizomes and Plateaus', 193–8. The opening of Braxton's 'The Bell' from his album *3 Compositions of New Jazz* (1968)

understood or accepted by the mainstream jazz community. In the mid 1970s, he was roundly chastised for his passion for avant-garde concert music, a trait perceived as an espousal of decadent European affinities and evidence of pretentiousness. Famously, Braxton was instructed by one jazz critic, John Storm Roberts, to 'stop Messiaen about'.[65]

More generally, French culture may still be perceived as contributing to, even tainted by, the complex underlying issue of Eurocentricity. Some argue that jazz education and scholarship have, at least until 'new jazz studies' of the 1990s onwards, been distorted by adherence to European classical and musicological models. Others claim that to resist or deny any European role is falsely simplistic and perpetuates old binaries. From an improvisational stance, George Lewis has argued eloquently and persuasively for a strong upholding of the Afrological dimension; more recently, Tony Whyton has attempted to mediate these domains, tackling stereotypes, re-examining identities and advocating a new, flexible mode of European jazz studies.[66]

Intertextuality

At this point, it makes sense to outline suitable approaches to the music that will be lightly invoked, sometimes more implicitly than explicitly, and developed in the case studies: the intention is to combine hermeneutic, critical enquiries with an accessible – loosely formal – analysis, often as a way in. Given the broad topic of interactions between French music and jazz (which, as we have seen, may connote matters of cultural identity, otherness, modernism, gender, music techniques and so on), it would be neither feasible nor desirable to separate the musical from the sociocultural or historical, or to concentrate on one to the exclusion of another. All are contingent.

For similar reasons, no single methodology is endorsed and many approaches may theoretically be implicated, pertaining to eclecticism, orientalism (Edward Said),[67] associated exoticism (Ralph Locke),[68] and

quotes the Bach motive at pitch: B♭, A, C, B; association with Satie's dadaism is found in 'Silence', from *Silence/Time Zones* (1969/1976): 196.

[65] John Storm Roberts, 'Anthony Braxton', *Melody Maker* (7 February 1976), 47. Quoted by Ronald M. Radano, in a chapter on 'Black Experimentalism as Spectacle' within his *New Musical Figurations: Anthony Braxton's Cultural Critique* (University of Chicago Press, 1993), 255. See too Ronald M. Radano, 'Critical Alchemy: Anthony Braxton', in Krin Gabbard (ed.), *Jazz among the Discourses* (Durham, NC: Duke University Press, 1995), 201.

[66] George E. Lewis, 'Improvised Music after 1950: Afrological and Eurological Perspectives', *Black Music Research Journal*, 16/1 (1996), 92–122; Tony Whyton, 'Europe and the New Jazz Studies', in Cerchiari, Cugny and Kerschbaumer (eds.), *Eurojazzland*, 366–80.

[67] Edward W. Said, *Orientalism* (New York: Pantheon, 1978).

[68] Ralph Locke, *Musical Exoticism: Images and Reflections* (Cambridge University Press, 2011).

'conceptual blending' (Gilles Fauconnier and Mark Turner, Nicholas Cook).[69] Equally, to assert that all things are possible is neither helpful nor useful. Apart from anything else, the problematics of mixing too many metaphors in expressing relations between artistic entities, such as dialogue, translation, cross-fertilization, intersection, exchange, collage and fusion, would quickly become apparent.[70] In case-study practice, certain approaches prove much more conducive than others.

Therefore, the book's theoretical apparatus is presented within an overarching framework that extends from a default position of working with the concept of (trans)cultural flow, as an inclusive, flexible and often subliminal intertextuality, through to acknowledging more precise instances of historical influence, or conscious borrowing. We might also perceive a loosely parallel *esthesic–poietic* notion (listener- or receiver-based, through to composer- or creator-based) or, more generally, a sense of implicit–explicit. In turn, these notions of intertextuality and borrowing create a variety of effects (embracing elements of commonality, reinflection, transformation and, occasionally, a balanced hybridity: see below) and cultural meanings. Theoretically, there is a third domain of active artistic collaboration, which can be hugely important and fruitful. However, given the general time lag involved in these exchanges and my case study choices, it is less relevant, since one artist is more often a silent, posthumous partner. Apart from the evident cross-fertilization between Gershwin and Ravel (Chapter 5), the nearest we get to a collaborative relationship is that between Milhaud and Brubeck (Chapter 9).

Historically, much musicological discourse on intertextuality emanates from literary critical studies and is indebted to the French theorist-philosopher Roland Barthes (1915–80), especially his seminal essay 'The Death of the Author': 'We know now that a text is not a line of words releasing a single "theological" meaning (the "message" of the Author-God) but a multi-dimensional space in which a variety of writings, none of them original, blend and clash. The text is a tissue of quotations drawn from the innumerable centres of culture.'[71] Another deeply influential literary figure

[69] Gilles Fauconnier and Mark Turner, *The Way We Think: Conceptual Blending and the Mind's Hidden Complexities* (New York: Basic Books, 2002); Nicholas Cook, 'Theorizing Musical Meaning', *Music Theory Spectrum*, 23/2 (Fall 2001), 170–95.

[70] See George Lakoff and Mark Johnson, *Metaphors We Live By* (University of Chicago Press, 2003), but also David L. Ritchie, 'Lost in "Conceptual Space": Metaphors of Conceptual Integration', *Metaphor and Symbol*, 19 (2004), 31–50.

[71] Roland Barthes, 'The Death of the Author', in *Image, Music, Text*, Eng. trans. Stephen Heath (London: Fontana Press, 1977), 142–8: 146. See, too, a useful essay collection discussing Barthes and intertext, Julia Kristeva, Bloom and others: Michael Worton and Judith Still

on texts and intertexts is the American theorist of poetry Harold Bloom (b. 1930), his work often being contrasted with the earlier inclusive stance of the poet-critic T. S. Eliot (1888–1965): their approaches are discussed a little later.

Among an abundant body of musicological literature, we may foreground the writings of scholars including Kramer,[72] Abbate (*Unsung Voices*), Klein (*Intertextuality*), Georgina Born[73] and Cooke, whose sensitive contribution to the reciprocal relations between classical music and jazz, focused upon Ellington, is especially notable.[74] Similarly, Klein's intertextual musical webs prove fitting since he interprets 'Western art music' sufficiently broadly to encompass comparison between Joplin's *Original Rags* (1899) and Witold Lutoslawski's Study No. 1, as part of a larger web.[75] I also tend to concur with Klein's basic distinction between influence and intertextuality, whereby 'the former implies intent of a historical placement of the work in its time or origin, and the latter implies a more general notion of crossing texts that may involve historical reversal'.[76] David Meltzer's quirky and wide-ranging anthology, *Reading Jazz*,[77] also proves pertinent, especially in Chapter 4. (For analytical exploration of intertextuality, see discussion below of Tymoczko's *A Geometry of Music*.)

Beyond these specifics, Kramer's groundbreaking work from the early to mid 1990s onwards remains relevant, with certain provisos: we are concerned with what music expresses and what it *means* in the context in which it was or is heard, as well as with the musical *means* by which it achieves this goal. Such matters connect with music's representational and narrative qualities, including Abbate's 'unsung' voices or Claudia Gorbman's 'unheard'

(eds.), *Intertextuality: Theories and Practices* (Manchester and New York: Manchester University Press, 1990).

[72] Salient texts include Lawrence Kramer, *Music as Cultural Practice, 1800–1900* (Berkeley and Los Angeles, CA: University of California Press, 1990) and his *Classical Music*: see particularly the chapters 'From the Other to the Abject' and 'Consuming the Exotic'. His ideas were re-established and developed in *Musical Meaning: Toward a Critical History* (Berkeley and Los Angeles, CA: University of California Press, 2002), especially 'Powers of Blackness: Jazz and the Blues in Modern Concert Music'; and *Interpreting Music* (Berkeley and Los Angeles, CA: University of California Press, 2010).

[73] Georgina Born and David Hesmondhalgh (eds.), *Western Music and Its Others: Difference, Representation, and Appropriation in Music* (Berkeley and Los Angeles, CA: University of California Press, 2000). Ideas explored in the editors' substantial introduction include 'Postcolonial Analysis', 'Othering, Hybridity, and Fusion in Transcultural Popular Musics', 1–58.

[74] Cooke, 'Jazz among the Classics'.   [75] Klein, *Intertextuality*, 8–9.   [76] *Ibid.*, 4.

[77] Gottlieb's equivalent *Reading Jazz* contains much fascinating critical material, but frustratingly, especially given its large size, it lacks an index.

melodies.[78] For Kramer, music is 'an object constituted in representation' and 'a cultural trope produced by musical aesthetics, imaginative literature, and, reflexively, by musical composition'.[79] I would qualify, however, that this seemingly incidental sonic presence via composition still matters a good deal. We should also bear in mind Kramer's useful characterization of music history as 'the logic of alterity',[80] one founded upon perceptions of opposition or contradiction between a dominant self and others: such reversals of assumption will be pursued later in the book.

Arguably the most important tenet of Kramer's work is its upholding of the value of subjectivity and culturally defined musical experience, especially that of the receiver. A possible corollary of this might be that, conceivably, anything goes. This is, however, probably an unfair assessment since, as early as 1993, Kramer was defining a 'structural trope' – his most potent type of 'hermeneutic window' – as 'a structural procedure, capable of various practical realizations, that also functions as a typical expressive act within a certain cultural historical framework'.[81] In his most recent *Interpreting Music*, he distinguishes between two kinds of interpretation. The first may be characterized as 'closed': it is an everyday, generalized interpretation such as a fixed opinion or statement of belief, which produces merely 'the mirror of a settled understanding. Its conclusions lie in its premises.'[82] By contrast, the second is defined as an 'enriched', 'open interpretation' and here Kramer does point up the significance of frameworks and relevance of matters analytical, in the widest sense: 'open interpretation is a relatively rare and specialized practice. It is analytical, articulate, and reflective. It brings the interpreter as subject into contact, and sometimes conflict, with the subject(s) – both the agents and the topics – of what is interpreted.'[83] Kramer's approach proves especially relevant to Chapter 3, in conjunction with that of Metzer (not to be confused with Meltzer).

Recognizing the subjective is crucial, but preserving some referential, empirical framework to ensure a measure of objectivity is just as important.

---

[78] Claudia Gorbman, *Unheard Melodies: Narrative Film Music* (Bloomington, IN: Indiana University Press, 1987).

[79] Kramer, *Classical Music*, 35.   [80] *Ibid.*, 34, 35.

[81] Kramer, *Music as Cultural Practice*, 10. In turn, a 'structural trope' may be seen to denote a development of the French philosopher Pierre Bourdieu's notion of 'habitus'; see Pierre Bourdieu, *Outline of a Theory of Practice*, Eng. trans. Richard Nice (Cambridge University Press, 1977), 72. 'Citational inclusions', as one version of 'textual inclusion', presents as another 'hermeneutic window', and thus is also potentially relevant to the section on Borrowing.

[82] Kramer, *Interpreting Music*, 2.   [83] *Ibid.*

We may relate here to Nicholas Cook's musical take on conceptual blending (see too below): a useful mediation between the subjective and objective is proposed whereby interpretation is linked to salient musical 'attributes',[84] which may be expressed graphically.[85] To be manageable and meaningful, there must be a limit upon the number of attributes that may be realized in any given interpretation, performance, or reception study. There are in fact parallels between Cook's approach and that of Kramer in differentiating between 'originary' meanings and new ones resulting from the confluence of particular entities, such as French music and jazz.

Borrowing

Whilst none of these terms is watertight or fixed, to probe the detail and diversity of French music–jazz interplay, it is purposeful to consider certain relational techniques as a subset of a much larger intertextuality. Such techniques extend from a more traditional, historically documented perception of influence to embrace a spectrum of borrowings: from allusion to genre, or style, through to modelling, paraphrase and quotation. In these latter instances where causality (and authorial intention) may plausibly be established, it can still be apt and illuminating to think in terms of a historically evidenced source–product relationship, an idea furthered below.

The starting point for these enquiries is inevitably the well-tested, yet still pertinent, Eliot–Bloom dialectic,[86] with its largely opposed literary ideas upon the nature of influence. Such critical strategies may be characterized, respectively – albeit rather essentially – as 'generosity' versus 'anxiety' towards the past. For Eliot, in 'Tradition and the Individual Talent' (1919), the main stance was one of a beneficial embrace of history and heritage, involving 'a continual surrender of himself [. . .] to something which is more valuable'.[87] Paradoxically, it often turns out that 'the most individual parts of his work may be those in which the dead poets, his ancestors, assert their immortality most vigorously'.[88] Conversely for Bloom, in the early to mid 1970s, engagement with the past cues an 'anxiety' or struggle. In the 'Introduction: A Meditation upon Misreading' to his

---

[84] Cook, 'Theorizing Musical Meaning', 178–9.

[85] Several of my articles have experimented with graphic CIN-style notation, such as: Deborah Mawer, 'Jazzing a Classic: Hylton and Stravinsky's *Mavra* at the Paris Opéra', *Twentieth-Century Music*, 6/2 (September 2009), 155–82. Here, I have preferred to keep a more accessible, prose-based approach.

[86] Eliot, 'Tradition and the Individual Talent', 36–42 (page run from the *Perspecta* reprint); Bloom, *The Anxiety of Influence* and *A Map of Misreading*.

[87] Eliot, 'Tradition and the Individual Talent', 39.   [88] *Ibid.*, 37.

second book, which offers an application of his poetic theory of influence, Bloom declares that 'Reading [...] is a belated and all-but-impossible act, and if strong is always a misreading.'[89] In fact, in his essay on 'The Metaphysical Poets', Eliot too notes this phenomenon as the wilful creation of 'new wholes'.[90] And behind such activity what is at stake is the ascribing of literary, or artistic, meaning itself. In discussing influence, Bloom distinguishes between 'the passing-on of images and texts from earlier to later poets', which he does not recognize as influence, and the idea of intertextuality where 'there are *no* texts, but only relationships *between* texts. These relationships depend upon a critical act, a misreading or misprision that one poet performs upon another'.[91]

From Bloom's stance there is thus no such thing as an independent text: all are composites of many others (I would argue strongly, however, that such a stance should not in any sense reduce the value of texts or the validity of textual analysis). Their multiple reinvocation involves a revisionary act whereby 'the revisionist strives to *see* again, so as to *esteem* and *estimate* differently, so as then to *aim* "correctly"'.[92] Bloom's theories were subsequently brought into musicology by Joseph Straus, himself criticized for Bloomian 'misprision',[93] and by Kevin Korsyn.[94] Conversely, Eliot's stance may be seen as broadly emulated by Leonard B. Meyer.[95] For my purposes, the main tenets of Bloom's ideas do enable a meaningful characterization of relationships around Russell (Chapter 7), with Eliot's ethos especially congruent with Brubeck's practice (Chapter 9). More often, the approach involves a blending of some Bloomian traits with aspects of Eliot's ideas (chapters 5 and 8).

As a much more recent development, attention may be drawn to an intriguing study by Matthew Brown about the impact of Debussy's music upon popular culture.[96] His work is relevant to mine on at least three counts. Firstly, his notion of impact comprises a mix of relationships from

---

[89] Bloom, *A Map of Misreading*, 3.

[90] T. S. Eliot, *Selected Prose*, ed. Frank Kermode (New York: Harcourt Brace, 1975), 64.

[91] Bloom, *A Map of Misreading*, 3. (The italics are original.)   [92] *Ibid.*, 4.

[93] Joseph N. Straus, *Remaking the Past: Musical Modernism and the Influence of the Tonal Tradition* (Cambridge, MA: Harvard University Press, 1990). See too Richard Taruskin, 'Revising Revision', *Journal of the American Musicological Society*, 46/1 (1993), 114–38.

[94] Kevin Korsyn, 'Towards a New Poetics of Musical Influence', *Music Analysis*, 10/1 (1991), 3–72.

[95] Leonard B. Meyer, 'Innovation, Choice, and the History of Music', *Critical Inquiry*, 9/3 (1980), 517–44, and *Style and Music: Theory, History, and Ideology* (University of Chicago Press, 1989, reprinted 1997).

[96] Matthew Brown, *Debussy Redux: The Impact of His Music on Popular Culture* (Bloomington, IN: Indiana University Press, 2012).

intertextual parallels, through to closer causal connections involving an original and its arrangement, or transcription.[97] The latter is pursued in an attractively titled study 'In the Moog', which considers Debussy's re-presentations of his own music, in aesthetic, publishing and financial terms, as well as Moog-synthesizer recreations of Debussy's music by Isao Tomita.[98] Secondly, Brown's French subject matter crosses cultural boundaries in a similarly reciprocal manner: he considers how Debussy 'appropriated material from Asian culture in works such as "Pagodes" (*Estampes*)' and how 'Clair de lune' has been 'recast in an exotic mold', both in Japanese film and in Tiki culture.[99] Parallels exist with my dual approach to Milhaud (chapters 4 and 9). Brown also raises the inevitable follow-on question about 'the degree to which it is possible to understand works from other cultures and other time periods',[100] since their meanings are culturally defined. Thirdly, his approach achieves a largely successful balance between the cultural and the analytical (on the latter, see below).

Useful research on the act and role of music quotation has been undertaken by writers such as Metzer[101] and the composer John Oswald, in his 'Bettered by the Borrower'.[102] Early on, Metzer clarifies that his interest lies in discovering 'how quotation has served as a cultural agent in twentieth-century music',[103] the idea of agency holding currency in this book, too. His intention is to view 'borrowing not as a single practice [. . .] but rather as a larger mode of music-making comprising different practices, such as quotation and parody, as well as allusion, modeling, and paraphrase'.[104]

These theoretical distinctions prove germane here too, even though they do feel less differentiated in compositional practice, since several techniques may be employed in a single locus: Coltrane's 'Impressions', for instance, uses quotation, paraphrase and modelling (see page 37). Nevertheless,

---

[97] *Ibid.*, 9, 12.   [98] *Ibid.*, 66–79.

[99] *Ibid.*, 13, and chapter 8, 'Other Cultures, Other Sounds', 134–53.   [100] *Ibid.*, 10.

[101] Metzer's reading of Ellington ('Black and White: Quotations in Duke Ellington's "Black and Tan Fantasy"', in *Quotation and Cultural Meaning*, 47–68) may be compared with that of Cooke.

[102] John Oswald, 'Bettered by the Borrower: The Ethics of Musical Debt', in Christoph Cox and Daniel Warner (eds.), *Audio Culture: Readings in Modern Music* (New York: Continuum, 2004), 131–7. On a similar theme, we find Marjorie Perloff, *Unoriginal Genius: Poetry by Other Means in the New Century* (University of Chicago Press, 2012), advancing from Benjamin's manifesto on art in an era of mechanical reproduction to its digital equivalent.

[103] Metzer, *Quotation and Cultural Meaning*, 3.

[104] *Ibid.*, 4. This stance may be contrasted with an earlier, more generalized yet still relevant, approach adopted by Jean-Claude Klein and J. Barrie Jones, 'Borrowing, Syncretism, Hybridisation: The Parisian Revue of the 1920s', *Popular Music*, 5 (1985), 175–87.

expanding on my Introduction, provisional correlations may be offered between musical loci and such borrowing techniques. Quotation is used by: Debussy in 'Golliwogg's Cake-Walk' (Wagner, 'Tristan chord' or motive); Milhaud in *La Création* (Handy, *St. Louis Blues*); Evans in 'Peace Piece' (Leonard Bernstein, 'Some Other Time'); and on a larger scale by Hylton in his many arrangements. Paraphrase is employed especially by Satie in 'Rag-time du paquebot' from *Parade* (Irving Berlin, *That Mysterious Rag*). Modelling is used by Ravel in the 'Forlane' of *Le Tombeau* and arguably by Russell in analysing Ravel's 'Forlane' and Debussy's 'Ondine'. Hermeneutic arguments favour a modelling of Chopin's *Berceuse* in Evans's 'Peace Piece', akin to that of Chopin's Prelude in E minor in 'Young and Foolish' from *Everybody Digs*.

Back with Metzer, other central tenets include the following: quotation is usually presented briefly in relief, rather than being concealed; the practice of quotation relates past and present, but also creates a 'significant cultural site in itself'.[105] Occasionally, resonating with Born's pursuit of 'appropriation' in *Western Music and Its Others* or with Oswald's 'plunderphonics',[106] such an act of quotation may even constitute one of theft. Nonetheless, in respect of covered songs and elsewhere, strictly speaking, 'The original is the fragment as it exists in that [external] source [. . .] it never sounds in the new work, for there is always some degree of alteration.' By extension, the 'transformation is the borrowing as we hear it',[107] though I would qualify that the context too is transformed by means of the borrowing.

If we return to my proposed source–product relationship, which may involve quotation, modelling or other allusion, this is essentially what Metzer, talking expressly about quotation, identifies as a 'two-part gesture: the original and its transformation'.[108] And while no one would look to fall foul of Foucault's accusation of 'ransack[ing] history',[109] I would argue that there is nevertheless intrigue in the search for sources that have then been retreated – what Korsyn refers to as a 'central precursor-text'.[110] Two points should, however, be emphasized. Firstly, a source–product relationship need not be exclusive, or absolute: sources may themselves be products of

---

[105] Metzer, *Quotation and Cultural Meaning*, 4, 10.

[106] John Oswald, 'Plunderphonics or Audio Piracy as a Compositional Prerogative' (Paper presented to the Wired Society Electro-Acoustic Conference, Toronto, 1985). *Plunderphonics* was also the title of Oswald's large-scale recorded album in 1989.

[107] Metzer, *Quotation and Cultural Meaning*, 5.

[108] *Ibid.*, 11. Incidentally, while there is much to commend in Metzer's book, it does have several flaws. Many thought-provoking ideas are raised, some of which should be developed further rather than just restated; repetitiousness is a related concern.

[109] Foucault quoted in Klein, *Intertextuality*, 3.   [110] Korsyn, 'Towards a New Poetics', 18.

previous practice, and products may serve as future sources. Secondly, identifying such eclectic practice has no negative connotation of itself: it is simply that any creative artist flourishes within a given cultural context, as does any reader or listener.

Analytical approaches

Both cultural hermeneutic and music analytical means of enquiry are implicated in pursuing matters intertextual, as well as those more precise relationships of quotation, paraphrase and modelling. Moreover it is a vitally important part of the brief for this book to engage with the *musical* workings of the French music–jazz intersection. Quite apart from missing out on the main substance, there could otherwise be a real danger that 'sidestepping of discipline-specific technical issues perpetuates a false sense of mystery and mystification'.[111] Cook's approach in 'Theorizing Musical Meaning', introduced earlier, offers an appropriate bridging by virtue of the premise that cultural-critical interpretation should relate to a selected framework of defining musical attributes, or conceivably tropes. This is a similar distinction to that existing between a 'signifier' and a variety of connoted 'signifieds', as embodied in a given sign. As Cook acknowledges, any kind of comparison-contrast exercise between two or more entities requires a measure of 'enabling similarity'[112] (and some salient differences) in order to function. A range of musical features are relevant to this process of assessing commonality through to difference, or, for a source–product instance, extents of alteration and transformation.

These parameters include formal characteristics, such as the AAB schema of twelve-bar blues form, or division into front-line melody and rhythm sections. In theory, there is an interesting meeting place in neoclassicism between the French baroque and 1930s jazz in a technical-cum-aesthetic equivalence between *notes inégales* and swung rhythms. Of primary importance, given the entities being related, are the workings of scalic and wider modal collections: for example, Dorian, Lydian, or the so-called blues scale, with flexible third and seventh. By extension, enquiries may embrace pitch-rhythm motives, or separated intervallic shapes and rhythmic patterns (*objets sonores*): a favoured four-note 'Gershwin motive', D–E–D–F, or the augmented fourth/'flatted' fifth relation (see Chapter 7). Special attention may be paid to shared harmonic constructs: chains of dominant sevenths, dominant minor ninths, or half-diminished ('Tristan') chords.

---

[111] Gary Tomlinson paraphrased in Barham, 'Rhizomes and Plateaus', 173.
[112] Cook, 'Theorizing Musical Meaning', 181.

Crucial to this analytical process is an ascertaining of the sonic dimension: particular instrumentations, orchestrations and their timbral qualities.

Given the diverse musics being considered, it follows that a range of musical sources will be invoked, including music scores, jazz transcriptions and audio recordings pertaining to both genres. While issues of edition are generally not problematic for this relatively recent French repertory (frequently, there is only one accepted main edition), questions of jazz transcription are more complex. Inevitably a transcription of a jazz recording is much less of a fixed entity than a composer's score, especially when there may be several, different recorded takes or improvised performances spanning several years, during which a jazz musician's aesthetic and style will have developed. One might imagine the great potential diversity in seeking to reconstruct a French music score aurally from any one of a wide variety of performance interpretations. Even when dealing with a single take, there remains significant interpretative scope, judgement and responsibility on the part of a transcriber.

This point may be illustrated by reference to Evans's intense portrayal of 'Peace Piece', as recorded in December 1958 on *Everybody Digs*. The main notational source employed in the case study (Chapter 8) is the classic transcription by Jim Aikin.[113] But even this well-respected transcription raises questions, especially where registral extremity is concerned. One high-tessitura passage around bars 66–7 (*c.*5.25–5.30) involves a pitch discrepancy as to whether a reiterated decorative note is an F♯ (f♯^{4}), or conceivably a G (g^4), possibly fractionally out of tune in the recording (see Example 8.6a). Another intricate treble passage for pitch notation is around bars 58–9 (*c.*4.45–4.53). Conversely, at the very end of this piano piece, the acoustic overtones vibrating above a bass fifth interval: C–G may suggest the existence of an extended fifth construct: C–G–D, though the D was probably not sounded by Evans (see Example 8.7a). Pedalling contributes to the complexities. Precise rhythmic placements cue similar debate: whether to notate a gesture such as a slight anacrusis in the bass or a pause in the treble line, which may be the product of localized rubato rather than strictly inherent, particularly where the material itself comprises an external quotation. Such matters become the topic of further discussion.[114] More

[113] Jim Aikin, 'Bill Evans: *Peace Piece*. Transcription', *Contemporary Keyboard*, 6/6 (June 1980), 46–9.

[114] Personal conversation with Brian Priestley, Leeds International Jazz Conference (25–26 March 2010). Fausto Borém kindly created a Portuguese translation of an earlier version of Chapter 8: Deborah Mawer, 'A música francesa reconfigurada no jazz modal de Bill Evans' ('French Music Reconfigured in the Modal Jazz of Bill Evans'), *Per Musi*, 28 (2013),

recently, the jazz pianist William Hughes has produced a transcription of Evans's recording,[115] relating in turn to his performance interpretation.

The provision of the majority of this data does not require specialist methodologies: much can be achieved via standard principles of formal, harmonic and motivic analysis, with basic annotations. There are, however, several recent analytical studies that have inspired the current enquiries and which may be viewed, up to a point, as models. Especially in a jazz domain, aural investigation of diverse recordings proves very pertinent. Indeed it is increasingly recognized that 'Over the last hundred years [. . .] the primary means of musical dissemination has shifted from scores to recordings.'[116] Texts such as Barry Kernfeld's jazz listening guide prove highly relevant and eminently readable.[117] Kernfeld addresses salient parameters: rhythm, form, arrangement, improvisation and chordal notation in Roman numeral style and along the lines of so-called fake-books (some more commercialized, simplified or casual transcriptions are notoriously unreliable).[118] Specific mention should be made of Jack Reilly's practical guide to Evans's harmonic traits, which considers typical voicings and their notation.[119]

One analytical approach to jazz, with obvious potential for mediating with French music, is that advocated by the much-missed Steve Larson (1955–2011).[120] Larson's impressive manifesto for cultural-analytical *mélange* involves detailed questions of jazz transcription and subsequent analysis along Schenkerian lines.[121] Case studies are presented on Monk's ''Round Midnight', an associated piano solo of the celebrated Oscar

---

7–14. It is accompanied by Borém's revision of Aikin's transcription: 'Score of *Peace Piece*, for solo piano by Bill Evans', *Per Musi*, 28 (2013), 15–20.

[115] See http://drwilliamhughes.blogspot.co.uk/2012/09/complete-transcription-bill-evans-peace.html#!/2012/09/complete-transcription-bill-evans-peace.html. I had the pleasure of meeting William Hughes and hearing him perform a variety of Evans's music at the International Conference on Music since 1900/LancMAC (Lancaster University, 28–31 July 2011).

[116] Tymoczko, *A Geometry of Music*, 394.

[117] Barry Kernfeld, *What to Listen for in Jazz* (New Haven, CT and London: Yale University Press, 1995).

[118] *Ibid.*, Appendix 1, 200ff.

[119] Jack Reilly, *The Harmony of Bill Evans*, 2 vols. (Milwaukee, WI: Hal Leonard Corporation, 2010), vol. II.

[120] See the special issue of *Music Theory Online*, 18/3 (September 2012): *Festschrift for Steve Larson*, with articles by David J. Heyer, 'Applying Schenkerian Theory to Mainstream Jazz: A Justification for an Orthodox Approach' (http://mtosmt.org/issues/mto.12.18.3/mto.12.18.3.heyer.php) and Mark McFarland, 'Schenker and the Tonal Jazz Repertory: A Response to Martin' (http://mtosmt.org/issues/mto.12.18.3/mto.12.18.3.mcfarland.php).

[121] Steve Larson, *Analysing Jazz: A Schenkerian Approach*, Harmonologica, Studies in Music Theory, 15 (Hillsdale, NY: Pendragon Press, 2009). See too Larson's preceding studies: 'Schenkerian Analysis of Modern Jazz: Questions about Method', *Music Theory Spectrum*

Peterson (1925–2007), and ensemble performances by Evans, so creating a set of intricate variations on the main locus. Larson has been criticized by some jazz scholars for imposing a method from classical music upon jazz because, it is argued, jazz will therefore be found wanting.

To an extent, I am sympathetic to this view since I express certain misgivings about imposing a Lydian chromatic reading on Ravel (Chapter 7). Heinrich Schenker's ideas were conceived in relation to a spectrum of music colloquially known as the 'three Bs': Bach, Beethoven, Brahms, with all the canonic baggage of such common tonal practice within high-art German hegemony. However, much depends upon exactly how such methods are implemented and their usefulness in a given context. When sensitively employed, extended or post-tonal voiceleading still has much to offer early twentieth-century French music, as I argued in *Darius Milhaud* (see too Chapter 4). Insensitively applied, French music, too, would be found wanting. Brown argues similarly in *Debussy Redux*. Following a series of motivic, thematic, formal and multimedia comparisons, his study culminates (*pace* Roger Parker, Abbate and McClary)[122] in a Schenkerian analysis of the opening of Queen's wonderful *Bohemian Rhapsody* (1975).[123] Furthering a claim of Michael Long,[124] Brown perceives this passage as Freddie Mercury's reconception of Debussy's *Rêverie*; he concludes that high/low cultural divisions have been overplayed and that more nuanced, close analysis of the music is needed.[125] I strongly concur. Moreover, in a bid to reveal relations across any two domains, one or more means of analytical bridging is needed, whether Schenkerian, Lydian chromatic-based, or otherwise. In the absence of some wholly new system, analytical approaches are likely to emanate flexibly from one domain or the other.

Despite mixed reviews, a recent study that offers arguably the strongest sense of a technical model and inspiration for the current book is Tymoczko's fascinating quest for *A Geometry of Music*.[126] Whilst his motivation is that of a composer-theorist envisaging future tonal compositional possibilities, Tymoczko promises something of a flexible third way. The clue lies in his subtitle about harmony and counterpoint (as vertical and linear parameters) viewed within an 'extended common practice'. In encompassing repertory

20/2 (1998), 209–41; 'Composition versus Improvisation?' *Journal of Music Theory*, 49/2 (2005), 241–75; and 'Rhythmic Displacement in the Music of Bill Evans', in David Gagné and Poundie Burstein (eds.), *Structure and Meaning in Tonal Music: Festschrift in Honor of Carl Schachter* (Hillsdale, NY: Pendragon Press, 2006), 103–22.

[122] Brown, *Debussy Redux*, 160, 162–3.   [123] *Ibid.*, 154–65.

[124] Michael Long, *Beautiful Monsters: Imagining the Classic in Musical Media* (Berkeley and Los Angeles, CA: University of California Press, 2008), 226.

[125] Brown, *Debussy Redux*, 168.   [126] Tymoczko, *A Geometry of Music*.

from the Renaissance, through Chopin, Robert Schumann, Leoš Janáček, to jazz, The Beatles, Michael Nyman and beyond,[127] Tymoczko attempts theoretical thinking of a similar magnitude and ambition to that of Allen Forte in seeking to bridge tonal and atonal practices in his audacious theory of pitch-class set genera.[128]

A five-point theory for working with an extended tonal music comprises 'conjunct melodic motion' (principles of voiceleading again), 'acoustic consonance', internal 'harmonic consistency', 'limited macroharmony' (a restricted tonal palette) and centricity.[129] Upon this basis, Tymoczko observes wide-ranging patterns of practice; while intriguing, the wealth of geometric graphing – featuring chordal networks, rotations, symmetries, two- and three-dimensional shapes – is less applicable here. Like Russell, albeit through different means, Tymoczko views chromaticism positively, rather than as connoting a slippery path to tonal self-destruction and inevitable atonality. In a thoroughly intertextual manner, he observes voice-leading similarities, from relative consonance to dissonance, in examples from Schubert, Schoenberg, Wagner's *Tristan und Isolde* and Debussy's *Pelléas et Mélisande*. A specific finding is that, in its voiceleading treatment launched by a dominant seventh chord, Chopin's late Mazurka in F minor exists as 'a virtual rewriting of one of [. . . his] most famous pieces – the E minor Prelude, Op. 28 No. 4'.[130] The point is demonstrated by a comparative chart of four procedures, as a shared improvisatory recipe, similar to my approach to Ravel's adaptation of blues form (see Table 5.2).

In a study of scales that references Davis's 'Freedom Jazz Dance', chordal progressions in The Who's 'I Can't Explain' are compared with Bob Seeger's 'Turn the Page', so creating 'a kind of dorian-mode dual'.[131] (Modal connections also constitute a foundation for almost all my case studies.) Moreover, the use of a 'single-semitone change over a fixed tonic' links the verse and chorus of The Who's song with the beginning of Debussy's 'Des pas sur la neige'. Another striking intertextual coupling, not necessarily audible, is that of The Beatles's 'Help' and Stravinsky's 'Dance of the Adolescents' from *Le Sacre du printemps*, by virtue of 'more abstract intervallic patterns'.[132] The loci also 'exploit melodic material that is deliberately simple or even primitive', with surprisingly comparable fixed pitch or intervallic elements.[133]

---

[127] *Ibid.*, 394.
[128] Allen Forte, 'Pitch-Class Set Genera and the Origin of Modern Harmonic Species', *Journal of Music Theory*, 32 (1988), 187–270.
[129] Tymoczko, *A Geometry of Music*, 4.   [130] *Ibid.*, 287–8.   [131] *Ibid.*, 340.
[132] *Ibid.*, 346.   [133] *Ibid.*, 347.

Finally, while we may legitimately have trouble with loaded terms such as *classical music* and with defining jazz, incontestably both partake of tonality in distinctive and innovative fashions. Thus Tymoczko posits a 'modern[ist] jazz synthesis', which 'unites impressionist chords and scales, chromatic voice leading, and the functional harmony of the classical era',[134] his focus culminating in a full reading of the choruses from Evans's version of 'Oleo' on *Everybody Digs*. He considers harmonic constructs, voicings, modality (altered scales, including Lydian varieties) and polytonality, practices of tritone substitution, 'side-stepping' (semitonal shifting) and a deliberately unsynchronized ensemble playing.[135] In linking the music of Debussy (*Prélude à l'Après-midi*, 'Sirènes', 'La Danse de Puck' and *Six épigraphes antiques*), Ravel (*Pavane pour une infante défunte, Jeux d'eau*, 'Ondine' and *Le Tombeau*), Alexander Scriabin (1872–1915) and others, with that of Evans, Davis, Coltrane and Jarrett, this rich chapter offers a kind of launch pad for my study.

Within the analytical dimension of my own readings, I thus posit a balance between establishing broad intertextual relations (after Tymoczko and Klein) and investigating more specific types of borrowing (after Metzer and Brown).

Potential effects and emergent meanings

Before summarizing a range of potential outcomes from interactions between French music and jazz (to be witnessed in the case studies), it is prudent to stress a few caveats. Firstly, we have to admit the sheer challenge of being presented with a creative entity that one then attempts at some level to unpick and effectively reconstruct. Alternatively, it is as though we are in receipt of an answer, but then try to work out in reverse exactly what the question might have been. Rarely is one domain tacked onto the other with an obvious, neat join, and sometimes it may feel inappropriate or impossible to deconstruct such intricate, composite entities. Except where actual quotation or modelling is involved, there is no true experimental baseline or control for comparison, as the one without the other. This situation is especially acute where the fluidity of jazz as improvisation is concerned.

Secondly, but closely connected, there are extraneous variables and other compromising factors: those elements that obstruct, or blur, what one is attempting to measure and which may affect the validity of what can be deduced. Some ostensibly French features within modal jazz may result as much from jazz predecessors, such as stride pianists with their own classical

---

[134] *Ibid.*, 27.   [135] *Ibid.*, 374ff.

experience, as from French music directly. Similarly, aspects of Brubeck's polytonality and polyrhythm are seemingly intrinsic, as well as being traits held in common with Milhaud; moreover, where classical impact on Brubeck is established, it pertains as much to non-French sources, especially Bach, as it does to Milhaud. Meanwhile, Ravel is arguably as influenced by Gershwin as by jazz directly, if not more so. In response to these problematics, it is crucial to advocate flexibility, sensitivity and an appreciation of plurality: hence, too, why an *esthesic* perception of intertextuality is the default response.

As for the effects created by the interplay, or blending, of the chosen domains with their selected attributes: in theory, these apply to all music parameters and operate across several spectra: from similarity to difference; from disjunct to synthesized presentations; from ambiguity, tension, even contradiction, through to possible resolution;[136] at a surface level through to being deeply embedded in the structure of a piece; on small and large scales. Generally, and unsurprisingly, given the respective authorial (musicianly) positionings, such effects may be characterized as resulting in jazz-inflected French music in the central portion of the book and French-inflected jazz in the latter portion. Nevertheless, the strength of inflection may vary from a subtle tingeing of the main entity by the other (Ravel's music remaining French, its jazz accent firmly Gallicized and personalized) through to a rather deeper reconfiguration (Evans's cosmopolitan jazz conception). More interesting perhaps is, within the confines of a single work, how fluid, divergent and multifaceted the relationship between French music and jazz may be, mixing those elements of commonality amid contrast, inflection through to transformation. (Transformation may result from a conscious eclectic assimilation and individualization of features of the other domain, or from misconception or unwitting distortion.) Sometimes these processes may unfold diachronically, at other times synchronically through a simultaneous layering of effects.[137]

In parts II and III of this book, there is a sense of Milhaud and Brubeck, independently among their respective French modernist and jazz peers, coming closest to inhabiting a fragile realm of a true, balanced hybridity. This notion of a hybrid, and associated processes of hybridization, enjoys much currency and differentiation across several disciplines, including botany, art, linguistics, postcolonial and post-structuralist cultural

---

[136] See Brown, *Debussy Redux*, 8.
[137] In turn, we might liken this layering to Mikhail Bakhtin's borrowed notion of 'polyphony' in literary-cultural hybridity theory, as pursued in *Problems of Dostoevsky's Poetics*, ed. and Eng. trans. Caryl Emerson (Minneapolis, MN: University of Minnesota Press, 1984.)

studies.[138] Essentially, I regard it as a positive, special and rare musical phenomenon. We might posit pieces such as Milhaud's 'Fugue' from *La Création* or Brubeck's 'The Duke' as examples of genuine, one-off trans-cultural fusions or syntheses – extraordinary and unrepeatable, for which there could be no direct creative offspring (biologically sterile).

Similarly, the multiplicity of cultural meanings resulting from such blending practices, as determined across time by numerous critics, listeners, composers and performers, in theory ranges hugely from negatives to positives across many different themes. Such meanings, therefore, are never closed or complete: there will always be scope for new ones arising from a particular whole. As Kramer has advocated aptly, 'When we interpret hermeneutically we can neither stick to the facts nor adhere to fixed assumptions. If we don't go forward we go nowhere.'[139] Richly divergent responses have already been noted, in the Introduction and above. This spectrum extends from perceptions of mimicry or caricature, unethical appropriation or even theft at one extreme, through to those of sincere tribute or homage at the other. It ranges from accusations of frivolity, pretentiousness or uninspired banality, through to an applauding of creative expression and real originality, as recognition of vibrant scope for future artistic enquiry.

---

[138] See again n. 40.   [139] Kramer, *Interpreting Music*, 2.

PART II

The impact of early jazz upon French music
(1900–1935)

3 Debussy and Satie: early French explorations of cakewalk and ragtime

In their artistic forays into the precursors of jazz, Debussy and Satie were firmly positioned within the France of the later Belle Époque with all its associated cultural values.[1] These values were based upon a prevailing confidence that Paris represented the pinnacle of artistic culture; that exoticism, especially of a variety pertaining to the French colonies (euphemistically termed 'protectorates') could be invoked to enhance a sophisticated and luxuriant, decadent Frenchness. As detailed in Chapter 1, the experiences of the 1889 Exposition and the whole ensuing climate of human and technological endeavour nonetheless contributed to the unfolding of what Charles Sowerwine has termed a 'Cultural Revolution'.[2] This was cultural modernism: the emergent response to a need for profound change that was brutally confirmed by the sheer senselessness of World War I. Such was the broad landscape in which Debussy and the notably anti-establishment, idiosyncratic Satie found themselves: one that in France, especially, was also profoundly influenced by the influx of Russian art, as a consequence of revolution at home, in the shape of the Ballets russes, Diaghilev and Stravinsky.

Contextual genres: ragtime, cakewalk and *musique nègre*

Contemporaneously, on the other side of the Atlantic, American ragtime was developing predominantly as a genre for piano (see again Chapter 1). Within the output of ragtime's most celebrated composer, Joplin, a path may be traced from the phenomenally successful – commercial yet still highly artistic – *Maple Leaf Rag* (1899) through to *Magnetic Rag* (1914),[3] which also encompasses a shift from the standard usage of 2/4 metre through to 4/4. By contrast, some rags involved song, as exemplified by the American Jewish songwriter Irving Berlin (1888–1989) in *Alexander's Ragtime Band* and *That Mysterious Rag* (both 1911). Additionally, a close

---

[1] I am very grateful to Roy Howat for his insightful feedback on the Debussy-related portion of this chapter.

[2] Sowerwine, *France since 1870*, 99.

[3] For sensitive, classically measured interpretations, see recordings by the pianist-musicologist Joshua Rifkin, as compiled on *The Entertainer: The Very Best of Scott Joplin* (New York: Nonesuch Records 7559 79449-2, 1996).

cousin of ragtime, but one with a much more overt plantation slavery background, was the dance genre of the cakewalk. Originating in the Southern States of the mid nineteenth century, the cakewalk supposedly provided an annual opportunity for slave workers to satirize their white masters with impunity by strutting their stuff within the confines of an entertaining dance competition for the prize of a cake. At worst, however, the donning of Sunday best, top hats, bow ties, canes and general clowning could readily be interpreted as self-parody, even as comically futile attempts by black workers to emulate their masters, so reinforcing profound prejudice and rigid power relations. There were also later connections to white minstrel shows. Nonetheless, the prevalent view among musicians was that 'It was a vigorous and exciting dance, and as a musical form, like ragtime, transcended the racial stereotypes that surrounded it.'[4] Although the two terms were used freely and often interchanged, as a dance the cakewalk tended to be less musically complex or sophisticated than ragtime.

Back in France, Debussy and Satie were increasingly interested in expanding their compositional horizons in a new, eclectic fashion. Debussy had already explored and exploited much of the potential to be gleaned from more traditional oriental sources with his pioneering usage of pentatonic and wholetone sonorities, while the popular music of the circus, music hall, café-concert and street, not to mention 'furniture music', saw Satie very much in his element and as one who still deserves wider acknowledgement as an innovator in this respect.[5] Seemingly, Satie capitalized on the ragtime potential in a wider cabaret context before Debussy:[6] his ragtime-inspired cakewalk march *Le Piccadilly* appeared in 1904, together with a rag song *La Diva de l'Empire*, described as an 'American intermezzo' for Paulette Darty.[7] In fact,

---

[4] Waldo, *This Is Ragtime*, 25.

[5] Satie's profile has already been raised significantly by several rich studies, including: Robert Orledge, *Satie the Composer* (Cambridge University Press, 1990); Perloff, *Art and the Everyday*; and Steven Moore Whiting, *Satie the Bohemian: From Cabaret to Concert Hall* (Oxford University Press, 1999). Caroline Potter (ed.), *Erik Satie: Music, Art and Literature* (Aldershot: Ashgate, 2013) appeared late in the research process for this current book.

[6] See Peter Dickinson, review of John Hasse (ed.), *Ragtime: Its History, Composers and Music* (London: Macmillan, 1985) in *Music & Letters*, 68/1 (1987), 78–9: 78; and Dickinson, 'The Achievement of Ragtime: An Introductory Study with Some Implications for British Research in Popular Music', *Proceedings of the Royal Musical Association*, 105 (1978–9), 63–76: 69.

[7] Erik Satie, *A Mammal's Notebook: Collected Writings of Erik Satie*, ed. Ornella Volta, Eng. trans. Antony Melville (London: Atlas Press, 1996), 13. See too Robert Orledge, 'Satie and America', *American Music*, 18/1 (Spring 2000), 78–102: 81.

Steven Moore Whiting has discovered an earlier raglike experiment dating from spring 1900 contained in a piano overture: 'Prélude de *La Mort de Monsieur Mouche*'.[8]

It is highly probable that Debussy was introduced to a menu of marches, raglike pieces and the associated cakewalk, at one remove, by Sousa's band at the 1900 Exposition. (In addition, there may conceivably be contributory European popular sources to Debussy's ragtime, since Roy Howat has detected a distinct hint of cakewalk rhythms in pieces as early as the 1880s, including the songs *Pantomime* (1881, published posthumously) and 'Chevaux de bois' from *Ariettes oubliées* (1885–7), and 'Ballet' from the *Petite Suite* (1886–9).)[9] Jackson notes that, in a Paris concert of 1903, Sousa's final act was explicitly billed as showcasing 'Songs from the American plantation'.[10] Furthermore, although Debussy was clearly highly enthusiastic and receptive to the compositional potential of ragtime, as demonstrated by his innovatory, imaginative pieces that draw on the genre, his attitude like those of his contemporaries could be ambivalent – even contradictory – and his tone at times decidedly caustic. Witness his documented response to Sousa's music, published in *Gil Blas* of April 1903, which rather damns through faint praise: 'At last! [...] the king of American music is within our walls! [...] If American music is unique in putting into rhythm the indescribable "cakewalk", I admit that at the moment this appears to me its sole merit over other music [...] then Mr. Sousa is undoubtedly its king.'[11] One crucial word is the qualifying adjective for cakewalk[s], 'indicibles', which has received totally opposed translations: 'unspeakable'[12] versus a

---

[8] Whiting, *Satie the Bohemian*, 257; and see discussion in Orledge, 'Satie and America', 80–1.

[9] Howat, *The Art of French Piano Music*, 256. It is noteworthy that Louis Moreau Gottschalk (1829–69), a virtuoso pianist-composer from New Orleans, of Creole and Jewish parentage, was performing his Louisiana-inspired raglike pieces, such as *Bamboula*, *Danse de nègre*, Op. 2 (1844–5) at the Salle Pleyel in Paris, as early as 1849.

[10] See Jackson, *Making Jazz French*, 83. For further programme details, see Barbara Heyman, 'Stravinsky and Ragtime', *The Musical Quarterly*, 68/4 (October 1982), 543–62: 545.

[11] Claude Debussy, *Monsieur Croche et autres écrits*, ed. François Lesure (Paris: Gallimard, 1971), 153: 'Enfin! [...] le roi de la musique américaine est dans nos murs! [...] Si la musique américaine est unique à rythmer d'indicibles "cake-walk", j'avoue que pour l'instant cela me paraît sa seule supériorité sur l'autre musique [...] et M. Sousa en est incontestablement le roi.' (The copy referred to here is part of the Edward Lockspeiser Collection at Lancaster University, affectionately inscribed in blue ink: 'À Edward Lockspeiser, ces textes qui ne lui apprendrant rien mais avec toute mon amitié, F.L.)

[12] Quoted in Heyman, 'Stravinsky and Ragtime', 545, from Léon Vallas, *The Theories of Claude Debussy*, Eng. trans. Maire O'Brien (London: Oxford University Press, 1929), 165.

softened 'famous'.[13] My more neutral 'indescribable' aims to preserve interpretative scope, but otherwise one might propose 'notorious'.

This issue of ambivalence may be probed further through Debussy's early piece, now known as *Le Petit Nègre* (1906, published 1909). If the title now feels to us very uncomfortable, even translated in its least offensive form as 'The Little Negro', Debussy's original title, in his usual mangled English, was 'The Little Nigar'.[14] Verbally and musically, though, this was part of a widely used and accepted language relating to the cult of *art nègre* – 'black art' – that generated its own double-edged reception of celebration and rejection.[15] Ravel, for instance, who had socially progressive views for his time, used the diminutive term 'négrillons' without anxiety for 'blacked-up' boys in his own scenario for *Ma mère l'Oye* (1908–11).[16]

Poulenc composed his five-movement *Rapsodie nègre*, Op. 1 (1917) for baritone and a mixed chamber ensemble of flute, clarinet, violins, viola, cello and piano. Dedicated to his spiritual mentor Satie, generally it partakes of a stereotypical otherness: the 'Prélude' features mock-oriental modal resonances, while the strident finale, 'Violent', has distinct resonances of *Shéhérazade* by Nikolai Rimsky-Korsakov (1844–1908). Its second movement, a lively 'Ronde', however, opens with accented dotted rhythms combined with a plausible bluesy third/seventh within E♭ minor: G♭/G, D♭/D. A shift from triple to duple metre cues a bitonal procedure between the piano's left hand (flattened) and the remaining texture (naturalized or sharpened). Interestingly, this technique prefigures moments of Ravel: the witty exchange between the black Wedgwood Teapot and the Chinese Cup in the ragtime-foxtrot of *L'Enfant*, or the black-versus-white tensions in 'Aoua!' from *Chansons madécasses* (1925–6). The *Rapsodie* centres on a vocal intermède, 'Honoloulou': a nonsense 'pseudo-Malagasy' poem by a fictitious writer, Makoko Kangourou.[17] Poulenc's setting is very static, with an ironic repeated vocal intoning over reiterated added sixth and seventh chords, presented in contrary, conjunct motion. With its hints of music hall,

---

[13] Richard Langham Smith and François Lesure (eds.), *Debussy on Music: The Critical Writings of the Great French Composer Claude Debussy* (London: Martin Secker & Warburg, 1977), 181.

[14] McKinley, 'Debussy and American Minstrelsy', 250.

[15] For a comprehensive appraisal, see Blake, *Le Tumulte noir*.

[16] See Mawer, *The Ballets of Maurice Ravel*, 36, 47, 48. Ravel also used 'Negro' in connection with *L'Enfant* and meant it positively, as was its usage at the time, simply as black: see Arbie Orenstein (ed.), *A Ravel Reader: Correspondence, Articles, Interviews* (New York: Columbia University Press, 1990), 188.

[17] Supposedly found by Poulenc in a second-hand bookshop, this poem appears in a make-believe collection *Les Poésies de Makoko Kangourou* (1910), created by Marcel Ormoy and Thierry Sandre (also known as Charles Moulié): Schmidt, *Entrancing Muse*, 43, 44.

its melodrama and its unabashed potpourri of exotic clichés, this surrealist piece again foreshadows Ravel's zany declamation, admittedly much more characterized, of the Chinese Cup in *L'Enfant*.

Most famously, Josephine Baker exploited, and was exploited by, the *art nègre* label in her hugely successful *Revue nègre* (1925). What then should we make of Debussy's labelling of *Le Sacre du printemps* as 'une musique nègre'?[18] Stravinsky's icon of modernism and *art nègre* itself could both be embraced collectively in a dynamic definition of cultural primitivism as a powerful and fundamental creative force,[19] but this seems unlikely to have been Debussy's express intention. Rather outside his comfort zone,[20] Debussy effectively distanced himself from the avant-garde *Le Sacre* by likening it to 'a black music', so arguably transferring negative connotation to 'musique nègre'.[21] More neutrally, we might interpret Debussy's comment simply as his relating to part of the other world that also provided ragtime. Such equivocation and manoeuvring was not atypical of Stravinsky too, but was complicated in Debussy's case by the creation of his critical *alter ego* 'Monsieur Croche'.[22] Nevertheless, Debussy's music inspired by ragtime and cakewalk speaks convincingly of these sources,[23] in much more affirmative terms.

Critical-analytical perspective

This is an appropriate point to reinvoke and begin to apply some of the main critical-analytical principles outlined in the previous chapter. To emphasize: a holistic approach is required that marries the sociocultural-historical and the analytical within a broadly hermeneutic, critical enquiry. The main tenets of Kramer's interpretative ideas seem especially applicable: his notions of 'the logic of alterity'[24] and the importance of challenging and

---

[18] Igor Stravinsky and Robert Craft, *Memories and Commentaries* (London: Faber and Faber, 1960; reprinted 2002), 77, and mention in Watkins, *Pyramids at the Louvre*, 66.

[19] See Watkins's coverage of *Le Sacre* and 'Musique nègre: Cakewalk and Ragtime' under a larger umbrella of 'The Primitive', in Watkins, *Pyramids at the Louvre*, 84–111. Debussy wrote a section on the primitive in music within a substantial article entitled 'Le Goût', *Revue musicale de la S.I.M.* (November 1912).

[20] See Langham Smith and Lesure (eds.), *Debussy on Music*, 262.

[21] Intriguingly, there are two clear passing quotations from *Le Sacre* in Debussy's piano music: Debussy, *Préludes* (Book II, No. XI), 'Les Tierces alternées' (bars 75–8) and *Berceuse heroïque* (bars 59–60) of 1914: Howat, *The Art of French Piano Music*, 27–8, 348.

[22] Langham Smith and Lesure (eds.), *Debussy on Music*, ix–xii.

[23] On Debussy's engagement with this topic, though less so for its music analysis, see again McKinley, 'Debussy and American Minstrelsy'.

[24] Kramer, *Classical Music*, 28.

reversing assumptions (while still heeding my earlier tempering). Beyond these general principles, the chosen music by Debussy and Satie highlights the role of quotation – in conjunction with paraphrase – as a most precise cultural borrowing explored by Metzer.

More specifically, Metzer refers to a 'cultural provocation' that can result from borrowing and how, in jazz (and to some extent rag) contexts, such music may employ 'the African-American rhetorical practice of signifying'.[25] In turn, he recalls a classic definition of the practice by Henry Louis Gates Jr as 'the trope of tropes'.[26] While some tropes, such as ironizing, are already implicit from a French perspective, the scope may potentially be expanded 'from the classical oratorical modes of metaphor and irony to the black practices of testifying and rapping. In its myriad forms, signifying outlines the basic strategy of "repetition and revision". Practitioners draw upon existing formal structures and concepts and continually rework them to create new versions that break away, often ironically, from the originals.'[27]

Debussy, cakewalk and quotation: ragging Tristan

'Golliwogg's Cake-Walk' is the final movement of the *Children's Corner* suite (1906–8) for solo piano, dedicated to Debussy's daughter Claude-Emma, nicknamed Chou-Chou – 'a *Siegfried Idyll*-like gift',[28] as Schuller neatly remarks given the Wagnerian association. Evocative and nostalgic of childhood, rather than written expressly for children, its preceding movements adopt the following sequence: 'Doctor Gradus ad Parnassum', 'Jimbo's [*sic*] Lullaby', 'Serenade for the Doll', 'The Snow Is Dancing' and 'The Little Shepherd'. The usage of English-language titles probably reflects the fact that Claude-Emma's governess was herself English.

Invoking a certain classicism, the first piece alludes to the volume of graded piano exercises by Muzio Clementi (1752–1832), while the second,

---

[25] Metzer, *Quotation and Cultural Meaning*, 49.

[26] Henry Louis Gates Jr, *The Signifying Monkey: A Theory of African-American Literary Criticism* (New York: Oxford University Press, 1988), 52. Among a sizeable repertory of writings on signifying in jazz, see Gary Tomlinson, 'Cultural Dialogics and Jazz: A White Historian Signifies', *Black Music Research Journal*, 11 (1991), 229–64, reprinted in Katherine Bergeron and Philip V. Bohlman (eds.), *Disciplining Music: Musicology and Its Canons* (University of Chicago Press, 1992), 64–94; and Robert Walser, 'Out of Notes: Signification, Interpretation, and the Problem of Miles Davis', *The Musical Quarterly*, 77/2 (1993), 343–65.

[27] Metzer, *Quotation and Cultural Meaning*, 49.

[28] Schuller, 'Jazz and Musical Exoticism', 283.

featuring a compound pentatonic exoticism at its core,[29] presents a lullaby for Jumbo, a French-Sudanese elephant who briefly inhabited the Jardin des Plantes, the Parisian botanical garden. Two other items contrast appropriately children's love of snow with a playful, pastoral idyll of summer: note the affectionate diminutive for the shepherd with his flute, or pipe. The third and sixth pieces reference children's toys, specifically dolls, and are surely meant as innocent and playful. Both, however, also exhibit a typical association with prevailing imperial attitudes, as discussed above. 'Serenade for the Doll', in triple metre, evokes a generic oriental china doll, with much use of pentatonic collections; the balancing, concluding cakewalk dance alludes to what was in this prewar era a fashionable, but heavily caricatured, black-faced doll: the golliwog,[30] with its clownlike eyes and lips, wild hair and gaudy-coloured clothing, featuring that now most derogatory suffix 'wog'. Furthermore, it was a doll that likely related to the performance practice of minstrelsy, or blacking up – again typical of its period and for some time thereafter, but considered highly offensive today. Bearing the date July 1908, designed and signed by the composer,[31] the original cover of Debussy's piece published by Durand may now cause some concern: the Sudanese elephant tethers a long cord leading to a child's balloon, which in turn becomes the face of the golliwog.

'Golliwogg's Cake-Walk' reveals Debussy as a French composer very well versed in the aesthetic and musical characteristics of American cake-walk and ragtime.[32] As Langham Smith and Lesure remarked some time ago: 'Those acquainted with the piano preludes, with "Golliwogg's Cakewalk," will realize that before the jazz band had made its mark on classical composers [...] Debussy had himself absorbed a good deal from its precursors, the cakewalks of the Negro minstrels, and the brassy circus

---

[29] Howat, *The Art of French Piano Music*, 9–10.

[30] Howat remarks in personal correspondence (10 December 2013) that 'Florence Upton's original golliwogg was a thoroughly heroic and positive character [...] It was Enid Blyton who did the damage, charging him with negative connotations.' See Howat, liner notes to *Claude Debussy, Piano Music*: Roy Howat (pf.), 4 vols. (Tall Poppies TP165, 2004), vol. IV.

[31] Debussy made clear his wishes for the cover in a letter to Jacques Durand (6 August 1908): see Claude Debussy, *Letters*, ed. François Lesure, Eng. trans. Roger Nichols (London: Faber and Faber, 1987), 195. For a colour facsimile, see *Œuvres complètes de Claude Debussy*, eds. François Lesure and Denis Herlin, series 1–6 (Paris: Éditions Durand, 1998), series I, vol. II, ed. Roy Howat, 118.

[32] For an alternative reading of 'Golliwogg's Cake-Walk', directed mainly by 'a persona identified with that fetish of modernist art, the clown', see Caddy, 'Parisian Cake Walks', 308–315, 317. For an excellent recording, consult *Debussy, Complete Works for Piano*: Jean-Efflam Bavouzet (pf.), 5 vols. (Colchester: Chandos Chan 10421, 2007), vol. III.

Example 3.1 Debussy, *Children's Corner*, 'Golliwogg's Cake-Walk' (bars 1–4): raglike 'head' material

bands.'[33] Marked 'Allegro giusto', it is a fun and witty piece, set in the 2/4 metre typical of early ragtime and in an overall tonality of E♭ major, harmonically enriched with added sevenths and ninths. An incisive rhythmic identity is maintained through continual syncopation, displaying the classic cakewalk pattern: semiquaver-quaver-semiquaver plus two quavers (also used in *Le Petit Nègre*), pitted against a time-keeping quaver background. Given its regular metre and apparent simplicity, this opening section of an ABA ternary form (bars 1–46; 47–89; 90–128) might just about be danceable. But this is not really the point. It is primarily a portrait or representation of cakewalk and, in its sophistication, layering and mechanicity (bar 10 stipulates: 'très net et très sec', plus staccato and accent markings), the music nods more towards contemporary ragtime. Overall, both source genres remain relevant, often fused, which is not inappropriate given the scope for interchangeability between the original forms: for instance, Joplin's *Swipesy Cake-Walk* is a rag, while William Krell's *Mississippi Rag* of 1897 is arguably a cakewalk.

One measure of the music's sophistication is in its setting up of patterns with consequent expectations or implications,[34] which are played upon, often confounded (remaining 'unrealized') through processes of reversal or, later, interruption. A descending raglike 'head' melded with pentatonicism and a flattened sixth (bars 1–4; Example 3.1) tips into a silent anticipatory caesura (bar 5). A four-bar 'vamp till ready' gesture then features an offbeat-quaver-plus-two-semiquavers pattern in the right hand of bar 6, which is reversed as two semiquavers plus quaver in bar 8.

Similarly, in the closely derived main melody characterized as 'very clean and very dry' (bars 10–17; Example 3.2), an incipient blueslike motion on the

[33] Langham Smith and Lesure (eds.), *Debussy on Music*, 70.
[34] Reference may still be made to Eugene Narmour, *The Analysis and Cognition of Basic Melodic Structures: The Implication-Realization Model* (University of Chicago Press, 1990).

Example 3.2 Debussy, *Children's Corner*, 'Golliwogg's Cake-Walk' (bars 10–17): pattern reversal in the main melody

sixth scalic degree, C♭/C natural (bars 11–12), is balanced by its reversal: C/C♭ (bars 14–15). On the further significance of this non-diatonic C♭, see below. Four bars before the double-strain AABB is completed, the 'head' (bar 38ff., contracted to three bars) and vamping (extended to six bars) interrupt to cue change but, whereas previously these gestures signalled ensuing momentum, they now effect a reduction of energy and dynamic – a kind of fragmentation, even liquidation of material – ready for the central section (bar 47ff., 'Un peu moins vite'). Another twist of expectation lies in the tonality selected for this trio portion: G♭ major, the flattened mediant relation (i.e. the relative of the tonic minor): more a French than a ragtime manoeuvre.

So far the musical attributes of Debussy's opening have been compared to those of his source genres, but these attributes have their own wider hermeneutic resonances. The ploy of creating expectations that are then undermined through inversion – keeping us on our toes and avoiding predictability – cleverly mirrors those ambiguities inherent in our perception of the cakewalk spectacle itself: questions of white/black power relations and satire versus farce.[35]

---

[35] This idea may also be seen to anticipate Ravel's 'Aoua!', where, using Évariste de Parny's text, Ravel inverts standard white-oriented evocations of exoticism – Western views of the East – to identify with the islanders' warning: 'Beware white men, dwellers of the shore' ('Méfiez-vous des blancs, habitants du rivage').

Example 3.3 Debussy, *Children's Corner*, 'Golliwogg's Cake-Walk' (bars 59–64): Wagner's *Tristan* leitmotif and quipping

These reversals are one aspect of more far-reaching combinative and transformative processes that come to the fore in the central section: layering, liquidation and musical identity itself. The double-strain CC material presents a *sotto voce* vamping on Gb, with percussive, offbeat iterations above – plucked like a banjo, followed by hints of a walking string bass descending by step (bars 51–4). But, interrupting the final two bars of this would-be sixteen-bar strain, marked 'Cédez' and 'avec une grande émotion', there appears with suitable gravity the defining love-death leitmotif A, F, E, Eb from Wagner's *Tristan und Isolde* (bars 61–3; Example 3.3). It is combined with the now-ascending walking bass, which morphs wonderfully into Wagnerian chromaticism. As before, apt ambiguity is created through a deliberate confusion of antecedent and consequent: the quotation, effectively brought in as a consequent, becomes an antecedent.

The mainstay of this middle section (bars 61–78), in theory the double-strain DD, alternates a total of four close quotations of the *Tristan* material ('Cédez'), harmonized variously, with a bathetic banjo-like quipping ('a Tempo'). The stop-start cycle adds to the sense of mockery. Particularly intriguing are the additional 'Cédez'-type interpolations that transform the *Tristan* allusion into cakewalk guise, breaking the back of the sacrosanct motive with an accented syncopation on an upper Ab: A, F, Ab, G (bars 69–70); the second occurrence (bars 79–80) destroys the start of the motive, reduced to a tritone, before further extending and distorting the middle: D♭, A, C, B♭, at *ff* dynamic. Omission here of the 'Cédez' designation in the 1908 Durand edition (though later included in the *Œuvres complètes*)[36] might be seen as more evidence of Debussy's transformative *jeux* in changing one aspect of material identity, while retaining another. Cakewalk now wins out, combined with walking bass. And in a reversal of that liquidation which effected a transition between opening and middle sections (and which later governs the coda: bars 118–28), the main melody for the reprise in E♭ is restored from the reiterated fragment: B♭, A♭, B♭. Crucially, after a sense of 'shall we, shan't we?', this implication is allowed its realization. Even then, Debussy avoids any complacency by staggering the starts of the first four-bar phrase of the theme (bar 90, 'Toujours retenu') and the '1° Tempo' (bar 92, itself preceded by a caesura which breaks the phrase).

With reference back to Metzer,[37] Debussy's quoting of Wagner in the central section – very much set in relief – already involves a modicum of transformation in the source–product relationship. This point is picked up on by Kramer in his brief reading of the passage which focuses on its essential falsehood:[38] while the motivic pitches are consistent with the original, both harmony and metre-cum-rhythm are deliberately varied.[39] However, a bigger question concerning transformation may then be pondered about the emergent meanings from Debussy's piece, a notion congruent with Metzer's assertion that the act of quotation immediately invokes a cultural agency. The Wagner quotation, with its own small-scale autonomy, creates rich added meaning and functions as a kind of pivot that can articulate opposed perspectives.

From one perspective, quoting Wagner for satirical effect is a very French gesture.[40] Debussy's complex love-hate relationship with Wagner and all he stood for as German hegemony – yet, awkwardly, his undeniable catalytic role in French musical modernism – is well known. As Langham Smith and Lesure note, Debussy's attitude to Wagner in his writings is far from

---

[36] The 'Cédez' and 'a Tempo' markings (bars 79–80, 81) are not present in Debussy's manuscript, but do appear in a published orchestral transcription, supported by piano roll recordings: *Œuvres complètes de Claude Debussy*, series I, vol. II, 107.

[37] Metzer, *Quotation and Cultural Meaning*, 5.

[38] Lawrence Kramer, *Opera and Modern Culture, Wagner and Strauss* (Berkeley and Los Angeles, CA: University of California Press, 2004), 113–14.

[39] For more harmonic discussion, see Caddy, 'Parisian Cake Walks', 308, 310.

[40] Note Emmanuel Chabrier's irreverent *Souvenirs de Munich* (1880; a quadrille on themes from *Tristan*), or the Fauré and Méssager, *Souvenirs de Bayreuth* (themes from *The Ring* cycle): Howat, *The Art of French Piano Music*, 170–1.

transparent: 'he hides behind a mask that is frequently frivolous and only occasionally do real insights shine through'.[41] From his initial private denigrating of Wagner, despite his early, overt compositional embrace, Debussy moved on to admit that *Parsifal* and, significantly, *Tristan* did represent collectively the height of the composer's attainment. He remained adamant, however, that: 'Wagner is not a good mentor for the French.'[42] Satie went a stage further, disguising his distaste by claiming Wagner ironically for the French: 'the Germans get everything from France ... It's quite shameful! ... You know, don't you, that Wagner was French?'[43] Ravel's musical reactions were as or more acute, with his later lampooning of *Götterdämmerung, Das Rheingold* and other grand opera in a section marked 'Wagneramente' of an opening miniature fanfare of another children's work, the ballet *L'Éventail de Jeanne* of 1927.[44] It is possible that Debussy's quoting of *Tristan* was itself inspired by a memoir recalling a late nineteenth-century French circus act that did the same thing: 'Wagner was parodied on a tightrope, accompanied by a warped medley of his own leitmotiv played by the circus band.'[45] So the inclusion of a Wagner reference could be seen to consolidate a reading of this music as a French burlesque portrait of cakewalk-cum-ragtime and, on the larger scale, a beguiling, exotic colouring of French music.

Intriguingly however, from an opposed perspective, the lampooning of a classical music quotation also enables Debussy's music to be identified with ragtime, reversing its privileged French position and assumptions. It is as though Debussy, momentarily assuming the persona of a rag artist, is debunking the establishment that he was really a part of. (This strategy might resemble the Ravel/de Parny choice of positioning in 'Aoua!', mentioned above.) Effectively, this means regarding Debussy's cakewalk as a stand-alone piece, a status it already enjoys: having won the public's imagination, it is published and frequently performed separately from the suite.

---

[41] Langham Smith and Lesure (eds.), *Debussy on Music*, 66. On Debussy's related criticism, see his review 'M. Siegfried Wagner at the Concerts Lamoureux', *Gil Blas* (2 March 1903) and 'London Letters' review of 30 April 1903, *Gil Blas* (5 May 1903), plus 'Impressions of *The Ring* in London', *Gil Blas* (1 June 1903), 132–3, 188–91, 203–7.

[42] Langham Smith and Lesure (eds.), *Debussy on Music*, 66. On the strong dramatic connections between *Tristan* and Debussy's *Pelléas et Mélisande*, see 'Pelléas and Tristan' in Robin Holloway, *Debussy and Wagner* (London: Eulenburg Books, 1979), 60–75.

[43] Erik Satie, *The Writings of Erik Satie*, ed. Nigel E. Wilkins (London: Eulenburg Books, 1980), 70. As Roy Howat observes in personal correspondence (10 December 2013), this is an ironic matter of 'Satie acknowledging that Baudelaire's championship of Wagner [...] had in turn spawned a sort of autonomous French Wagnerian identity'.

[44] Mawer, *The Ballets of Maurice Ravel*, 212–13.

[45] Langham Smith and Lesure (eds.), *Debussy on Music*, 71, with reference to Albert de Saint-Albin, *Les Sports à Paris* (Paris, 1889).

Indeed, as identified by Howat, it is one of a dozen or so ragtime-related pieces written by Debussy between 1904 and 1915. Its relative sophistication is not out of kilter with Joplin's aspiration for classic rag to be revered as art music.[46] If its presentation may seem problematic from a black stance, it is mild in comparison with some of the cruder, caricatured images used by many American rag composers, including even the African-American rag composer Ben Harney to match public expectations for *The Cake-Walk in the Sky*.

From a rag perspective, quoting Wagner's *Tristan* motive exhibits very strong parallels with a veritable tradition of ragtime, blues and jazz quotations from Chopin's 'Funeral March', often used as a piece's concluding gesture. The ploy is illustrated by Felix Arndt's aptly titled *Desecration Rag* of 1914,[47] Armstrong's 1928 recording of *West End Blues* and Ellington's contemporary *Black and Tan Fantasy*. As Metzer comments, himself relating to Kramer's work,[48] the act of quoting Chopin may signify simultaneously the sincere and insincere. By the early twentieth century a second, mocking aspect was layered upon the sincere usage it already manifested for public funeral processions (including Chopin's own in Paris and in decorated format in New Orleans settings): 'It had become a cliché, a familiar and bombastic portent of death.'[49] In our reading of a cakewalk-ragtime that quotes and distorts – that 'rags' – Wagner, this observation nicely legitimizes the equivalent impossibility of separating the sincere and insincere in Debussy's love-hate reaction to Wagner. Similarly ambivalent, Stravinsky produced a distorted allusion to Debussy's cakewalk in his ensemble *Ragtime*: 'a harmonically out-of-focus, slightly askew, caricature of Debussy's opening measures'.[50]

As for the African-American dancing couples in the cakewalk competition, the more subdued central section may be viewed as a flirtatious interlude in the proceedings.[51] In this setting, the Wagner quotation might denote the amorous, earnest approach of a male suitor to his partner, and an irreverent response to it as female laughter rejecting his advances, or

---

[46] Waldo, *This Is Ragtime*, 58.

[47] Metzer, *Quotation and Cultural Meaning*, 63, 65. The short-lived Felix Arndt (1889–1918), who died in the New York flu epidemic of 1918, was a pianist and song composer for vaudeville, also influencing the young Gershwin.

[48] Lawrence Kramer, 'Chopin at the Funeral: Episodes in the History of Modern Death', *Journal of the American Musicological Society*, 54 (Spring 2001), 97–125.

[49] Metzer, *Quotation and Cultural Meaning*, 63.

[50] Heyman, 'Stravinsky and Ragtime', 557.

[51] As noted by Howat, an alternate interpretation is that this setting was inspired by a march played by the Grenadier Guards outside Buckingham Palace, which could fit with the descending tuba scale in the orchestral transcription.

the tittering of onlookers. The banjo simulation too is wholly consistent with this Southern States plantation image. Equally, Schuller's interpretation of this reaction is attractive as 'nose-thumbing Tin Pan Alley chuckles'.[52] Given that the Wagner motive conjoins notions of love and death (and bearing in mind the Chopin connotations), all may not, however, be simple jollity. Like early black ragtime music 'feigning happiness while masking underlying misery',[53] the inclusion of this double-edged motive, in keeping with the other reversals, might even be inferred as encompassing – possibly a fleeting 'testifying' to – the struggle of plantation existence and ongoing prejudice.

By extension, knowing there is one definitive quotation, we may wonder whether there are more. Since the main melody has such a familiar feel, it is easy to imagine we must have heard it somewhere before – another instance of signifying within popular practice? In part, we have of course because, as long noted elsewhere,[54] the infamous half-diminished 'Tristan chord': B, F, D♯, G♯, is recreated, enharmonically incognito, across that opening head of the tune: (B♭) A♭, F, E♭, C♭. But, while there are also distinct similarities of shape and rhythm with the main melodies of Joplin's *Pineapple Rag* and *Paragon Rag*, their respective compositional dates of 1908 and 1909 make clear that such relationships are generic. This further evidence of hybridizing Wagner and rag clinches the case for Debussy's impressive facility and familiarity with ragtime style.

Despite already being a well-documented example, 'Golliwogg's Cake-Walk' was chosen here because, as well as demonstrating Debussy's pioneering role in utilizing the cakewalk-ragtime other, it prompts added cultural meanings associated with quotation and maximizes opportunity for reading the music both ways. As remarked on above, it was not by any means the composer's only experience of musical mixing and, whilst the remaining repertory is far more obviously French-based, these other interactions with ragtime, minstrelsy and popular music still warrant mention. Two later examples – Schuller's 'ragtime-influenced delicacies'[55] – are located in the two sets of twelve *Préludes* (1910 and 1910–13), where exploration of timbre, modality and rhythm prove especially germane.

Firstly, continuing the cakewalk theme, in Book II (No. VI), we find the prelude that depicts 'Général Lavine – Eccentric', whose music is designated 'Dans le style et le Mouvement d'un Cake-Walk'. The likely subject is Edward Lavine, a vaudeville clown figure who appeared at the Théâtre

---

[52] Schuller, 'Jazz and Musical Exoticism', 283.   [53] Waldo, *This Is Ragtime*, 33.

[54] See for instance Caddy, 'Parisian Cake Walks', 309, 310.

[55] Schuller, 'Jazz and Musical Exoticism', 284. For superb recordings, again consult *Debussy, Complete Works for Piano*: Bavouzet, vol. I.

Marigny, Paris, in 1910 and 1912,[56] and who was immortalized as a stiff, limping puppet in a Folies Bergère show. But this is one very urbane French interpretation of cakewalk. The introduction sets up a 2/4 metre and a chromaticized F major, with the designations 'strident' and 'sec' (similar to 'Golliwogg's Cake-Walk') supporting a percussive, mechanical figuration: left-hand *gruppetti* preceding an accented dominant pedal, with minor–major quaver triads above. However, the characteristic syncopated patterning of cakewalk is downplayed. Following a pause (bar 10), the actual melody – now embraced within the subtle marking 'Spirituel et discret' – is imaginatively located in the bass, as the middle of an elaborate three-stave construction that is maintained for the duration of the piece (bars 11–19; Example 3.4). Vestiges of syncopation remain, with the offbeat chords, marked at *p* dynamic, in contrast with the melody at *pp*. Beyond its Debussyan pentatonic basis: C, D, F, G, A, there are hints of incipient blues third: A/A♭ (bars 16–17). Another defining attribute of this piece is its fitting flexibility of tempo, together with further evidence of quotation, this time from Mussorgsky – a ragging of *Boris Godunov* – as well as from Stephen Foster's *Camptown Races*, which may yet have a bearing back in 'Golliwogg's Cake-Walk'.[57]

Secondly, there is the final prelude from Book I (No. XII), which explicitly evokes 'Minstrels' and which may hold association with American vaudeville performers. Paul Roberts suggests that Debussy superimposes his experience of American minstrelsy – perhaps acquired on his trip to Eastbourne in 1905 – collage-like, upon a Parisian fairground, circus and music-hall background.[58] In this sense, Debussy moves beyond the direct one-on-one usage of any single external stimulus, creating a unique eclectic *mélange*. Like 'Général Lavine', this prelude adopts 2/4 metre in a chromaticized G major, with hints of blues third: B/B♭. Its highly percussive introduction, marked 'Nerveux et avec humour', with explicit instruction for the *gruppetti* to be placed on the beats, creates a comical, tripping effect. It also shares the temporal fluidity ('Cédez', 'Mouvement')[59] and pentatonic

---

[56] Siglind Bruhn, *Images and Ideas in Modern French Piano Music: The Extra-Musical Subtext in Piano Works by Ravel, Debussy, and Messiaen* (Hillsdale, NY: Pendragon Press, 1997), 118.

[57] Howat, *The Art of French Piano Music*, 135, 255.

[58] Paul Roberts, *Images: The Piano Music of Claude Debussy* (Portland, OR: Amadeus Press, 2001), 218.

[59] For more on issues of tempo in these evocations and their ragtime exemplars, see Roy Howat, 'Debussy's Piano Music', in Richard Langham Smith (ed.), *Debussy Studies* (Cambridge University Press, 1997), 87–88. Note too the similar coverage in Howat, *The Art of French Piano Music*, 255–6.

Example 3.4 Debussy, *Préludes* (Book II, No. VI), 'Général Lavine – eccentric' (bars 11–19)

tendencies in the main melody: D, E, G, A, B (bar 9ff.). Meanwhile, a reminiscence of 'Golliwogg's Cake-Walk' is found in the marking 'Moqueur' ('Mocking', bar 37) for a poignant chromatic phrase, presented in relief: Eb–D–Db–C, Eb–Bb (bars 37–40; see Example 3.5), supported by wholetone harmony.[60] Stravinsky and Wagner may be the subjects of this mockery, with a seeming chromaticized version of the start of the big tune that cues the conclusion of *L'Oiseau de feu* (also 1910). Although this

---

[60] On 'cakewalk revival' here, see Lawrence Kramer, 'Powers of Blackness: Africanist Discourse in Modern Concert Music', *Black Music Research Journal*, 16/1 (Spring 1996), 53–70: 65; reproduced in Kramer, *Musical Meaning*, 210. Roberts (*Images*, 218) interprets this passage through to bar 44 as a music-hall clowning routine.

Example 3.5 Debussy, *Préludes* (Book I, No. XII), 'Minstrels' (bars 34–40)

prelude too avoids standard ragtime rhythmic patterns, it offers a generally higher profile to syncopation than does 'Général Lavine'. One later detail, uncomfortably evocative of minstrelsy, is the repeated offbeat triplet semi-quaver figuration, which is to sound 'quasi tambouro' (bar 58ff.) – dry, like bones.

With a large amount of commonality, these loci do suggest a certain fixity of Debussy's sonic image in relation to ragtime-cum-popular-entertainment inspiration – rather like Stravinsky's evocations of ragtime, if less acute. Additionally, 'Hommage à S. Pickwick Esq., P.P.M.P.C.', with its climactic central melody preceding the 'Mouvement' section, and the opening of the final 'Feux d'artifice' may be identified as evidence of Debussy's interest in incipient blues-third relations, while 'Les Tierces alternées' form the subject matter of the penultimate prelude.

Satie (Stravinsky) and ragtime: paraphrasing Berlin

Continuing the issue of quotation posed by Debussy, this second study focuses on Satie's 'Rag-time du paquebot' and its implications. As already noted and as recognized by Cocteau,[61] 'the profound originality of a Satie' proved at least as innovative as Debussy and this episode from *Parade* was not his first ragtime excursion, though it was his first ballet experience. This 'Rag-time' should, however, also be seen in an immediate postwar context of similar pieces by other native French composers and Stravinsky. Although Stravinsky did not officially acquire French citizenship until 1934, his output was absolutely core to the flourishing Parisian artistic scene before and after World War I: indeed, as part of the wider Russian dimension, it was a catalyst for much of what happened.

It is useful to glean a little more about the nature of Satie's ragtime pursuit in *Parade* via comparison with Stravinsky in *L'Histoire du soldat* – a work that in Stephen Walsh's words offers 'a reflection of Stravinsky's enforced re-assimilation into the multi-faceted world of Western European culture'.[62] Both *Parade* and *L'Histoire* date from around 1917–18, although the four-hand version of *Parade* was performed as early as 19 November 1916.[63] Both stage works have strong Russo-French connections: as a surrealist ballet on a scenario of Cocteau, *Parade* was taken up by Diaghilev's Ballets russes, with choreography by Léonide Massine and cubist sets and costumes by Picasso – a collaborative first;[64] meanwhile, Stravinsky's *L'Histoire*, as a text-setting of the French-Swiss writer C. F. Ramuz, was 'to be read, played and danced'. Both are crucial as neoclassical prototypes, together with Ravel's *Le Tombeau*, each emphasizing chamber forces and closed forms, especially dances, and existing in variously scored versions. Both incorporate their ragtimes into larger structures, close to their work's centre: Satie's is contained within the second main number: 'Petite fille américaine' (Young American Girl); Stravinsky's is the last of 'Three Dances (Tango, Waltz, Ragtime)'. Each also presents ragtime as part of a wider traversing of musics. After an initial 'Choral'[65] and 'Prélude', Satie's first main number (Chinese Conjuror) invokes pentatonic *chinoiserie*, while the third (Acrobats) uses the waltz; Stravinsky's work references national dances, marches and chorales, resulting in 'stylistic plurality'.[66] Both ragtimes

---

[61] Cocteau, *Le Coq et l'arlequin*, reprinted in *Le Rappel à l'ordre*, 25: 'La profonde originalité d'un Satie'.

[62] Stephen Walsh, *The Music of Stravinsky* (Oxford: Clarendon Press, 1993), 95.

[63] According to Orledge ('Satie and America', 84), the 'Rag-time' was actually completed by 19 October 1916.

[64] For a detailed study of the interarts collaborative dimension of *Parade*, see Christine Reynolds, '*Parade*: Ballet réaliste', in Caroline Potter (ed.), *Erik Satie: Music, Art and Literature* (Aldershot: Ashgate, 2013), 137–60.

[65] See the full orchestral score of Erik Satie, *Parade* (New York: Dover Publications, 2000; originally published Paris: Éditions Salabert, 1917).

[66] Walsh, *The Music of Stravinsky*, 95.

display a machinist dimension, so connecting the genre with cultural modernism and modernity itself: Satie's in its passenger steamer allusion ('paquebot': an oblique reference to the liner *Titanic*, with its fateful trans-atlantic maiden voyage of 1912),[67] Stravinsky's in his continuing use of ostinati and mechanized accompaniment figurations. Elsewhere, Satie too employs ostinato and creates parts for Cocteau's noise-making instrumental additions, including a typewriter ('machine à écrire').

Beyond these shared features, there is substantive stylistic contrast, not least regarding the composers' handling of their ragtime inspiration: the 'external idiom', as Walsh puts it.[68] In addition to the wealth of experience Satie had accrued from popular entertainment performed in Paris and via his own early rag excursions, his inspiration for the product 'Rag-time du paquebot' had a definitive American source: Berlin's *That Mysterious Rag*.[69] By contrast, at least for the 'Ragtime' in *L'Histoire*, Stravinsky's experience was acquired through notation, as opposed to live performance or record-ings, via a bundle of unspecified sheet music brought to him by Ansermet in 1918, during his involuntary wartime exile from Paris in Switzerland. Neatly, it was also Ansermet who had conducted the premiere of *Parade* at the Théâtre du Châtelet on 18 May 1917.

While not pre-empting the enquiries below, where the cultural meanings of Satie's interaction are concerned I propose that his ragtime takes over Berlin's identity to a considerable degree yet, on a larger scale, remains French. In parallel, Stravinsky's ragtime still sounds very Russian; witness his later admission that 'The snapshot has faded, I fear, and it must always have seemed to Americans like very alien corn.'[70] Despite this, both formally, where it approximates Joplin's *Maple Leaf Rag*, and metrically, syncopated in 2/4 metre, Stravinsky's piece is quite close to the letter, if not the spirit, of early ragtime. His practice also shows a phenomenal ability to effect trans-formation: the tango theme morphs, via the waltz, into the ragtime material.

In brief, the zany (non-)plot for *Parade* involves three stage managers on the street outside a theatre, trying to promote their respective music hall

---

[67] Robert Orledge, 'Satie's Approach to Composition in His Later Years (1913–24)', *Proceedings of the Royal Musical Association*, 111 (1984–5), 155–79: 169, and Orledge, 'Satie and America', 84. Orledge points out that the piece was entitled 'Ragtime du Titanic' in an annotated piano duet score belonging to Serge Lifar and used for early rehearsals in 1917.

[68] Walsh, *The Music of Stravinsky*, 88.

[69] According to Volta, the precise source was very likely a Francis Salabert arrangement, dated 1913, of Berlin's song: Ornella Volta, *Erik Satie et la tradition populaire* (Paris: Fondation Satie, 1988), 28. Orledge remarks that Berlin's song appeared in a revue at the Moulin Rouge in the same year: 'Satie and America', 99n.

[70] Igor Stravinsky and Robert Craft, *Dialogues and a Diary* (Garden City, NY: Doubleday, 1963; Berkeley and Los Angeles, CA: University of California Press, 1982), 54.

acts – the Chinese Conjuror, Young American Girl and Acrobats – but unfortunately failing to persuade members of the public to enter the theatre to see the show. (Performatively, the premiere of *Parade* created similar misunderstandings and secured the scandal that Cocteau seemingly sought.) The start of the second number cues the entry of the second stage manager, while the third manager enters on a pantomime horse at the end of the 'Rag-time'.[71] In his essay on *Parade*, Apollinaire who strongly endorsed its 'esprit nouveau' commented that 'the American girl, by turning the crank of an imaginary automobile, will express the magic of everyday life'.[72] thus, she symbolizes a French perception of contemporary American life. Nancy Perloff points out that Cocteau's image of America was strongly founded upon its exported films, suggesting that his stage directions for the ragtime 'recall a Mary Pickford or Pearl White film in their dizzying display of a great range of activities: riding a horse, catching a train, driving a Model T Ford, swimming, and playing cowboys and Indians'.[73]

A substantial part of this American image is also furnished by reference to Berlin's *That Mysterious Rag* and so this is an appropriate moment to interpolate some detail about this prewar product of Tin Pan Alley. Born in Belarus, Berlin had emigrated from Russia to the United States with his Jewish family seeking asylum; as his fortunes rose, he became a prolific songwriter who enjoyed a sixty-year career. The song in question was one of an astonishing 1,500 or so, extending from his first hit *Alexander's Ragtime Band*, midst a host of film and Broadway show scores. For Gershwin, Berlin was simply 'the greatest songwriter that has ever lived'.[74]

That Mysterious Rag is notated in cut-common time, in C major, with a marking of 'Allegro moderato'. A regular eight-bar introduction, based on the chorus theme, leads via a repeated 'Till ready' vamping into the main verse (Example 3.6a). The jokey text questions: 'Did you hear it? Were you near it? If you weren't then you've yet to fear it' – 'it' being an earworm: one of those tunes that get stuck in your head. It is set to a catchy dotted rhythm and stepwise melody that explores the relative minor before ending on the dominant, to cue and then resolve onto the chorus (verse: bar 16). Announcing the title line (Example 3.6b), the chorus has a simple but power-ful melodic contour, encompassing an uplifting span of a major tenth: C–E: 'That mysterious rag / While awake or while you're a-slumbering'. Spoken

---

[71] The stage directions and titling of 'Rag-time du paquebot' occur only in the two-piano score.

[72] Apollinaire, quoted in Perloff, *Art and the Everyday*, 114–15.   [73] *Ibid.*, 113–14.

[74] Robert Wyatt and John A. Johnson (eds.), *The Gershwin Reader* (New York: Oxford University Press, 2004), 117.

delivery is reserved for the declamation: 'Look! Look!' (chorus: bar 15), warning the listener that he is inadvertently whistling the tune: a confident marketing ploy, with in-built performative dimension since the subject-matter and its means match up.

Characterized as 'Triste', to convey the emotions of a homesick Young American Girl and seemingly the tragedy of the *Titanic*, Satie's 'Rag-time' (Figs. 23–33^{+7}) operates at a moderate tempo in the same, modally expanded C major and cut-common time, also typical of later rags such as Joplin's *Magnetic Rag* (even if, strictly, the latter is in 4/4 metre).[75] Two renditions of a chorus in the tonic (Figs. 23 and 25; Example 3.7a) lead to a more chromatic, minor-key and accented verse section (Figs. 26–7; Example 3.7b), which is supported in the piano score by the direction 'au dehors et douloureux' ('projected and sorrowful'). Back in the tonic, an eight-bar condensed recurrence of the chorus material (Fig. 28; 'Au temps') contains the ominous direction 'Criblé' ('pierced', 'perforated'). A return to the 2/4 metre of the Young American Girl's music ensues, marked 'Trembler comme une feuille' (Tremble like a leaf), and includes what has been interpreted as a musical portrait of the engulfed *Titanic*, with a climactic wave of scalic sextuplet semiquavers (Figs. 30–1).[76]

Despite Satie's previous usage of pre-existing sources, many years passed before the close source–product relationship between Berlin's rag song and Satie's 'Rag-time' was remarked upon by Joseph Machlis: 'The melody duplicates almost verbatim that of Irving Berlin's *That Mysterious Rag*.'[77] In fact, the relationship is not one of straight quotation; had it been so, it would doubtless have been apparent much sooner (compare Examples 3.6 and 3.7 and the relevant scores). Nor is it simply confined to the melody – the bass line also is implicated. Instead, assuming the mysterious spirit of its source, Satie seems to have enjoyed covering his tracks or, like the engulfed ship, submerging Berlin's composition under his own. In her thorough formalist account, Perloff describes the connection as one of 'paraphrase'[78] and this is largely correct, though at times such paraphrasing approaches the original so closely that it borders on

---

[75] For a useful French recording, consult *Satie, Orchestral Works (Parade, Trois gymnopédies, Mercure, Relâche)*: Jérôme Kaltenbach (cond.), Orchestre symphonique et lyrique de Nancy (Nancy: Naxos, 8-554279, 1997).

[76] That the *Titanic* disaster had occurred only four or so years earlier begs questions about the role of such a portrayal: is Satie's allusion a concealed memorial, a neutral topical account, or a lighthearted reference in poor taste? It is probably a contradictory mixture.

[77] Joseph Machlis, *Introduction to Contemporary Music* (New York: Norton, 1961; reprinted 1979), 215.

[78] Perloff, *Art and the Everyday*, 132–43.

Example 3.6 Berlin, *That Mysterious Rag*
   (a) Verse (bars 1–5)
   (b) Chorus (bars 1–5)

(mis)quotation. What should we make of it? Does this major unattributed borrowing, concealed rather than Metzer's norm of being set in relief, mean that the connection verges on plagiarism,[79] or is it simply Satie's

---

[79] Metzer includes an interesting chapter on this, focusing on much more recent 'Sampling and Thievery', where he suggests the need for a further category of 'creative theft' to

Example 3.7 Satie, *Parade*, 'Rag-time du paquebot' (Satie's piano reduction)
(a) Fig. 23 (bars 1–5, chorus)
(b) Fig. 26 (bars 1–5, verse)

describe an American group 'Negativland', who sample existing recordings and openly admit to breaching copyright, but who justify their actions by the quality of their originality and creativity: Metzer, *Quotation and Cultural Meaning*, 161. This might prove an intriguing, if controversial, line of future enquiry for specific portions of Satie's art, but would need convincing documentary corroboration of artistic intent.

private joke?[80] Although Satie's intentions will likely remain elusive, we shall attempt some answers about the relationship, partly through a selective Satie–Berlin comparison, to probe its range and extremes.

Rhythmically, as the main determinant of ragtime, Satie's derivative is almost identical to its Berlin source, across the chorus and verse.[81] Similarly, exact formal repetitions of material are employed in both loci. Melodically, the antecedent of Satie's main chorus melody closely maintains Berlin's contour, starting out a third higher on E, played by a doubling of clarinets and first violins (Examples 3.7a and 3.6b); the consequents are, however, more contrasted. Orchestration and newly detailed articulation form part of this process. Berlin's melody reaches its peak on E (chorus, bar 6) before curving back downwards to the lower E (chorus, bar 8); Satie outdoes his source, employing an ascending minor ninth interval B–C on clarinets (Fig. 23, bars 4–5), then extending by a further tone to climax on a sustained upper D sounded by flutes, clarinets and strings (Fig. 24^{-2}).

When the two melody lines are compared directly, it looks almost as though Satie has engaged in a bizarre note-against-note species counterpoint exercise, with judicious amounts of contrary, similar motion and some unison, but also intervallic solecisms: parallel seconds and fifths. One nice touch is his usage of chromatic trombone slides (Fig. 25^{-4}) for Berlin's repeated question: 'Are you listenin'?' (chorus: bars 13–14). Where the bass lines are concerned, clear parallels exist, with Satie's rendition appearing as a kind of extemporisation upon Berlin's original (Examples 3.6b and 3.7a are especially close). Examples 3.6a and 3.7b demonstrate a modified transposition at the major second: G♯–A–B–A–G♯; F♯–G–A♭–G–F♯. In keeping, Satie's harmonic palette is also slightly extended, chromatically and modally. His verse melody too heightens the chromaticism and emboldens Berlin's initial ascent–descent melodic contour, at other times inverting the original contours. Both loci peak just before the return of the chorus, but once more Satie's represents an exaggeration, marked by the higher register with piccolo, the *ff* dynamic and 'ralentir' (Fig. 28^{-4}). As Perloff identifies, Satie's final occurrence of the chorus (Fig. 28) was Berlin's introductory material, reversed as a new ending: more subterfuge, yet imagination. However, credit for this reordering may be due to a French arranger rather than Satie directly, since Berlin's rag was available in arrangements that included this formal

---

[80]   As Orledge has remarked: 'He liked making jokes, but hated it when the joke was turned on him': Robert Orledge (ed.), *Satie Remembered* (London: Faber and Faber, 1995), xiv.

[81]   A point noted by Orledge, 'Satie's Approach to Composition', 169, crediting Peter Dickinson.

modification via the Parisian publisher Salabert seemingly from 1912 onwards:[82] thus, conceivably, another level of borrowing.

In summary, the Berlin–Satie source–product relationship encompasses a spectrum of effects: from duplication, or appropriation, of Berlin's rhythmic framework; through paraphrase, including variation techniques applied to melody and bass; to Satie's relative originality in recharacterizing the piece (and its context), developing its orchestration, articulation and to some extent harmony. Thus paraphrase represents the centre of the relationship, if not either extreme, but also enables a neat mediation, a further pivoting, between ragtime and classical practices to see how we might best position Satie's 'Rag-time'.

At one level, what Satie does is to improvise on a published standard, a familiar Tin Pan Alley tune. Kernfeld discusses the notion of 'paraphrase improvisation', a term introduced by Hodeir in the 1950s, which he defines as: 'the recognizable ornamentation of an existing theme'.[83] Of course, this practice also implies notions of signifying referred to above. Kernfeld continues: 'This restless, creative urge to keep altering things (however slight such alterations may be) has a great deal to do with what jazz is all about', and again involves a range of responses, from limited melodic decoration through to 'a highly imaginative reworking of that melody',[84] or changes of formal structure.

It would be attractive to interpret Satie's actions as temporarily emulating those of a ragtime-jazz musician, as advocated within bounds for Debussy. Several reasonably far-reaching changes have occurred: a sung rag has been instrumentalized; Berlin's introduction has been reordered as postlude (whether by Satie or Salabert); and recharacterization has, to some degree, recalled the melancholic African-American roots of the rag. It would, though, be a hermeneutic stretch to interpret this latter trait along Metzer's lines as a 'testifying' of black experience;[85] there is more mileage in pursuing an autobiographical angle. As Orledge explains: '[t]he concept of being like a "sad child" recurs in several reminiscences of Satie and there

---

[82] Thanks are due to Martin Guerpin for sharing this information (7 February 2014). An arrangement as a new 'one step ou pas de l'ours', held in the Library of Congress, has a printed date of 1912, hand-amended to 1913. Further research is needed to ascertain whether Satie did use one of these Salabert editions, but it is the most plausible scenario; compare with n. 69.

[83] Kernfeld, *What to Listen for in Jazz*, 131. For more detail on this topic, see the seminal text: Paul F. Berliner, *Thinking in Jazz: The Infinite Art of Improvisation* (University of Chicago Press, 1994).

[84] Kernfeld, *What to Listen for in Jazz*, 131.

[85] Metzer, *Quotation and Cultural Meaning*, 49.

can be no doubt that his chosen life of continual poverty and self-denial in the interests of his art made his existence profoundly unenviable'.[86] In the wake of *Parade*, Satie's melancholy was intensified by tensions that arose with the ailing Debussy.

On the main matter of jazz-type paraphrase techniques, there are also limitations: Satie's melodic response cannot readily be described as one of ornamentation or virtuosity; furthermore, Berlin's original melody was not recognizable, at least for an extended period. Significantly, the music creates a fixed paraphrase which never varies on repeat. In part, this limitation lies with Satie's choice of source, since Berlin's rag song relies on repetition and, unlike Joplin, does not feature the overt syncopations of classic ragtime, being rhythmically rather four-square. (The situation is analogous to Hylton's problems in seeking to jazz Stravinsky's *Mavra*.)[87] A third issue is Satie's concealment of his source, since ragtime or jazz reworkings typically function as a tribute and are explicit: for example, Armstrong's 1929 version of Handy's *St. Louis Blues*; or Davis's paraphrase on his album *'Round About Midnight* (1957) of Monk's ''Round Midnight' (1944).

At another level, the idea of paraphrase enables interpretation of Satie's practice within a history of classical music: it extends back to the Renaissance and related concepts of paraphrase, parody and *cantus firmus* mass, involving varied techniques for reusing existing materials. Paraphrase masses elaborated a single voice of a pre-existing source, generally redeployed across the new parts rather than being contained in a strict *cantus firmus*, whereas parody (imitation) masses reused more than one part – thus the closest equivalent to the Satie–Berlin interaction. Examples include the *Missa pange lingua* (paraphrase) and *Missa malheur me bat* (early parody) by the Franco-Flemish composer Josquin des Prez,[88] but, as evident from their titles, these works again acknowledge their respective sources.

Paraphrase also facilitates connection with other early twentieth-century practice: Ravel's *À la manière de ... Borodine* (1913)[89] and its ingenious double-paraphrase companion that imagines Emmanuel Chabrier's improvisatory handling of a melody from Charles Gounod's *Faust*; those incipient neoclassical loci *Le Tombeau* and *Pulcinella*; plus later occurrences such as Milhaud's *Suite d'après Corrette* (1937). But again, unlike Milhaud's

---

[86] Orledge (ed.), *Satie Remembered*, xiv–xv.   [87] See Mawer, 'Jazzing a Classic', 155–82.
[88] For detailed treatment, see David Fallows, *Josquin* (Turnhout: Brepols, 2009).
[89] See Michael J. Puri, 'Memory, Pastiche, and Aestheticism in Ravel and Proust', in Deborah Mawer (ed.), *Ravel Studies* (Cambridge University Press, 2010), 56–73.

credited paraphrase, Satie's practice does not come across as open, unequivocal homage; in this sense, it holds more common ground with Stravinsky's approach to *Pulcinella*. Interestingly, at the premiere Stravinsky had been presented as the arranger and orchestrator of original pieces by Giovanni Batista Pergolesi (and Domenico Gallo). By 1935, in his autobiography, he had become the composer, breathing life and coherence into what were supposedly mere scattered fragments by a short-lived composer.[90] In terms of Bloom revisited by Straus,[91] this may be seen as a remaking of history both of the eighteenth century and interwar period. So too we might interpret Satie as, initially, an arranger-orchestrator of *That Mysterious Rag* by the long-lived Berlin who needed no promotional help, but one who had subsequently, at least implicitly, raised the status of his contribution to that of composer.

Conclusion

This case study has sought to highlight contrasting treatments of cakewalk and ragtime by two crucial French pioneers of the Belle Époque and World War I period, especially in respect of quotation and paraphrase where Metzer's work has offered a pertinent angle. Debussy's and Satie's creative products both involve a complex *mélange* of French and ragtime attributes. However, while the *Children's Corner* suite generally remains a very French compendium of nostalgic childhood images, there is a sense in which the simple, supremely skilful, self-standing 'Golliwogg's Cake-Walk' with its ragging of Wagner may be fruitfully regarded, hermeneutically, as assuming a ragtime persona.

In its concealment, appropriation and large-scale reuse of its Berlin source, Satie's 'Rag-time du paquebot' presents a different case, delightfully ambiguous just like its composer and in keeping too with a surrealist fusion – sometimes contradiction – of fantasy and reality. On balance, it is surely best viewed as a French classicizing of ragtime. Its other prevalent traits may be comfortably embraced within a newly developing concept of neoclassicism, for which Satie should receive proper recognition: the fresh orchestration for chamber forces; a calculated fixity of rag treatment; placement of rag in a larger, topical context (with possible internal reordering of material); congruence with a modernist stance that celebrated the

---

[90] Igor Stravinsky, *Chroniques de ma vie* (Paris: Denoël et Steel, 1935); Eng. trans. as *Chronicles of My Life* (London: Gollancz, 1936); republished as *An Autobiography* (London: Calder and Boyars, 1975), 81, 109, 141.

[91] See Straus, *Remaking the Past*, chapter 3: 'Recompositions', 44–73: 58–64.

mechanical and machinelike; and, finally, the usage of rag as one distinct instance of eclecticism. In this spirit, a remark made by Mikhail Druskin apropos Stravinsky and *Pulcinella* may be reapplied fittingly to the enigmatic Satie: 'He studied and adapted, modified and adopted for his own purposes everything that was new to him.'[92]

[92] Mikhail Druskin, *Igor Stravinsky: His Personality, Works and Views*, Eng. trans. Martin Cooper (Cambridge University Press, 1983), 86–7.

4 Milhaud's understanding of jazz and blues: *La Création du monde*

After the highly productive phase of his wartime posting to Rio de Janeiro, the cultural context in which Milhaud found himself on his return to Paris influenced strongly his creative output in the early 1920s.[1] Primitivism, as exemplifying a Western perception of cultural otherness (introduced in Chapter 1), was a crucial artistic concept, already implicit in *L'Homme et son désir* (1918) and relevant to a case study on *La Création du monde*. Epitomized in its Russian inflection by Stravinsky's monumental *Le Sacre du printemps*, which cast such a daunting shadow across the second decade of the twentieth century, the complex origins of primitivism in early modernist 'high art' stretched back several decades.

At that famous Exposition of 1889, the Parisian public had been introduced to 'exotique' cultures of the Far East, most notably the Javanese gamelan. Orientalism and exoticism had emerged as potent forces in late nineteenth- and early twentieth-century Paris, although such notions also spawned more than their fair share of mediocrity in shallow, stereotyped Western constructions of the East.[2] At their most exemplary, the oriental and exotic were manifested in the music of Debussy, Ravel and Rimsky-Korsakov, whose *Shéhérazade* was produced in Paris in 1910; and in dramatic costume designs by Léon Bakst (1866–1924). Similarly, they were encapsulated by Paul Gauguin (1848–1903), whose Tahiti-inspired paintings were inextricably bound up with primitivism itself; and Auguste Rodin (1840–1917), whose watercolours of Cambodian dancers were created in 1906. Picasso, André Derain (1880–1954) and others became fascinated by artefacts brought back from tribal Africa and exhibited at the Musée ethnographique, while 1917 saw the celebrated exhibitions of *art nègre* organized

---

[1] This chapter is a modified, abridged version of parts of chapters 4 and 6 from my *Darius Milhaud: Modality and Structure in Music of the 1920s* (Aldershot: Scolar Press, 1997, reprinted 2000; copyright rests with the author). The reader is directed to the original for a full analytical account. The central portion on Milhaud's writings was presented in a more detailed account: 'Darius Milhaud, critique de jazz: les caractéristiques de ses écrits et son rôle', at an international colloquium: 'La Critique de jazz', Université Paris 7 (6–7 February 2014).

[2] Relate especially to Said, *Orientalism*. For a musical exposition, see Watkins, 'The Orient', in *Pyramids at the Louvre*, 13–60; and Elaine Brody, *Paris: The Musical Kaleidoscope 1870–1925* (London: Robson Books, 1988), 60–76.

by Paul Guillaume (1891–1934), who was perhaps the 'cheer leader for primitivism'.[3] *Art nègre*, as black American and African art, became a phrase with almost a cult significance, regarded by some as the essential primitivist source, somehow separated from European or oriental tradition, and so representing a possible means of bypassing Bloom's 'anxiety of influence' of the immediate past.[4] In fact, the temporal aspect to this chapter is more with the timeless: the idealism of apparent connection back to a primordium.

For many, including the poet-novelist Blaise Cendrars, with whom Milhaud would collaborate in *La Création*, there was celebration in the discovery of African and African-American culture; Cendrars's biographer, Monique Chefdor, talks specifically of this celebratory sense.[5] It was witnessed by the Pan-African Congress of 1921 and by Josephine Baker's success mid decade in *La Revue nègre*, presented, as was *La Création*, at the Théâtre des Champs-Élysées. In furtherance of our discussion from chapters 2 and 3, the response to *art nègre* was, however, deeply divided: artistic fascination, coexisting with a barely concealed racism, evidenced even in the poster design for *La Revue nègre*, which used gross racial caricature.[6] Not for nothing did Phyllis Rose entitle one chapter of her biography of Baker 'Savage Dance': for those fearful of cultural submergence, 'Degeneration was the dark underside of Darwinian thought.'[7] This ugly stance was adopted, for example, in Lothrop Stoddard's *The Rising Tide of Color*,[8] with its introduction by Madison Grant, whose own *The Passing of a Great Race* (1916) appeared in New York.[9] Sadly, Paris too was not immune, as evidenced by Maurice Muret's *Le Crépuscule des nations blanches* (1925).[10]

---

[3] Phyllis Rose, *Jazz Cleopatra* (London: Chatto & Windus, 1989), 45. On primitivism, see Watkins, 'Out of Africa and the Steppes', in *Pyramids at the Louvre*, 63–83; Christopher Butler, 'Subjectivity and Primitivism', in *Early Modernism*, 106–31; and Charles Harrison, *Primitivism, Cubism, Abstraction: The Early Twentieth Century* (New Haven and London: Yale University Press/Open University Press, 1993).

[4] See Straus, 'Toward a Theory of Musical Influence', in *Remaking the Past*, 1–20.

[5] Monique Chefdor, *Blaise Cendrars* (Boston, MA: Twayne, 1980), 74.

[6] See the reproduction in Michael Horsham, *'20s and '30s Style* (London: Grange Books, 1994), 76.

[7] Rose, *Jazz Cleopatra*, 33. More recently, see Andy Fry, 'Re-thinking the *Revue nègre*: Black Musical Theatre in Interwar Paris', in Julie Brown (ed.), *Western Music and Race* (Cambridge University Press, 2007), 258–75.

[8] Lothrop Stoddard, *The Rising Tide of Color against White-World Supremacy* (New York: Chapman & Hall, 1921).

[9] Madison Grant, *The Passing of a Great Race*, fourth edition (London and New York: G. Bell & Sons, 1921).

[10] Eng. trans. as *The Twilight of the White Races*, trans. Lida Touzalin (London: T. Fisher Unwin, 1926).

This is perhaps an apt point at which to pick up Meltzer's critical work in his stimulating, if idiosyncratic, sourcebook *Reading Jazz*. Meltzer sees jazz in terms of 'forms of permissible racism', to the extent that without racism there is no jazz: 'jazz as mythology, commodity, cultural display is a white invention and the expression of a postcolonial tradition'.[11] Similarly, Lynn Haney, another of Baker's biographers,[12] considers the role of jazz and perceptions of it. Both Meltzer and Haney point out that the word 'jazz' may have derived from 'jass' as a slang term for sex, while Howat hears an echo of the French verb *jaser* (to chatter, gossip), as in Paul Verlaine's poem *Mandoline* (1869): 'Et la mandoline jase / Parmi les frissons de brise.'[13]

Early experience of and experimentation with jazz

For Milhaud the world of jazz held a deep 'fascination', resonating to a limited extent with a much wider application of that term by Meltzer in the creative jottings of his 'Pre-ramble'.[14] The young composer visited the United States in 1918, 1922–3 and 1926 to experience it at first hand, in marked contrast to Stravinsky. Interestingly, he supplemented his understanding with recordings that he purchased in New York in 1922 and brought back to Paris,[15] including *I Wish I Could Shimmy Like My Sister Kate* and *The Wicked Five Blues*.[16] These recordings were issued by the Black Swan record company, a hugely influential venture, set up by Harry Pace and Handy to promote and disseminate African-American music. Very likely, Milhaud also heard early recordings or performances of other blues numbers that he references, such as Handy's *Aunt Hagar's Children Blues* and *St. Louis Blues*.[17] Perloff remarks that he 'probably had opportunity to hear recordings of *St. Louis Blues* on the Pathé, OKeh, and Columbia labels'.[18] Milhaud's first encounter with 'this school of rhythm' was, however, provided in Paris in 1918, by the arrival of jazz bands from

---

[11] Meltzer (ed.), *Reading Jazz*, 5 and 4, respectively.

[12] Lynn Haney, *Naked at the Feast: A Biography of Josephine Baker* (London: Robson Books, 1981).

[13] Personal correspondence with the author (10 December 2013).

[14] Meltzer (ed.), *Reading Jazz*, 9: 'Most of the texts [on jazz] reflect this fascination, the creating and re-creating of a romantic other; acts Aldon Lynn Nielsen calls "romantic racism". (Implying a dialectic that polarizes between racism of hate and racism of desire. Also suggestive of the impossibility of Romance; the participatory blindness of either two-way or one-way ardor.)'; and '"Fascination," another key word with roots in magic and magical empowerment.'

[15] Milhaud, *My Happy Life*, 116.   [16] Perloff, *Art and the Everyday*, 96.

[17] See Milhaud's comments in *Études*, where he refers attractively to a 'M. Andy' (57).

[18] Perloff, *Art and the Everyday*, 204.

New York.[19] His interest was further aroused, in 1920, by the visit of Billy Arnold's American Band to the new Hammersmith Palais de danse in London,[20] while he was also aware of (and initially enthusiastic about) Whiteman's slick contribution and Berlin's style.

Indeed, his experiencing of Arnold's band may have been the inspiration for *Caramel mou* (1920), created for a jazz band of clarinet, trumpet, trombone, piano, percussion and voice (or saxophone), to be performed in a show at the Théâtre Michel in May 1921; see Example 4.1. *Caramel mou* exhibits a curious stylistic mixture, reflecting Milhaud's increasing interest in jazz and the witty Parisian scene. It is subtitled 'Shimmy', as a lively American ragtime dance involving much gyrating of the shoulders and hips (Hindemith also composed an example in his Suite for Piano of 1922). The piece is dedicated to Auric and reveals a close paraphrase relationship to *Adieu New York!*, Milhaud having completed a four-hand transcription of Auric's work in December 1919.[21] An archetypal period piece of the 1920s, its absurdist text is that of Cocteau;[22] in translation:

> Take a girl,
> Fill her up with ice and gin,
> Shake it all about,
> To turn her into an androgyne,
> And send her back home to Mummy and Daddy.
>
> Hello, hello Miss, don't hang up . . . Miss, don't . . . don't hang up . . .
> Ah! Oh! Oh! How sad it is to be King of the Beasts,
> Nobody there.
> Oh, oh, love really sucks.
>
> Take a girl,
> Fill her up with ice and gin,
> Put a drop of angostura on her lips, Shake it all about
> To turn her into an androgyne,
> And send her back home to Mummy and Daddy.
>
> I once knew a guy really unlucky in love,
> Who played Chopin nocturnes on the drum.
>
> Hello, hello Miss, don't hang up, I was talking to . . .
> Hello, hello, nobody there.

---

[19] Milhaud, *Études*, 20: 'cette école de rythme'.   [20] *Ibid.*, 52.
[21] Perloff, *Art and the Everyday*, 174–6.
[22] See Cocteau's comments in Jean Cocteau, *Correspondance Jean Cocteau–Darius Milhaud*, eds. Pierre Caizergues and Josiane Mas (Montpellier: Université Paul Valéry, 1992), quoted in Perret, 'L'Adoption du jazz', 328.

Take a girl,
Fill her up with ice and gin,
Don't you find that art is a little . . . ?
Shake it all about,
To turn her into an androgyne,
And send her home to Mummy and Daddy.

You say to your kid, 'Wash your hands',
You don't say, 'Wash your teeth'.

Soft caramel.

Milhaud's writings about jazz

Much information about Milhaud's serious love affair with, in Meltzer's more provocative words, the 'sexual utopia' of jazz can be gleaned from his rich repertory of writings. These include an early dedicated essay: 'L'Évolution' – contrasting predominantly white jazz bands with African-American musics – published in May 1923 and already translated for an American readership by 1924.[23] A notated lecture at the Sorbonne, 'Les Ressources nouvelles de la musique', with its dual, connected focus upon jazz bands and mechanical instruments, was also published in 1924, aptly in the journal *L'Esprit nouveau*.[24] Meanwhile, 'L'Évolution' was reprinted in Milhaud's volume of *Études* (1927),[25] for which the series director was Cœuroy. This main essay was supplemented by inclusion of America and early jazz as a final, dynamic 'foreign influence' in Milhaud's opening essay on 'La Musique française depuis la guerre'.[26] The extent of the composer's involvement is evidenced further by a contemporaneous article, 'À propos du jazz', thought to have been unpublished, but which in fact appeared, intriguingly, in *L'Humanité*, as early as August 1926.[27] These writings, especially 'L'Évolution', acted as sources for Milhaud's much later coverage

---

[23] Milhaud, 'L'Évolution du jazz-band et la musique des nègres d'Amérique du nord'. According to Sandria Bouliane (personal communication, 7 February 2014), Milhaud's French article was published in Montreal as early as summer 1923.

[24] Darius Milhaud, 'Les Ressources nouvelles de la musique (jazz-band et instruments mécaniques)', *L'Esprit nouveau*, 25 (July 1924), n.p.

[25] Milhaud, *Études*, 51–9.   [26] *Ibid.*, 1–26: 20–2.

[27] Darius Milhaud, 'À propos du jazz', undated typescript (Basle: Paul Sacher Stiftung, Collection Darius Milhaud), 1–7; published in two parts in the official newspaper of the French Communist Party: *L'Humanité* (3 August 1926), 5; *L'Humanité* (4 August 1926), 5. Milhaud discusses his visit to Soviet Russia – Leningrad and Moscow – and the positive impact of jazz there, played by 'my companion [comrade?] Jean Wiéner, who would merit being black, so well does he play this music' ('mon camarade Jean Wiéner, qui mériterait

of the jazz phenomenon in his autobiography *Ma vie heureuse* (*My Happy Life*),[28] with some notable revision and personal repositioning highlighted below.

In his personal 'Rencontre avec le jazz', Milhaud makes crucial comparison with Bach, as he stresses the rhythmic parameter of jazz: 'syncopated music calls for a rhythm as inexorably regular as that of Bach himself, which indeed is firmly established on the same basis'.[29] He is intrigued by the improvisatory syncopation and rubato superimposed on this regular rhythmic background. Melody and timbre are also part of the appeal of jazz:

> the lyrical use of the trombone, glancing with its slide over quarter-tones in crescendos of volume and pitch, thus intensifying the feeling; and the whole, so vari[ed] yet not disparate, held together by the piano and subtly punctuated by the complex rhythms of the percussion, a kind of inner beat, the vital pulse of the rhythmic life of the music.[30]

In this way, prefiguring Goffin's approach of the early 1930s, Milhaud details the instrumental roles of piano, percussion, trombone, trumpet, saxophone, clarinet, banjo and violin within the jazz ensemble, and is captivated by the use of glissando, portamento, vibrato, tremolo, oscillation and the huge variety of timbral expression.[31] He is savvy about avoiding passing gimmicks, such as sirens and klaxons, while light classical arrangements are similarly regarded as tasteless!

Milhaud seems deeply drawn by the sense of tragedy and despair inherent in many spirituals and Creole folk songs, referencing collections by the African-American composer-singer Harry Burleigh (1866–1949), Mina Monroe and the musical ethnologist Nathalie Curtis Burlin (1875–1921).[32] These sources are viewed as the expression of a persecuted people, telling of prejudice and repression, the composer's empathy resulting in part perhaps from his Sephardic Jewish experience.[33] Indeed direct comparison is made

---

d'être nègre tellement il joue bien cette musique'). I am very grateful to Laurent Cugny for alerting me to its published status.

[28] *Ma vie heureuse* (Paris: Pierre Belfond, 1974; reprinted 1987) also has an evolutionary history, first appearing as *Notes sans musique* (Paris: René Julliard, 1949); Eng. trans. as *My Happy Life*.

[29] Milhaud, *My Happy Life*, 98.   [30] *Ibid.*   [31] Milhaud, *Études*, 20–1, 51–2.

[32] Harry Burleigh became well-known for his published arrangements of spirituals, such as 'Deep River' (c.1916–17), while Nathalie Curtis Burlin produced a four-volume collection of *Negro Folk-Songs* (c.1918–19). See too, Mina Monroe, *Bayou Ballads: Twelve Folk-Songs from Louisiana* (New York: G. Schirmer, 1921).

[33] On Milhaud's strong sense of Jewish rootedness ('enracinement'), see Barbara L. Kelly, *Tradition and Style in the Works of Darius Milhaud, 1912–1939* (Aldershot: Ashgate, 2003), 32–4.

with the biblical Jewish exile into Egypt.[34] In 'L'Évolution', he opines, ahead of Ravel, that blues style merits special attention: 'From this eruption in sound there followed a remarkable development of melodic elements: this was the age of the "blues".'[35] He continues by alluding to 'la mélodie depouillée':[36] a melody stripped of all inessentials, a notion usually associated with neoclassicism, but here suggestive of a potential commonality.

Milhaud's remarks also uphold the relevance of primitivism to his aesthetic outlook: 'The African primitiv[ist] side has remained deeply rooted in the black community of the United States and it is there that one must seek the source of this formidable rhythmic force.'[37] Developing this stance in connection with contemporary (mis)conceptions of 'the primitivist' as, at some level, necessarily synonymous with 'the ancient', we may note his admiration for the music of 'A Negress whose grating voice seemed to come from the depths of the centuries' (for full quotation, see pages 45–6).[38] The context was blues-jazz typically heard at the Capitol, on Lennox Avenue in New York's Harlem district;[39] and Milhaud may have been referring to the African-American singer Ethel Waters (1896–1977), although another candidate is Anna Pease.[40] We might perceive something of an idealized blackness here, along Panassié's later lines (but Milhaud's stance was much more balanced). In any event, he is quick to credit African-American musicians Blake and Noble Sissle (1889–1975) for their Broadway revue hit *Shuffle Along* (1921) and rates Maceo Pinkard (1897–1962), composer of 'Sweet Georgia Brown', for *Liza* (1922). Special insight is revealed in his recognition of the expressive importance of improvisation, operating within a complex of melodic lines and harmonies, and that this was very much an African-American domain, beyond dance music.[41]

Milhaud considered that in the early 1920s most American musicians had not realized the value of jazz as an art form, and comments that his own views were regarded with some astonishment: '"Milhaud admires Jazz", or "Jazz dictates the future of European music"'.[42] These quotations are apparently the titles of interviews given with New York journalists, though no

[34] Milhaud, *Études*, 56–7, 59.
[35] *Ibid.*, 53: 'À cette cataracte sonore a succédé une mise en valeur remarquable des éléments mélodiques: c'est la période des "Blues".'
[36] *Ibid.*
[37] *Ibid.*, 56: 'Le côté primitif africain est resté profondément ancré chez les noirs des États-Unis et c'est là qu'il faut voir la source de cette puissance rythmique formidable.'
[38] Milhaud, *My Happy Life*, 110.   [39] Milhaud, *Études*, 59.
[40] Information from Madeleine Milhaud: Perloff, *Art and the Everyday*, 95; Milhaud, 'À propos du jazz' (4 August 1926), 5.
[41] Milhaud, *Études*, 57–8.   [42] Milhaud, *My Happy Life*, 109.

exact sources are provided. Milhaud's perception here is one that has since been regularly confirmed, including by Meltzer: 'Europeans, especially French, British, and German, were first to fully receive jazz as art, as an aesthetic and expressive practice worthy of serious creative and intellectual engagement. America's initial difficulty with the music may have been due to vestigial nineteenth-century republican rigidities, its anti-urbanism, anti-intellectualism.'[43] Following his fervent quest as posed in *Études* – 'So here we have to the fore sonorous and rhythmic elements [that are] completely new and apt [...], but how should I use them?'[44] – Milhaud became convinced about wanting to employ these timbres and rhythms in a chamber work, which would prove to be *La Création*, but first he needed to further his formal and technical understanding.[45]

As he explains towards the end of 'Rencontre avec le jazz', his creative thinking was also supported by avant-garde Parisian shows, such as that put on by Pierre Bertin in May 1921, in which Satie's extraordinary play *Le Piège de Méduse* was performed, together with *Caramel mou*. Such imaginative ventures acted as catalysts, leading to new means of musical expression.[46] That the opportunities for technical experimentation which Milhaud so valued here existed in equal measure within his perception of jazz is revealed by his opening statement in the essay from *Études*: 'The strength of jazz comes from the novelty of its technique in all parameters.'[47] Thus he seeks to develop the sources of his inspiration. He is not interested in pastiche, but in rethinking, reworking and intensifying what he finds, often increasing the complexity within rhythmic and modal domains: hence, as a possible misreading, his treatment of so-called polyrhythm criticized by Hodeir in the 'Fugue' of *La Création* (see below).

Some years later, Milhaud apparently disappointed American reporters by informing them that his interest had waned because jazz had 'become official and won universal recognition'.[48] He explains that, by 1926, there were even instructional manuals that analysed and dissected jazz as, in the apt words of Meltzer, 'bagged difference',[49] with the consequence that the popularity and explanation deprived this music of its spontaneous appeal. Interestingly, in Milhaud's corresponding comments in *Études*, he refers more ambivalently to the implicitly white music resulting from such

---

[43] Meltzer (ed.), *Reading Jazz*, 37–8.
[44] Milhaud, *Études*, 54: 'Les voici à la tête d'éléments sonores et rythmiques absolument nouveaux [...], mais comment les utiliser?'
[45] Milhaud, *My Happy Life*, 98.   [46] *Ibid.*, 98–9.
[47] Milhaud, *Études*, 51: 'La force du jazz vient de la nouveauté de sa technique dans tous les domaines.'
[48] Milhaud, *My Happy Life*, 146; see too *Études*, 22.   [49] Meltzer (ed.), *Reading Jazz*, 40.

instruction as 'this mechanized music, just as precise as a machine'.[50] (In 'À propos du jazz', his stance is surprisingly extreme, to the extent that, having previously been 'deceived', he now 'detests' the perfected commercial style of Whiteman's orchestra, as part of the whole encroachment – 'this invasion' – of Americanization.)[51] Whatever the inappropriateness of 'mechanized music' here, Milhaud's awareness of a machinist concept is still relevant to his music, including the staging of *La Création*.

While represented in both main sources, the idea of jazz instruction was welcomed in *Études* – 'these treatises are valuable', '[they are] of remarkable technical interest'[52] – yet disparaged in his autobiography, once it has served its compositional purpose. This latter thinking may conceivably have been tempered by wider, complex concerns of an implicit Eurocentricity, whereby to gain institutional recognition and 'genre prestige' jazz was seemingly compelled to ape classical music.[53] On the one hand, Milhaud was part of that institutional conservatoire framework; yet, without it, we might not have had the likes of Brubeck (see Chapter 9). In his detailed descriptions of jazz teaching, Milhaud nevertheless demonstrates his familiarity with jazz structures, again anticipating Goffin. That he knew of the following techniques, and may have incorporated them compositionally, is valuable from an analytical stance:

> The various ways of assimilating jazz were taught [by the Winn School of Popular Music], as well as jazz style for the piano, and improvisation; its freedom within a rigid rhythmic framework, all the breaks and passing discords, the broken harmonies, arpeggios, trills and ornaments, the variations and cadences which can return *ad lib.* in a sort of highly fantastic counterpoint.[54]

Milhaud adds regretfully that, even in his beloved Harlem, 'White men, snobs in search of exotic colour and sightseers curious to hear Negro music had penetrated to even the most secluded corners. That is why I gave up going.'[55] Evidently he does not classify himself as a (white) musical tourist! His view, nonetheless, resonates well with that of Meltzer, who considers that 'jazz was mythologized, colonialized, demonized, defended, and ultimately neutralized by white Americans and Europeans. This is about the

---

[50] Milhaud, *Études*, 56: 'cette musique mécanisée et aussi précise qu'une machine'; see too 53.

[51] Milhaud, 'À propos du jazz' (4 August 1926), 5.

[52] Milhaud, *Études*, 55: 'Ces traités sont précieux'; 'd'un intérêt technique remarquable'.

[53] See David Ake, 'Learning Jazz, Teaching Jazz', in Cooke and Horn (eds.), *The Cambridge Companion to Jazz*, 255–69: 265.

[54] Milhaud, *My Happy Life*, 146.   [55] *Ibid.*, 146–7.

white invention of jazz as subject and object.'[56] It is worth emphasizing Milhaud's staunch upholding of interracial understanding and harmony; we may witness his troubled remarks on observing racial segregation: 'In New Orleans, the gulf between Whites and Blacks was even deeper, and their ways of life lay quite apart.'[57]

From the composer's creative stance, it is unfortunate that he did not maintain his interest long enough to hear the emerging genius of Armstrong, who had a significant presence from about 1918, joining King Oliver at Lincoln Gardens in 1922 and setting up his Louis Armstrong's Hot Five in 1925. The two would surely have found a meeting point in *St. Louis Blues*, recorded so brilliantly by Armstrong at the Savoy Ballroom in Harlem on 13 December 1929,[58] and previously quoted by Milhaud in 1923 (see case study, page 113).

Overview of Milhaud's early jazz practice

Milhaud's jazz-inspired practice embraces a spectrum of eclectic works. Strictly speaking, it might be deemed to focus upon *Caramel mou*, *La Création* and the Sixth Chamber Symphony (1923). However, it also includes those works initiated by ragtime, especially *Trois rag-caprices* (1923) for solo piano, while incipient blues-related processes may be observed in the preceding Brazilian repertory, including *L'Homme*, the *Cinéma-fantaisie: Le Bœuf sur le toit* (1919)[59] and *Saudades do Brazil* (1920–1; solo piano, partial orchestration). It is a substantially larger repertory than that credited to Milhaud by Kramer.[60]

Ternary structures predominate in these jazz-related works, as in the 'Romance' and 'Final' of *Trois rag-caprices*, or the tangos of *Saudades*, with extended derivatives, as found in *Caramel mou* (ABABA, coda). Rondo also finds many applications: the 'Scherzo' from *La Création*, the 'Sec et musclé'

---

[56] Meltzer (ed.), *Reading Jazz*, 4.   [57] Milhaud, *My Happy Life*, 148.

[58] This recording may be heard, recreated in stereo by Robert Parker from the 78 r.p.m. original, on Louis Armstrong, *Great Original Performances 1923–1931* (Louisiana Red Hot Records RPCD 618, 1997).

[59] *Le Bœuf* is so regarded in Milhaud scholarship that postdates my original chapter: for example, Perret, 'L'Adoption du jazz', 332–4 (albeit slightly ahistorically, especially in using the expression 'big-band' to refer to typical New Orleans instrumentations). Equally, it provides further evidence of Milhaud's attraction to musical borrowing, as revealed in an excellent, substantive article by Manoel Aranha Correa do Lago, 'Brazilian Sources in Milhaud's *Le Bœuf sur le toit*: A Discussion and a Musical Analysis', *Latin American Music Review*, 23/1 (Spring/Summer 2002), 1–59.

[60] Kramer, 'Powers of Blackness', 61: 'Milhaud's contribution (aside from a little shimmy) is only a single work, the ballet *La Création du monde*.'

from *Trois rag-caprices* (modified as AB/AC/ABA), or 'Gavea', 'Corcovado' and 'Tijuca' from *Saudades*; meanwhile, *Le Bœuf* presents a loosely structured rondo-fantasy, sometimes simply suggesting a medley of ideas. Significantly, this repertory does employ stylized blues forms, such as the modified twelve-bar form used in the 'Romance' of *La Création*; additionally, prelude and fugue occur there in an ultimate synthesis of jazz and Bachian techniques.

Similarly, Milhaud's jazz-related works are strongly centric, exhibiting less modal ambiguity than elsewhere in his early output. Pentatonicism seems to act as a compositional source for the development of this idiom, appearing in the Fourth Quartet (1918) composed in Rio, at the close of the first movement: F, G, A, C, D. In most pentatonic collections, one of the missing scalic degrees is the leading note, while the minor third between $\hat{6}$ and $\hat{1}$ is especially prominent: this phenomenon applies to parts of Milhaud's Fourth Quartet, the end of his 'Scherzo' from *La Création*, and several traditional negro spirituals. (Thus, Milhaud's jazz and loosely folk-influenced works may share a common source in pentatonicism.) The wholetone scale constitutes a localized reference, with its tritonal framework: melodic and harmonic perspectives are well illustrated in *Caramel mou* (bars 186–96) involving a collection on B♭: B♭, C, D, E, F♯, A♭, which introduces foreign pitches F and G, used chromatically.

Undoubtedly the most important modal collection is a blues scale, whose salient features are its melodic blues third, as well as seventh.[61] This oscillation between minor and major inflections – a microtonal bending – is best suited to vocal technique and can only be parodied on instruments with fixed pitches. Instances of blues third pervade the majority of Milhaud's works across 1918 to 1926. Only a horizontal expression suggests close affinity with jazz, the vertical expression more redolent of pastiche and frequently linked to large-scale third relations emerging from bimodality. The essence of the blues third principle is found in the opening of *Caramel mou* (bars 1–6): D/C♯ upon a B♭ basis, as shown in Example 4.1. The use of post-tonal voiceleading (as an analogous, yet contextually inverted, quest to that of Larson) suggests the prolonging of an initial upper line structural $\hat{3}$ (an important sustaining of the third scalic degree), with major–minor modal mixture. Clear examples also occur in *Trois rag-caprices*, the second and third movements of the Sixth Chamber Symphony (and 'Sorocaba', 'Tijuca' and 'Sumaré' from *Saudades*), with this horizontal expression enjoying a much higher profile in Milhaud's compositions than in those

---

[61] See J. Bradford Robinson, 'Blue Note (i)', in Kernfeld (ed.), *The New Grove Dictionary of Jazz*, vol. I, 245–6.

Example 4.1 Milhaud, *Caramel mou* (bars 1–6): blues third and seventh

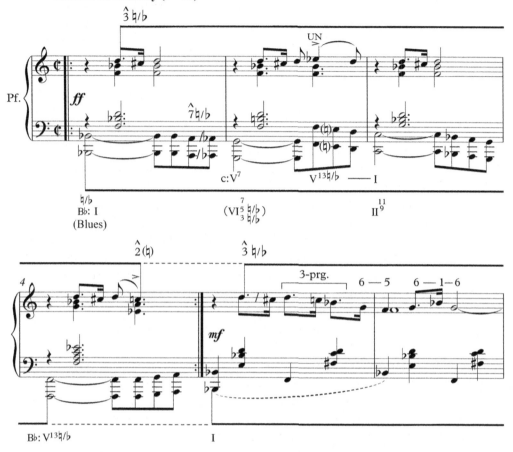

of his contemporaries. Again, an ultimate fusion of vertical and horizontal presentations occurs in *La Création*.

As a non-authentic, personal extension, Milhaud creates large-scale blues third progressions across whole movements or works: for example, his songs for voice and violin *Quatre poèmes de Catulle* of 1923: G–B♭/B–G, or the suite version of *La Création*: D–d–F/F♯–D. Even after his interest in jazz had waned, vestiges of blues third persist in the Seventh Quartet, *Les Malheurs d'Orphée* and the *opéras-minute*, as an instinctive part of his vocabulary. Apart from mixture at the third, the trait is commonly encountered at the seventh, often resulting from modal ambiguity between centres a fourth apart: a phenomenon exploited in the 'Fugue' of *La Création* (bars 22–6). Other instances include the opening bass line of *Caramel*

Example 4.2 Milhaud, Sixth Chamber Symphony, III (bars 25–7): blues seventh

mou (see again Example 4.1), the ending of the slow, final movement of the Sixth Chamber Symphony (Example 4.2) and the second movement of the Fifth Chamber Symphony (1922).

There are several means of extending modal structures in the jazz-related repertory, some shared with more overtly neoclassical loci. Tonic and dominant pedals abound (as in 'Sumaré' from *Saudades*); another way of securing larger-scale modal coherence is via a (dominant) seventh chordal axis. V^7 and I^7 constructs (vertical or horizontal) are prominent in the concluding of main sections, particularly in ending the second of a three-movement work. This is an identifiable trait of traditional jazz, as an expression of the flattened seventh of Mixolydian or blues modes: a seventh axis, C, E, G, B♭ proves relevant to the F-based 'Romance' of *La Création*. (A large-scale tonic seventh axis is applicable across 'Ipanema' from *Saudades*.)[62] Other

---

[62] See Mawer, *Darius Milhaud*, 134–44, in conjunction with Joseph N. Straus, 'Stravinsky's Tonal Axis', *Journal of Music Theory*, 26 (1982), 261–90: especially 265.

strategically placed dominant seventh chords occur in the second movement of the Flute Sonatina (1922) and that of *Trois rag-caprices*, together with a significant tonic major seventh sonority at the end of *La Création*.

As introduced in Chapter 1, the riff – melodic or accompanimental – is an acknowledged rhythmic-pitch formula for extending blues and jazz structures, as an equivalent of ostinato.[63] A favoured pattern for Milhaud is tonic–supertonic–tonic, this substitution of supertonic for dominant in 'passages of vamping for example (especially in connection with Latin-American rhythms)' first being observed in Milhaud's operas.[64] Almost as a mannerism, this clichéd gesture usually begins section A of a dance, after which the pattern changes (many occurrences are found in *Saudades*); more sophisticated patterns operate in the 'Final' of *La Création*.

Discussion of techniques influenced by jazz (and Brazilian popular music) must include metric and rhythmic parameters, their processes being closely linked to the exigencies of particular dances. The most frequent metres are 2/4 and 4/4. Metric changes within a movement are uncommon but can be striking: in the finale ('Précis et nerveux') of *Trois rag-caprices*, 4/4 metre alternates firstly with 3/4 bars to form seven-beat groupings, and then with 2/4 metre. A 5/4 bar is introduced (bar 85), as a metric suspension, before the recapitulation (bar 86). Anacrusic patterns favour three quavers in 4/4 metre, as in the 'Fugue' of *La Création*, or the same pattern in double augmentation, as in its 'Romance'. The first (and third) of *Trois rag-caprices* uses this three-quaver motive, followed by the three-crotchet version, in a slower section beyond bar 30 (this latter characteristic shared by its central 'Romance'). Beyond the tango's main rhythmic prerequisite (dotted quaver, semiquaver, two quavers) in 2/4 metre, Milhaud's examples in *Saudades* exhibit great variety. Similarly, the samba's simple syncopated pattern (semiquaver, quaver, semiquaver), also in 2/4 metre, occurs in augmentation in *Le Bœuf* and in fourfold augmentation (crotchet, minim, crotchet) in the 'Scherzo' of *La Création*. Tied note-values may contribute to the effect: the first of *Trois rag-caprices* features a crotchet tied over the barline to a quaver. Although the rumba developed somewhat later (with its 3 + 3 + 2 pattern of dotted crotchet, dotted crotchet, crotchet, in 4/4 metre), the second movement 'Souple et Vif' of the Sixth Chamber Symphony (composed in New York) nicely anticipates a distorted rumba in 7/4 metre, divided into 2 + 3 + 2.

[63] See Robinson, 'Riff', 415–16.
[64] Jeremy Drake, *The Operas of Darius Milhaud* (New York and London: Garland Press, 1989), 213.

Mixing primitivism, jazz and blues in *La Création du monde*

This case study serves to examine interactions between primitivism, early jazz, blues and French music (and between music, dance and design). As a *tour de force* of jazz ballet, *La Création* exists in two versions: the original ballet score (1923; Op. 81) and an extracted *Suite de concert* for piano quintet (1926; Op. 81b), conducive to analytical study (but not the version usually performed, as stated by Kramer).[65] The ballet was first performed on 25 October 1923 by the highly inventive and avant-garde Ballets suédois,[66] directed by Vladimir Golschmann (1893–1972), at the Théâtre des Champs-Élysées in Paris, while the Suite was premiered in 1927 by the Kolisch Quartet at the annual Festival for Contemporary Music in Baden-Baden. The work is dedicated jointly to Milhaud's lifelong friend and biographer Paul Collaer, and to the conductor Roger Desormière (1898–1963). Tellingly, given its evocation of African mythology, the first performance (of any serious ballet) with African-American dancers did not take place until 22 January 1940, when Agnes de Mille choreographed the work as *Black Ritual* at the (American) Ballet Theatre, New York.

Given the common origin of ideas for both versions, it is desirable to outline the dramatic collaboration behind *La Création* and its musical genesis. The scenario, focusing on African myths of creation, was developed by the prolific French (Swiss-born) poet-cum-novelist Cendrars, whose collected writings extend to some eight volumes. Early on, Cendrars's name was frequently associated with Apollinaire and Léger, and like Milhaud he was a very keen traveller, viewing his journeys as literary allegories. He derived the scenario from his own *Anthologie nègre* (1921), which in turn, and with historically inevitable colonial association, was heavily indebted to folk tales collected by a nineteenth-century missionary, Father H. Trilles.[67] The poetic expression of this exotic and fanciful mythology certainly generated part of the initial momentum for the collaborative project: 'The couple embraces. The [dancing] circle quietens, checks itself and slows and starts to die down peacefully all around. The circle breaks up into little groups. The couple is separated off in an embrace, which carries it along like a wave. It is springtime.'[68]

---

[65] Kramer, 'Powers of Blackness', 62.

[66] See Bengt Häger, *Ballets Suédois* (London: Thames and Hudson, 1990).

[67] See Chefdor, *Blaise Cendrars*, 74; she also discusses 'Cendrars and the Ballets Suédois' (75ff.).

[68] Scene V of Cendrars's scenario, quoted in Paul Collaer, *Darius Milhaud* (Paris and Geneva: Éditions Slatkine, 1982), 121: 'Le couple s'est étreint. / La ronde se calme, freine et ralentit

Meanwhile, the visual dimension was shaped by the painter and aesthetician Fernand Léger (1881–1955), an exponent of cubism and new classicism, who produced the sets and costumes; his most famous collaboration was probably that with Antheil on the *Ballet mécanique*, but his finest sets are undoubtedly those for *La Création*.[69] Léger was strongly interested in Futurism, as represented in its second wave by the journal *L'Esprit nouveau*, and in the powerful potential inherent in industrial mechanization. His ideas sprang from a concern with geometry, abstraction and space. He was fascinated by the innovative possibility of 'mechanical theatre'[70] and introduced radical, dramatic strategies for rethinking the conventional relationship between actors, or dancers and their sets. The shallow stage was conceived as a moving image, in effect almost anticipating video art, and the sets and figures were to be as one. Characters wore animal costumes and masks, as illusory African sculptures; the gods of creation were huge figures, several metres in height. In accordance with Léger's concept, no recognizable human figure was to be seen. The aim was to depict the very processes of creation, with partly formed creatures: insects, birds, animals and man himself, developing before one's eyes. Form from chaos. The choreography of the disguised dancers was then created by Jean Börlin (1893–1930), the leading dancer of the Ballets suédois, who had made his name with a stunning solo display in the highly acclaimed *Sculpture nègre* (1920). Sympathetic to Léger's aims, Börlin sought a new approach to dance and movement that would be in keeping with the new technological age.

So, in collaboration with these artists, Milhaud looked to portray the creation as suggested by African(-American) legend and ritual, without the innate violence of *Le Sacre*, and yet embracing somewhat similar oppositions of the primitivist and the modern.[71] He had acquired the necessary musical and project expertise through earlier collaborations, including that

---

et vient mourir très calme alentour. / La ronde se disperse par petits groupes. Le couple s'isole dans un baiser qui le porte comme une onde. / C'est le printemps.' This fantasy aspect does not of itself, however, provide grounds for any devaluing of the ensuing work, as implicitly suggested by Kramer, 'Powers of Blackness', 62: 'The fit between this fantasy [claimed to be 'black Africa as a primitive Eden'] and Milhaud's *La Création du monde* is so perfect it is almost disconcerting.' After all, the strongest artwork frequently emerges from creative imagination rather than imitation, and the presenting of an alternative image of creation may be regarded positively as a revisionary act. There is no reason to doubt Milhaud's respect for African culture.

[69] For an illustration of one of Léger's main sets, see Häger, *Ballets Suédois*, 192–3.

[70] See Fernand Léger, 'The Invented Theater' (1924), in Henning Rischbieter (ed.), *Art and the Stage in the Twentieth Century*, Eng. trans. Michael Bullock (Greenwich, CT: New York Graphic Society, 1968), 97.

[71] Watkins (*Pyramids at the Louvre*, 112–33) offers thorough coverage of the primitivist stance behind *La Création*.

with the dramatist Paul Claudel on *L'Homme*, itself a celebration of Latin American primitivism and legend, and another production of the Ballets suédois, in 1921. For the composer, 'At last [. . .] I had the opportunity I had been waiting for to use those elements of jazz to which I had devoted so much study'[72] – particularly those of the blues.

Milhaud's inspiration derived from diverse sources outlined earlier: from Harlem jazz heard in 1922 and previously via Billy Arnold's Band, from those Black Swan recordings, from Parisian nightlife – the ambience of the rue de Lappe or boulevard Barbès – and indirectly from his Latin American experiences. In his autobiography, he explained that for *La Création*, 'I adopted the same orchestra as used in Harlem, [with] seventeen solo instruments'.[73] As he conceded in *Études*, this instrumentation was directly inspired by Pinkard's *Liza*: that contemporary musical from which he borrowed the idea of a string quartet, with viola replaced by alto saxophone, plus double bass.[74] The emerging music nevertheless connects transcultural discourses of jazz and neoclassicism: American, French and Germanic traditions, via Bachian fugue. For Milhaud, this inherent mixing was thus expressed: 'I made wholesale use of the jazz style to convey a purely classical feeling.'[75]

The ensuing commentary restricts itself to these meeting points, particularly in the first three of five movements: 'Prélude', 'Fugue' and 'Romance' (these titles appearing only in the suite). Critically, it engages mainly with the views of the early jazz critics Hodeir and Sargeant,[76] important historically and conceptually. Hodeir offers the most detailed early analysis of Milhaud's practice and is usefully provocative in highlighting certain classical–jazz problematics, while Sargeant's treatment of blues scalar formations is pertinent. Brief reference is made to the approach of Carine Perret, which postdates the first publication of this analysis (for detailed treatment, see Chapter 5).

I 'Prélude'

This introductory portion of the ballet serves as a kind of overture prior to the rise of the curtain. Its main material comprises Theme A on the piano (originally alto saxophone marked 'chanté') and Counterthemes 1 and 2 on violin plus viola, as shown in Example 4.3. Whereas Theme A (with its ascending perfect fourth motive and stepwise descent via the flattened

---

[72] Milhaud, *My Happy Life*, 118.   [73] *Ibid.*   [74] Milhaud, *Études*, 57.
[75] Milhaud, *My Happy Life*, 118.
[76] Sargeant, *Jazz: Hot and Hybrid*. Subsequent references are to the 1959 edition.

Example 4.3 Milhaud, *La Création du monde (Suite de concert)*, I (bars 1–11): themes and modality

seventh) favours the upper segment of the Aeolian on D: A–D, the counter-themes (with derived, balancing third progressions) utilize the lower segment: D–A.

Mixture at the third scalic degree is immediately evident, but is simply a major plus minor superimposition and so, for Hodeir, does not yet justify the term *blues*. In any case, Hodeir argues, this is too early for harmonic instability in a piece where tonality later becomes important.[77] In response, I would concede that this blues third treatment is not authentic, but instead parodies jazz practice. However, it has echoes in rag-inspired repertory, as Milhaud himself theorizes, finding 'the perfect simultaneous major and minor chord' in 'Zez' Confrey's *Kitten on the Keys* (1921).[78] Moreover, it can be countered that the work's basis upon D is still clearly established by its tonic pedal (bars 1–30), and that its ambiguous *mélange* creates an appropriate expectancy; see again Example 4.3. Roman numeral chordal designations are given, with a freer interpretation of likely jazz chordal symbols above – in some sense, a reversal of Larson's invocation of voice-leading for mainstream jazz. Most chords of tonic modality feature added sevenths, ninths or thirteenths, which Milhaud comments on as fashionable in Tin Pan Alley music, referencing *Ivy* (1922) by songwriter Isham Jones (1894–1956) and pianist James P. Johnson:[79] again, suggestive of a close theory–practice correlation.

Another complexity concerns phrasing: while Theme A is constructed in three-bar phrases with supporting bass, the counterthemes utilize two-bar units – almost like a 'secondary ragtime' procedure, which applies also to the rhythmic relationship between the counterthemes. Even where a twelve-bar blues form might be envisaged, it is invariably this parody of four three-bar units, rather than a traditional blues pattern of three four-bar units.

Within a second section (bars 31–55), Theme A is reiterated by the string quartet with added tonal warmth, the character of its melodic contour and accompaniment being reminiscent of the first of Gustav Mahler's *Lieder eines fahrenden Gesellen*, also D-minor-based: a shared Jewish wistfulness, perhaps. Embraced too is a favourite developmental device (bars 41–6): multiple sequential transpositions of a second-inversion chord, heralded in the original by slithering glissandos and blue notes on trombone, resolving climactically onto a tonic pedal (bars 46–7).

Significantly, Countertheme 2 hones its jazzed rhythmic identity of three anacrusic quavers with syncopation, plus major–minor third (bars 56–64),

---

[77] Hodeir, *Jazz*, 255.
[78] Milhaud, *Études*, 55: 'l'accord parfait majeur et mineur à la fois'.   [79] *Ibid.*

from which the fugal subject is derived, while its $F^7/B\flat$ harmonic constructions (bars 75–80) set up an affinity with the 'Romance'. Among other
details, a smoothing of the join into a recapitulation, with a phrase marked
'Cédez' (bars 81–2), is similar in effect to a brief jazz 'break'.[80] A raised
leading note (C♯) is reserved for the final cadence (bars 105–6), with a
seemingly overt allusion to baroque practice: the V^{4-3} dissonance (which
might yet be read as a jazz 'sus4') in the piano resolves onto a pure D minor
chord.

II 'Fugue'

The initial portion of the corresponding scenario begins as follows: 'The
curtain rises slowly on a dark stage. In the middle of the stage, we see a
confused mass of intertwined bodies: chaos prior to creation. Three giant
deities move slowly round the periphery. These are Nzame, Medere and
N'kva, the masters of creation. They hold counsel together, circle round the
formless mass, and utter magic incantations.'[81]

Musically, Milhaud's main fugal subject (Theme B) reveals the authentic
handling of a blues collection on D, as shown in Example 4.4. It features
motives from Theme A: motive b' (inv.), as a stepwise minor third in ascent;
its extension β (inv.), as an ascending fifth progression; and motive c' (retr.),
a mordent-like decorated third, originally cadential. This classic illustration
of a flexible blues collection of pitches enables major–minor inflections and
microtonal bending, particularly of the third and seventh degrees.[82] Up to a
point, it correlates with Milhaud's professed understanding of 'the use of
perfect simultaneous major and minor chords and quarter-tones obtained
by a mixture of techniques of glissando and vibrato' in African-American
improvisation.[83] The first four pitches of the subject, D–E–D–F, were, in
Hodeir's words, 'particularly prized by composers "inspired" by jazz',[84]

---

[80] A 'break' cues a brief improvised solo (unaccompanied), interpolated between the lines of a
verse, or between a verse and a chorus, which serves to dovetail different sections.

[81] Cendrars, trans. Ruth Sharman, in Häger, *Ballets Suédois*, 190. 'Rideau' is marked in the
orchestral score at the start of the fugal portion, but the exact subsequent correlation
between the ballet scenario and the music is not clear-cut.

[82] See Sargeant, 'The Scalar Structure of Jazz', in *Jazz: Hot and Hybrid*, 147–72.

[83] Milhaud, *Études*, 58: 'l'emploi d'accords parfaits majeurs et mineurs simultanés et de
quarts de tons obtenu par un mélange de la technique du glissando et du vibrato'. As
noted by Perloff (*Art and the Everyday*, 98), however, Milhaud conflates some distinctions
between African-American and American (white) jazz. Compare his observation here with
n. 78, and with his comments about jazz bands like that of Billy Arnold, given in Chapter 2,
nn. 33, 34.

[84] Hodeir, *Jazz*, 254.

Example 4.4 Milhaud, *La Création du monde (Suite de concert)*, II (bars 1–6)

(a) Main fugal subject

(b) Motives, voiceleading and modality

including Gershwin in *Rhapsody in Blue* (see too Example 5.2 and
Example 8.1, for commonality with the riff in Davis/Evans, 'All Blues').
The first part of the subject works within the span D–A, to which it returns
after a short excursion to the upper tetrachord A–D.

The voiceleading interpretation of the subject and countersubjects
heeds basic principles of jazz, as embraced in Walter Stuart's practitioner-
orientated *Encyclopedia of Improvisation*;[85] see Example 4.4b. This includes
the premise that 'neighbor notes [i.e. appoggiaturas . . .] precede the principal tones they embellish. If a neighbor note [i.e. mordent] should follow its
principal tone, then the principal tone must be returned [to]'.[86] The subject
features a melodic blues third with its main pitch as F (bars 2–3: preceded
by F♯), then F♯ (bar 4: preceded by E♯). A flattened seventh is also introduced
(bar 4), with a confirmatory C♯/C gesture (bar 5). Even Hodeir opines that
'the composer got close here to the true significance of the blue note – its
instability'.[87] From a rhythmic perspective, Perret makes intertextual comparison with a New Orleans locus: Morton's *Black Bottom Stomp* (1925),
slightly postdating Milhaud's 'Fugue', where a syncopated melody also
emerges from a varied rhythmic accompaniment that is set out as a background foundation.[88] Certainly the subject's rhythmic identity contributes
to its effectiveness, with a dynamic drive afforded by that all-pervasive
three-quaver anacrusic grouping, so typical of early jazz.

Hodeir finds the way that Milhaud brings the subject around to its
subdominant at the phrase-end (bar 6) especially telling: 'The harmonic
climate and evolution of the blues do not depend solely on the more or less
frequent use of blue notes. They result above all from a perpetual interplay
between the tonic and subdominant. Darius Milhaud seems to have understood this perfectly.'[89] This move of a fifth interval across the subject
embodies a certain irony, since it is both a feature of jazz and one that
operates very naturally in the alien, neobaroque context of fugue, as part of
the cycle of fifths. Within the jazz domain lies a second incongruity in that,
while melodic transposition to a new tonic a fourth higher is common,[90]
both African-American music and Milhaud's fugal subject tend to avoid

[85] Walter Stuart, Stan Applebaum and 'Bugs Bower', *Encyclopedia of Improvisation* (New
York: Charles Colin, 1972).

[86] Stan Applebaum, 'How to Improvise for All Instruments', in Stuart, Applebaum and
'Bower', *Encyclopedia*, 3.

[87] Hodeir, *Jazz*, 253.

[88] Perret, 'L'Adoption du jazz', 330–1. Rather perpetuating a linguistic divide, Perret seems
unaware of my earlier analysis.

[89] Hodeir, *Jazz*, 254.

[90] Sargeant, *Jazz: Hot and Hybrid*, 147–72 (especially 160, 163, 167), 203.

melodic reference to the fourth scalic degree because of the former's heavy reliance on the pentatonic collection.[91]

The countersubject, in a flexible blues scale on E, also features the main motives, and incorporated within it and the free part is an exact five-note quotation – surely deliberate – of that most famous of blues themes, Handy's *St. Louis Blues*;[92] see Example 4.5. This is Handy's head motive for the verse, to the lyrics 'I hate to see [de ev'nin' sun go down]', which is closely echoed by *Aunt Hagar's Children Blues* of 1921 (bars 2–3). Interestingly, the introduction and 'bridge'[93] of *St. Louis Blues* – known as the 'Spanish tinge' – feature habanera dotted rhythms and were viewed by Handy as tango, thus also aligning nicely with Milhaud's Brazilian affinities. In this source–product relationship, it is almost as if Milhaud is questing for a musical partnership, building in Handy's signature, in tandem with his own (see below), along the lines of jazz 'licks'.[94] A second free part (bars 17–21) restates the quotation in the blues collection on D. Furthermore, the pattern of fugal entries in the exposition is consistent with that of a basic jazz riff, reused in the 'Final': D (I), Subject (bars 1–6, cello); E (II), Answer (bars 6–11, viola); A (V), Subject (bars 11–16, violin II); and D (I), Answer (bars 16–21, violin I).

Most harmonic movement occurs in the middle section (bars 22–43), starting with a varied countersubject that is preoccupied mainly with the upper tetrachord A–D; see Example 4.6. This countersubject involves motive a', as the initial perfect fourth in descent; its compound motive α', as the fourth with incorporated major second; plus motive d', as its intervallic expansion, which in turn creates part of Milhaud's signature 'Triad motive'. Although first heard in a blues collection on D, the possibility of a localized centre on A becomes increasingly feasible: the main figure is D–C♯/C–A, and the classic ambiguity concerns whether C♯/C is the blues seventh of D, or the third of A. Again, Milhaud's modulatory technique is congruent with jazz practice, whereby a blue note on the third is transformed into one on the seventh of a new tonic (as occurs in the 'Romance'). This practice relates to that concept of 'perpetual interplay', which, in Hodeir's apt view, the composer develops to create a 'complex of blue

---

[91] *Ibid.*, 149, 151, 166.

[92] See the 1914 sheet music in the Digital Collections of Duke University Libraries: http://library.duke.edu/digitalcollections/hasm_a1311/.

[93] This 'bridge' is a contrasting, sixteen-bar section, which links and articulates the verse and chorus.

[94] 'Licks' are the typical melodic-rhythmic gestures of any given jazz musician that constitute their hallmark or signature.

Example 4.5 Milhaud, *La Création du monde* (*Suite de concert*), II (bars 7–11)

(a) Main fugal answer and countersubject

(b) Motives, voiceleading and modality

Example 4.6 Milhaud, *La Création du monde* (*Suite de concert*), II (bars 22–5): varied countersubject

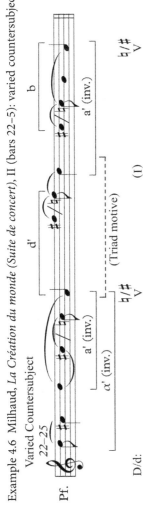

notes',[95] exploiting tonal ambiguity. Ironically, Milhaud's music explores the blues phenomenon more thoroughly than the sources he sought to emulate. Intriguingly and ahistorically, his constant fluctuation between lowered and raised seventh degrees 'creates an harmonic relation that Duke Ellington came across on his own several years later and used as one of the bases of his dissonant system'.[96]

Beneath the piano's varied countersubject (bar 22ff.), the cello plucks a five-beat walking-bass riff, which spans four bars and operates in a localized C major, its inclusion signalling a more persistent conflict and disruption in the bass (bars 44–56). Material becomes fragmented, creating a mosaic-like, imitative texture. A recapitulatory final section (bar 43ff.) maintains, with impressive consistency, the contrapuntal intricacy and semblance of improvisation: Milhaud's striving for what he admires in jazz as 'a linear [inter]play often of a disconcerting complexity'.[97] Polyrhythmic groupings now reach their culmination: six simultaneous patterns of differing lengths stress unexpected beats, particularly the second quaver of the bar: Cendrars's 'confused mass of intertwined bodies', perhaps.

Failing fully to appreciate Milhaud's programmatic brief in portraying 'chaos prior to creation' and his right to an independent jazz-inspired aesthetic, Hodeir criticizes this rhythmic accentuation and linear conflict: 'The resulting impression of disorder is undoubtedly intentional, even though the composer does not always seem to be completely in control of the forces he unleashed.'[98] More damning is a pronouncement that, rhythmically, Milhaud's practice bears no more than passing resemblance to a valorized, contemporary 'good jazz'.[99] Hodeir considers this treatment inauthentic because the jazz beat has been compromised in Milhaud's outdoing of his source: 'By introducing a certain type of polyrhythm, he destroyed the very bases of jazz rhythm.'[100] Ironically, it was this very polyrhythm, and his prediction of a polytonal jazz harmony,[101] that would make Milhaud so attractive to Brubeck. Presumably Milhaud would have much objected to an accusation of destroying the pulse since the 'inner beat' was one of the main traits he found attractive.[102] Equally, there is no reason why he should not exaggerate or distort the rhythmic component as a particular misreading within his own 'revisionary strategies'.[103]

---

[95] Hodeir, *Jazz*, 254.   [96] *Ibid.*, 255.
[97] Milhaud, *Études*, 58: 'un jeu de lignes souvent d'une complexité déconcertante'.
[98] Hodeir, *Jazz*, 258.   [99] *Ibid.*   [100] *Ibid.*, 260.
[101] Milhaud, *Études*, 55: 'dans quelques années, les harmonies polytonales et atonales seront du domaine courant des danses qui succéderont aux shimmys de 1920'.
[102] See n. 30 above.   [103] Straus, 'Toward a Theory of Musical Influence', 16–17.

As regards the two scorings, the 'Fugue' probably loses something in its quintet transcription: the first subject entry is definitely more novel and jazzlike when played by double bass (rather than cello),[104] and answered by heterogeneous timbres of trombone, saxophone and trumpet. Another original strength lay in the primitivist percussive backing of this fugal material, with muted bass drum (in a conflicting triple metre), *tambourin*, snare drum, and very dry, 'nervous' arpeggios on the piano.[105] Additionally, the timpanist dovetailed the join between the 'Prélude' and 'Fugue' with a dramatic roll to mark the raising of the curtain.

III 'Romance'

The next portion of scenario runs thus: 'There is movement in the central mass, a series of convulsions. A tree gradually begins to grow, gets taller and taller, rising up straight, and when one of its seeds falls to the ground, a new tree sprouts.'[106] In the ballet, this section commences with a reprise of the 'Prélude' that links to the 'Romance'.

Musically, this locus most closely approaches blues chordal progressions and forms, within an elaborated overall ternary form.[107] Its main melodic material reworks and recharacterizes the fugal subject (combined with a cadential formula: motive c, from Theme A), hence the labelling as Theme B in Example 4.7 and Example 4.8a. Although the harmonic content is based around the Mixolydian on F, ambiguity in respect of centres on C and B♭ is created by a jazzlike alternation of $F^{♭7}$ and C^9 chords (bars 4–12), combined with a melodic line centred on C (albeit as the upper tetrachord of F) and a significant perfect cadence in B♭ (bars 13–14). At some level, *Aunt Hagar's Children Blues*, which exhibits a very similar fluidity around $F^{♭7}$ and B♭, offers an apt model. As Example 4.7 shows, Milhaud's opening is also a skilful stylization of a classic three-line blues formula, sharing an AAB phrase construction within a twelve-bar form (plus two-bar extension), and

---

[104] As Kelly notes (*Darius Milhaud*, 174), Milhaud's use of the double bass mediates well between the jazz idiom and his modernist 'interest in the solo potential of this neglected instrument'.

[105] One of the most rhythmically tight, dynamic and percussive recordings is that by the then young Simon Rattle, with John Harle on alto saxophone: *Simon Rattle, The Jazz Album*, Simon Rattle (cond.), London Sinfonietta (EMI 7 47991-2, 1987). For a more leisurely recording, including of four dances from *Saudades do Brasil*, see Milhaud, *La Création du monde*, Leonard Bernstein (cond.), Orchestre nationale de France (EMI 7 47845-2, 1978).

[106] Cendrars quoted in Häger, *Ballets Suédois*, 190.

[107] See Barry Kernfeld, 'Blues Progression', in Kernfeld (ed.), *The New Grove Dictionary of Jazz*, vol. I, 255–6.

Example 4.7 Milhaud, *La Création du monde (Suite de concert)*, III (bars 1–17): thematic material and modality

Example 4.8 Milhaud, *La Création du monde (Suite de concert)*, III
(a) Theme B (bars 1–17): motives and voiceleading
(b) Subsidiary thematic fragment B' (bars 42–6): motives and voiceleading

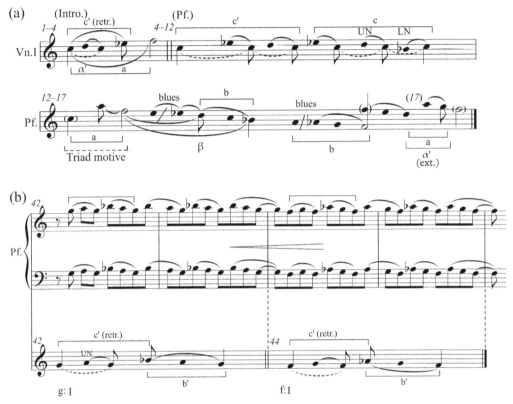

emphasizing the subdominant relation, B♭ (bar 14). The more wide-ranging third phrase (bars 12–17), with expressive sixth and seventh intervals, does not finish, but hangs inconclusively mid-air. In keeping with the blues formal analogy, a two-bar scalic break leads to a modified repeat of the piano's solo (bars 20–31). Additionally, Milhaud cleverly replicates the AAB idea on a larger scale: section A (bars 1–19), A (bars 20–34), and B (bars 35–51).

Example 4.8b shows a figuration (bars 42–6), with a subsidiary thematic fragment B' (including motive b') derived from the 'Fugue' and 'Prélude' and foreshadowing the 'Scherzo' (bars 18–24), which would appear strongly influenced by Gershwin's *Rhapsody in Blue*, except that Milhaud seemingly got there first. But, although the *Rhapsody* only appeared in 1924, Milhaud may well have heard Gershwin songs in 1921 played by Jean Wiéner and others at the Parisian bar Gaya (soon superseded by its Cocteau-Milhaud namesake Le Bœuf sur le toit).[108] (On this ubiquitous musical tic, see too page 156.) In relation to the prevailing crotchet–minim motion, this figure creates another secondary ragtime gesture. Equally, the neoclassical device of sequence cannot be overemphasized, with Theme B on violin heard twice on G^7 (bars 35–8, 39–42), then on F^7 (bars 43–4), $E\flat^7$ (bars 45–7), and directed through B♭ minor ('Cédez'), back to the pillar chord of $F^{\flat 7}$ (bar 51).

To fast-forward: the final cadence, as those of other sections, concludes on an F^{11} chord, still with a hint of dominant function. Once more, this recurrent bivalence (paralleling the fugal instance) between E♭ as the third of C minor, or seventh of F, reflects an intrinsic trait of jazz modality.[109] On the large scale, nonetheless, the Mixolydian on F remains the appropriate collection.

IV 'Scherzo' and V 'Final'

Most jazz-related elements have now been brought into play, thereafter to be reinvoked and combined, and so receive only brief further coverage. The next portion of scenario, congruent with the 'Scherzo', is as follows:

> Each creature, with a dancer bursting from its centre, evolves in its own individual way, takes a few steps, then gently begins to move in a circle, gradually gathering speed as it revolves round the initial three deities. An opening appears in the circle [. . .] two torsos straighten, cling together: this is man and woman, suddenly upright. They recognize one another; they come face to face.[110]

In contrast to the lyrical 'Romance', the 'Scherzo' displays a stark neo-classicism and is generally less relevant to our crossover agenda. Nonetheless, a few noteworthy details persist: its chordal opening features simple dance-like syncopations: crotchet–minim–crotchet and two-quavers–minim–crotchet, which propel a melody derived from the first countertheme (Theme C). Insistent interjections of a contrasting contrapuntal episode (bars 17–24) generated from the 'Fugue' and 'Romance' again suggest an intertextuality with the jazz-derived sequential motives that were to ensure Gershwin's fame. Later on, a more vivacious episode (bars 41–54) incorporates other earlier elements, including the three-crotchet versus three-quaver formula: a musical depiction of 'the formless mass seething. Everything vibrates'. It tumbles into a descending scalic break on piano (bars 44–6), then extemporized on by the strings (bars 51–4): this is the climactic point,

---

[108] Milhaud, *Études*, 51, and Perloff, *Art and the Everyday*, 92–3.   [109] Hodeir, *Jazz*, 254.
[110] Cendrars in Häger, *Ballets Suédois*, 190.

plausibly matching the creation of man and woman in the scenario. In a brief coda (bars 63–7), an unexpected melodic twist occurs with a tetrachor-dal formula: A♯–C♯–D♯–E–A♯–F♯, which exhibits characteristic ambiguity between C♯ and F♯ centres and minimizes reference to the leading note or fourth degree: B. Its authenticity in a jazz setting is supported by Sargeant, who quotes a remarkably similar shape when discussing typical endings of African-American melody that 'coincide with the principle of melodic movement peculiar to the blues tetrachordal grouping: A, C, D, E♭, (E)'.[111]

Fittingly, the 'Final' draws together previous ideas, commencing in the suite version with allusion to the languorous 'Prélude' and 'Romance', including its parody of blues form. The 'Animé' marking (bar 16) likely corresponds to the climactic text: 'And while the couple perform[s] the dance of desire, followed by the mating dance, all the formless beings that remained on the ground stealthily creep up and join in the round dance, leading it at a frenetic, dizzy pace.'[112] Cendrars's 'dance of desire' makes syncopated reference to the 'Scherzo' reconfigured within a new melody (Theme D, on piano), the extension of which (bar 25ff.) develops the fugal subject. Similarly, its accompaniment – a New Orleans-like rhythm section – evokes the rhythms and blue notes of the 'Fugue' on strings and may be construed as parodying a riff; see Example 4.9. A repeating four-bar harmonic pattern: $I–II^7–V^{11}–I^7$ (bars 16–19) underpins a directed chromatic descent. Percussive, part-pizzicato chords remind us that, in the ballet, this is where cymbal, *tambourin*, snare and bass drum return most effectively to strengthen the sonic texture. Consonant with the drama, this is Milhaud's 'round dance'.

Cued by 'Cédez' (bars 60–5), the solo cello mimics another jazz break in pensive recollection of the 'Romance' (bars 42–5), with elaborated chordal punctuation courtesy of the upper strings: $I^7–II^{♯9}–V^{13}(–I^{6/5})$, as shown in Example 4.10. Additionally, we find further mixture at the third and seventh, stylized blues structures and more violent spasms in the piano's adoption of the three-quaver anacrusic riff (bar 79ff.). A recapitulation (bars 116–52) combines Theme D, the varied fugal countersubject and riff: this music thrives on mesmeric repetitions of mosaiclike patterns, creating its own momentum and a mock improvisatory effect. It makes for the period of most intense activity, with continual reinforcement of the tonic modality

---

[111] Sargeant, *Jazz: Hot and Hybrid*, 203; see also 167 and 175. Given his passionate advocacy of African-American jazz, Sargeant's usage of 'Negroid' simply shows how far societal attitudes have since shifted.

[112] Cendrars in Häger, *Ballets Suédois*, 190.

Example 4.9 Milhaud, *La Création du monde (Suite de concert)*, V (bars 16–19): chordal riff

of D in the bass, supporting myriad blues inflections above (and reiterated percussive flourishes in the ballet score): Cendrars's 'frenetic, dizzy pace'. An inexorable building leads to the most forceful and ecstatic *fff* climax (bar 147), after which the music inevitably subsides.

A slow, expressive and intimate coda (bars 166–90) – effectively an epilogue after the close of the action – corresponds with Cendrars's text

Example 4.10 Milhaud, *La Création du monde (Suite de concert)*, V (bars 60–5): jazz break and riff

cited earlier:[113] the couple is transported in its embrace and spring has arrived. A final chromatic gesture highlights the blues seventh: C/C♯, ending with a deliciously subtle dissonance: $I^{♯7}$: in keeping with the real blues, there is no resolution. It is, however, surely no coincidence that the pitch centres across the suite's movements create the pattern: D–d–F/F♯–D. This is the ultimate blues progression writ large, yet the irony is that no actual piece of jazz would be so prescriptive, or in Hodeir's words show 'such faithfulness to the letter'![114]

A mixed critical reception

Although the first performance of *La Création* did not meet with the riots that had marked the premiere of *Le Sacre*, the Parisian critical response was still decidedly mixed. Some were shocked by the ballet, particularly its staging and unconventional use of dancers, while others complained that the music especially was not shocking enough! Émile Vuillermoz (1878–1960) commented in uncompromising fashion, in *La Revue musicale* of December 1923, that 'The scenario by Blaise Cendrars and the décor and costumes by Fernand Léger seemed intent on making of this evening an audacious manifestation of the avant-garde. This did not happen, however.'[115] Meanwhile, the typically conformist ballet critic Levinson was shocked by the outlandishness of the concept, writing in *Comœdia* of 28 October 1923:

> What an aberration, taking on living dancers to imitate the formulas of exotic sculptors by contorting themselves. No one can ever create a work for dancers by translating the conventions peculiar to the plastic arts by means of saltatory movement . . . the glamour of Negro sculpture, exalted to the skies by some great modern artists and adopted by the snobs.[116]

It is worth highlighting the derogatory nuances concerning the 'exotic', and the scepticism with which the primitivist enterprise was viewed; there are unwitting misconceptions and veiled hints of racism.

While Vuillermoz complained that Milhaud's music 'becomes meeker with each passing day', another critic, Pierre de Lapommeraye, declared in *Le Ménestrel* of 2 November 1923 that: 'The feeling one gets listening to Darius Milhaud's latest productions is rage . . . Going back to tom-toms, xylophones, bellowing brass and noise is not progress.'[117] Again, the inaccuracies contained in this account, for instance regarding the nonexistent

---

[113] See again n. 68.   [114] Hodeir, *Jazz*, 252.
[115] Quoted in Watkins, *Pyramids at the Louvre*, 126.
[116] Quoted in Häger, *Ballets Suédois*, 44.   [117] *Ibid.*

tom-toms, suggest a preconceived and prejudiced stance that does not trouble itself with the facts. As quoted in Chapter 2, Milhaud summed up this early reception by exposing the short-sightedness and hypocrisy of those critics who, having totally discounted his work on first hearing, were pretentiously applauding its success a decade later.[118]

Conclusion

With this work, Milhaud became one of the first composers to assimilate successfully and imaginatively a variety of jazz techniques within classical repertory. Thus far, as he himself noted, most had confined themselves to 'interpretations of dance music', by recreating the rhythms and formulae of ragtime.[119] Stravinsky had written his ragtime pieces and those with a wider range of popular allusion, including *L'Histoire du soldat*, but Milhaud went further: he approached his subject at first hand and with much technical and anthropological seriousness, as well as passion, fully appreciating the crucial African-American dimension. Consequently, he was able to incorporate elements of the timbre, instrumentation and scalic forms of ragtime, blues and New Orleans styles within his developing neoclassical aesthetic, his main priority having been to absorb the emotional spirit of jazz, especially the melancholic, vocal inflections of the blues. Additionally a machinist-technological dimension finds expression here, largely in the visual dimensions of Léger's avant-garde 'mechanical theatre' and Börlin's choreography, but also in Milhaud's employment of unrelenting musical mechanisms, particularly the circular, contrapuntal devices in the 'Fugue' and the punctuating riff in the 'Final'.

While this is Milhaud's jazz masterpiece and surely the work by which he is best known, any practising jazz musician would assert that his assimilation of jazz and blues scale is still a far cry from the real, spontaneous art.[120] And this is part of the point. Composing for a classically trained ensemble, with music fully notated, such a task would have been impossible: true jazz exists only in improvised performance – albeit planned, to a greater or lesser degree – and Milhaud recognized this. He was not attempting to compose a genuine piece of jazz: such would be a contradiction, and the work would have been far less successful and durable had he done so. Although he had previously written pieces more in keeping with early jazz, including *Caramel mou*, these have not captured the public imagination in the manner of *La Création*. In collaborating with Cendrars and Léger on a

---

[118] Milhaud, *My Happy Life*, 120.   [119] *Ibid.*, 98; Milhaud, *Études*, 54.
[120] Hodeir, *Jazz*, 250.

ballet that evoked creation visually – as African-styled folklore – and aurally, Milhaud must presumably have intended a mix of European modernist, African and African-American cultures from the beginning.

Beyond this cultural opposition is that of the inherent technical vocabularies. Much discussion has focused on the jazz element as the more remarkable achievement of a (neo)classical composer; what remains is to stress some incongruities, even polarities. There is a wonderful absurdity to Milhaud's using fully developed fugue – the epitome of baroque rigour and restraint, exemplifying 'high art' – as the structural framework for one of his most bluesy themes, itself part-quoted from the music of Handy. In the 'Romance', reconfigured twelve-bar blues structures engage with and potentially contest a refined, classical ternary form. However, *La Création* only works because such elements are melded and developed within processes that are seemingly organic. The high profile of third relations in Milhaud's handling of jazz and neoclassical texts provides some of the necessary common ground.

Stylistically, too, we can envisage bizarre contrasts. In the original staging, ballet dancers trained in Europe's most exclusive schools engage in role-play as creatures from exotic regions, which most could only hope to visit in their imaginations. Caucasian classical musicians, trained at the conservatoire, act out a role, giving a semblance of the improvisatory freedom of the African-American jazz musician. In the concert suite, the double incongruity of a European piano quintet enacting a jazz role in a tightly controlled neoclassical framework is perhaps yet more striking. In the spirit of *Le Sacre*, the audience who witnessed these rites also entered a fantasy world, far from their ordered twentieth-century Parisian lifestyles.

La Création is certainly the jazz prototype in stage or concert music of the 1920s – French or otherwise, with many attempted sequels. With the notable exception of Gershwin, it is doubtful whether even successors such as Copland (Concerto for Piano and Orchestra, 1926), Křenek (*Jonny spielt auf*, or *Der Sprung über den Schatten*, 1924), or Weill (*Die Dreigroschenoper*, 1927–8; *Mahagonny*, 1927–9) had the same understanding and compositional skill within the elusive world of early jazz. Their works fall much more readily into categories of pastiche or parody than that of a developed assimilation.

The attraction and strength of *La Création* lie in its exploration of oppositions (cultural, stylistic and technical, including processes of modal complementation) that are subsequently synthesized as a superb *mélange* of differing worlds. The music provides a compelling instance of intertextuality, but more specifically, along Metzer's lines, it demonstrates a full spectrum of techniques from quotation, paraphrase-parody, potential modelling, allusion and looser textual associations and transformations. Milhaud's case exemplifies a rare hybridity: truly cosmopolitan, international. His assimilation of blues modality, jazz harmonies, rhythms and timbres transforms his French compositional practice, which simultaneously inflects and recharacterizes his jazz borrowings. In this respect, he is unlike Ravel or Satie, but – with the two sharing a Bachian link – much more a forerunner of Brubeck.

5 Crossing borders: Ravel's theory and practice of jazz

Within the contexts of popular musics and European modernist eclecticism, this case study considers Ravel's reading of jazz through assessment of his writings and letters, followed by analytical exploration of selected works.[1] It argues that Ravel translated an American jazz into his vernacular, creating a French-accented and personalized practice, and that this was an important aspect of his aesthetic and musical identity in the later 1920s. While we typically regard Ravel as embracing his French history along Eliot's lines, in conveying 'a feeling that the whole of the literature of Europe from Homer and within it the whole of the literature of his own country has a simultaneous existence',[2] aspects of his jazz theory also resonate with Bloomian traits.[3] As the final chapter of Part II, this Ravelian topic forms a significant part of the larger quest by various twentieth-century French musicians to revitalize their national music; paradoxically, it is predominantly a reinvigoration of French identity through the foreign.

To this end, and cued by Ravel's crossing of borders between America and France on his 1928 tour, I probe an intriguing double relationship that embodies transformative processes across a spectrum from minor to major change. The first relationship is between Ravel's 'theory' or views of early jazz – especially the associated blues – and the historical actualities, as interpreted by jazz scholars past and present (with the benefit of hindsight). Although there is much congruity, a modulation between actuality and theory is underpinned by intricate dynamics which relate to broader processes of Gallicizing jazz, as in Jackson's *Making Jazz French*, and to Ravel's

---

[1] This chapter is a slightly modified reprint of that published in Deborah Mawer (ed.), *Ravel Studies* (Cambridge University Press, 2010). Small changes reflect the essay's new context, with cross-referencing and removal of any substantive duplication with the current book. Earlier versions were presented at 'Musique française: esthétique et identité en mutation, 1892–1992', Université Catholique de l'Ouest, Angers, France (29–30 April 2008) and at the joint conference of the Society for Musicology in Ireland and the Royal Musical Association, Dublin (9–12 July 2009). I am grateful for feedback and suggestions from Carolyn Abbate, Andy Fry, Jacinthe Harbec, Julian Horton, Barbara Kelly, Danièle Pistone, Jan Smaczny and others.

[2] Eliot, 'Tradition and the Individual Talent', 37. Succinctly, he writes of upholding 'the mind of his own country', 38. It is worth noting that Eliot's essay of 1919 is roughly contemporary with Ravel's own writings.

[3] Bloom, 'Introduction: A Meditation upon Misreading', *A Map of Misreading*, 3–6.

artistic aesthetic and experience. While not underplaying the very real challenges in defining early jazz, which has meant different things to different people and even to the same people across time (see Introduction and Chapter 1),[4] I claim that idiosyncrasies within Ravel's positioning can be revealed. The second relationship is between Ravel's theory and his practice across the 'Blues' movement of the Violin Sonata, the ragtime from *L'Enfant et les sortilèges*, *Boléro*, the Left Hand Concerto (1929–30) and the Piano Concerto in G (1929–31). Again, this process is marked by complex dynamics: although theory and practice relate closely, one is not synonymous with the other. I suggest that more occasional idiosyncrasies emerge and that Ravel's compositional stance – the *poietic*, to use Jean-Jacques Nattiez's terminology – is not in any case synonymous with our analytical *esthesic* stance in seeking to understand his music.

Topical research literature relating to the American–French jazz background, both African-American culture in Paris and jazzing the classics/ classicizing jazz, has largely been covered earlier in the book. It only remains to add that, more historically, Hodeir's incisive if eccentric views still hold some merit and offer a controversial foil (also pursued in Chapter 4).[5] Other pertinent resources include Perret's fascinating article which compares American jazz and French compositions, concentrating upon expressivity and spirituality, and more specific treatment of Ravel's 'Blues' by Robert Orledge and by Mark DeVoto, the former making comparisons with Gershwin, Jerome Kern (1885–1945) and Joe Venuti (1903–78).[6]

Although some records were imported during World War I, essentially early jazz arrived in Europe towards the end of the war, courtesy of American troop entertainment. And since much has been written on this topic, I shall confine myself here to summarizing matters relevant to Ravel.[7] Many white and a few African-American bands were heard in Paris – or the 'Transatlantic Terminus' as it was known.[8] Billy Arnold's

---

[4] These problematics are confronted in many jazz histories; see, for instance, Gunther Schuller, *Early Jazz: Its Roots and Musical Development* (New York: Oxford University Press, 1968; reprinted 1986), 4: jazz is 'a hybrid that evolved through many stages of cross-fertilization over a period of more than a century'.

[5] Hodeir, *Jazz*.

[6] Perret, 'L'Adoption du jazz'; Robert Orledge, 'Evocations of Exoticism', and Mark DeVoto, 'Harmony in the Chamber Music', in Mawer (ed.), *The Cambridge Companion to Ravel*, 27–46: 42–3; 97–117: 115–16.

[7] For detail see Jackson, *Making Jazz French*, 19, 20, 111, 120–1; Perret, 'L'Adoption du jazz', 311–20; and Deborah Mawer, '"Parisomania"? Jack Hylton and the French Connection', *Journal of the Royal Musical Association*, 133/2 (November 2008), 270–317: 280–4.

[8] Sisley Huddleston, *Back to Montparnasse: Glimpses of Broadway in Bohemia* (Philadelphia, PA and London: J. B. Lippincott, 1931), 47.

white band featured in the Concerts Wiéner in December 1921 and was much enjoyed by Ravel (as it was initially by Milhaud): the musicians were 'marvellous'.[9]

In Le Bœuf sur le toit, whose convivial atmosphere appealed to Les Six, Ravel most likely first heard Gershwin numbers,[10] including perhaps 'The Man I Love', the opening verse of which Perret proposes as a model for Ravel's practice.[11] Léon-Paul Fargue offers an attractive image of the composer as 'a sort of debonair wizard, buried in his corner at the Grand Écart or Le Bœuf sur le toit, telling me endless stories which had the same elegance, richness, and clarity as his compositions'.[12] By contrast, in uncharitable and disdainful fashion, Hodeir talked of Ravel's 'jumping on the latest thing, regardless of where it came from, eager to exploit this novelty, slightly shopworn though it may have been, after he had followed Debussy and flirted a moment with Schoenberg'. He continued: 'There is no dearth of anecdotes in some of which he is shown applauding Jimmie Noone, in others the orchestra at the Moulin Rouge.'[13] A better balance is achieved by Arbie Orenstein, who notes that, although Ravel was intensely private when composing, 'he enjoyed Parisian nightlife, the conversations, the lights, the jazz, and the crowds'.[14]

On his American tour, there is evidence that Ravel visited the still-segregated Cotton Club in Harlem where Ellington appeared on stage,[15] though Ravel's priority seems to have been to play and hear Gershwin's renditions of 'Tea for Two', *Rhapsody in Blue*, '"My Blue Heaven", and other jazz tunes [sic]'.[16] Indeed Ravel and Gershwin met several times and much admired each other's work, to the extent that, according to the singer Eva Gautier, Gershwin sought composition lessons from

---

[9] Jean Wiéner, *Allegro Appassionato* (Paris: Pierre Belfond, 1978), 83.

[10] See Sachs, *Au temps du bœuf sur le toit*.

[11] Perret, 'L'Adoption du jazz', 323–34. Ravel's practice echoes more obviously Gershwin's dotted figuration that begins the chorus (bar 21ff.).

[12] Quoted in Orenstein (ed.), *A Ravel Reader*, 15.

[13] Hodeir, *Jazz*, 246–7. Jimmie Noone (1895–1944) was a New Orleans clarinettist, taught by Sidney Bechet, who from 1927 led a band at the Apex Club, Chicago. His style, blues-influenced yet lyrical and polished, would likely have appealed to Ravel.

[14] Orenstein (ed.), *A Ravel Reader*, 15.

[15] Joseph Roddy, 'Ravel in America', *High Fidelity Magazine* (March 1975), 58–63, quoted in Perret, 'L'Adoption du jazz', 322. The Cotton Club was for whites only, though there were African-American performers.

[16] Marie Dunbar, 'Maurice Ravel, Napoleon of World Music, Plays Popular Numbers', *Seattle Post Intelligencer* (13 February 1928), quoted by Perret, 'L'Adoption du jazz', 320. 'Tea for Two' was the hit from the New York musical *No, No Nanette* (1925), with music by Vincent Youmans and lyrics by Irving Caesar.

Ravel.[17] At New York's Liederkranz Hall, Ravel heard Paul Whiteman's Orchestra recording with Beiderbecke.[18]

Within his record collection Ravel amassed a diverse repertory, including occasional jazz-related numbers such as *Tiger Rag*, numerous chansons or music-hall songs – Gaston Claret's 'Si petite', Scotto's 'Tu m'fais rire', Mireille's 'Le Petit Chemin' and Maurice Yvain's 'Pourquoâ' (sung by the 'chansonnier montmartrois' or cabaret singer Paul Colline) – together with popular piano music, notably that by the British musician Billy Mayerl (1902–59).[19] For many modernist composers, to jazz up their classical style, as one type of eclecticism, enabled a significant means of inflecting their authorial voice; in addition to Ravel, Milhaud especially wrote about the impact of jazz upon his practice.[20]

Relations between Ravel's theory and the actualities of early jazz

Ravel's theory of jazz is evidenced primarily from his notated lecture-cum-pamphlet entitled *Contemporary Music* of April 1928 for the Rice Institute in Houston, rehearsed in his article 'Take Jazz Seriously!'[21] and supplemented by interviews and correspondence. Certain ideas recur across several years and sources and have been abstracted as themes in my constructing and presenting of this theory. On the one hand, a substantial part of the writing reveals Ravel as a connoisseur of American-French jazz, reflecting contemporary realities (so that criticisms by Hodeir may seem grudging and unfounded) and presenting, up to a point, an untransformed (more Eliot-like?) perspective.

Theme 1: Americans are urged to appreciate jazz as a cultural asset rather than something to be taken for granted. Interviewed by Olin Downes early in 1928,[22] Ravel declares how much he admires jazz, claiming that he values it more than many American contemporaries. Witness to this is the title of his article 'Take Jazz Seriously!' in which he chides Americans for regarding

---

[17] Eva Gautier, 'Reminiscences of Maurice Ravel', *New York Times* (16 January 1938). Ravel's enthusiastic account about Gershwin is given in a letter to Nadia Boulanger (8 March 1928), in Orenstein (ed.), *A Ravel Reader*, 293. On the matter of teaching Gershwin compositional technique, Ravel asks Boulanger, 'Would you have the courage, which I wouldn't dare have, to undertake this awesome responsibility?'.

[18] See Ravel seated at the piano with Whiteman standing, in Thomas A. DeLong, *Pops: Paul Whiteman, King of Jazz* (Piscataway: New Century Publishers, 1983), plate at 272–3.

[19] Bruno Sébald's listing in Orenstein (ed.), *A Ravel Reader*, 601–11.

[20] See Milhaud, 'Les Ressources nouvelles de la musique', *Études* and *Ma vie heureuse*.

[21] For full references, see 'French critical discourse and jazz', in Chapter 2.

[22] Olin Downes, 'Mr Ravel Returns', *New York Times* (26 February 1928), section 8, 8.

jazz as 'cheap, vulgar, momentary'.[23] We may argue that it is all very well Ravel being indignant and slightly self-righteous, but he is late on the trail in comparison with Milhaud, or Auric. Nonetheless, he feels justified in contrasting American lack of interest with a European perspective, whereby '[jazz] is influencing our work'. His knowledge of early jazz and French colonialism is such that, in a letter to Mme Fernand Dreyfus, he talks of his intention to look in affectionately on jazz's birthplace, New Orleans.[24] (By this point, he had seemingly had fleeting contact with Harlem jazz, and had written to his brother Édouard about experiencing African-American theatre in New York and jazz in Omaha, en route to Minneapolis.)[25] On the topic of the Gallicizing of jazz, Ravel paints a lively picture of New Year's Eve entertainment aboard the liner named the *France*, which took him literally and figuratively from Europe to New York. Writing to French friends, he exclaims, in anticipation of William Shack's *Harlem in Montmartre*: 'We are supping joyously in a dance hall which is hardly level: jazz, paper streamers, balloons, champagne, a Russian quartet, drunk Americans – all the local color of Montmartre.'[26]

In writings that postdate his tour, Ravel generally upholds the value of jazz for himself and fellow classical composers.[27] He presents a typical *Zeitgeist* stance in which jazz is seen to embody the modernist age: 'In jazz rhythms, it is often said, the pulsation of modern life is heard.' Such a view echoes that of Mendl: 'The energy, industry, the hurry and hustle of modern American methods find their counterpart in the [. . .] jazz orchestra.'[28] Ravel qualifies his position, saying that jazz is not the only influence, and should be seen in conjunction with that exerted by machines, industry and technological endeavour: this alignment with a machinist aesthetic, especially

[23] Ravel, 'Take Jazz Seriously!', 49.

[24] Letter to Mme Fernand Dreyfus (4 April 1928), in Orenstein (ed.), *A Ravel Reader*, 294.

[25] See Orenstein (ed.), *A Ravel Reader*, 293n, 288, 293. Omaha has long been a jazz centre, frequented by Armstrong, Ellington, and others; the Omaha Riverfront Jazz and Blues Festival continues this tradition.

[26] Letter to Nelly and Maurice Delage (31 December 1927), in Orenstein (ed.), *A Ravel Reader*, 287; William A. Shack, *Harlem in Montmartre* (Berkeley and Los Angeles, CA: University of California Press, 2001).

[27] See [unsigned interview], 'Factory Gives Composer Inspiration', *Evening Standard* (24 February 1932), in Orenstein (ed.), *A Ravel Reader*, 490–1: 490. The exception occurs in [unsigned interview], 'Problems of Modern Music, From a Conversation with Maurice Ravel', *Der Bund* (19 April 1929), in Orenstein (ed.), *A Ravel Reader*, 465–6: 466, where Ravel purportedly exclaimed: 'Jazz might serve many of us as entertainment, but it has nothing in common with art.' No other source expresses negativity, which may raise questions of authenticity.

[28] [Unsigned interview], 'Problems of Modern Music'; Mendl, *The Appeal of Jazz*, 97–8.

following *Boléro*, reflects another popular Parisian cult from the early 1920s. Although by 1931 Ravel suspects, as had Milhaud five years earlier, that 'jazz influence is waning', he still credits it as a major factor in his late music, including the Concerto in G.[29] And he does not want to let go, reasserting, 'It is not just a passing phase [...] It is thrilling and inspiring'; as late as August 1932, in a little-known interview for *Rhythm* magazine entitled 'Jazz – Democracy's Music!', he reaffirms the influence of jazz and popular music.[30]

Theme 2: ragtime is credited as a specific entity, and is the first style or genre on which Ravel comments, aptly given its role as a precursor of jazz. As Waldo cautions however, 'Ragtime [...] is a much more eclectic term [than rag] and could be said to apply to almost any music that is syncopated.'[31] Nevertheless, Ravel's usage of foxtrot characteristics within ragtime in *L'Enfant* makes apparent his familiarity with a technique dating from around 1913. In a letter to Colette (27 February 1919), he asks her view of 'the cup and the teapot, in old Wedgwood – black – singing a ragtime?' His appreciation of raglike forms is evident from his remark that 'the form – a single couplet, with refrain – would be perfectly suited to the gestures in this scene: complaints, recriminations, furor, pursuit'.[32] An unconventional, politically savvy approach is highlighted in his good-humoured intention for a vocal ragtime to be given by two African-American singers at the then somewhat stuffy Paris Opéra. Ravel's use of the word 'nègres', while troubling for us, is typical of its time. (The first so-called jazz-band performance at the Opéra did not happen until Jack Hylton and His Boys appeared in February 1931, and this performance only featured white players; see Chapter 6.) Ravel also makes mention in *Contemporary Music* of the 'rags',[33] with perceptive quotation marks, of composers such as Hindemith and Alfredo Casella.

Theme 3: in Ravel's theory, the blues deserves a special status, though as today's jazz scholars caution, this term has no one concrete definition.[34] (Unlike ragtime, blues has continued in parallel with various jazz styles

---

[29] [Special correspondent], 'A Visit with Maurice Ravel', *De Telegraaf* (31 March 1931), in Orenstein (ed.), *A Ravel Reader*, 472–5: 473.

[30] [Unsigned interview], 'Factory Gives Composer Inspiration', 490; the interview in *Rhythm* (not listed by Orenstein) was drawn to my attention by John Watson, a music historian who researches into 'rhythm and novelty' pianists of the interwar years: personal communication (21 April 2008).

[31] Waldo, *This Is Ragtime*, 4.   [32] Orenstein (ed.), *A Ravel Reader*, 188.

[33] Ravel, *Contemporary Music*, 140; Waldo, *This Is Ragtime*, 4: 'A rag, strictly speaking, is an instrumental syncopated march.'

[34] Paul Oliver and Barry Kernfeld, 'Blues', in Kernfeld (ed.), *The New Grove Dictionary of Jazz*, vol. I, 247–55: 247.

through to the present. But although authors such as Shipton consider the interrelationship between early jazz and blues, and although Cooke classifies blues, with ragtime, as a precursor to New Orleans jazz,[35] the relationships are not straightforward. While the blues is 'widely assumed' to have impacted on early jazz, more documentary research is necessary to clinch the case.)[36] In a further interview with Downes, Ravel demonstrates his earnest intent, stating, 'I take this "blues" very seriously,' and questioning, 'Why have not more of the important American composers turned to this "blue" material [...]?'[37] This stance is stressed in *Contemporary Music*, where he extols the inherent expressivity and emotional content of the blues, and reveals his deep enthusiasm for the genre: 'the "blues" is one of your greatest assets, truly American, despite earlier contributory influences from Africa and Spain'.[38] The Spanish connection resonates strongly with Ravel's own background and compositional practice (his writing of blues focusing the second part of this case study).

   Theme 4: jazz should relate to larger questions of national identity. Ravel has a subtle understanding of such issues, influenced by his French identity. On various occasions,[39] he talks of the typically mixed sources of national musics arguing that, whatever its strict and varied origins, jazz is unequivocally American. A perceptive, detailed discourse is developed on American identity, with Ravel looking forward to experiencing more of 'those elements which are contributing to the gradual formation of a veritable school of American music'.[40] He debates 'high' versus popular art and American versus European music, perceiving two camps: those who believe folklore to be essential to national music and those who think that a national music will emerge from the music of the day. His tone is, however, disparaging when referring to the first group's agonizing over exactly which folklore, Native American traditions, spirituals or blues are authentically American 'until nothing is left of national background'. Nevertheless, French traditions and background remain crucial to Ravel. Ravel talks of the lure of European tradition versus the criticism faced by American composers whose music is seen as overly European. For him, the answer to this conundrum is to revisit the past and see how so-called nationalist composers held true to their

---

[35] Shipton, *A New History of Jazz*, 31–2; Cooke, *Jazz*, 192–3. See also Lewis Porter, 'The "Blues" Connotation in Ornette Coleman's Music – and Some General Thoughts on the Relationship of Blues to Jazz', *Annual Review of Jazz Studies*, 7 (1994–5), 75–99.

[36] Oliver and Kernfeld, 'Blues', 248. For these reasons, unlike Perret, I would not use the terms jazz and blues interchangeably: Perret, 'L'Adoption du jazz', 311.

[37] Olin Downes, 'Maurice Ravel, Man and Musician', *New York Times* (7 August 1927), X6.

[38] Ravel, *Contemporary Music*, 145, 140.   [39] For example, Downes, 'Maurice Ravel', 49.

[40] Ravel, *Contemporary Music*, 142–3.

individual conscience, surprisingly singling out Wagner.[41] His prediction
is that, whatever the origins of 'negro [*sic*] music', it will have a significant
role in establishing an 'American school'; the final rhetoric exhorts,
showing seeming familiarity with the differences between jazz, blues and
spirituals, that a new American music should contain much of 'the rich
and diverting rhythm of your jazz [. . .] the emotional expression of your
blues, and [. . .] the sentiment and spirit characteristic of your popular
melodies and songs'.[42]

On the other hand, and more interestingly, distortions and oversimpli-
fications sometimes justify Hodeir's criticisms and reveal transformation of
actuality in Ravel's theory (more of a Bloomian repositioning). The reasons
for this include Ravel's entitlement to his own aesthetic and his role as a
Frenchman in espousing his national identity. He is already selecting what
he wants and reading jazz in relation to his artistic (and scholarly) needs.
But perhaps the most significant reason is that, for much of the 1920s, his
experience of jazz was indirect. Although we find in his record collection the
classic *Tiger Rag*,[43] by 1927 Ravel, unlike Milhaud, had still not heard jazz
on American soil. In a letter to Prunières of September 1927, Ravel exclaims
in slightly contrived fashion: 'As for my feelings about America, it would be
better to limit yourself to the strict truth: never having been there, I would be
happy to see it [. . .] you may add that I like jazz much more than grand
opera.'[44] So Hodeir has something of a point when he says of Ravel (as of
Stravinsky and even Milhaud), that errors of understanding stem from 'an
insufficient acquaintance with authentic jazz'.[45] Conversely, current scholarship would argue for a more inclusive definition of jazz and regard claims
of exclusivity or authenticity with suspicion.

Theme 5: Ravel's discussion of jazz can be rather vague and generic. *Tiger
Rag* apart, it is unclear which rags or types of ragtime (cakewalk, two-step,
'coon' song, or folk ragtime) he was familiar with. While he must have
known well Debussy's reading in his early 'Golliwogg's Cake-Walk', Ravel
never mentions Joplin[46] with his classics such as *Magnetic Rag*, or Berlin
with his vocal *Alexander's Ragtime Band* (though this is not a true rag).
(Here again, Ravel differs from Milhaud.) There is no acknowledgement of
those we now regard as the leading exponents of early, New Orleans jazz:
Oliver, the composer of *West End Blues*, or the young Armstrong. In fact
Ravel explains that his thematic inspiration for the Violin Sonata came from

---

[41] *Ibid.*, 143–4.   [42] *Ibid.*, 145.
[43] *Tiger Rag* (Pathé X 94428), coupled with 'Tyrolian Song', sung by the Kentucky Singers.
[44] Orenstein (ed.), *A Ravel Reader*, 280.   [45] Hodeir, *Jazz*, 250.
[46] See Berlin, *King of Ragtime*.

Parisian cabaret, though perhaps wisely he gives no more away;[47] elsewhere he refers to 'jazz idioms' which remain unspecified.[48]

Theme 6: Ravel's usage of the term 'picturesque' lays him open to Hodeir's criticisms of superficiality. Obvious comparisons may be drawn between his childlike utterance that 'It is to me a picturesque adventure in composition' and Hodeir's accusation that the foxtrot of *L'Enfant* exhibits a mere 'picture-postcard exoticism'.[49]

Theme 7: there are issues of seeming oversimplification and misconception. Ravel suggests that jazz is synonymous with 'American popular music',[50] though to be fair he later qualifies his response, alluding to the influence of 'so-called' popular music and referring in *Contemporary Music* to the blues as 'this popular form of your music'.[51] A revealing misconception – or perhaps a statement of preference – is about Gershwin's status as somehow representative of jazz, when his position was much more that of a 'middleman', rather like Tin Pan Alley itself. In making the valid point about being attracted to melody, Ravel juxtaposes Gershwin and jazz, announcing: 'Personally I find jazz most interesting: the rhythms, the way the melodies are handled, the melodies themselves. I have heard some of George Gershwin's works and I find them intriguing.' (His expression, 'the melodies themselves', may refer to notated jazz standards.) Just as tellingly, if we can trust the source, Ravel is quoted as saying: 'The best jazz is *written* by good musicians.'[52] We may then understand Hodeir's disparaging attitude to what he saw as indiscriminate attraction to 'commercial counterfeits' and his exclamation, 'The surprising thing is that someone like Ravel was able to take even as much interest as he did in such obvious trash.'[53] But in a sense Hodeir too misses the point since Ravel, like Milhaud before him, was not aiming for any real portrayal of jazz, rather to use his take on an inspirational source to develop his own voice. Furthering Ravel's defence, as mentioned above it is well recognized these days that the term 'jazz' was applied very loosely in the 1920s to a range of musics. And it was perfectly legitimate for Ravel, as a creative artist, to favour what he perceived as Gershwin's refined stance: one that accorded well with his own aesthetic,

[47] [Unsigned interview], 'Ravel Says Poe Aided Him in Composition', *New York Times* (6 January 1928).

[48] Downes, 'Mr Ravel Returns'.   [49] *Ibid.*; Hodeir, *Jazz*, 256.

[50] Downes, 'Mr Ravel Returns'.

[51] Ravel, 'Take Jazz Seriously!', 49; *Contemporary Music*, 140.

[52] [Unsigned interview], 'Famous French Composer in London', *The Star* (16 October 1923), in Orenstein (ed.), *A Ravel Reader*, 428–30: 429 (my italics).

[53] Hodeir, *Jazz*, 251.

including the centrality of writing for the piano which would be asserted ultimately in the concertos.

Finally, theme 8: African-American origins are sometimes downplayed. While there is no evidence that Ravel was in any way racist, indeed his views were distinctly left-wing, this occasional understatement does present as a distortion.[54] There was an unfortunate expression in a British newspaper interview of 1923, where Ravel apparently damned jazz with faint praise, though it is unclear what, if any, editorial control he had: 'Jazz from America is not wholly to be despised.' More concerning is a comment about jazz harmonies: 'They come from the Negroes, no doubt, but I'm not sure their real origin is not partly English and partly Scotch.'[55] Apropos these mixed origins, Ravel's thinking is consistent with the likes of Schuller, for whom jazz 'developed from a multi-colored variety of musical traditions brought to the new world in part from Africa, in part from Europe'.[56] Nonetheless, in relation to Ravel's special concern with the blues, more recent jazz scholarship is clear where the lion's share of credit should go: 'Blues is in essence an African-American music, with its roots in African-American culture'; crucially, 'its most profound expression' results from the oppressed position of its people, existing like a minority group within 'a dominant white society'.[57] In 1928, hints of Ravel's partial denial of origins persist as, overplaying his national quest, he presents a curious claim about an ostensible jazz from nineteenth-century France. This line of argument could be misconstrued, although Ravel's point about extensive syncopation and the ability of material to mutate whilst retaining a sense of its origin is well made.[58]

Relations between Ravel's theory and practice of jazz

So, even in spring 1928, Ravel's theoretical stance was a little removed from a first-hand experience of improvised jazz, but, importantly, his writings also advocate a set of transformational principles. His sophisticated engagement is plain, questioning the extent of influence and necessary reshaping needed for his compositional purposes. Here I find a little inconsistency in the argument of Perret, who talks rightly of the desirability of 'a marriage

---

[54] As introduced in Chapter 2, the attitude was taken to extremes by contemporary critics such as Suarès (and Hoérée), whereas for Ravel it seemingly arose through considering national identities and musical mutations.

[55] 'Famous French Composer in London', 429.   [56] Schuller, *Early Jazz*, 3.

[57] Oliver and Kernfeld, 'Blues', 249.

[58] Ravel, 'Take Jazz Seriously!', 49. He also makes a pertinent point about common ground between classical and popular musics. See too Chapter 3, n. 9.

between jazz and western music, two musical worlds that one is more accustomed to oppose', but later claims that 'Ravel's step is constantly driven by a desire for confrontation between a foreign cultural language and his own style'.[59] Such a view perhaps overplays opposition and downplays *mélange*,[60] a point that will be clarified through analysis below. The following principles derive from Ravel's account of his ultimate jazz-inspired piece, the slow 'Blues' of the Violin Sonata.

Firstly, some borrowed elements are 'adopted' (an Eliot-style engagement with one's cultural surroundings, yet still suggestive of borrowing).[61] Within the eclectic approach there has to be assimilation of, or allusion to, the chosen external source(s), but such elements usually act simply as initial 'materials of construction'. Despite Ravel's problematizing of folklore in relation to national musics mentioned above, Perret considers that he still upholds the blues as folklore to be drawn upon.[62] (Her thinking matches that of Paul Oliver, who has long argued for this music as 'the creation of the people and not separate from the whole fabric of living'.)[63] In this context, we can reasonably assert that paradigms likely to be invoked are a scale with bended pitches,[64] especially at the third and seventh degrees, and the twelve-bar blues form. On the wider importance of certain fixities or predetermined elements which await melodic inspiration, we learn that Ravel's Violin Sonata 'was clearly outlined in his mind before the themes of the first and third movements had taken shape'.[65]

Secondly, materials must be subjected to 'minute stylization' and 'manipulation' (emergent hints of Bloom and his rewriting).[66] In 'Take Jazz Seriously!' Ravel refers to a 'stylized jazz, more French than American in character, but nevertheless influenced by your so-called "popular music"', and here Hodeir's limitations surface in his naïve surprise that composers 'betray a desire to adapt and stylize it [jazz]'.[67] Back in *Contemporary Music*, Ravel explains that the artwork requires gestation to create a 'mature conception where no detail has been left to chance'; concurring

---

[59] Perret, 'L'Adoption du jazz', 313: 'une cohabitation entre jazz et musique occidentale, deux mondes musicaux que l'on a plutôt coutume d'opposer'; 335: 'La démarche de Ravel est constamment mue par un désir de confrontation entre un langage culturel étranger et son propre style.'

[60] *Mélange* is achieved partly through Ravel's noting of an important commonality in national identity, whether from an American or a French perspective.

[61] Ravel, *Contemporary Music*, 140.   [62] *Ibid.*, 143; Perret, 'L'Adoption du jazz', 335.

[63] Paul Oliver, *The Story of the Blues* (London: Barrie & Rockliff, 1969), 6.

[64] For a perspicacious, early study, see again Sargeant, *Jazz: Hot and Hybrid*.

[65] 'Ravel says Poe Aided Him in Composition'; see too Ravel, 'On Inspiration' (1928), in Orenstein (ed.), *A Ravel Reader*, 389.

[66] Ravel, *Contemporary Music*, 140.   [67] Ravel, 'Take Jazz Seriously!', 49; Hodeir, *Jazz*, 251.

with Perret, we could argue that Ravel's approach opposes at least one fundamental feature of jazz: its improvisatory nature. Such improvisation is itself, however, a complex, finely nuanced matter. Kernfeld recognizes various contexts and types: 'solo'; 'collective', as employed in New Orleans style by the 'front line' players typically of trumpet, clarinet and trombone; 'paraphrase improvisation' or thematic ornamentation, as explored by Hodeir; a wide-ranging 'formulaic improvisation' with personalized hallmarks or licks; and lastly 'motivic improvisation'.[68] Furthermore, the notion of a completely spontaneous improvisation, without any pre-determined framework or deeply embedded harmonic knowledge, is itself a myth.[69]

Finally, 'national characteristics' and 'individualities' are imposed upon the borrowed material,[70] which is enveloped within a larger whole. In February 1928, Ravel stresses that 'my musical thinking is entirely national', and in *Contemporary Music* he develops this idea, hypothesizing about other composers, American and European, utilizing the same material, yet emerging with very different results.[71] In this extension of Ravel's notion of origins, the composers' national identities are privileged over those of the sources; in shaping ideas to their own ends, the 'individualities' of Milhaud or Stravinsky outweigh any debt to the 'materials appropriated' – inevitably again, at some level, a Bloomian misreading, whether through accident or design. Indeed, as Ravel noted elsewhere, faithful copying would be impossible but, fortuitously enough, originality often emerges through 'unintended unfaithfulness to a model'.[72] And beyond his most obvious exemplar, it is worth summarizing Ravel's assessment of the impact of jazz: 'No one can deny the rhythms of today. My recent music is filled with the influence of jazz. The "fox trot" and "blue" notes in my opera *L'Enfant et les sortilèges* are not the only examples'; in the Concerto in G too 'one can recognize syncopation, although it is refined'.[73] So, according to Ravel's theory, his compositional techniques involve a mixture of adoption (appropriation) and adaptation (distortion), followed by incorporation within individualized forms. Still viewed within that early jazz

---

[68] See Kernfeld, 'Improvisation', in *What to Listen for in Jazz*, 119–58; Hodeir, *Jazz*, 161–7. (See also my Chapter 3 on improvisation and Chapter 4 on the application of licks.)

[69] See Berliner, 'Introduction: Picking Notes Out of Thin Air?', in *Thinking in Jazz*, 1–17.

[70] Ravel, *Contemporary Music*, 140.

[71] Downes, 'Mr Ravel Returns'; Ravel, *Contemporary Music*, 140.

[72] Quoted by Roland-Manuel, 'Des valses à *La Valse* (1911–1921)', in Colette, Maurice Delage [et al.], *Maurice Ravel par quelques-uns de ses familiers* (Paris: Éditions du tambourinaire, 1939), 141–51: 145. (For full quotation, see page 205.)

[73] 'A Visit with Maurice Ravel', 473.

context, these principles may now be tested analytically across the parameters of instrumentation, timbre and texture; ragtime rhythm and form;
blues form and melody.

Instrumentation, timbre and texture

'A pliable set of sounds is at the heart of jazz,'[74] and on these instrumental
and textural fundamentals Ravel's practice demonstrates well his idea of
assimilation combined with adaptation. Although ragtime is often associated with piano (as immortalized on piano rolls), instrumental and sung
versions were also created: so in *L'Enfant*, Ravel's ragtime-foxtrot is introduced by a small bandlike ensemble (Fig. 28ff.). Three trombones, bass
clarinet, contrabassoon, bass drum, percussion, voice and piano are supplemented by upper wind (flutes, clarinet, trumpet and horns), before the
orchestral palette expands to embrace strings with their banjo- or guitarlike
plucked chords (Fig. 31ff.). Similarly, in the 'Blues', a banjo or guitar sound
is adopted, then adapted, as the violin's opening pizzicato triads (developed
at Figs. 7 and 10) are transferred to piano with increased percussive edge
(Fig. 1ff.). Fixity and precision in the piano are contrasted by pitch fluidity
and timbral variety in the violin: glissandos, 'sul tasto', 'sul ponticello' and
'sul Sol'. As Ravel pointed out, 'What I wanted to do in the violin sonata was
to accentuate the contrast between the percussive piano accompaniment
and the weaker violin melody.'[75] (The ultimate expression of this articulation is *Boléro* where the front-line melody players become consumed by a
rhythm section which finally destroys the work.) But while the piano
simulates a rhythm-bass section, this does not preclude its exploring subtle
timbres, notably the '[con] sord.' indications (Fig. 3ff.): thus this rereading
also confounds expectation. In the Concerto in G, Ravel felt he had
addressed the same issue through different means. Orenstein observes the
enactment of orchestral versus solo contrast in the first movement through
the presenting of harp and woodwind cadenzas – in jazz parlance, 'breaks' –
before the pianist finally gets his turn.[76] Additionally, a jazz-influenced
instrumentation is used to reiterate the main theme (Fig. 2ff.): trumpet,
supported by trombone (plus horns) and percussion, supplemented by
pizzicato strings. The second subject group also foregrounds a jazzlike
ensemble of E♭ clarinet, muted trumpet, piano and percussion (Fig. 5ff.),

---

[74] Kernfeld, *What to Listen for in Jazz*, 159.
[75] [Unsigned interview], 'Ten Opinions of Mr Ravel', *De Telegraaf* (6 April 1932), in
Orenstein (ed.), *A Ravel Reader*, 492–5: 494.
[76] *Ibid.*, 495.

while subjugated strings sustain a chord beneath. Instrumental combinations apart, Ravel revels in characterizing sound, such as the flutter-tonguing effects on winds in the recapitulation (Fig. 24ff.).

Ragtime rhythm and form

In contrast to Hodeir's dismissive view of Ravel as carried away in *L'Enfant* by 'picture-postcard exoticism', Orledge finds this work to be 'the most successful eclectic amalgam of jazz with different types of "otherness"'.[77] Certainly Ravel's rich fantasy vision was not a purist one, but there are, nonetheless, allusions to ragtime and foxtrot (Figs. 28–37). Similarly, Hodeir's further comments seem unduly negative, though conversely they point up Ravel's personalization: 'Maurice Ravel seems to have assimilated the rhythmic procedures of jazz [only] in a very elementary way.'[78] Granted that those distinctive dotted rhythms in *L'Enfant* derive from foxtrot rather than the syncopated patterns of a classic rag and so denote some transformation of the source, nevertheless foxtrot was an accepted variant in later rags from around World War I. Elsewhere, syncopated rhythms do find a place in the 'Blues' of the Violin Sonata, the first movement of the Concerto in G (Figs. 1, 4, 7 and 10) and the opening of the Left Hand Concerto (Fig. 1ff.). Within *L'Enfant*, at the 'Allegro non troppo' (Figs. 28–9; introduction) a striking rhythmic locus occurs which serves to mark time, to feature a vamping on the lugubrious tones of the contrabassoon, third trombone and bass drum, and to create a backing for the casual banter between the Teapot (black Wedgwood) and the Cup (Chinese). In correspondence with Colette, Ravel wondered: 'Perhaps you will object that you don't usually write American Negro slang. I, who don't know a word of English, will do just like you: I'll work it out.'[79] The result is a delightfully zany few bars whose English stresses are reversed and set against the metre, but whose nonsense declamation approaches the spirit of a 'Satchmo' scat, combined as Colette observed with the world of music hall. Benjamin Ivry suggests that the neat inclusion of 'How's your mug?' may have been courtesy of Victor de Sabata, *L'Enfant*'s original conductor.[80]

Formally, instrumental rags, operating in a 2/4 or 4/4 marchlike metre, tended to be built up in units as AABBCC and so on, comprising at least three different sixteen-bar themes or strains, each consisting of four

---

[77] Hodeir, *Jazz*, 256; Orledge, 'Evocations of Exoticism', 43.   [78] Hodeir, *Jazz*, 257.
[79] Orenstein (ed.), *A Ravel Reader*, 188.
[80] Benjamin Ivry, *Maurice Ravel: A Life* (New York: Welcome Rain, 2000), 130.

Table 5.1 *Comparison of raglike forms*

(a) Typical rag form		(b) Ravel's form in *L'Enfant* (Figs. 29–32)	
Music	Fig.	Music	Lyrics
A (16 bars – occasional minor key)	Fig. 29 (8 bars)	Theme A: Antecedent – melody on B♭ minor; A♭ minor: V^7	a: Black, and costaud, Black and chic,
		A♭ minor: [V^7]–I	a: Black, black, black, jolly fellow, jolly fellow, black,
		Consequent; V^7–I	b: I punch, Sir, I punch your nose,
		[I]	b: I punch,
A (16 bars – exact repetition)	Fig. 30 (7 bars)	Theme A': Antecedent – melody on E♭ major; A♭ minor: I	b: I knock out you, stupid chose!
		C♭ major: I (relative)	a': Black, black and thick, and vrai beau gosse,
		Consequent; shifting C major: V–I^7	b': I boxe you, I boxe you, b': I marm'lad' you.
B (16 bars – relative major)	Fig. 31^{-1}	Trio: Theme B – pentatonic (F major: V^7 – raised subdominant of relative)	c: Kengçafou, Mahjong, c: Kengçafou, Puis'kongkongpranpa, d: Çaohrâ, Çaohrâ, d: Çaohrâ, Çaohrâ [...]

four-bar phrases. Their themes were subjected to repetition and later reprise, and might feature introductions and brief interludes (both elements adopted by Ravel); extended patterns yielded formulae such as 'AABBAACC, AABBCCDD, and AABBCCA', starting in the tonic before moving to the subdominant for a trio section.[81] While Ravel's raglike conception was a free one, he theorizes nevertheless about 'a single couplet with refrain'[82] to which he adheres closely in practice. In miniaturist fashion, he halves the quantities of a standard raglike recipe and brings expected modulations forward; in fact, the small-scale lyric patterns may be seen as quartered, creating a hierarchy of relations as illustrated in Table 5.1. A truncated fifteen-bar section for the Teapot (Figs. 29–31) is portrayed

---

[81] See Edward A. Berlin, 'Ragtime', in Stanley Sadie (ed.), *The New Grove Dictionary of Music and Musicians*, 29 vols. (London: Macmillan, 2001), vol. XX, 755–9: 756. See too Chapter 1.

[82] Orenstein (ed.), *A Ravel Reader*, 188. (See 'Theme 2' above.)

literally as a black A♭ minor – the minor key being much rarer in ragtime – with the maximal seven flats. Theme A (Fig. 29), with its antecedent focused initially upon B♭ minor, is balanced by a modified repeat (Fig. 30) on its subdominant major, E♭ (for the pitch detail, see under 'Blues form and melody' below). Other subtle customization includes the overlaying of a lyric couplet, 'nose/chose', across a musical articulation. The ensuing Theme B for the Chinese Cup occupies a twenty-bar trio section (Figs. 31–3: sixteen bars, plus a four-bar interlude), which again is characterized literally as a much paler F major with one flat – effectively a Bloomian semitonal misreading of classic rag theory that would favour the subdominant of the relative, i.e. F♭. After Ravel reaches the expected relative – C♭ major, as the dominant of F♭ (Fig. 30^{+3}) – he pushes up a further chromatic step to C^7 (Fig. 31^{-2}), as the dominant of F. His extended reprise offers a nice twist in combining the main themes bitonally (Figs. 33–7), ultimately favouring the tonality of F. Tellingly, a similar black versus white musical conceit is played out in 'Aoua!', from *Chansons madécasses*, to denote the tensions between black and white peoples, which remain sadly irreconcilable in de Parny's text presented from a black perspective.

Blues form and melody

On the large scale, Ravel's 'Blues' movement employs a ternary, or modified sonata form,[83] but might there be evidence of localized blues form? Although Orledge perceives 'no signs of the conventional chord progressions associated with the twelve-bar negro blues', I want to test this idea further in relation to the introduction. Certainly there is profound manipulation, but the opening violin strumming does provide a kind of blues harmonic structure in simple crotchet pulses, as a paradigm, or primed canvas on which to paint. Kernfeld offers a model here in relating a basic blues structure to customized versions by Parker – *Blues for Alice* (1951) – and Mingus – 'Goodbye Pork Pie Hat' (1959).[84] Thus Table 5.2 compares a standard, schematic twelve-bar blues form[85] with Ravel's truncated ten-bar structure. Standard four-bar phrases are contracted to three-bar phrases

---

[83] Unlike Perret ('L'Adoption du jazz', 344), I do not perceive a separate development section at Fig. 5 (bar 63ff.), but this point still marks a B section on the dominant(s). Section A' (Fig. 9; bar 110) then recapitulates ideas from both earlier sections.

[84] Kernfeld, 'Blues Progression', 256. For recordings, see *Charlie Parker: The Complete Savoy and Dial Studio Recordings (1944–1948)* (Savoy 92911-2, 2000), and Charles Mingus, *Mingus Ah Um* (New York: Columbia 1959; reissued Columbia/Legacy CK 65512, 1998).

[85] See Kernfeld, 'Blues Progression', 255, and Richard Middleton, *Studying Popular Music* (Milton Keynes and Philadelphia, PA: Open University Press, 1990), 197–8.

Table 5.2 *Comparison of blues forms*

(a) Standard 12-bar blues				(b) Ravel's 10-bar blues				
| I	| (IV)	| I$^{(7)}$	| — |	| I	| I IV	| I V	|	
| IV$^{(7)}$	| —	| I$^{(7)}$	| — |	| I	| —	| —	|	
| V$^{(7)}$	| (IV)	| I$^{(7)}$	| V$^{(7)}$ ||	| I	| I IV	| I	| I V ||	

and, while the main I–IV–I–V–I progression is maintained, initially without added sevenths, the rate of harmonic change ebbs and flows. But Ravel's reading still employs a common blues-form variation known in the trade as the 'quick to four' – an early move to the subdominant – in bar 2 and ends with a dominant (bar 10), to effect what is aptly called a 'turnaround'.[86]

By contrast, across bars 11–26 (Figs. 1–2), Orledge privileges a sixteen-bar verse structure more akin to the songs of Gershwin or Kern, with a gentle rhythmic syncopation 'in the character of Gershwin's sanitisations of authentic rough jazz'. But consistent with Ravel's interventionist theory, Orledge identifies the end of this passage as classic Ravel: 'a cycle of fifths pattern typically spiced up with sevenths, ninths and judiciously spaced bitonality',[87] in the keys of A♭ and G. So we have more evidence of Ravel transforming and individualizing those 'constructive materials'; we shall return to these bars presently.

On the crucial expressive and fluid blues melody, Hodeir's observation, apropos the concertos, of 'appreciable melodic borrowings from the language of blues and spirituals' still holds sway.[88] Incipient blues third gestures, linear but spatially separated, are found in *L'Enfant* in the Teapot's line: a dotted minor phrase: B♭–C–D♭–C, B♭–C–D♭ (Fig. 29; 'Black, and costaud, Black and chic') is balanced by a major phrase a fourth higher: E♭–F–G–F, E♭–F–G (Fig. 30; 'I knock out you, stupid chose'), anticipated in the second half of the first phrase. Rag-cum-blues theory is closely played out – as major–minor mixture and partitioning between

[86] Blues association is highlighted in a recording where articulation of the piano's dotted rhythms approaches a kind of tripletized swing: Gérard Jarry (vn.), Georges Pludermacher (pf.), on *Maurice Ravel: Musique de chambre* (EMI 7243 5 69279-2 6, [recorded 1973] 1991). Conversely, the treatment in a more recent recording approximates a neobaroque double-dotting: Chantal Juillet (vn.), Pascal Rogé (pf.), on *3 Sonates pour violon* (London: Decca 448 612-2, 1996).

[87] Orledge, 'Evocations of Exoticism', 42. Even here, Ravel creates three phrases as a reconfigured blues form: A (1 + 5 bars), B (5½ bars), B (4½ bars), rather than AAB.

[88] Hodeir, *Jazz*, 252.

Example 5.1 Ravel, Piano Concerto in G, I: blues third treatment
   (a) Start of second subject, solo piano (Fig. 4, bars 1–5)
   (b) Second subject group (continued), solo piano (Fig. 8, bars 1–4)

lower and upper scalic segments – and is therefore less transformed. Similarly, in the Left Hand Concerto, an opening minor idea on contra-bassoon is balanced by a major reinflection (Fig. 2; see Example 5.2a and 5.2b). Later, we find a neat reworking of blues third combined with scalic partitioning, noted as 'one of the melodic lines most frequently used by old-time singers and players of the blues'.[89] Above a plucked string pedal on C, with oscillating major–minor third, E/D♯ (on viola), an 'espressivo' bassoon repeats the lower scalic segment: E♭–D–C (Fig. 28ff.), followed by the upper segment which emphasizes the flattened seventh: (G) B♭–A–G. But a doubled melodic/harmonic emphasis of the flattened seventh (Fig.1) shows Ravel effectively outdoing, or transforming, any blues model (rather like Milhaud): the ending of the contra's theme outlines a seventh chord, C, E, G, B♭, the root of which is the flattened seventh of the tonic, D. Meanwhile, in the Concerto in G, a vertical blues third occurs near the start of the poignant second subject on solo piano (first movement, Fig. 4; Example 5.1a): based harmonically upon the seventh degree, F♯, the major third, A♯, is asserted in the bass arpeggiation and pitted against a melodic A within a Phrygian collection on F♯ (i.e. F♯, G, A, B, C♯, D, E). But a more authentic linear expression is adopted with the resumption of the piano texture (first movement, Fig. 8ff.; Example 5.1b): in A major, set beneath an exquisite, accented seventh degree which falls to the sixth, G♯–F♯, the

---

[89] *Ibid.* Ravel commented on 'this jazz music' being brought to the fore in the scherzo: Michel-Dimitri Calvocoressi, 'M Ravel Discusses His Own Work', *Daily Telegraph* (11 July 1931).

bass arpeggiation presents the minor blue note resolving onto the major third: B♯/C♯.[90]

The ultimate locus is, however, the 'Blues', to which we return. Ravel surely understands the flexible melodic bending of seventh and third scalic degrees (horizontally, within a phrase), as demonstrated in the main theme (Figs. 1–2). We could categorize linear blue notes as an element 'adopted' (perhaps as Orledge suggests after Venuti and, following transfer of the bending to the piano, after Paul Whiteman's Orchestra), then 'stylized' and controlled. Pitch bending is particularly effective on violin, akin to the voice, where Ravel details the use of the A string and the playing of F/F♯–G (bars 12–13) with the second finger alone, the gesture reiterated and balanced on A–B♭/B (bars 15–16).

Still aligned with Ravel's theory, further manipulation and personalizing is revealed when the bitonal violin and piano parts are combined (bars 11–18; see Example 5.5a). The antecedent part of the melodic phrase: G–F/F♯–G, may be read as 8–7/7♯–8 in an upper modality on G. Alternatively, F♯–G might just be heard as G♭/G: an expressive, lingering blues seventh gesture in the lower modality of A♭, which is after all the key signature. The 'nostalgico' marking, apt given the innate melancholy and seriousness of the blues, also indicates something elusive or unattainable – 'real' jazz?[91] The consequent of this phrase (bars 14–16) emphasizes the minor seventh, F, via upper and lower neighbour notes (i.e. G and E♭), thence to the A–B♭/B gesture, which does feel to be a blues minor–major third inflection in G, supported by the repeated G, B dyad in the central texture. Of course, B may conceivably be heard as C♭, a flattened third in terms of the bass on A♭. So in a clever transformation, and with deceptive economy, Ravel achieves a blue effect with a theoretical single pitch: B [C♭], in relation to tonics on G and A♭.[92] Similarly, in the second phrase (bars 17–22), a major–minor third: C♭ [B]/B♭, in G (bars 17–18) coexists with a minor–major gesture: C♭/C, in A♭. A distinct blue-note complex emerges: see Table 5.3.

---

[90] This idea was rehearsed in the Left Hand Concerto (Fig. 8[+4]), where an F♯ arpeggiation features a major third falling to the minor: A♯/A, a gesture replayed on D♯/D within a B[7] harmony (Fig. 9[+2]).

[91] Abbate has questioned, in personal discussion, why Ravel used 'nostalgico' here if his motivation in adopting jazz was essentially modernist. Ravel's music is temporally complex and invariably engages with the past in some way. Despite his claim that the 'Blues' was more Parisian than American, the very title might reasonably indicate empathy with the history of an oppressed people (as in the *Chansons madécasses*, composed concurrently). The music also layers the serious and the more frivolous.

[92] Harmonically, Ravel's use of combined fifths a semitone apart (A♭–E♭; G–D) apes that of the typical flattened fifth in jazz (albeit notated as A♭–D). I am grateful to Julian Horton for this point.

Table 5.3 *Ravel's melodic-harmonic blue-note complex*

Blue notes:	Minor–major thirds		Minor–major sevenths	
Pitches:	B♭/B	B [C♭]/C	F/F♯	F♯ [G♭]/G
Tonality:	G	A♭	G	A♭

On a larger scale, malleability of material is pursued through five variant readings of the main 'Blues' theme,[93] as a composed-out improvisation – a contradiction in terms, yet implying a greater heeding of this fundamental jazz concept in Ravel's practice than in his theory (as discussed above). Varied repetition also occurs in the Concerto in G (first movement), where a higher profile is afforded to improvisatory notions courtesy of the harp's *Quasi cadenza* designation (Fig. 22), followed by the *Cadenza* proper (Fig. 26). It is a special factor in the Left Hand Concerto, where the thematic material only gradually becomes focused. Until confirmed by a forthright orchestral repetition (Fig. 5), we wonder whether the piano's cadenzalike entrance (Fig. 4), as an early jazz break, denotes a more distant derivative of the contrabassoon's opening melody (with intervallic expansion through to an octave), or the arrival point of 'true' thematic identity. This variation process is illustrated in Example 5.2.

Discrepancies in practising jazz

Since Ravel's theory generally postdates his practice, extensive correlation is unsurprising, but interestingly elements of his practice are glossed over in theory: in particular several overt cross-references between his music and that of others, as unmediated 'adoption' – almost quotation. So, as with the first relationship investigated in the first half of this case study, we find some untransformed aspects, although they are more exceptional here.

On predictable territory, there are striking similarities between Ravel's jazz practice and Gershwin's: one dimension in which Ravel's music is notably Americanized. We can compare a piano figuration in the 'Blues' (Fig. 5ff.), featuring reaccented three-quaver groupings as a melodic third progression: (F♯–G♯) A–G♯–F♯, with a repeated three-quaver accompaniment

---

[93] Perret too discusses 'variation thématique': 'L'Adoption du jazz', 344. As for a blues-form complex, we might view the first three variants of the main theme that comprise section A as a medium-scale rereading of blues form (or indeed the complete ternary structure in the same way).

Example 5.2 Ravel, Piano Concerto for the Left Hand: thematic variation
  (a) Introductory theme – minor (bars 2–4; contrabassoon)
  (b) Introductory theme – major (Fig. 2, bars 1–2)
  (c) First subject proper (Fig. 4^{+3}; piano)

from *Rhapsody in Blue*: B♭–A–G; B–A–G (Figs. 9–11); see too Example 4.8b.[94] Ravel's dotted figure on piano: C♯–D♯–C♯–E[♮] (Fig. 6ff.) echoes the refrain from Gershwin's 'The Man I Love' (or is it the opening verse of 'Fascinating Rhythm', or possibly Milhaud's 'Fugue' from *La Création du monde*?). Equally, we could relate it back to the woodwind (bass clarinet, flute) and vocal figurations of the Teapot in *L'Enfant* (Figs. 28–31), or forward to the opening theme of the Left Hand Concerto: E–F♯–E–G (–F♯–A). These loci all derive from, or extend, that inspirational 'four-note figure' identified by Hodeir, and introduced in Chapter 4.[95] Other close Gershwin references include the syncopated rising melody in E major, with a prominent sixth scalic degree, from the Concerto in G (first movement, Fig. 7) and an idea in A minor from *Rhapsody in Blue*, as compared by David Schiff.[96] Beyond their shared overall contour, both four-bar phrases are subdivided as 1 + 1 + 2.

We also find unexpected, untheorized similarities, for example the resemblance of the 'espressivo' imitative theme in the second subject group of the

---

[94] Ravel uses other three-note hemiola figures, ostinato-like, near the start of the Concerto in G (Fig. 1ff.): G–E–D, in even quavers on upper woodwind and: C–E–D(–C), in a counterpointed dotted augmentation on bassoons and horns. See too Schiff, *Gershwin: Rhapsody in Blue*, 18, 20.

[95] Hodeir, *Jazz*, 254. See too Examples 4.4 and 4.5, and Example 8.1.

[96] Schiff, *Gershwin: Rhapsody in Blue*, 20.

Example 5.3 Comparison between Ravel, Concerto in G and Bruch, Violin
Concerto

(a) Ravel (I, Fig. 5, bars 1–2)

(b) Bruch (II, Adagio, bars 16–20)

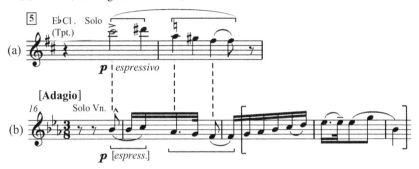

Concerto in G (first movement, Fig. 5ff.) to the powerful 'Adagio' theme
from Max Bruch's Violin Concerto No. 1 in G minor; see Example 5.3. The
main intervallic relations and stresses are very similar, with the tritonal
descent around the apex of Ravel's melody suggesting an expressive exaggeration of Bruch's major third, 'jazzed' à la Gershwin.

Further unexpected correspondence exists between Ravel's 'Blues' and a
lighthearted piano piece by Mayerl: his 'Marigold' (1927), an item held in
Ravel's record collection in a performance by Carmen Guilbert.[97] Since
Guilbert's Paris recording was not made until July 1931,[98] it is reasonable to
assume that the similarities are effectively generic within a raglike mould,
rather than connoting Mayerl's influence upon Ravel, though Ravel might
conceivably have heard the former's music live in 1927. Whatever the cause
and effect, from a hermeneutic stance, Ravel's raglike dotted, descending
figuration (Fig. 3ff.: bars 43–5 of the piano part) may usefully be compared
with Mayerl's main theme (bar 5ff., following a brief introduction), as

[97] Billy Mayerl, 'Marigold', from *Syncopated Impressions*; Carmen Guilbert, piano (Pathé X
98042). Guilbert also recorded Ravel's 'Alborada del gracioso' in 1935 (Pathé (Fr) PAT23);
see Orenstein (ed.), *A Ravel Reader*, 611.

[98] Personal communication from John Watson (21 April 2008). Watson, who compiled the
discography for Peter Dickinson, *Marigold: The Music of Billy Mayerl* (Oxford and New
York: Oxford University Press, 1999), describes Guilbert's renditions of Mayerl's pieces
as 'competent, if perhaps slightly cautious, performances'. Ravel's apparent appreciation
of Mayerl was reciprocated by Mayerl on BBC Radio's *Desert Island Discs* in 1958 when
he requested 'Laideronnette' from *Ma mère l'Oye*, plus works by Stravinsky and
Milhaud.

Example 5.4 Comparisons between Ravel, Sonata for Violin and Piano, 'Blues' and Mayerl, *Syncopated Impressions*, 'Marigold'
(a) Melodic comparison: Ravel (bars 43–5) and Mayerl (bars 5–7)
(b) Harmonic comparison: Ravel (bar 46) and Mayerl (bar 8)

demonstrated in Example 5.4. Apart from the general melodic-rhythmic contour, commonalities include an upper neighbour-note figure, the motive C, B♭, G and dotted notes F–E♭ (amid a fondness for major seconds and fourths). Another instance concerns the harmonic gestures which follow: Ravel's E♭^{9} bass treatment (bars 46–7) and Mayerl's more characterized, fruity chromatic reading on B♭^{13} (bars 8 and 16). Both feature the chordal root in the bass (beat 1), followed by a tenor stepwise descent (beats 2–4), with inner pedal notes that span a major second: the two sets of bars could comfortably belong to the same piece.

As for possible setting of agendas, Ravel's main 'Blues' theme (Fig. 1ff.) cannily anticipates Gershwin's 'Summertime' aria from his opera *Porgy and Bess* (1935). This idea develops Orledge's suggestion of stylistic similarities between Ravel's 'Blues' and Kern or Gershwin songs, though it must be remembered that such songs were never strictly jazz or blues. We might argue for a more finely nuanced triangulation of similarity.[99] Undoubtedly,

---

[99] Sonic similarities are especially compelling when comparing the Violin Sonata recording by Juillet and Rogé (see n. 86) with a 1941 recording of 'Summertime' by Mabel Mercer (voice) and Cy Walter (pf.), reissued on *'S Wonderful: Songs of George Gershwin* (Naxos Nostalgia 8.120828, 2005). One of the most respected studies of Gershwin's music, with

Example 5.5 Ravel's apparent anticipation of Gershwin
   (a) Ravel, Sonata for Violin and Piano, 'Blues' (bars 12–16)
   (b) Gershwin, *Porgy and Bess*, 'Summertime' (Fig. 17^{-1})

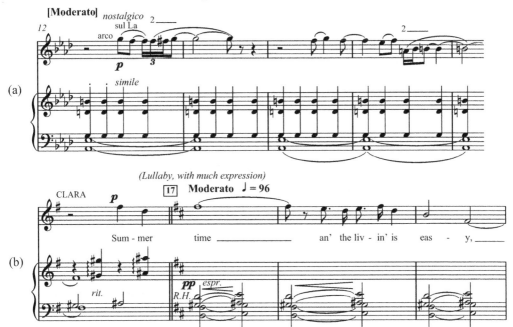

the melodic influence of songs from Gershwin's *Lady, Be Good* (1924), including 'Fascinating Rhythm' and 'The Man I Love' – in fact discarded from the show – is felt in Ravel's 'Blues' (heard by Gershwin in 1928), which seemingly then acts as a catalyst for Gershwin in 'Summertime'; see Example 5.5a and 5.5b. (Intriguingly, as an extra link, Mayerl had been the soloist for the London premiere of *Rhapsody in Blue* in October 1925.) Ravel's marking of 'nostalgico' well befits the bittersweet recollections of summer, and is maintained in Gershwin's marking of Clara's lullaby 'with much expression'. The two loci share a quiet, spacious lyricism and gentle 'Moderato'. Melodically, both open with a sustained pitch, reinforced from beneath – by a second or third interval, respectively – to form the antecedent, which leads to a syncopated (or dotted) descending consequent. Portamentos act as final expressive gestures in each piece. Harmonically, both are supported by significant fifth intervals.

a chapter on *Porgy and Bess*, does not mention these similarities: Steven Gilbert, *The Music of Gershwin* (New Haven, CT and London: Yale University Press, 1995), 182–207. Gilbert does, however, note references in *Porgy* back to *Rhapsody in Blue*: 194, and so the triangulation continues.

As a second triangulation, while Ravel's guitarlike plucking in the 'Blues' surely betrays the influence of typical Spanish models, in turn it looks forward to the jazz manouche practice of Reinhardt. Balancing this, Ravel's violin treatment may, according to Orledge, reveal the influence of Venuti, but it neatly anticipates the young Grappelli. An American number by Walter Donaldson with lyrics by Gus Kahn entitled 'I've Had My Moments', recorded in September 1935 by Grappelli and His Hot Four, features a very similar punctuated rhythmic-chordal background on guitar which supports a languid, floating melody on violin.[100]

Conclusion: jazz Gallicized and 'Ravelized'

Scrutiny of Ravel's theory in relation to the complexities of early jazz has shown how the composer's impressive cultural grasp makes for close correspondence (Eliot-like?), coupled with some transformation: a few distortions may have been unintentional; other idiosyncrasies are in line with his argument for compositional 'individuality' (more Bloom-like?). In the main theory–practice(–actuality) relationship, analysis of Ravel's compositional techniques has confirmed his stated transformative principles, amid some untheorized similarities between his music and potential sources. Ultimately, this sophisticated theory–practice of jazz (broadly interpreted) needs to be understood as part of a necessary response and contribution to modernism itself and as one privileged form of eclecticism. It operates in a similar fashion to Ravel's fascination with machines, or his lifelong love of Spain and the Basque Country. Despite, or perhaps because of, his strong attraction to Gershwin's example, Ravel was not looking to convey an authentic jazz; instead he used his enthusiastic reaction to it as a way of accessing new exotic colourings and timbral-textural finds to inflect his own voice.

The result of this border crossing, and the arrival point of Ravel's theory, is a further developed French music which retains its national core. It exists within what was already becoming, thanks especially to members of Les Six, a distinctly Gallic tradition of jazzed art music. Blues acts as an expressive vehicle for Ravel to pursue an archetypal French musical concern with 'la mélodie' while, harmonically, his seventh chords and certain textures owe much to Debussy, the violin pizzicato in his 'Blues' being reminiscent of 'Ibéria' from *Images*.[101]

[100] Original recording (Paris: Decca P77538, F 6150, 1935); reissued on *Stéphane Grappelli*, 2 vols. (Naxos Jazz Legends 8.120688, 2003), vol. II: *Swing from Paris, Original Recordings 1935–1943*.
[101] DeVoto, 'Harmony in the Chamber Music', 115.

As important, the jazz-inspired repertory maintains a personal core and so is 'Ravelized': the frequent harmonic fifth intervals in the 'Blues', A♭–E♭ combined with G–D, act as a hallmark in Ravel's musical language from *Daphnis et Chloé* (1912) onwards.[102] This versatile fifth object serves to connote the ancient and, even more widely, a blended otherness not only of the past and the exotic, but of the classical and the popular. (Ravel's literalism in *L'Enfant* or in 'Aoua!', in portraying black and white relations, is another stylistic hallmark.) And if we criticize Ravel for his unacknowledged near-quotation of others, we should at least recognize this as part of his own aesthetic of recycling – especially postwar, since he also quotes himself. In the 'Blues', both the effective strumming, which anticipates *Boléro*, and the raglike, melodic fifth tic that begins and ends the piano part are rereadings of *L'Enfant* (Figs. 31–7).

Crucially, Ravel's engagement with jazz gives as much as it takes. While the American premiere of the Violin Sonata, played by Joseph Szigeti and the composer at the Gallo Theater in New York, offered a most convenient springboard for the 1928 tour, Ravel's invocation of jazz was of longer-term consequence. It created an impetus for, and a key to our understanding of, his late works from *Boléro* to the piano concertos. Arguably, it played a role in his final work before terminal illness silenced his creativity: the third song, 'Chanson à boire', from *Don Quichotte à Dulcinée* (1932–3) opens with a prominent melodic outline of a seventh chord that echoes the Left Hand Concerto (Fig. 1). Furthermore, aspects of Ravel's 'Blues' anticipate wider developments of the 1930s, both American and French (hints of Klein's 'historical reversal'): the main melody has been shown to resonate with Gershwin's 'Summertime', yet to come, and the combination of jazzed violin lyricism plus strumming accompaniment presages the captivating soundworld of Grappelli and Reinhardt. But for all his adopting and adapting of elements of American jazz, the last word should be this: 'I venture to say that nevertheless it is French music, Ravel's music, that I have written.'[103]

---

[102] Other reminders of *Daphnis* in jazzed contexts include the rippling LH accompaniment of sextuplet semiquavers (down–up contour) in the cadenza of the Concerto in G (first movement, Figs. 26–8) and the primordial opening of the Left Hand Concerto, where a quartal harmony in cellos and basses, pitched as the bass open strings (E, A, D, G), is 'horizontalized' as sextuplet semiquavers (up–down contour). With its foreboding start, the Left Hand Concerto continues a fatalistic strand in Ravel's writing, apparent in *Daphnis* and resurfacing in *La Valse* and *Boléro*.

[103] Ravel, *Contemporary Music*, 140.

PART III

The impact of French music upon jazz (1925–1965)

6 Hylton's interwar 'jazzed' arrangements of French classics

In contrast to the French concert-music-based chapters and their early jazz enquiries (Part II), this case study turns the tables by exploring the imaginative usage made of French music by the significant interwar British jazz/dance bandleader Jack Hylton. Although Hylton was much influenced by American cultural and commercial precedent – in short, Americanization[1] – this inclusion still points up that America did not have an exclusive monopoly on jazz. It also acts as a pivot, to articulate the two halves of this French music–jazz project, in terms of time frame and approach. Across a more extended canvas, this study picks up from my earlier coverage of Hylton and France between the two world wars,[2] including his compromised attempt to create a 'jazzed' dance band version of Stravinsky's *Mavra*, presented at the Paris Opéra in 1931.[3] The former article urged further study of Hylton's 'jazzed' rereadings of classical pieces, to contribute 'to a central, ongoing debate about the nature of boundaries and (con)fusion between so-called classical and popular musics'.[4] Part of that brief was fulfilled by my narration of the story of *Mavra* and examination of the associated interactions via theories of conceptual blending, while this case study constitutes the second response to that call.[5] Among arrangements of Rachmaninoff, Gershwin and Křenek's *Jonny spielt auf*,[6] French

---

[1] See James J. Nott, *Music for the People: Popular Music and Dance in Interwar Britain* (Oxford and New York: Oxford University Press, 2002), 225.

[2] Mawer, '"Parisomania"? Jack Hylton and the French Connection'.

[3] Mawer, 'Jazzing a Classic'. The main portion of *Mavra* selected for arrangement was from Figs. 44–92.

[4] Mawer, '"Parisomania"? Jack Hylton and the French Connection', 306.

[5] This study is a further research outcome of a Jack Hylton and France Project at Lancaster University, which houses the Jack Hylton Archive (JHA). It does not revisit the previous theoretical discussion, for which readers are referred to the 'Critical approach' and subsequent analysis in Mawer, 'Jazzing a Classic', 160–1, 162ff. A later section on 'Hylton and Ravel's *Boléro*' is reprinted, with kind permission of the *Journal of the Royal Musical Association*, from Mawer, '"Parisomania"? Jack Hylton and the French Connection', 302–3.

[6] See Jack Hylton (in interview with Perceval Graves), 'Taking or Inflicting Pains', *Melody Maker and British Metronome* (May 1928), 513–14, in Jack Hylton Press Cuttings 1928–31, JHA. Hylton recorded two double-sided 10-inch discs from Křenek's jazz opera *Johnny Strikes Up*, following a request from the German firm Elektron, despite being sceptical about the venture, since in his view 'the work is hopelessly old-fashioned in its rhythmical aspects, and altogether too discordant for *my* ears' (original italics): 514.

pieces subsequently 'jazzed' within a source–product relationship included those by the French-naturalized Chopin, Georges Bizet (1838–75), the female salon composer Cécile Chaminade (1857–1944), Massenet and Ravel.

Hylton and jazz

The identification of Hylton's material as loosely jazz-based is itself problematic and largely dependent upon later 1920s perceptions of dance band music, such as that of the American Paul Whiteman, or fellow Briton and director of the BBC Dance Orchestra Jack Payne, as a kind of jazz. With reference to such bands, Messager, known for his lighthearted operettas, enthused: 'J'adore le jazz';[7] meanwhile, the English-speaking press dubbed Hylton, as they did Whiteman, the 'Czar of Jazz' and Hylton's rereading of Stravinsky as a 'Jazz Version of [an] Operatic Excerpt'.[8] Similarly, the French press promoted the equivalent expression 'le roi du jazz' when Hylton received the prestigious Légion d'honneur in 1932,[9] and announced Hylton's début at the Palais Garnier as 'Le Jazz à l'Opéra'.[10]

Part of the reason, historically, for blurred boundaries between jazz and dance band in Britain and France, especially during the 1920s, was because African-American early jazz was still relatively unknown outside America.[11] Ellington was not heard in Paris (or Britain) until summer 1933, when Hylton helped to arrange his European tour.[12] Equally, what reception there

---

[7] André Messager cited in Maurice Montabré, 'J'adore le jazz ⋯', *L'Intransigeant* (12 June 1926).

[8] See an uncredited review, 'Czar of Jazz', *The People* (22 January 1928), and 'Stravinsky and Jack Hylton: Jazz Version of Operatic Excerpt', *The Times* (29 January 1931), in Jack Hylton Press Cuttings, 1928–31. Although the JHA provides a very rich resource, the many volumes of press cuttings were set up for promotional not scholarly reasons and often lack author credits, or page numbers.

[9] Uncredited review, 'Jack Hilton [*sic*] a le ruban rouge', *Indépendant* ([Pau], 14 January 1932). Coverage by Le Loup de Dent[elle], 'Cours et leçons', *Comœdia* (14 January 1932) presented Hylton in glowing terms: 'L'animateur de jazz le plus prestigieux de notre époque, le légendaire Jack Hylton, roi du rythme syncopé' ('The most prestigious animator of jazz of our time, the legendary Jack Hylton, king of syncopated rhythm').

[10] Clément Vautel, 'Le Jazz à l'Opéra', *Cyrano*, 350 (1 March 1931), 1, in Jack Hylton Continental Tours, 1930–35. See too an uncredited review: 'Jack Hylton à l'Opéra', *La Baune* ([Paris], 18 February 1931): 'La Révolution est un événement, le jazz en est un autre [⋯] La musique de jazz est souvent une conversation: le xylophone rit; le banjo bavarde [⋯] Jack Hylton connaît leur langage mystérieuse' ('The Revolution is one event; jazz is another [⋯] Jazz music is often a conversation: the xylophone laughs; the banjo chatters [⋯] Jack Hylton understands their mysterious language').

[11] Nott, *Music for the People*, 129.

[12] See Tucker (ed.), *The Duke Ellington Reader*, 67, 73, 75, 76, 82, 87.

was proved distinctly mixed: some deep appreciation of this improvisatory art and a thinly veiled racism.[13] This background helps to explain Hylton's own early equivocation over the term, confiding that: 'Whenever you see quotations marks round the word "jazz" you can depend upon it that a dance musician is talking.'[14] Hylton's likely fear was that his typical audience, with its relatively conservative tastes, would be alienated by the categorization.[15] His initial distancing also highlights the distinctiveness of his British-based musical contribution: his concern to give repertory 'the British touch'.[16] This same scepticism operated in reverse in respect of African-American jazz musicians' perceptions of commercialized dance band music. Despite his early caution, Hylton's attitude softened alongside those of his listeners as jazz gained in popularity, as can be detected across articles that he wrote between 1927 and 1939.[17] By 1932, in 'Naissance et vie du jazz', Hylton was explicitly acknowledging the black American, African origins of his band's repertory, while offering plausible reworkings of 'hot' items such as Handy's phenomenal *St. Louis Blues* and the ubiquitous *Tiger Rag*, as well as arrangements of Ellington's music.[18]

As for the dance band genre, Jackson refers in a circumspect way to an 'upbeat orchestral music called jazz', alluding to a review which opined that

---

[13] On the complex perceptions of jazz in France, see Jackson, *Making Jazz French*, 89–97, and the precursor text: Jeffrey H. Jackson, 'Making Jazz French: The Reception of Jazz Music in Paris, 1927–1934', *French Historical Studies*, 25/1 (Winter 2002), 149–70.

[14] Jack Hylton, 'Jazz Music: Is the Expression Objectionable?' *Midland Daily Telegraph* (6 March 1931), n.p., including a section on 'The Development of Jazz' in the form of dance music.

[15] It was crucial to Hylton's entrepreneurial strategy to give an audience what it wanted. Hylton ('Taking or Inflicting Pains', 513) considers 'hot' records the domain of 'highly sophisticated' listeners and that, if one analysed English gramophone record sales, 'the sales of the "sweet melody" numbers [would] easily exceed those of the "hot" records'.

[16] Jack Hylton, 'The British Touch', *Gramophone* (September 1927), 146.

[17] See Jack Hylton, '"Jazz Only in Its Infancy": Mr Jack Hylton Replies to Mr Gillespie', *Nottinghamshire Guardian* (4 February 1927), in Jack Hylton Press Cuttings, 1926–7; Jack Hylton, 'Naissance et vie du jazz', *Le Courrier musical et théâtral* (15 March 1932), n.p.; Jack Hylton, 'Jazz: The Music of the Masses – An Appeal to the Critics', *News Chronicle* (22 February 1933), n.p., and Jack Hylton, 'The High Finance of Jazz', *Rhythm*, 13/136 (January 1939), 3–7.

[18] *St. Louis Blues*, arranged by Ternent; vocalist Billy Munn (Decca F-3239: recorded London, 5 October 1932). *Tiger Rag*, in *Good Old Dances* (HMV C-1784: recorded Small Queen's Hall, London, 15 October 1929); arranged by Léo Vauchant (HMV B-5789: 10 January 1930); arranged by Major Williams (HMV BD-5128: 24 August 1936). Hylton also acted as compère for a series of recorded *Jazz Histories*: No. 1 *Tiger Rag*, No. 2 *St. Louis Blues*, showcasing excerpts of American and British recordings (HMV C-2885: Autumn 1936). The JHA holds an *Ellington Medley* and an arrangement entitled *Ellingtonia* (Decca F-3764: recorded London, 18 November 1933).

'Hylton's approach to jazz resembled more traditional European forms of music in spite of his clowning on stage'.[19] In fact, this latter observation supports the relevance of the Jack Hylton Orchestra (JHO) to this enquiry, since one main criterion for the selection and treatment of jazz loci is the inherent strength of reference to French classical repertory.

Certainly, this is to propose a more inclusive usage of the term *jazz* than some today would vouch for, but I would counter that there is no single, authentic definition – such would be to construct a historical falsehood; that one of the strengths of jazz is its sheer diversity and ability to keep reinventing itself through time, location and cultural context: African-American and white; art music and commercial. While not downplaying what are profound differences, I argue that Hylton's 'modern syncopated music'[20] still has a place historically at one end of an extended spectrum called jazz.[21] Nuancing things further, we might posit that Hylton's popular brand of 'sweet' jazz mediated between light classics, on the one hand, and so-called 'hot' jazz, on the other.[22] Arguably, his practice also contributed to making early jazz more accessible, preparing the ground in France for the extraordinary creative jazz forces of Ellington, Armstrong, Hawkins and others.[23]

Hylton's mixing of musics and affinity with France

Mixing jazz, popular and classical musics, French or otherwise, was for Hylton as much a canny entrepreneurial move as an interest in intertextuality, stylistic fusion, or any 'deliberate attempt to bridge the gap between popular and classical music'.[24] In response to changing circumstance, Hylton 'appeared to know how to develop his band when they moved

---

[19] Jackson, *Making Jazz French*, 111; Edmond Wellhoff, 'Le Jazz et la vie', *Vu* (14 May 1930), n.p.

[20] See Leighton Lucas, 'What I Hate in "Jazz"', *Melody Maker and British Metronome* (February 1928), 137–9: 137.

[21] Otherwise, it is surprisingly easy for this dance band category to become the ignored domain of musicology and sociocultural history, not quite 'fitting' either at the jazz or classical ends. In that scenario, we lose much rich material for enquiry. See Derek B. Scott, 'Music, Culture and Society: Changes in Perspective', in Derek B. Scott (ed.), *Music, Culture, and Society: A Reader* (Oxford University Press, 2000), 1–19; and 'Incongruity and Predictability in British Dance Band Music of the 1920s and 1930s', in *From the Erotic to the Demonic: On Critical Musicology* (New York: Oxford University Press, 2003), 80–100.

[22] On a triangulation between classical music, popular music ('sweet' jazz) and ('hot') jazz, see Mawer, '"Parisomania"? Jack Hylton and the French Connection', 280–4.

[23] Both Hawkins and Henderson were members of Hylton's band in May 1939, while Robeson was a vocalist for the band as early as September 1931. See Band Members list in JHA.

[24] Quoted from Peter Faint: www.jackhylton.com/ (section on Hylton and Stravinsky).

from the dance halls onto the concert platform and one tactic he and his team of arrangers used was to borrow from the "classical" world, producing what became known as "light classics".[25] Thus he endeavoured to keep giving his increasingly diverse audiences a little of what they particularly liked: 'The public rightly expects from a dance band good music and a certain amount of extraneous entertainment,' including showmanship.[26] In so doing, he potentially widened the appeal of classical music, with a variety of approachable and at least half-familiar repertory presented in bite-sized chunks, like an early version of Classic FM!

While not Hylton's main priority, such compositional borrowings still constituted a kind of cultural eclecticism, resulting in a range of effects, including stylistic blending, collage or even contradiction, in tandem with new emergent meanings. Association between jazz/dance music and classical music could create a sense of cachet or nostalgia.[27] In this spirit, we might include Rachmaninoff's preludes in C♯ minor and G minor, 'specially arranged for Jack Hilton's [sic] orchestra' by Peter Yorke which, together with Stravinsky's *Mavra* (see Appendix 6.1 to this chapter), were conceived as part of the 'concert of jazz' programme for February 1931 'when jazz is making its entry at the Opéra'.[28] In their recorded versions, these preludes – especially the C♯ minor – presented as somewhat bizarre pastiche, featuring a serious Russian string sound with strict tempi, yet emphasizing syncopation and showcasing a Wurlitzer organ (see Appendix 6.1).[29] At the cusp of the classical–jazz intersection, we find effective rereadings of George Gershwin, with a detectably British accent: the Gershwin/Whiteman *Rhapsody in Blue*, compressed to meet the confines of a 10-inch disc (R27: Appendix 6.1);[30] a *Valse moderne* (Appendix 6.1); *Gershwin Medley*;[31]

---

[25] *Ibid.*

[26] Jack Hylton, 'Over Hurdles – Into Ditches: What Bands Should Avoid and What's Wanted', *Melody Maker* (October 1929), 921.

[27] See Mawer, '"Parisomania"? Jack Hylton and the French Connection', 282–3.

[28] Louis Schneider, 'Music and Musicians', *New York Herald* ([Paris] 15 February 1931). It is interesting that Yorke did still arrange the C♯ minor prelude, despite the misgivings of fellow arranger Lucas ('What I Hate in "Jazz"'), who dismissed the work as a 'pseudo-classic'.

[29] Such arrangements were part of a wider tradition: George Linus Cobb paraphrased the C♯ minor prelude in what became *Russian Rag* (1918); the repertory of the Southern Syncopated Orchestra (c. 1920) included a 'ragged' performance of the piece, which was also quoted in Whiteman's 'Hot Lips' (1922).

[30] *Rhapsodie* [sic] *in Blue* is included in various continental programmes, including one for a 'Concert donné par Jack Hylton et son Orchestre', at the Exposition internationale de Liège (21–22 August 1930): loose programme, JHA.

[31] *Gershwin Medley* (JHA file no: G43) comprises published portions of 'The Man I Love' and ''S Wonderful', plus MS sections.

instrumentalized songs from *Lady, Be Good*;[32] plus "'S Wonderful' from *Funny Face* (1927).[33] *Lady, Be Good* and *Funny Face* were two of the Broadway musicals that Gershwin co-wrote with his brother Ira Gershwin. I shall explore further the use of French repertory to create nostalgia and accrue prestige for the band.

Theoretically, and quite commonly in strict jazz practice, classical stereo-types could be parodied for comedic effect – another crucial dimension since Hylton's fare involved entertainment. 'Meadow Lark'[34] quotes the famous opening figure of 'Morning' from Grieg's *Peer Gynt* suite, with its 6/8 running rhythm swung as a crotchet plus two quavers, thereby high-lighting what Derek Scott would identify as an 'incongruity', presented amid a flurry of whistling larks; in this way, Hylton conspires jokingly with his audience that this light approach 'is also our preferred style of music'.[35]

Hylton's music was received by audiences and critics,[36] in dance and concert halls, as well as in the parlour via the gramophone, and inevitably it created questions about the blending of styles, genres and consequent meanings. While it was enthusiastically received by many, who praised Hylton's discernment in selecting his band's classical repertory – 'Let's also note the respect shown by these musicians to classical music in sup-pressing entirely from their programme those detestable transcriptions of famous pieces for dance band'[37] – sceptics still perceived a high/low

---

[32] *Lady, Be Good*, Selection, Part 1, including 'I'd Rather Charleston' (HMV C-1261); Selection, Part 2, including 'Little Jazz Bird' and 'Fascinating Rhythm' (HMV C-1261: both recorded Hayes, Middlesex, 14 April 1926). MS in JHA. There is also an earlier vocal arrangement (HMV B-5042: recorded 29 March 1926). 'Lady, Be Good' and 'I'd Rather Charleston' were programmed at the Royal Albert Hall concert 'The Happy New Year' Ball in aid of the Middlesex Hospital on 31 December 1926: JHPR9701275.

[33] "'S Wonderful' featured vocalists Jack Hylton, Hugo Rignold and Chappie d'Amato (HMV B-5536: recorded Hayes, Middlesex on 24 August 1928). MS in JHA. Hugo Rignold (1905–76), who was primarily a violinist, later became quite well known as a classical conductor (including of the City of Birmingham Symphony Orchestra). I wish to thank Arnold Whittall for making this connection.

[34] 'Meadow Lark' (HMV B-5199: recorded 13 January 1927).

[35] Scott, 'Incongruity and Predictability', 95. Greig's 'Morning' also begins Hylton's satirical version of 'Run, Rabbit, Run!' (HMV BD-5523: recorded 14 September 1939), corrupted to 'Run, Adolf, Run!' following the lead of Flanagan and Allen, who sang in the original show, *The Little Dog Laughed*.

[36] Audiences too had opinions on the dance band/popular music they heard; it was not merely 'a mass audience passively consuming the mass-produced commodities of a "culture industry"': Scott, 'Music, Culture and Society', 1.

[37] Stéfan Cordier, 'Jack Hylton', *La Revue musicale* ([Brussels] 29 January 1929): 'Remarquons aussi le respect que témoigne ces musiciens à la musique classique en supprimant tout à fait de leur programme ces détestables transcriptions de morceaux célèbres pour orchestre de danse.'

incompatibility.[38] Pierre Leroi's assertion constitutes one of the more extreme critiques and, while I would argue that its conclusions are unjustified (despite the real difficulties in jazzing *Mavra*),[39] it is useful as a provocative foil: 'The mixing of different genres always turns out badly. The jazz version of *Mavra* has just confirmed this truth in striking fashion. Let jazz stay as it is, played by specialist musicians who know the technique; and let other musicians keep to their own genres where they are sufficiently distinguished.'[40] Conversely, another French reviewer perceived an intriguing connection between Hylton's jazz and Satie's modernism: 'Let's add that one finds there certain effects of ultra-modern dissonance which, after all, are not so far from those thrown up, before jazz, by certain French contemporary composers like Erik Satie.'[41]

Congruent with Hylton's many successful French tours within his European schedules through the later 1920s and 1930s, a significant portion of his repertory involved French light classics and chanson arrangements.[42] There was a very strong, seemingly reciprocal, bond forged between Hylton and France, especially Paris. Consider the 'Parisomania' quip in a review that accompanied Hylton's being awarded the Officier de L'Instruction publique in 1930: 'It's that Jack Hylton [...] has caught "Parisomania"'; the piece concluded that 'This [award] is absolutely justified [...] and very Parisian.'[43] Contemporaneously, this strong association was reinforced by a member of Hylton's band: 'Hylton empathised with Paris completely; and there can be little doubt that Paris reciprocated in the same way. He seemed

---

[38] F. E. Baume, 'How Jazz "Symphony" Failed', *Daily Guardsman* (11 February 1927): review of Albert Hall concert (19 December 1926), where the compilation included an arrangement by Eric Coates and Gershwin's *Valse moderne*.

[39] See Mawer, 'Jazzing a Classic', 155–82.

[40] Pierre Leroi, 'Jack Hylton à l'Opéra', *L'Édition musicale vivante*, 37 (February 1931), 12–13: 'La confusion des genres aboutit toujours à un résultat mauvais. *Mavra* en jazz vient d'illustrer de façon frappante cette vérité première.' Sources: Jack Hylton Continental Tours, 1930–35 and Collection Rondel, Ro. 586.

[41] A. D., 'Le Jazz Jack Hylton', *Grand Écho du Nord* ([Lille] 5 February 1933): 'Ajoutons qu'on y trouve certains effets de dissonances ultra-modernes qui, après tout, ne sont pas si loin de ceux lancés, avant le jazz, par certains compositeurs français contemporains comme Erik Satie.' Source: Foreign Press Cuttings, October 1928 – February 1933.

[42] For a substantive listing, see Mawer, '"Parisomania"? Jack Hylton and the French Connection', Appendix, 308–17.

[43] L. R., 'Deux artistes américains [*sic*] "bien parisiens" sont décorés par le gouvernement français', *Paris Presse* (24 August 1930), International News Cuttings (Jack and Band), 1 March 1930 – 15 August 1930 (JHA): 'C'est que Jack Hylton [...] est atteint de "parisomanie" [...] Jack Hylton [est] officier de l'Instruction publique! C'est très juste ··· et très parisien.'

happy to spend more time there than anywhere else; and of course we had to be there with him.'[44]

Archival finds in support of Hylton's French affinity

Research in the Jack Hylton Archive (JHA) has unearthed additional materials, as yet uncatalogued,[45] which extend Hylton's interest in French-related classics beyond pieces known to have been transcribed, arranged, or recorded by his band. Some repertory is particularly intriguing because by today's standards it is unfamiliar – even obscure – and surprisingly serious in character. While these works do not appear to have been arranged, their conservation indicates that they were valued and had potential application, so expanding our view of light French classics beyond the time-filtered obvious.

In the little-known, serious category, we encounter evocative early songs by the naturalized French composer and critic Reynaldo Hahn (1874–1947). A pupil of Massenet and one-time lover of Marcel Proust, Hahn composed his settings of Verlaine's melancholic *Chansons grises* around 1893. These songs for female voice and piano: 'Chanson d'automne', 'Tous deux', 'L'Allée est sans fin', 'En sourdine', 'L'Heure exquise', 'Paysage triste' and 'La Bonne Chanson' were published in Paris by Heugel. The first song 'Chanson d'automne', marked 'Lent et triste', reveals an expressive, late romantic style, in C♯ minor. A restricted vocal span (major sixth) and dynamic range (*p*, *un peu plus f*, *pp*), decorated by circumscribed chromaticism, suits its opening text: 'Les sanglots longs / Des violons / De l'automne, / Blessent mon cœur / D'une langueur / Monotone'. Also found in this repertory is Schumann's *Frauenliebe und Leben* (1840), in its French edition: *L'Amour et la vie d'une femme*, Op. 42. While eminently mainstream, these romantic, passionate lieder might seem curious candidates for potential band transcription, but then in 1928, the celebrated singer Lotte Lehmann (1888–1976) had successfully recorded the full eight-song cycle with salon orchestral accompaniment on the Parlophone Odeon Series (four-disc set, commencing R20090).

We rediscover Vuillermoz, well known as a supportive critic – both of Ravel and of Hylton's Paris concerts – as a composer and musicologist-editor. As former fellow pupils of Fauré, we might compare Vuillermoz's

---

[44] Les Carew, 'How Are the Mighty ⋯ ?' *Nostalgia*, 10/40 (October 1990), 19–21: 19; quoted by Faint: www.jackhylton.com/ (section on Hylton and Stravinsky).

[45] In January 2012, most music discussed here was shelved in an unsorted 'Box 4'.

Chansons populaires, françaises et canadiennes (1910),[46] with Ravel's *Chants populaires* of the same year, or *Cinq mélodies populaires grecques* (1904–6). Amid studies and dances – especially bourrées – the *Chansons populaires* was one of Vuillermoz's main undertakings, comprising seven songs with traditional texts. Only the music for the second is present, with its obscure title 'Une perdriole ⋯ ', dedicated to the French poet-scholar Paul-Louis Couchoud. Marked 'Joyeusement', this simple folk melody with much stepwise motion and arching contours is harmonized around an Aeolian mode on E, though Vuillermoz enjoys added sevenths and occasional ninths and varies the lilting metre (6/8, 9/8, 12/8) to match the text. With shades of 'The Twelve Days of Christmas', the song contemplates presents for a beloved across the first five days of May ('Le premier jour de mai que donn'rai-je à ma mie? [⋯] Une perdriole qui va, qui vient qui vole, une perdriole, qui vole dans les bois').

A further obscure find involves the French composer-conductor Alexandre Luigini (1850–1906), whose career focused on the Opéra-Comique and who, in 1899, conducted the premiere of Massenet's *Cendrillon*. Contemporary with Bizet's *Carmen* and written just four years after Verdi's *Aïda*, Luigini's *Ballet égyptien* (1875)[47] was dedicated to 'Monsieur Jules Pasdeloup' of the well-known Parisian Pasdeloup Concert series. As light stage music, in a stereotypical exotic mode, this ballet was very much a product of colonial interests, from Napoleon onwards. It became very popular in a concert suite version, following its incorporation within the second act of *Aïda* in a production given in Lyon in 1886. Abstracted items might well have been envisaged as a nostalgic reminiscence of the Belle Époque and as potential companion pieces for selections from *Carmen* or *Thaïs* (see below) for one of Hylton's French tours since, despite an equivalent British colonial activity, this work would have had less impact for a British audience.

On an even lighter classical note is evidence of the thriving tango phenomenon in 1920s Paris: firstly, a 'Tango chanté' from Messager's 'comédie musicale' *L'Amour masqué* (1923).[48] A typical 'Mouvement de Tango', the music operates in 2/4 metre, with suitable syncopation, within F♯ minor. A loud raglike 'head' phrase on the piano in doubled octaves leads *subito piano* to three bars of vamping before the Baron declaims a silly text: 'Valentine a perdu la tête! / C'était pourtant un'femme honnête / Mais elle a fait une

---

[46] The edition held in the JHA, carefully backed with brown paper, is A. Z. Mathot, Paris, 1921.

[47] 'Nouvelle édition', transcribed for four hands by Aristide Hignard (Paris: L. Grus et Cie, n.d.).

[48] André Messager, 'Tango chanté (Le Baron)', arr. Sacha Guitry (Paris: Éditions Francis Salabert, 1923).

conquête / En dansant le tango!' Secondly, we find *Planisphère* No. 4 (1928): 'Argentines', from a set of eight piano pieces by Pierre Vellones (1889–1939). Marked 'Largo (T° di Tango)', it is a most effective dance: accented and rhythmically tight, yet smouldering at very quiet dynamic levels. Although these French tangos do not seem to have been arranged, the band did play Jacob Gade's famous *Tango tzigane jalousie* of 1925.

French classics and the process of 'jazzing'

The repertory treated by the JHO is rich and moderately varied, ranging from early nineteenth-century pieces, including Chopin's Étude in E major, Op. 10, No. 3, composed in Paris in 1832, through to Ravel's *Boléro*, written almost a century later. While usually popular, the repertory spanned an emotional range: from the serious, poignant and sometimes unashamedly sentimental, through to lighthearted fare, including the more satirical side displayed by Jacques Offenbach's *Orphée aux enfers*. Selection favoured later romantic through to *fin-de-siècle* repertory, in an extended tonal style, within which melody remained the defining feature: the big tunes from *Carmen* (the 'Toreador Song'), or Massenet's *Thaïs* (the 'Méditation') make this point. Generally, the repertory was familiar to the audience and could thus be enjoyed in a nostalgic fashion. Much material was drawn from staged works: comic opera or ballet, usually in suite format, while some derived from orchestral, instrumental or piano pieces.

Hylton rarely arranged this material himself, though he normally conducted the band and sometimes acted as vocalist. Given the quantity of repertory required and frequency of gigs, he engaged a team of arrangers across the interwar period. French classics were jazzed from 1925 (Chaminade's 'Pas des écharpes') to 1939 (Chopin's Étude, recorded in a new guise). Personnel included Major Williams, employed as band arranger (1926–33); Yorke, pianist-cum-arranger (1929–33); Phil Cardew, arranger and tenor saxophonist (1930); Leighton Lucas, arranger (1925–31); and Freddy Bretherton (May 1939). Most important was William (Billy) Ternent (1899–1977), a multi-instrumentalist and Hylton's main arranger from 1927 to 1940, when the JHO was disbanded because its membership was called up for service in World War II. Ternent was viewed as 'one of the band's star hot arrangers. Truly a born musician. How lucky it is that he has been able to find expression for his talents in the "Jazz Age". What a waste if he had been born 50 years ago!'[49]

---

[49] Uncredited article, 'Our Cover Portrait: The Multiple-Instrument Man', *Melody Maker* (March 1930), 237.

Materials for analysing the French arrangements and extent of their jazzing vary: in most instances, manuscript band parts survive, sometimes with a separate lead sheet or full score; an arrangement may be coupled with its precise printed source, sometimes itself an arrangement, so aiding comparative study. This is the case with Massenet's 'Méditation' and Stravinsky's *Mavra*, although, unfortunately, there are no matching recordings. Conversely, there may be 78 r.p.m. recordings – generally His Master's Voice (HMV) or Decca – but no matching manuscript arrangement, as with 'Pas des écharpes', foregrounding aural analysis in comparison with a printed source. Sometimes, an ideal situation pertains with arrangement(s), original source(s) and recording(s), creating valuable scope for exploring the detail of changes and gaps, as with *Boléro*. Equally, dates and authorship may be clear-cut: a signed, dated MS, or a recording dated via Brian Rust's superb catalogue;[50] or more obscure: a matter of comparing arrangers' handwriting and correlating given data with concert programmes and employment dates, where player names are indicated.

The process of jazzing these French pieces essentially meant modifying their image to conform to the bold sound and slick style which denoted Hylton's (British) band brand, but the degree to which an original was remade, occasionally transformed, depended on several factors. Firstly, there was limited improvisatory scope for individual players, especially solo violinists, harpists or drummers, so that scored arrangements and recorded performances rarely match up exactly. Eric Little, a member of Hylton's Kit-Cat Band, responded to the issue of notation for drummers, saying: 'the monotony which would ensue from playing these "straight" parts absolutely as written is very obvious, and [···] one of the first duties of a real dance drummer is to know how and when to improvise upon such parts *in a proper manner*'.[51] Similarly, for Lucas, 'In most cases where a solo break is required it is better to leave it entirely to the discretion of the soloist rather than write one out for him.'[52] More generally, this improvisatory scope relates to performance style: rhythms may be swung or otherwise decorated (dotted or scotch-snap patterns; accelerando through semiquaver groupings); portamentos and tempo rubato may be maximized.

---

[50] Brian Rust and Sandy Forbes, *British Dance Bands on Record, 1911–1945 and Supplement*, revised edition (Harrow: General Gramophone Publications, 1989).

[51] Eric Little, 'Should Drummers Use Parts?', *Melody Maker and British Metronome* (March 1927), 263 (original italics).

[52] Leighton Lucas, 'Arranging on the Stand', *Melody Maker and British Metronome* (March 1927), 264. A *Poème* from the 1890s by the Czech composer Zdeněk Fibich (1850–1900), arranged by Ternent, involves much freedom for the harpist, especially in non-notated cadenzas (P26; see Appendix 6.1).

Secondly, each band arranger had his quirks: Lucas was more orchestral in his scoring and more adventurous with chromatic harmony than Ternent, who favoured bolder blocks or sections of sound (differences which came to a head over *Mavra*).[53] This French repertory had to be rescored for the band's instrumentation, which itself varied across time; conversely, arrangements needed to heed special original sonorities, such as those created by a piano accordion or harp. So the extent of difference, even 'dissonance', depended partly on the original instrumentation. Apart from the important saxophone sound, often doubling violins, distinctive band touches included the banjo and glockenspiel; most arrangements involved piano and a range of percussion for added rhythmic drive. As a consequence of new instrumentation, especially brass, the original key and pitch of a piece might be modified: Massenet's 'Méditation' in D major, conducive to its violin solo, is transposed in band arrangements to E♭, F and even B♭ major.

The character of a piece could be further modified. To make an instrumental work more versatile, accessible and topical for its audience, lyrics might be added, with the vocal range impacting upon key. Some recordings exist in separate instrumental and vocal versions; alternatively, a single recording often features an instrumental introduction, vocal verse and instrumental postlude. The addition of text, or creation of new text, may exaggerate or profoundly change the original associations of an instrumental piece (for example, Chopin's E major Étude), creating new cultural meanings. Other recharacterizations involve metric and rhythmic changes – especially added syncopation important to the new jazzed identity (Chopin and Chaminade) – and altered dynamic schemes (Stravinsky and Massenet).

A final fundamental issue in these jazzed arrangements was a technical one concerning the crucial recordings: the playing duration of a 10-inch 78 r.p.m. disc during this period was approximately 3½ minutes per side. Many arrangements thus underwent significant compression and cutting of material; compression and cuts became almost an aesthetic trait since they connected to issues of accessibility and mass audience attention span. A substantial original piece (for instance, *Boléro*) would inevitably be more radically remade than one which was of suitable length to begin with. Sometimes, this practice created the metonymic effect of presenting part of a work as a new whole, since this part might well constitute an audience's total experience. A related variable that also impacted upon the extent of difference involved the production of new material: links between what were originally separate sections, or a new introduction where the arranged

---

[53] See Mawer, 'Jazzing a Classic', 162–4.

portion had been abstracted from the middle of a larger work (for example, Massenet).

'Jack Hylton presents': a short history of light French classics

In the spirit of Hylton's later television productions[54] what follows is a selective history of the lighter side of French music as directed by the JHO's repertory choices and by my interpretation of the intrinsic interest of any one arrangement. This history is presented chronologically by the dates of original composition to give coherence to the rereading of a French musical story, rather than by the dates of band arrangement, though the latter trajectory may be largely reconstructed and the entries may be read in a different order.

Hylton's interpretation of French history, as a series of source–product relations, starts with music by an adoptive Frenchman: Chopin's Étude, Op. 10, No. 3, in E major for piano, first published in France in June 1833. (Having arrived in Paris in 1831, Chopin acquired French citizenship in 1835; his father Nicolas was French, originally from Lorraine. Chopin is also relevant to Evans, in Chapter 8.) This ternary-form étude is highly melodic, with a strong sense of *cantabile* line or contour that is immediately emotive – elusively evocative and with more than a hint of melancholy (a composerly patriotic yearning). Chopin's final choice of tempo, 'Lento ma non troppo', means there is time to shape this music, which has distinctly nocturne-like introverted qualities, commencing at *p* dynamic and marked *legato*. Less imediately obvious, and unusually for 2/4 metre, the piece uses irregular phrase lengths, especially as a contra(di)ction of expectation. Aptly, as indicative of potential for rereading, there is a constant bass syncopation. A central section ('Poco più animato'), which develops a more dramatic characterization – its greater momentum coupled by increased fluidity, urgency and virtuosity – is followed by a shortened reprise of the opening.

Interestingly, the transcriptive potential of the Étude, especially its vocality, had become apparent by the mid 1830s: Chopin, apparently, heard the operatic legend Maria Malibran singing his piece in London and liked the effect.[55] Nicknamed 'Tristesse', though not by Chopin, the piece has since become a victim of its own popularity, its compact duration rendering it

---

[54] *Jack Hylton Presents* was the title of a television series that Hylton presented in the mid 1950s and of a subsequent book by Pamela W. Logan (London: British Film Institute (BFI) Publishing, 1995).

[55] See Frédéric Chopin, *Studi per pianoforte*, ed. Alfredo Casella (Milan: Edizioni Curci, 1946), 21.

suitable for music boxes everywhere! Much later, Tino Rossi (1907–83), a cabaret tenor working in Paris during the 1930s, popularized the Étude further in its sung form as 'Tristesse', in 1939. Meanwhile, a contemporaneous instrumental version created for Hylton's band by Bretherton relates to a vocal arrangement by Cardew, which uses the text 'So Deep is the Night' (T95; Appendix 6.1). Thus those inherent nocturnal qualities have also come to the fore.

Bretherton provides a flamboyant, nineteen-page full score of a working nature, transposed into F: it is rather messy, at one point requiring an 'Insertion to be made' (p. 7), but his detailed markings allow us to glean useful insight, as shown in Figure 6.1. An initial designation, 'Rubato' followed by 'A Tempo. Slightly quickens' (Fig. 1), combined with that for solo violin 'À la Tzigane', makes clear the scope for flexibility in performance, though this version was not apparently recorded. Timbral variety is evident via the hat mutes for trombones; the alto saxophone presenting its 'Solo sweetly' (Fig. 12); the direction to 'Make harp prominent in this cho[rus]' (Figs. 8–9); and the inclusion of drums, 'Tymp.' [sic] and even celesta.

Hylton's recording (HMV BD-5554) corresponds closely with Cardew's printed version in E♭, except that a new handwritten introduction featuring solo violin has been added and that the violin continues with a melodic preview, in preference to the trumpet designated in the printed short score. The violin's audible position-shifts lend a poignant, if sentimentalized, quality. Temporally speaking, Chopin's music has become even more malleable, incorporating pauses, much tempo rubato, and a sense of being slightly swung, foxtrotlike: the notation is only a guide. A tutti string-wind rendition of the material includes punctuation from the piano (a crucial thread from the original), with the use of thirds and the maximizing of tension and intensity creating a film-music-like trait. At times, the music is faster than expected, contrasted by a substantial slowing into the vocal rendition.

Sung by the crooner Sam Browne, the refrain (in D♭) with English lyrics by Sonny Miller begins: 'So deep is the night, No moon tonight, No friendly star / To guide me with its light'. The text tells of love and heartache from a distance, but with initial musical emphasis on the possibility of his lover 'returning'. Attractively, the setting involves a textual segue between the verses, reminiscent of that need to press on in the B section of Chopin's original (the only vestige of that section). Initial hope fades with an amended textual-musical repeat that admits to 'lonely night', 'broken wings' and that any return may only be in dream form. The musical climax extends to the line end: 'Will your mem'ry haunt me till I die?', while the final stanza lays it bare: 'Alone am I [···] Deep is the night'. An instrumental

Figure 6.1 Bretherton's manuscript score of Chopin, *Tristesse* (T95, p. 1).
Reproduced by kind permission of the Jack Hylton Archive, Lancaster University.

postlude rounds off the number, with notable syncopation (a forced levity?), through to a quiet finish, congruent with the original.

While not wholly attributable to Hylton's remaking, this Chopin 'cover' does embody a significant measure of transformation: changes of genre, ensemble and form (AA'A); the addition of lyrics; a double retitling with language shift ('Tristesse', 'Reviens mon amour', in the original French lyrics of Jean Marietti and André Viaud, to 'So Deep is the Night'). This enterprise polarizes the earliest music to be arranged and the latest band recording. In part, new meanings have been drawn and developed from the original: nocturne and melancholy, while the recording of this song in late December 1939, well after the declaration of World War II, accrues added sociocultural meanings about love, the long nights of the blackout, sacrifice and loss, including the imminent end of the band. From an exclusive, virtuosic, 'high' art source has emerged an inclusive, accessible, popular product.

Hylton's historical survey then takes us to the mid-nineteenth-century Parisian stage world for highlights of opera and ballet. Offenbach's hugely successful operetta *Orphée aux enfers*, on a text of Ludovic Halévy, was first performed at the Théâtre des Bouffes-Parisiens in 1858, during the Second Empire of Napoleon III. It was a satire, which would become notorious, upon Christoph Gluck's *Orfeo ed Euridice* of 1762 – itself adapted for Parisian tastes at the Académie Royale de Musique (as the Opéra was formerly known). The 'Gallop infernal' that denotes the gods having their party in hell (Act II, scene 2) is commonly abstracted as the infamous music for the 'Can-can'. Among sheet music in the JHA is a full set of printed parts for *Orphée*, including the first violin/conductor lead sheet.[56] This is quite a virtuosic violin-centred arrangement, marked up for use with cuts and starts indicated, and represents a classic parodic inclusion, appropriate in a jazzed context: *Orphée* may be seen as an earlier, more lighthearted equivalent of *Mavra*.

The next major phenomenon, aptly picked up in Hylton's practice, is that of *Carmen*, composed by the short-lived Bizet with a libretto by Henri Meilhac and Halévy again, the premiere of which at the Opéra-Comique in March 1875 was attended by Offenbach, Léo Delibes and Massenet.[57] With its emphasis on realism and emotional empathy with an exotic, Romani

---

[56] Jacques Offenbach, *Orphée aux enfers* (Orpheus in the Underworld), arr. W. H. Myddleton (London: J. R. Lafleur and Son Ltd/Boosey & Hawkes, 1915).

[57] The JHA also holds a full set of printed parts for Georges Bizet, 'Galop', from *Petite Suite: Jeux d'enfants* (1871), arr. Arthur Wood (London: W. Paxton & Co Ltd., 1965).

heroine, whose story is set in 1820s Seville, Bizet's powerful work challenged the boundaries of serious and comic opera and their associated traditions of sung versus spoken dialogue. Despite an uncertain start, from the 1880s onwards it became one of the most popular operas – French or otherwise – with portions extracted from the four-act epic for frequent concert suite performance and song recitals, including the 'Toreador Song' and the schmaltzy 'Habanera'.

Within this tradition, in the early 1930s Yorke created a manuscript arrangement (O3; Appendix 6.1) with full score and piano part: a Franco-Italian *Opera Selection*. Possibly catalysed by British contemporary films of *Carmen*, it includes three *Carmen* items in its diverse seven-movement sequence: 'Carmen Overture', 'Toreador's Song', '[La] Donna è mobile', '[Il] Trovatore', 'One Fine Day' [*Madam Butterfly*], 'Carmen Duet', ending inevitably with Rossini's 'William Tell'.[58] The instrumentation is wonderfully diverse: four violins, the usual complement of saxophones and brass, clarinet, drums, timpani, banjo, bass and piano. Bizet's brief 'Prélude' contains music from the Act IV bullfighting preparations that leads into the Toréador's material (and motivic reference to Don José's infatuation with Carmen), so creating a sequence that is maintained in the band arrangement. The opening page of Yorke's score is reproduced in Figure 6.2.

In a further act of compression, however, the opening item featuring strings and saxophones is reduced to sixteen bars – little more than a fanfare! The original 'Chanson du toréador' develops its big triumphant tune with surging climaxes and, like the prelude, is suitably brief for the purposes of abstraction and arrangement, again using the string–saxophone blend. Puccini's 'One Fine Day' features solo muted trumpet, while the ensuing melodic 'Carmen Duet' leads with alto saxophone, later joined by tenor, accompanied by pizzicato strings. Limited dynamics appear in the working score, but are missing in the parts although 'rall.' markings and the string indication '8va on repeat' are included, again implying flexibility in performance. Yorke's easily digested menu of operatic treats was essentially a crowd-pleaser – all the big tunes without any of the waiting around – but it did expand typical music hall and dance band repertory for concert-hall

---

[58] 'La donna è mobile' (Woman is Fickle) is from Verdi's *Rigoletto* (1851), while the ensuing song from *Il Trovatore* (The Troubadour) shares *Carmen*'s Spanish Romani theme and was first heard in Paris, in 1854. Rossini's *William Tell* was first performed at the Opéra in 1829, with the finale of its four-part overture often heard independently, including, from 1933 onwards, as the signature tune of the American radio and later TV show *The Lone Ranger*[!].

Figure 6.2 Yorke's manuscript score of *Opera Selection* (O3, p. 1). Reproduced by kind permission of the Jack Hylton Archive, Lancaster University.

performance, while buying into the nostalgia and grandeur of romantic opera.[59]

Meanwhile in ballet, Delibes's *La Source*, choreographed by Arthur Saint-Léon with a scenario by Charles Nuitter, premiered at the Opéra in 1866. In the JHA we encounter isolated parts, including that for first violin of a first Ballet Suite:[60] the opening number is 'Pas des écharpes' (Scarf Dance), followed by a 'Scène d'amour', 'Variation' and 'Danse circassienne'. Also present is a printed piano edition of Delibes's famous *Coppélia*,[61] premiered at the start of the Third Republic in 1870, and later becoming the most performed ballet at the Opéra.[62] This repertory is fascinating for its interconnections: a version of the *Coppelia* story occurs in Offenbach's later opera *The Tales of Hoffmann*,[63] while the 'Pas des écharpes' balletic theme – of colourful silk scarves, flowing veils and exotic mystique – is picked up again in Hylton's arrangement of Chaminade's music.

As a child, Chaminade played some of her earliest compositions to Bizet who thought she had much ability; she made her English concert début as a pianist in 1892 and gained renown in America following her successful tour of 1908. Despite being the first female composer to be awarded the Légion d'honneur in 1913, her music has generally descended into obscurity, with the exception of the Flute Concertino, Op. 107 (1902) and piano pieces such as 'Pas des écharpes', which have acquired a lasting, popular appeal: hence Hylton's involvement. This particular Scarf Dance is the third of *Cinq airs de ballet*, Op. 37 (1888), which also include a 'Danse orientale', 'Pas des amphores', 'Callirhoé' and 'Danse pastorale'.[64]

---

[59] The JHA also holds printed parts for Charles Gounod, 'Waltz Song', *Romeo and Juliet* (1867), arr. R. H. Just (Chicago: Lyon and Healy, n.d.). Later operetta items include a 'modern symphonic arrangement' of Franz Lehár's *La Veuve joyeux* (The Merry Widow, 1905; Decca K-620) and '[O] Maedchen' from *Frédérique (Friederike*, 1928), arranged by Ternent, and presented on European tours in 1930–1.

[60] Léo Delibes, *La Source*: Ballet Suite, arr. Charles Woodhouse (London: Lafleur/Boosey & Hawkes, 1915).

[61] Léo Delibes, *Coppelia Ballet Music*, arr. Ernest Reeves (London: Walsh Holmes & Co. Ltd., 1927).

[62] Another popular ballet was *Les Millions d'arlequin* (1900), composed by Ricardo Drigo (1846–1930) and choreographed by Marius Petipa: specifically, its 'Sérénade' waltz, which exists in instrumental and vocal arrangements, including that sung by the tenor Richard Tauber. Lucas created an imaginative version for Hylton's band that included organ and cor anglais (M4; see Appendix 6.1).

[63] Hylton's take on *Les Contes d'Hoffmann* was appreciated by Émile Vuillermoz, 'La Musique: Jack Hylton et ses "boys" au Théâtre des Champs-Élysées', *Excelsior* ([Paris] 7 April, 1930), International News Cuttings (Jack and Band), 1 March 1930 – 15 August 1930.

[64] See Marcia J. Citron, *Cécile Chaminade: A Bio-Bibliography* (Westport, CT: Greenwood Press, 1988).

Chaminade's original, marked 'Mouvement modéré de Valse', adopts a gently lilting triple metre in A♭ major. Four-bar phrases commence with an instantly memorable melodic line, to be played *legato*, which features an ascending arch-contour accentuated by a dynamic swell – an unashamedly romantic gesture within this salon-style piece. The melody rises by an expressive fourth interval: C–F, then falling back a fifth (to B♭), before moving chromatically via B natural to the first of many melodic repeats (bar 5). The opening two bars of each phrase establish a reiterated crotchet pattern, decorated by quaver diminution. Anticipating later waltzes by Ravel, Chaminade makes effective use of hemiola, adding interest to the second half of a phrase through cross-rhythms, with two-beat treble-part groupings set against the triple bass metre; alternatively, the bass sometimes emphasizes the second beat, as in a crotchet–minim syncopation (bar 7). Typically the harmony is straightforward, built upon dominant–tonic progressions, but attractive twists occur, such as a passing modulation to the mediant C minor (bar 9) emphasized by the *forte* marking, before arriving, softly once more, at the expected dominant, E♭ (bars 15–16). Repetition operates at a local level with those reiterated crotchets and, formally, with bars 17–32, marked initially 'poco rubato', a close repeat of 1–16. A more dramatic, chordal middle section is followed by a reprise of the opening, producing a ternary form.

Hylton's restyled music was recorded in December 1925 by his early Kit-Cat Band, led by Al Starita and with Little on drums (Appendix 6.1). At a fast pace, it incorporates a brief introduction and enjoys a distinct tempo rubato for the repeated crotchets of the main melody, especially the second bar of each four-bar phrase. Ironically, it adopts a classic Johann Strauss Viennese mannerism: moving very early to the second beat and then fractionally delaying the third, so creating a greater syncopation. Notable are the sonorities of the banjo, played by Len Fillis;[65] wide wind vibrato; characterful nasal trumpet iterations; and the percussion's punctuating cymbals and sweet bell-like chimes (glockenspiel?). Subsequent swung portions in the B section and a maximizing of Chaminade's swell effects in the reprise create a sound even more Parisian than the original. This band orchestration varies the tonal colour of the much-repeated melody, thereby increasing the interest over that of the piano version. What results is an attractive reworking that exaggerates and updates the Belle Époque original. Arguably the overriding visual image from listening to Hylton's recording is one of a smooth, slick Palm Court orchestra, performing in a grand Riviera hotel

---

[65] See Len Fillis Discography: www.jabw.demon.co.uk/fillis.htm.

foyer,[66] amid suitable greenery, for the backdrop of an Agatha Christie mystery, especially one of her interwar Hercules Poirot series. Other orchestrations of 'Pas des écharpes' included that of the Victor Salon Orchestra and, in 1928, a response to this performed by the Columbia Symphony Orchestra (Columbia 1658-D), conducted by Robert Hood Bowers (1877–1941), under whose baton the piece is more serious-minded and slower than in Hylton's hands.

Hylton's history continues with a grand *fin de siècle* stage work which had already rather fallen into obscurity. Massenet's three-act opera *Thaïs* – to a libretto of Louis Gallet derived from the novel by Anatole France – was first produced at the Opéra in 1894 and at the Opéra-Comique in 1898. Subsequently, however, with the exceptions of revivals of *Manon* (a five-act work given at the Opéra-Comique, 1884) and *Werther* (a four-act lyric drama, 1892), plus the abstracted 'Méditation', his music has been little heard. Like *Aïda* and Luigini's *Ballet égyptien*, *Thaïs* perpetuates an exotic Egyptian theme.[67] More like *Carmen*, however, it reverses stereotypical assumptions and blends genres: Thaïs, a non-Christian Alexandrian courtesan turns out to have far higher morals than Athanäel, a Christian monk of lustful tendency. Struggling with her conscience, she engages in an extended meditation, after which she decides to follow Athanäel to the desert. Sadly, the ending is tragic: both die, she in a convent, he in despair. This 'Méditation' occurs as an entr'acte for violin (representing the heroine) and orchestra, between the two scenes of Act II: it is often presented independently as a concert item and has been much arranged. The essence of Massenet's piece comprises a long, sweeping melody in common metre within D major, featuring arpeggio and scalic figuration and temporal flexibility – indicative of improvisational potential. Marked 'Andante religioso', the music contrasts an intimate start and close with impassioned outbursts; formally, it adopts a ternary structure – with internal melodic repeats, plus coda.

---

[66] On the contemporary fortunes of 'Riviera Rose', recorded by Hylton (HMV B-1808: 9 April 1924), see uncredited review, 'A New Waltz Success', *The Ball Room*, 5/4 (May 1924), JHCU970002: '"Riviera Rose", which the best judges of music [···] declare to be a triumph for Mr Nicholls. The superb orchestra at the Café de Paris at Monte Carlo, played this composition as a valse [*sic*], with such immediate success that a leading French publishing house at once secured the publishing rights for France. Since then, it has been played by all the leading English bands, including the Savoy Orpheans and Savoy Havana, Jack Hylton's, L'Oonie's etc.'

[67] Its Wagnerian penchant was noted by the Parisian salon hostess and singer Marguerite de Saint-Marceaux, who referred to it uncharitably as '*Parsifal* with white sauce': quoted in Roger Nichols, *The Harlequin Years: Music in Paris 1917–1929* (London: Thames and Hudson, 2002), 199.

Several connected arrangements exist in the JHA (T47; Appendix 6.1), which relate to a French 'transcription pour piano seul' published by Heugel in 1922 and involve the services of a commercial outfit: 'Mackey and Lowry: Arrangers & Orchestrators'. Although there is no obvious recording and the generally detailed manuscript score (no. 175) is undated, from the arranger's signature and players' names on parts (including Ternent's), we can deduce that Williams rebranded the 'Méditation' sometime between April 1927 and February 1930.[68] While the violin sonority offers an important constant, the orchestral original is arguably less diverse than the dance band instrumentation: 2 violins, viola,[69] 3 alto saxophones, 1 tenor saxophone, 2 trumpets, 2 trombones, bass, banjo, piano (and a disparate glockenspiel part). From the conductor's lead sheet combined with the score, we can summarize the remaking. Transposition from D into E♭ major creates a more mellow effect, coupled by a double rhythmic augmentation in cut-common metre that offers a more spacious feel.[70] An eight-bar 'All in' (tutti) introduction marked *forte*, utilizing the dramatic, accented appoggiatura link into the reprise, acts as a signal to the audience, like the lead-in for a congregational hymn. Gone is the *sotto voce* beginning. Through blending violin and saxophone, Williams upholds a Hylton band hallmark, also bringing a new timbral quality to the big tune at *mf* dynamic, rather than *ppp* (Fig. A). Projecting the upper octave, the violin remains, however, very much the soloist.[71]

Ironically, this arrangement omits some of the original flexibility of 'rall.' followed by 'a Tempo', instead emboldening the central section (Fig. B) as 'Animando', with new character also injected by the trumpet assuming the melody. Instrumental turn-taking (thus timbral variety) is maximized as a jazz-type feature, with trumpet passing to saxophones and strings, thence to brass and back to the string–saxophone blend. The build-up to climax is well managed: 'poco più appassionato' at *ff* dynamic is ringed in black ink in the manuscript score, which exploits the high violin register up to G♯ (eighth

---

[68] The deduction is supported by inclusion of the *Méditations* [sic] *de Thaïs* in a programme for a 'Concert donné par Jack Hylton et son Orchestre', Exposition internationale de Liège (21–22 August 1930).

[69] Harry Berly, of the Pougnet String Quartette, is listed as the viola player in a programme by 'Jack Hylton and His Boys' at the Théâtre des Champs-Élysées, Paris (22–23 March 1929): JHPR9701279. Another item involving viola was Handel's *Passacaglia* for violin and viola duo, listed in programmes for 1930.

[70] This practice also occurs in Lucas's *Millions d'arlequin* 'Serenade' arrangement, where an original 3/8 is converted to 3/4.

[71] Hylton's band recreated various romantic classics that featured solo violin: *Valse célèbre* (1884) by Moritz Moszkowski (1854–1925; Chaminade's brother-in-law), probably arranged by Yorke, and Fibich's *Poème* (see Appendix 6.1).

bar of Fig. C), while the intense transition is heightened as 'Agitato', with the second trombonist warned: 'not too rough'. Volume and instrumentation then reduce to 'violins alone'. Williams inserts 'Dolce' for the reprise (Fig. D), where the melody, in its lower octave, is taken by solo tenor saxophone. A comment: 'Not as written here: alto silent' makes clear the score's working nature and small gaps between notation and performance. The melodic repeat is enriched with chordal thickening ('All in'), but the remainder is congruent with Massenet's original, focusing upon the virtuosic violin and exaggerating the quiet conclusion as *ppp* dynamic.

Hylton and Ravel's *Boléro*

In autumn 1936, Hylton recorded that most malleable balletic candidate Ravel's *Boléro* (Appendix 6.1). Bearing in mind *Boléro*'s close association with its sister (Viennese-inspired) ballet *La Valse*, we may regard as rather apt the coupling of *Boléro* on Hylton's record with Ternent's reading of 'Vienna, City of My Dreams' (HMV BD-393). That Hylton was well aware of Ravel's significance is apparent from an article he had penned five years earlier, which declared that 'dance musicians lean hard on the teachings of the modernistic school. Ravel, Delius, Stravinsky are some of the masters who influence the harmonic character of dance band orchestration.'[72] There is, however, no evidence that Ravel was ever involved in Hylton's enterprise and, although he lived until December 1937, he was already seriously ill.

Conceptually, while *Mavra* and *Boléro* share similar notions of construction and distancing, the latter's popular, melodic aesthetic with hints of exoticism proved much more promising. Its brand of mechanization suited Hylton's slick machine, and of course his version exists within a rich tradition of *Boléro* transcriptions.[73] Ravel's inclusion of three saxophones, trombones and trumpets, playing glissandos and grace notes and generally indulging in showmanship and turn-taking, made his piece conducive to dance band rendition, even if it reduced the interpretative potential. In fact the two different arrangements (B39) ordered by Hylton derive from another version for small symphonic or jazz orchestra made by 'Roger Branga'[74] and published by Durand in the same year as the Ravel original, 1929. Ravel must have known of and presumably endorsed this version, at

---

[72] Hylton, 'Jazz Music: Is the Expression Objectionable?'.

[73] Jack Payne produced a version of *Boléro* on the Columbia label: see Julien Vedey, *Band Leaders* (London: Rockliff, 1950), 45.

[74] As pointed out to me by Nigel Simeone, 'Branga' is an anagram of the surname of Ravel's friend Lucien Garban. That Garban might have been the arranger of this somewhat compromising version is most intriguing.

least in principle, though it entails extraordinarily dramatic cuts that almost halve the original length from 340 to 198 bars (potentially it is even shorter if repeats are omitted) and a crescendo rather than his careful dynamic terracing. Surprisingly perhaps, the first (short, piano) score of Hylton's arrangements, which is in Williams's hand, restores the terraced dynamics and some of the length. It echoes Ravel's orchestration with solos for tenor sax followed by soprano sax (Williams, letter B–B2; Ravel, orchestral score, rehearsal Figs. 6–7), plus a duo for sax and violin, but the notation of ties is careless and, crucially, it removes the dissonance within the climax.

As was the case with *Mavra*, the second score, undertaken by Ternent, is the more pragmatic and bold. Closely modelled on 'Branga', it reduces the music to 108 bars and adopts a forthright dynamic trajectory: *pp, mf, ff.* Some sonorities recall Ravel's original: the opening muted trumpet solo (cf. Ravel, Fig. 5), the four-part block violins (Ternent, letter C; Ravel, Fig. 16) and a later blending of saxophones and violins, as shown in Figure 6.3. Unlike Branga, however, Ternent includes clarinets and reinstates in his instrumentation the guitar (in preference to banjo) that Ravel had sought to evoke through violin strumming.

Interestingly, Hylton's recording is very similar but not identical to Ternent's arrangement. Such gaps, or small differences, between scores and recordings are fascinating for what they can reveal about performance practice of notated arrangements and the potential for some improvisation, or 'jazzing it up'. As Scott comments more generally, 'while the score may appear predictable, the performance may not be so [⋯] even for dance band records with little or no improvisation, the score is an inadequate representation of the music'.[75] Most astounding is the tempo: Ravel's original has a metronome mark of crotchet = 72 (though his recording is as slow as approximately 63),[76] the 'Branga' version has 76, but Hylton's performance (as recorded on HMV BD-393) adopts a very swift 94. Even given the disc restrictions of approximately 3½ minutes per side, this is dramatic, and creates perhaps the shortest *Boléro* ever (a duration of *c.*3.20). (The pitch is only fractionally sharp.) In performance, the oboe is the initial melodic protagonist: an apt change in relation to Ternent's score, since the trumpets already have a high profile with the ostinato. The oboe sonority is followed by the effective block violins with overt vibrato and the saxophone–violin blend, true both to Hylton's doubling practices and to Ravel's original. By virtue of the guitar and radical tempo – which Ravel surely would

---

[75] Scott, 'Incongruity and Predictability', 87.

[76] See Ronald Woodley, 'Style and Practice in the Early Recordings', in Mawer (ed.), *The Cambridge Companion to Ravel*, 236.

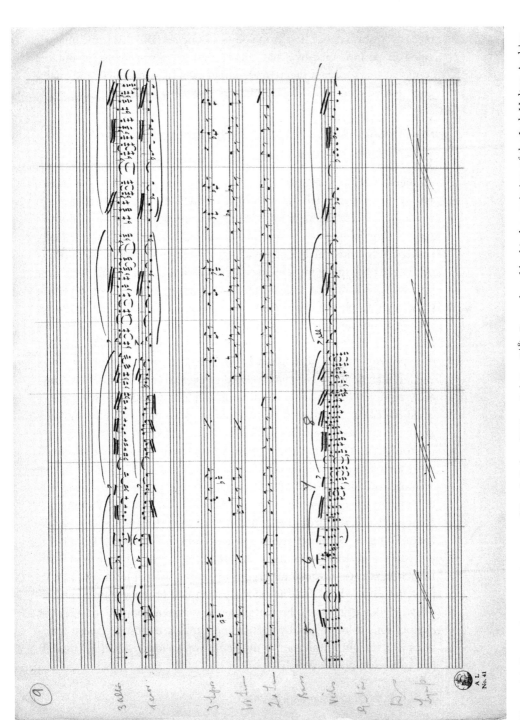

Figure 6.3 Ternent's manuscript score of Ravel, *Bolero* (B39, p. 9, letter F^{+8}). Reproduced by kind permission of the Jack Hylton Archive, Lancaster University.

have deplored, as he did Arturo Toscanini's liberties with the New York Philharmonic in May 1930[77] – Hylton to some extent renaturalizes this piece as Spanish dance. In the melody's second section, this sonic image is aided in performance by what comes close to a tripletizing of notated semiquavers (see again Figure 6.3), emblematic of Spanishness and analogous to the practice of swinging quavers.

Conclusion

The 'jazzifying' of French classical repertory by Hylton's band and his arrangers has been relatively circumscribed: any claim that the source musics have been totally transformed through the product(ion) process would be an overstatement; the closest we approach this is with Chopin's piece. In theory, there is greater improvisational potential than is actually realized. It is more a matter of French music receiving a customised update: one which – via the homogenizing effect of Hylton's dance band machine – unifies quite a diverse stylistic menu, extending across a century from Chopin to Ravel. We can support this argument by codifying the *Boléro* arrangement: the essential attributes of the original are its mock-Arabian melody; the ostinato/harmonic accompaniment; and the recharacterizing of repeated material through new instrumentation. Crucially, Hylton's version maintains the two pitch-related categories; timbral variety is, however, reduced with the more standardized block sound, the Spanishness of bolero as dance is re-emphasized and, most dramatically, the music is greatly compressed – a trait exaggerated by the extremely fast tempo.

From Hylton's stance, engagement with French music has been much more an act of affectionate tribute and nostalgic entertainment than one of humorous or satirical intent. And while his dance band music was undeniably a canny commercial product akin to that of Whiteman – completely different from the contemporaneous African-American artistry of Ellington, whom Hylton supported both in France and Britain – it nonetheless distinguishes itself in providing a rich intersection with French light classics. For our larger purposes, this chapter has sought to join parts of the book (and to offer a substantial primary source component). Hylton's jazzing of French music was contemporary with interwar explorations of early jazz by French modernist composers. It also functions as a transition through to the definitive, serious pursuit of (modal) jazz following World War II.

[77] See Orenstein (ed.), *A Ravel Reader*, 305–6.

Appendix 6.1 *Select list of Hylton's 'jazzed' classics*

This appendix is arranged alphabetically by music title, following the Jack Hylton Archive (JHA). French items are marked with an asterisk.

JHA title, composer, arranger	JHA band file no., materials, comments	Recording date, place, label/no.
Boléro, Maurice Ravel, arr. Roger Branga [Lucien Garban?] (Paris: Éditions Durand, 1929); two arrs.: Billy Ternent and another in Major Williams's hand (unsigned)	B39: MS score, large parts; MS small parts (including pf. part/short score); printed parts	13 Nov. 1936, London; HMV BD-393 (reissued on *Jack Hylton and His Orchestra: A Programme of Light Orchestral Favourites*, EMI SH-269, 1978); Victor 25533
Mavra (Parts 1, 2, 3), Igor Stravinsky (London: Édition russe de musique, 1925); two arrs.: Leighton Lucas and Billy Ternent (1930–1)	Separate box: MS score (Parts I, II: Lucas, Figs. 44–92; 97–112), parts; MS score (Ternent, Figs. 44–92), parts; two copies of printed vocal score (one signed Stravinsky: 'le 17 V 30'), orch. score	17 Feb. 1931, performed by JHO and broadcast from Paris Opéra; not recorded
'[Les] Millions d'arlequin serenade' (waltz), Ricardo Drigo (*Sérénade: tirée du ballet*, London: J. & W. Chester, n.d.); arr. Leighton Lucas	M4: MS short score and parts (including Wurlitzer organ part, for Claude Ivy); printed pf./short score	11 Nov. 1927, New Gallery Cinema, London; HMV B-5391 (also Zonophone 6049)
Opera selection: 'Carmen Overture', 'Toreador's Song', '[La] Donna è mobile', '[Il] Trovatore', 'One Fine Day', 'Carmen Duet', 'William Tell'; arr. Peter Yorke	O3 (orig. No. 870): MS score (P.Y.; rather messy hand); neat parts (including pf.)	No recording found
*'Pas des écharpes' (Scarf Dance), from *Cinq airs de ballet*, Cécile Chaminade; syncopated arrangement	No MS score or parts found	21 Dec. 1925, Hayes (Kit-Cat Band); HMV B-5004 (reissued on *Jack Hylton and His Orchestra*, EMI SH-269, 1978)
Poème, Zděnek Fibich; arr. Billy Ternent	P26 (orig. No. 1021): MS score; two sets of parts (A4 and cards)	14 Sept. 1933, London; Decca K-708 (take 1)
Prelude in C♯ minor, Op. 3, No. 2, Sergei Rachmaninoff; arr. Peter Yorke	No MS score or parts found	19 Feb. 1930, Kingsway Hall, London (Herbert Dawson, organ); HMV C-1864 (reissued on *Jack Hylton and His Orchestra*, EMI SH-269, 1978)

Appendix 6.1 (*cont.*)

JHA title, composer, arranger	JHA band file no., materials, comments	Recording date, place, label/no.
Prelude in G minor, Op. 23, No. 5, Sergei Rachmaninoff; arr. Peter Yorke	Loose MS in box (shelved at Jack Hylton Memorabilia): orig. No. 421; MS score (A3, skeleton); two sets of parts: A5 in Williams's hand, plus A4	19 Feb. 1930, Kingsway Hall, London (Herbert Dawson, organ); HMV C-1864 (reissued on *Jack Hylton and His Orchestra*, EMI SH-269, 1978)
Rhapsody in Blue, George Gershwin/Paul Whiteman; arr. Billy Ternent(?)	R27: MS score (8pp., incomplete); set of parts (small cards)	18 Nov. 1933 (Parts 1, 2; Alec Templeton, pf.); Decca: F-3763 (reissued on *'S Wonderful: Songs of George Gershwin – Original Recordings 1920–1949*, Naxos Nostalgia 8.120828, 2005)
Thaïs: 'Méditation', Jules Massenet ('transcription pour piano seul', Paris: Heugel, 1922); arr. Major Williams [pre-1930]; stamped 'Mackey and Lowry: Arrangers & Orchestrators'	T47: MS score (green booklet); MS score (skeleton); two sets of parts (including pf.): Nos. 105, 175	Performed on 1930 tours; no recording found
(*) *Tristesse* (orig. Étude in E major, Op. 10, No. 3), Frédéric Chopin (arr. Phil Cardew and Mario Melfi, as 'So Deep is the Night', Paris: Max Eschig, 1939); arr. Freddy Bretherton	T95: MS score (19pp., in F); one set of parts; MS intro. to Cardew printed parts (in E♭); second set of printed parts (in F)	22 Dec. 1939, London (voc. Sam Browne); HMV BD-5554
Valse célèbre, Op. 34, No. 1, Moritz Moszkowski (arr. Adolf Schmid, New York: G. Schirmer, 1924); arr. Peter Yorke(?)	V4: Mixed MS and printed parts, including pf./short score	No recording found
Valse moderne, George Gershwin; arr. Claude Ivy	V7: No score; incomplete set of MS band parts, signed Claude Ivy	30 Dec. 1926 (Arthur Young, Claude Ivy, pf. duet), HMV rejected; second recording 26 Jan. 1927, HMV rejected

7 (Re)Moving boundaries? Russell's Lydian jazz theory and its rethinking of Debussy and Ravel

Even within the discipline of musicology, the cultural persistence of some ring-fenced subdisciplines that exert their own territorial control has to some extent impeded musical analysis of interactions between jazz and French concert music – that label of compromise.[1] This is a stance supported by the likes of Tymoczko, who has sought to dissolve rather arbitrary distinctions between notated and improvised musics, and who begins his chapter on jazz by wondering 'whether we make too much of the boundaries between styles'.[2] For Barham too, there is a quest to 'break down prescriptive and restrictive generic boundaries and cultural-intellectual insularities that threaten to cloud rather than clarify musical understanding'.[3]

Ironically, the surge of popularity towards so-called Third Stream music around the later 1950s and early 1960s (see Chapter 1), followed by the subsequent waning of interest, may not have helped this situation. There is a sense that we have already been there and know all we need to know; that the pursuit of such musical relations is at best somewhat passé and at worst tainted by the historical baggage of European hegemony. Indeed there are some danger signs of 'lapsing into unreasoning academic prejudice' here.[4] While there is a sizeable body of research into the impact of early jazz upon French music – more in recent years from a sociocultural than a strictly musical stance, notably less has been done to assess in real detail the impact of French music upon jazz, specifically that of pre-World War I and interwar French music upon 1950s modal jazz. This is not a matter of pursuing some crude, naïve contest or artistic power struggle, but rather an opportunity to explore in depth the complex musical relations between the two: sometimes involving acts of transformation, but also revealing substantive common ground. A study exploring the analytical usage, as an unusual source–product relation, of two pieces of Debussy and Ravel by the

---

[1] An earlier version of this chapter was presented at the Annual Conference of the Royal Musical Association, aptly entitled 'Boundaries', held at Senate House, University of London (15–17 July 2010). I am grateful for feedback from Benjamin Davies, Nicholas Gebhardt and Justin Williams. A central portion was given as a guest paper at 'Maurice Ravel et son temps: tradition, exotisme et modernité', University of Montreal (15–16 November 2012), organized by Michel Duchesneau.

[2] Tymoczko, *A Geometry of Music*, 352.   [3] Barham, 'Rhizomes and Plateaus', 171.

[193]   [4] *Ibid.*, 174.

jazz composer-theorist George Russell in a treatise designed for jazz impro-visers (and still little known outside this circle) proves instructive and perhaps surprising. Indirectly, it also challenges some of our less tenable assumptions.

Positioning Russell and his music

Although Russell was perhaps a maverick figure, as a close contemporary of Miles Davis, Bill Evans and John Coltrane he undoubtedly had a major influence – as a kind of catalyst – upon the development of modal jazz, as immortalized in the albums *Milestones*,[5] or *Kind of Blue*. In respect of *Milestones* and modal jazz, according to Davis:

> The composer-arranger George Russell used to say that in modal music C is where F should be. He says that the whole piano starts at F. What I learned about the modal form is that when you play in this way, go in this direction, you can go on forever. You don't have to worry about changes [. . .] You can do more with the musical line. The challenge here, when you work in the modal way, is to see how inventive you can become melodically.[6]

Similarly, for fellow trumpeter Arthur 'Art' Farmer (1928–99), who played on several of the composer's recordings, Russell's Lydian concept 'opens the doors to countless means of melodic expression. It also dispels many of the don'ts and can'ts that [. . .] have been imposed on the improviser through the study of traditional harmony.'[7] Russell also came to develop close, long-term connections with Gunther Schuller, sharing some of the latter's Third Stream philosophy, while maintaining his own African-American identity.

Born in Cincinnati, Ohio in 1923, and adopted at an early age, George Allen Russell did not have a very happy upbringing and, like many of his peers, he experienced racial discrimination from his schooldays onwards.[8]

---

[5] Miles Davis, *Milestones* (New York: Columbia CL 1193, 1958; reissued Not Now Music NOT2CD339, 2010).

[6] Davis, *Miles: The Autobiography*, 215.

[7] Art Farmer quoted in Dom Cerulli, 'George Russell', *Down Beat*, 25/10 (29 May 1958), 15–16: 15.

[8] Duncan Heining, *George Russell: The Story of an American Composer* (Lanham, MD: Scarecrow Press, 2010), 2. Like Russell's music, this well-researched, substantial biography deserves to be better known. For an enlightened early source that acknowledged Russell's position as an African-American composer, see David N. Baker, Lida Belt and Herman C. Hudson (eds.), *The Black Composer Speaks* (Metuchen, NJ and London: Scarecrow Press, 1978). Baker, originally a trombonist in Russell's ensemble and editor of *New Perspectives on Jazz* (Washington DC: Smithsonian Institution Press, 1990), developed his own com-poserly notion of 'Africlassical' style.

He emerged from humble musical beginnings as a drummer in the Wilberforce College Band, directed by jazz composer Ernie Wilkins. Swiftly, however, he developed a fascination with music theory, a fascination which in turn extended to embrace matters of philosophy and spirituality,[9] a trait that gained intensity during extended periods of hospitalization as a young man in 1941 when receiving treatment for tuberculosis. Russell later recounted that: 'I knew I had to make use of this time to educate myself. From the scraps of advanced harmony I'd learnt, I knew that my answer didn't lie in traditional theory. I'd experimented a bit with polytonality, but on the piano in the hospital library I began a really intensive research into tonality.'[10] Like the contemporary classical music figures Morton Feldman (1926–87) and Charles Wuorinen (b. 1938), Russell later studied composition with the modernist German-Jewish émigré composer Stefan Wolpe (1902–74),[11] who had been director of music at Black Mountain College during the early 1950s and who then moved to New York. For Max Harrison, it was perhaps as a result of this study with Wolpe that Russell's own compositions revealed 'the most sophisticated of jazzmen, more aware than others [. . .] of the larger world of music'.[12]

Russell's significance as a mature artist is both as one of the earliest jazz theorists to publish a substantial treatise – regarded by Lewis as 'the first contribution made by jazz to the theory of music'[13] – and as an African-American composer and musician.[14] The first opportunity to put his early tonal theories into compositional practice resulted in what would become something of a hit: the two-part Afro-Cuban fusion piece *Cubana Be, Cubana Bop* (1947), commissioned and performed by the legendary trumpeter 'Dizzy' Gillespie and His Orchestra. This work, which featured the phenomenal Cuban conga drummer Chano Pozo, was premiered in the hallowed Carnegie Hall. While the performers' achievements were easily recognized, critics were initially unsure what to make of the ensemble parameter of the music: the issue was most acute in respect of 'the music's discontinuity, its juxtaposition of very different textures and types of

---

[9] Within the intellectual climate of Third Stream, Darius Brubeck ('1959: The Beginning of Beyond', 181) considers that Russell 'might indeed qualify as a "cabalist" and "metaphysician"'.

[10] Russell quoted in Cerulli, 'George Russell', 15.

[11] For confirmation of this pupil–teacher relationship, see Heining, *George Russell*, 81.

[12] Max Harrison, 'George Russell – Rational Anthems, Phase 1', *The Wire*, 3 (Spring 1983), 30–1: 31.

[13] John Lewis quoted in Harrison, 'George Russell – Rational Anthems', 30.

[14] Russell is among seven featured musicians in Christopher George Bakriges, 'African American Musical Avant-gardism', PhD dissertation (York University, 2001).

motion [...] its violently unpredictable rhythmic life'.[15] In short, it was highly original and unconventional. Significantly, in 1949 Russell wrote *A Bird in Igor's Yard*, a piece recorded by the jazz clarinettist Buddy DeFranco (b. 1923) and his large band, which cleverly brought together in tribute aspects of the art of the jazz saxophonist-composer Charlie Parker and Igor Stravinsky. Fittingly, Parker too was fascinated by Stravinsky's music. *A Bird in Igor's Yard* marks a further development in Russell's ideas, revealing a complexity and intensity – sometimes simultaneity – of musical material which belies its short duration.[16]

Russell's relationship with Evans (the subject of Chapter 8) was that of an informal teacher–pupil nature. His group the George Russell Smalltet, which contributed to the RCA *Jazz Workshop* series, included Evans among its players,[17] and he had also, around the mid 1950s, invited Davis into his ensemble. Davis recalls that:

> After I did the Birdland gig, I think I recorded with Lee Konitz [b. 1927], as a sideman for Prestige. Max Roach [1924–2007] was on that date and George Russell and some other guys I have forgotten. We did some of George's compositions and arrangements; he was always a very interesting composer. The playing as I remember it was good, but not startling.[18]

The success of his album within *The Jazz Workshop* series led indirectly to Russell being commissioned to write for the first Brandeis Jazz Festival at Brandeis University in 1957, together with contributors such as Schuller, the jazz composer Charles Mingus and, intriguingly, the serial/electronic composer-theorist Milton Babbitt (1916–2011). The result was the three-movement orchestral suite *All About Rosie*, the finale of which again featured Evans.

In his contemporaneous critique of Third Stream, Harvey Pekar identifies the Brandeis *Modern Jazz Concert* album recorded by Columbia (WL 127), which showcased the work of some six composers, as an important achievement.[19] But while rating Russell's prototype piece *Lydian M-1* (recorded on Teddy Charles's *Tentet* LP album in 1956), with its 'complex contrapuntal sections, brilliant orchestration and tense, staccato lines',[20]

---

[15] Harrison, 'George Russell – Rational Anthems', 30.

[16] The piece inspires a full chapter in Heining, *George Russell*: 'A Bird in Igor's Yard' (chapter 5), 87–112.

[17] Information from sources including: James G. Roy Jr, Carman Moore and Barry Kernfeld, 'George (Allan) Russell', in Kernfeld (ed.), *The New Grove Dictionary of Jazz*, vol. III, 474–5: 474; Edward Murray and Barry Kernfeld, 'Bill Evans (ii)', in Kernfeld (ed.), *The New Grove Dictionary of Jazz*, vol. I, 723–6: 723.

[18] Davis, *Miles: The Autobiography*, 136.   [19] Pekar, 'Third Stream Jazz', 9.   [20] *Ibid.*, 7.

Pekar is less sure about *All About Rosie* since, in his view, exciting surface-level complexities initially distract the listener from a problem of melodic triteness and 'jazz clichés'. Conversely, Harrison highlights a 'most imaginative use of borrowed material', namely of an Alabama children's song-game, 'Rosie, Little Rosie'. In the first movement, he remarks on 'a quasi-Stravinskian superimposition of phrases of unequal length, tension arising from conflict between the regularity of the underlying beat [. . .] and the irregular way the accents of these phrases fall around it'; meanwhile, the second movement pursues 'the feeling of the blues without the form', creating a 'jazz polyphony'.[21] Either way, the work has withstood the test of time. Another major landmark for the emerging composer was his extended album *New York, New York*, recorded in 1958 and released by Decca in 1959, with poetry by Jon Hendricks and with Russell acting both as band arranger – including of Rodgers and Hart's 'Manhattan' – and conductor. As Darius Brubeck has acknowledged, Russell's music while relatively unknown 'remains controversial, influential and respected within professional circles'.[22]

Across 1964–9, however, rather jaded by the overtly commercial and still racially prejudiced American scene, Russell left New York. Instead, he developed his European connections, undertaking a tour with his highly productive Sextet in autumn 1964 and working particularly with Swedish Radio, supported by its imaginative jazz director Bosse Broberg. Towards the end of the decade, however, Russell's relationship with Schuller, which had begun back in the Brandeis days, was rekindled: in 1969, as President of the New England Conservatory of Music in Boston, Schuller invited Russell to teach in the institution's newly set up jazz department.[23] This Russell did for many years, employing his own treatise among his teaching materials for elucidating jazz improvisation and composition.

Russell's Lydian chromatic concept

The *Lydian Chromatic Concept of Tonal Organization* was self-published in 1953, cannily anticipating the modal jazz movement, while Russell himself had been inspired by the bebop developments of Gillespie, Parker and

---

[21] Harrison, 'George Russell – Rational Anthems', 31.

[22] Darius Brubeck, '1959: The Beginning of Beyond', 191.

[23] To establish accurate information, I have cross-referenced various sources, including: Olive Jones, 'Conversation with … George Russell: A New Theory for Jazz', *Black Perspective in Music*, 2/1 (Spring 1974), 63–74; Roy, Moore and Kernfeld, 'George (Allan) Russell', 474–5; and Keith Shadwick, *Jazz: Legends of Style* (London: Quintet Publishing, 1998), 289; www.georgerussell.com/.

others. For the young composer-theorist, the years around 1950–3 were totally absorbed by this Lydian theoretical quest: 'It [the theory] was a live, growing thing with a constantly expanding logical life of its own [...] a concept with a soul, born out of jazz and its needs, yet embracing all music created in the equal temperament system.'[24] The resulting treatise-cum-instructional-manual reappeared in revised, enlarged editions in 1959, 1964 and finally 2001.[25] At one stage Russell contemplated plans for other large-scale theories, but this treatise effectively became his life's work, and his attitude towards it therefore verged at times on the obsessive, or at least became slightly out of proportion. On the inside flap of the jacket of the book, major ambitions – some of which are perhaps less supportable, self-promotional claims – are harboured for his theory: 'His [Russell's] work stands head-to-head with Arnold Schoenberg's "liberation" of the twelve-tone scale, the polytonal work of Stravinsky, and the ethnic-scale explorations of Bartók and Kodály.'

Nevertheless, we should examine critically the main tenets of his ideas.[26] In brief, Russell argues that it is the Lydian (F) scale, created through superimposed Pythagorean fifths, which should be regarded as the basis for tonal music, rather than the Ionian (C), traditional major scale. He strongly asserts the importance of scale in rebalancing, and correlating with, the jazz community's previous preoccupation with chord (especially chord changes), to the extent that 'the basic principle of chord–scale is now pervasive'.[27] In his invocation of notions of 'tonal gravity' and 'the linear, goal-oriented horizontal aspect of harmony',[28] he, perhaps surprisingly, adopts a somewhat Schenkerian tone: the two share underpinning meta-physical dimensions. We might also perceive parallels with Allen Forte's bold quest for a system of pitch-class set genera that could encompass both atonal and tonal music.[29] Similarly, in presenting their substantial theories, both Russell and Forte faced challenges in needing to call upon a sizeable body of specific technical language, which 'sometimes resulted in unread-ably turgid discourse burdened with jargon'.[30] There is surely also an

[24] Russell quoted in Harrison, 'George Russell – Rational Anthems', 30.

[25] George Russell's *Lydian Chromatic Concept of Tonal Organization*, fourth edition (Brookline, MA: Concept Publishing, 2001; orig. publ. 1953), vol. I: *The Art and Science of Tonal Gravity* [of two projected volumes]. I am grateful to Alice Norbury Russell, George's widow, for her generosity in permitting the reproduction of selected excerpts from Russell's book without charge.

[26] For a recent detailed account, from a jazz perspective, see Heining, *George Russell*: 'On Conceptual Thinking' (chapter 11), 283–320.

[27] Darius Brubeck, '1959: The Beginning of Beyond', 192.

[28] Russell, *Lydian Chromatic Concept*, 223.   [29] See Forte, 'Pitch-Class Set Genera'.

[30] Darius Brubeck, '1959: The Beginning of Beyond', 191.

Example 7.1 Russell, 'The Lydian Chromatic Order of Tonal Gravity' (reproduced from Russell, *Lydian Chromatic Concept*, 14)

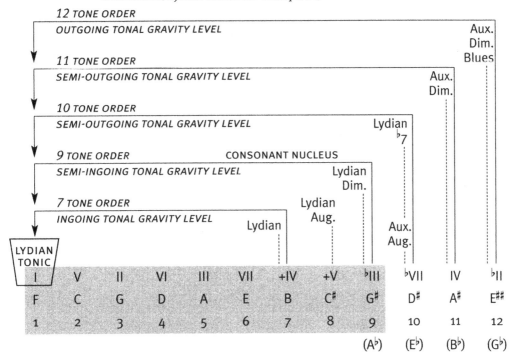

equivalence with the theorizing, modal constructions and creativity of Messiaen, articulated in his earlier manifesto, *Technique de mon langage musical* (refer to Chapter 1).

Having created a seven-note diatonic scale: F–C–G–D–A–E–B (i.e. through to the raised fourth, +IV), reduced within an octave, Russell brings in the remaining chromatic pitches, building a little idiosyncratically upon the raised fifth (+V) – C♯ – to generate a series of further fifths, excepting the final augmented fifth interval: C♯–G♯–D♯–A♯–E♯♯[*sic*]; see Example 7.1. The various incorporated scalic abbreviations, such as 'Lydian Aug.', are explained below. Although Russell's Lydian Chromatic scale does not map directly onto any of Messiaen's modes, in its commonly invoked nine-note version (see below) – F, G, G♯, A, B, C, C♯, D, E – it is intriguingly similar to the French composer's third mode, when transposed onto F: F, G, G♯, A, B, C, C♯, D♯, E.

By extension, Russell comes to recognize 'eleven [subsidiary] member scales' of his Lydian Chromatic scale. The criteria that are provided by him to support the introduction of C♯ here, rather than say F♯, are essentially subjective, although they are presented as being objective: his first criterion

Table 7.1 *Russell, 'The Seven Principal Scales of the F Lydian Chromatic Scale' (adapted from Russell,*
Lydian Chromatic Concept, 13)

1. Lydian scale	I II III +IV V VI VII	F G A B C D E
2. Lydian augmented	I II III +IV +V VI VII	F G A B C♯ D E
3. Lydian diminished	I II bIII +IV V VI VII	F G A♭ B C D E
4. Lydian flat seventh	I II III +IV V VI bVII	F G A B C D E♭
5. Auxiliary augmented [wholetone]	I II III +IV +V bVII	F G A B C♯ E♭
6. Auxiliary diminished [octatonic: 0, 2]	I II bIII IV +IV +V VI VII	F G A♭ B♭ B C♯ D E
7. Auxiliary diminished blues [octatonic: 0, 1]	I bII bIII III +IV V VI bVII	F G♭ A♭ A B C D E♭

Note: Russell's underlining of F and D highlights I and VI as respective major and minor 'tonic station
chords', unified within his Lydian system (i.e. his inflection of traditional linkage between tonic major and
relative minor).

Table 7.2 *Messiaen's modes of limited transposition*

1. C D E F♯ G♯ A♯ C [wholetone]
2. C D♭ E♭ E G♭ G A B♭ C [octatonic: 0, 1]
3. C D E♭ E G♭ G A♭ B♭ B C
4. C D♭ D F G♭ G A♭ B C
5. C D♭ F G♭ G B C
6. C D E F F♯ G♯ A♯ B C
7. C D♭ D E♭ F G♭ G A♭ A B C

concerns 'a [member] scale's capacity to parent chords considered important in the development of Western harmony'.[31] (What is more interesting, however, in the light of later ambivalence is the seeming endorsement
here of features of European harmony.) These members comprise both
'principal', also referred to as 'parent', and 'horizontal' scales. Where
the 'principal' scales are concerned, four Lydian modes, including 'augmented' and so-called 'diminished' versions, are supplemented by three
'auxiliary' ones; see Table 7.1. As already hinted at, there are fascinating
parallels and some commonalities, including the wholetone and octatonic
(0, 1) collections, with Messiaen's original identification of seven modes
of limited transposition (numbers 5 and 7 of which he later discarded);[32]
see Table 7.2.

[31] Russell, *Lydian Chromatic Concept*, 12.
[32] I am grateful to Chris Dingle for our fruitful discussion of Messiaen's modes.

Russell's audacious and single-minded theory has been regarded seriously across the years, as evidenced by the responses of Davis and others.[33] Furthermore, it still ranks highly, especially among jazz-based composers and practitioners, both in North America and Europe: for instance, his ideas continue to carry much weight for the jazz-based composer and pianist Hans Koller (b. 1970), who teaches at Birmingham Conservatoire. As the Swiss jazz pianist-writer André Jeanquartier has commented: 'Russell's contribution to developments in the melodic area of jazz, for example in the provision of Lydian scales [. . .] should not be underestimated.'[34] In spite of this support, his theory does still present problems of inconsistency, some arbitrariness, slips and sheer complexity that have also been documented and critiqued, particularly in *Jazzforschung* by Alfons Michael Dauer, Jeanquartier and others.[35] The treatments in these articles are thorough – with systematic charts and tabulations – if somewhat dry. Dauer does, however, include some analytical application and testing of Russell's theory in *Kary's Trance* by Konitz and in Parker's recording of 'Lady, Be Good', made in December 1940.[36] Meanwhile, Jeanquartier incorporates brief examples, such as 'Love for Sale' from the Broadway show *The New Yorkers* (1930) by Cole Porter (1891–1964) and Russell's own, loosely derived, 'Ezz-thetic' (dedicated to a boxer called Ezzard Charles), the title track of his album from 1961.[37]

(Mis)Reading French music

As mentioned earlier, Russell had already created *A Bird in Igor's Yard* and would later develop strong Scandinavian connections. Equally, on the front flap of his book jacket, if mainly for justificatory purposes, he makes clear

[33] See an early supportive critique of Russell's Lydian theory in John Benson Brooks, 'George Russell', *Jazz Review*, 3/2 (February 1960), 38–9; and John Howard Riley, 'A Critical Examination of George Russell's Lydian Concept of Tonal Organization for Improvisation', MA dissertation (Indiana University, 1967).
[34] André Jeanquartier, 'Kritische Anmerkungen zum "Lydian Chromatic Concept"', *Jazzforschung*, 16 (1984), 9–41: 41 (abstract, in English).
[35] Alfons Michael Dauer, 'Das Lydisch-Chromatische Tonsystem von George Russell und seine Anwendung', *Jazzforschung*, 14 (1982), 61–132; Jeanquartier, 'Kritische Anmerkungen zum "Lydian Chromatic Concept"'. See too Ingrid Monson, 'Oh Freedom: George Russell, John Coltrane, and Modal Jazz', in Bruno Nettl and Melinda Russell (eds.), *In the Course of Performance: Studies in the World of Musical Improvisation* (University of Chicago Press, 1998), 149–68.
[36] Dauer, 'Das Lydisch-Chromatische Tonsystem', 96–9, 106ff.
[37] Jeanquartier, 'Kritische Anmerkungen zum "Lydian Chromatic Concept"', 33, 34–5. See George Russell, *Ezz-thetics* (New York: Riverside RLP 9375, 1961).

that his theories find precedent in Western concert music: 'Radical as it may be, the theory is more than one person's eccentricity, having considerable precedent in the work of Ravel, Scriabin, Debussy, and in some of the learned works of Bach.' But, once we get inside the covers of the book, things feel to be inflected rather differently.

On the one hand, it is intriguing and unusual practice that Russell devotes special attention – implying special status – to analyses of Debussy's 'Ondine', from the second volume of *Préludes*, and Ravel's 'Forlane', the third movement of the composer's neoclassical prototype *Le Tombeau de Couperin*. On the other hand – and perhaps anticipating trends in jazz scholarship that sought (with some rationale) to neutralize European hegemony, or to bypass and move beyond this issue – Russell's analyses seem in practice to reverse any crediting of influence made on the jacket by subsuming, possibly subjugating, these pieces within his theory and reading of history. In a complementary fashion, Olive Jones makes the point that 'he [Russell] found the constraints of traditional music theory useless to explain music beyond Wagner and, more significantly, totally inadequate for the analysis of Afro-American music, particularly blues and jazz'.[38]

Association may be made here with notions of misreading and rewriting in one's own image or experience, at least loosely along the lines of the poetry theorist and critic Harold Bloom, and thus an apparently neutral traversing of boundaries may prove a little deceptive. With reference to Bloom's *Anxiety of Influence*, it would hardly be surprising if Russell were to feel the sheer weight of European musical tradition as somewhat oppressive: a cause of anxiety in his search for an artistic voice and quest to 'clear imaginative space'[39] for himself. Moreover, in writing any book, an author is susceptible to a certain temptation to overstate his or her case slightly,[40] not least to overcome that deep anxiety and justify having assumed the task in the first place.

Bloom's second, balancing book, *A Map of Misreading*, seems especially apt for our current purposes. It is worth recalling his crucial adage (quoted in Chapter 2), that: 'Reading [. . .] is a belated and all-but-impossible act, and if strong is always a misreading.'[41] Also relevant is his statement about artistic revisionary practice: 'These [intertextual] relationships depend upon

[38] Jones, 'Conversation with . . . George Russell', 63.
[39] Bloom, *The Anxiety of Influence*, 5.
[40] On this theme, Jonathan Dunsby refers to W. V. Quine's apt consideration of 'diffidence': Jonathan Dunsby, 'Criteria of Correctness in Music Theory and Analysis', in Anthony Pople (ed.), *Theory, Analysis and Meaning in Music* (Cambridge University Press, 1994), 77–85: 77.
[41] Bloom, *A Map of Misreading*, 3.

a critical act, a misreading or misprision that one poet [or musician] performs upon another.'[42] Drawing upon the revisionary tradition of the Kabbalah, as well as upon Freud and Nietzsche, Bloom considers that 're-seeing is a *limitation*, re-estimating is a *substitution*, and re-aiming is a *representation*'.[43] The central portion of his book sets out a 'Map of misprision',[44] with a table consisting of five columns. The first column comprises his 'Dialectic of revisionism' (*limitation, substitution, representation*), while others relate to 'Images in the poem' (including presence and absence), 'Rhetorical trope' (including irony, metonymy and metaphor), 'Psychic defense' (including reaction-formation, reversal, undoing, regression, repression) and a 'Revisionary ratio' (six ratios termed *clinamen, tessera, kenosis, daemonization, askesis* and *apophrades*).[45] Bloom tests this map, effectively piloting it, in Robert Browning's *Childe Roland* and later employs it more broadly in understanding John Milton, Ralph Waldo Emerson and others. Albeit in a much freer fashion, I shall touch on several of Bloom's ideas in the case studies.

Case study 1: Ravel's 'Forlane' as read by Russell, in light of Ravel's reading of Couperin

This focus upon the 'Forlane' acts as a neat vehicle for time travel and reinterpretation. The piece connotes two levels of modelling: firstly (and treated more briefly), that enacted by Ravel and followed up by the Ballets suédois around 1920; secondly, after Ravel's death, that enacted by Russell. In terms of a theoretical apparatus, although reference to Bloom provides the mainstay, Eliot's idea of generosity to a past still has some applicability, while we also recognize Ravel's own writings, some of which do favour quite a revisionary process in the act of composition, particularly his *Contemporary Music* lecture of 1928. In his creative response to inspirational external resources such as jazz, Ravel talks about necessary assimilation, but also about the imperative of treating source materials to 'minute stylization', 'manipulation', national redefinition, and individualization (for detail, see Chapter 5).

   Ravel is seen to have composed his Couperin suite as a multifaceted act of homage: firstly, to French classicism and the eighteenth-century master himself; secondly, as an evolving tribute from his own time to friends lost in World War I (with the 'Forlane' dedicated to Lieutenant Gabriel Deluc). In practice, it also constitutes a memorial to his beloved mother who died in 1917. This dimension of homage is illustrated literally by his nicely honed

---

[42] *Ibid.*   [43] *Ibid.*, 4.   [44] *Ibid.*, 83–105.   [45] *Ibid.*, 84.

black-ink sketch of a funerary urn, which appeared as the frontispiece to the first edition of the piano suite in 1918.[46]

Effectively as a preparatory exercise, Ravel had been involved in transcribing Couperin: specifically the 'Forlane' from the *Quatrième concert royal* (1722), undertaken in spring 1914, though unpublished during his lifetime. As Scott Messing points out, Ravel's actions had probably been motivated by Albert Bertelin's transcription of this 'Forlane', which appeared in Jules Écorcheville's article of the same title published in *Revue musicale de la SIM* in April 1914.[47] Barbara Kelly offers a useful comparison of these editorial sources, combined with Ravel's own 'Forlane' from *Le Tombeau*.[48] It may reasonably be concluded that Ravel's transcription, while overall presenting a faithful rendition of its Couperin source, still enjoys a measure of artistic licence: fittingly, baroque embellishment. In the fourth couplet marked 'mineur', we may note that gesture of a grace note plus octave descent which recurs on the third and sixth quavers of bars 5–8.

In respect of his own composition of *Le Tombeau*, Ravel distanced things slightly by maintaining that: 'The homage is directed less in fact to Couperin himself than to French music of the eighteenth century.'[49] But there are undoubtedly many strong parallels with, and occasionally conceivable misreadings of, the *grand maître* of the Ancien Régime. Messing and Orenstein perceive close rhythmic links between the Couperin and Ravel forlanes. For Kelly, too: 'Certainly, Ravel retained the rhythmic gestures, ornamentation and formal scheme of refrain and couplets from the original.'[50] Kelly remarks upon a particularly clear correspondence of phrasing, articulation and tonality between Ravel's E major section and Couperin's refrain, added to by melodic similarity apropos Couperin's third couplet.[51] This dimension of the relationship may be summarized as essentially 'reverential'.[52]

What should we make, though, of that most characteristic gesture of Ravel's 'Forlane': the strongly assertive rising major seventh with offbeat stress, set against block harmonies, within the opening phrase? Do we construe this as originality and/or an ironic misreading of an arpeggiation?

---

[46] For a reproduction of Ravel's drawing, see Mawer, *The Ballets of Maurice Ravel*, 189.

[47] *Ibid.*, 186.

[48] Kelly, 'History and Homage', 19–22. The reader is referred to Maurice Ravel, *Le Tombeau de Couperin*, urtext edition by Roger Nichols (London: Edition Peters, 1995).

[49] (Alexis) Roland-Manuel, 'Une esquisse autobiographique de Maurice Ravel [1928]', *La Revue musicale*, 19 (special issue, December 1938), 17–23: 22: 'L'hommage s'adresse moins en réalité au seul Couperin lui-même qu'à la musique française du XVIIIe siècle.'

[50] Kelly, 'History and Homage', 19.   [51] *Ibid.*

[52] Martha Hyde, 'Neoclassic and Anachronistic Impulses in Twentieth-Century Music', *Music Theory Spectrum*, 18/2 (1996), 200–35: 206–10.

Especially in its orchestrated form, imbued with distinctive cor anglais sonority, timbral combination and piquant dissonance, the modernist credentials become more apparent. As I have argued previously, 'the twentieth-century imprint is nonetheless quite audible'.[53] Similarly, Abbate talks of a dynamic process of 'reanimation' from within, while Andreas Dorschel perceives deformation of a model, as testimony to an unavoidable gap between present and past.[54]

To this musical time travel may be added that of the Ballets suédois in choreographing three of Ravel's four orchestrated movements of *Le Tombeau* in 1920, supported by delicate designs of Pierre Laprade (1875–1931).[55] Ironically, for historical reasons, French classical, or so-called 'style', dances – exported to Sweden by French dancers in the eighteenth century and venerated in the Swedish Royal Court – had been much better preserved in Stockholm than Paris. Börlin's 'Forlane' was aptly conceived for a chamber-sized group of four couples: a single quadrille. Among early photographs taken around the time of the ballet premiere, we may refer to one of Börlin and Jenny Hasselquist in a studio pose that probably relates to the stately 'Menuet'.[56] Such images suggest a convincing portrayal of eighteenth-century dance, albeit with a neoclassical exaggeration of manners: decorum, emotional detachment, and an overt affectation.

Despite Ravel's admission that, in seeking originality, 'this something will never emerge more distinctly than in your unintended unfaithfulness to a model',[57] we tend to read Ravel's act in Eliot's terms as generosity to a French past: traditionalism. For Kelly, 'Ravel was less concerned with remaking the past than with responding to it, unlike Stravinsky';[58] he was undeniably more of an evolutionary than a revolutionary. Nevertheless, a work such as Stravinsky's ballet *Pulcinella* preserves rather more of an underlying model, whether Pergolesi's or Gallo's, than does *Le Tombeau*. Stravinsky was initially acknowledged merely as the arranger, rather than

---

[53] Mawer, *The Ballets of Maurice Ravel*, 187, 191.

[54] Carolyn Abbate, 'Outside Ravel's Tomb', *Journal of the American Musicological Society*, 52/3 (Fall 1999), 465–530; Dorschel quoted in Michael J. Puri, *Ravel the Decadent: Memory, Sublimation, and Desire* (New York: Oxford University Press, 2011), 209n. See too Puri's 'contrasting modes of memory' after Proust, with an unattainable, fixed 'nostalgic' mode, versus one with 'optimistic' re-creative potential: 15–21 and book jacket.

[55] See illustrations reproduced in Mawer, *The Ballets of Maurice Ravel*, 194–5.

[56] See photograph in *ibid.*, 200.

[57] Ravel quoted by Roland-Manuel, 'Des valses à *La Valse*', 145: 'ce quelque chose n'apparaîtra jamais plus clairement que dans votre involontaire infidélité au modèle'; translated in Deborah Mawer, 'Musical Objects and Machines', in Mawer (ed.), *The Cambridge Companion to Ravel*, 47–67: 56.

[58] Kelly, 'History and Homage', 26.

Example 7.2 Ravel, *Daphnis et Chloé*, 'Introduction' (bars 1–7, reduced score)

composer, of *Pulcinella*, yet he is typically and fashionably portrayed as a (re)visionary, as in Straus's *Remaking the Past* (see Chapter 3). For Ravel scholars, however, the important need to maintain the composer's congruence with a French national tradition seemingly imposes a certain restriction.

As the second, main part of this case study, we project forwards to Russell's reading. And the first thing to note about Russell's referencing of Ravel is where he avoids doing so. Near the beginning of the book, the Lydian scale's 'ladder of fifths structure' is graphed, as shown in Example 7.1, and this portion cries out for reference to the extraordinary opening of *Daphnis et Chloé*, premiered some forty years earlier; compare with Example 7.2. Ravel's distinctive seven-note ladder of 'Pythagorean' fifths: A–E–B–F♯–C♯–G♯–D♯ then melts into the ethereal flute melody of the nymphs. This omission of *Daphnis* suggests that the admission of precedent may be selective, possibly that there might be some act of suppression (Bloomian 'repression') or denial of boundary crossing. Equally, the idea of reference to Ravel being conspicuous by its absence comes close to an instance of emphasis through suppression à la Derrida. Specifically, it might be viewed as illustrating one of the two main interpretations of Derrida's concept of 'différance': that of deferral.[59]

Interestingly, the music of Ravel that Russell chooses to analyse – as an activity somewhat analogous to Ravel's editing of Couperin – is the 'Forlane' from *Le Tombeau*. And within Russell's modal agenda, it is surely the overtly Ravelian traits, those modernist qualities, which interest him most: what might be termed the chromaticism of the opening phrase(s), especially its melodic A♯ and prominent D♯. This focus upon the well-known bars 1–6 is followed by a detailed beat-by-beat explanation of the

[59] Jacques Derrida, 'Différance', in *Margins of Philosophy*, Eng. trans. Alan Bass (University of Chicago Press, 1982), 1–27.

Example 7.3 Russell's analysis of Ravel, *Le Tombeau de Couperin*, 'Forlane' (bars 1–6; reproduced from Russell, *Lydian Chromatic Concept*, 155)

Allegretto ♩. = 96

scales and harmonies, primarily from a Lydian Chromatic perspective;[60] see Example 7.3. This start of the 'Forlane' is revisited later in the book, with a second annotated quotation.[61] (In more than one way, the circumscribed rehearing of these bars of Ravel nicely correlates with Bloom's *limitation*.) The main treatment of the 'Forlane' example occurs in discussion of a 'Vertical Tonal Gravity' – a notion whereby 'the magnetic "pull" [. . . is] always being directed to fall on the Lydian Tonic',[62] again not so distant from a Schenkerian *Ursatz* ('fundamental structure'), or from Hindemith's idea of 'fundamental bass'.[63]

By way of a control, a typical post-tonal approach would acknowledge a flexible E minor modality, with mixture at the third: G/G♯, embellished by other chromatic touches, for example A♯ and B♯. Melodic prominence is given to the expressive seventh degree (D♯), while, harmonically, seventh

---

[60] Russell, *Lydian Chromatic Concept*, 155–8.   [61] *Ibid.*, 220.   [62] *Ibid.*, 14n.

[63] Hindemith is cited by Russell, as noted by Monson, 'Oh Freedom', 152. See Paul Hindemith, *The Craft of Musical Composition*, 2 vols., fourth edition (Mainz and London: Schott, 1942), vol. I: *Theory*.

and extended ninth and eleventh chords are common (together with some augmented and diminished constructs): E, G/G♯, B, D♯ (bar 1); F♯, A, C♯, E♯, G♯, B (bar 3). Russell's jazz-style harmonic analysis beneath the bass stave is generally congruent with this view, indicating an initial 'Em$^{maj\ 7}$' (bar 1) and 'F♯m$^{maj\ 7}$', followed by 'F♯m$^{9♭5}$' (bar 3). ('Am$^{maj\ 7}$' is brought forward from bar 2 to apply also to the second beat of bar 1, and would presumably then constitute an A$^{♯11}$ chord: A, C [B♯], E, G♯, [B], D♯.)

As the next stage, a Lydian view is superimposed or *substituted* – a strong reading in Bloomian terms that involves a measure of *kenosis* or breaking from the past – one that I shall now summarize. In Russell's theory, 'The E min ^{maj7} tonic station chord [...] indicates the tone G as the Forlane's overall Lydian Tonic.'[64] This produces the collection: G, A, B, C♯, D♯, E, F♯, but starting on the sixth degree (VI), i.e. E. (Confusingly in traditional terms yet consistent with the chord–scale rethinking, bracketed roman numerals as notated above the stave in bar 1 denote scalic degrees rather than chords. More fundamentally, we might favour a simpler option of Dorian on E, with a raised seventh.) Russell expands his point, commenting on 'the frequent use of B♯ and C♯ accidentals', and 'the tone A♯ in the melody indicating the nine-tone order [9 T.O.] of the G LC [Lydian Chromatic] Scale'. The designation of '9 T.O.' here denotes a counting up, primarily in perfect fifths, from G through to A♯: G, D, A, E, B, F♯, C♯, D♯, A♯.

In this manner, a higher-than-normal prominence is undoubtedly afforded to pitches that would generally be regarded as superficial chromaticism. (And so this work may be construed to have offered a positive foundation for much more recent theoretical rethinking, such as that advocated by Tymoczko, who seeks 'to present chromaticism as an orderly phenomenon rather than an unsystematic exercise in compositional rule breaking'.)[65] Indeed Russell goes on to claim 'the composer's conscious intent to exploit the nine-tone order itself as an official scale'.[66] If we set aside the dangers of assigning authorial intent for a moment, the invoked pitches are thus viewed as integral and essential scale members – in a sense, loosely equivalent to a Schoenbergian emancipation of dissonance. As a matter of detail, however, there is still a perception of 'harmonic polarities'

---

[64] Russell, *Lydian Chromatic Concept*, 155.

[65] Tymoczko, *A Geometry of Music*, 268. Interestingly, he refers to Ravel's 'Forlane' in connection with the jazz concept of tritone substitution: 355, 364. The first locus also features upper quartal voicings (bar 130), while the second involves 'a beautiful g♯[=d]– G^{7}–c–f♯–F^{7}–B♭ progression that embellishes descending fifths with tritone-related chords' (bars 19–24). Sensitively though, Tymoczko considers that 'tritone embellishment' might be a more appropriate term here.

[66] Russell, *Lydian Chromatic Concept*, 156.

or a 'counterbalance' between 'Augmented' fifth and 'Diminished [flat-tened]' third constructs, involving D♯ and A♯, respectively.[67]

The main cause for concern lies with the seeming ahistoricism of the bold commentary that accompanies the graphed music analysis. The implication and misreading, in a classic Bloomian sense (that term *clinamen*: Russell effecting a corrective 'swerve' to Ravel's example), is that if Ravel had had the benefit of knowing about the Lydian Chromatic Concept, he would have subscribed to it; that his music was somehow 'out of time', awaiting this point of arrival. An unequivocal assertion is made that 'Ravel is clearly relating to the nine-tone order of each chord's parent LC Scale in the manner prescribed by the Law of Vertical Tonal Gravity'.[68]

Instead of appearing influenced by Ravel, by engaging strongly with his precursor, Russell creates a reversal of meaning that almost suggests he has influenced the earlier work. More generally, but still with Ravel as the exemplar, it is argued that: 'some composers obviously were applying their own vertical tonal organization, which had to be somewhat along the lines of the LC Concept, years before the Concept's initial 1953 publication, in spite of the fact that Western music pedagogy did not and does not recognize chord/scale unity as the basis for the vertical principle of Western harmony'.[69] We can relate to Bloom's final concept of *apophrades*,[70] whereby an author who may feel burdened by his solipsism holds up his work for scrutiny supposedly by the precursor, yet the result still tends towards a viewing of the former work within the image of the latter. Ravel is remade through a Lydian prism or Bloomian misprision: an intentional or witting 'infidélité au modèle' – modernity? (Of course, Ravel's *Le Tombeau* was itself a remodelling of Couperin, albeit a rather different kind of influence.) What emerges is a *representation* that embraces some sense of seeking to overpower one's precursors. In his general critique, Jeanquartier voices similar concerns, challenging Russell's claim to have created a wholly new theory, and that 'everything previously created in music, as well as still to be created, can be better explained with it'.[71]

Case study 2: Debussy's 'Ondine' as read by Russell

Russell's coverage of Debussy's water goddess 'Ondine' extends to four pages of annotated score (bars 1–20 and 50–7),[72] plus two or so pages of text.[73] This analysis was authored jointly with the jazz musician William

[67] *Ibid.*, 156.   [68] *Ibid.*, 158.   [69] *Ibid.*, 157.   [70] Bloom, *A Map of Misreading*, 84.
[71] Jeanquartier, 'Kritische Anmerkungen zum "Lydian Chromatic Concept"', 41.
[72] Russell, *Lydian Chromatic Concept*, 199–203.   [73] *Ibid.*, 198–9, 203.

(Bill) J. Geha (1921–2010), former bandleader of the Bill Geha Orchestra and, like Russell, associated with the New England Conservatory of Music, Boston. As with *Le Tombeau*, a Bloomian revisionist dialectic embracing *limitation*, *substitution* and *representation* may readily be discerned. Similarly, this illustration occurs within, and is limited by, the context of 'Vertical Tonal Gravity', with Russell arguing convincingly for Debussy's combinative melodic-harmonic conception, in support of his own quest for 'chord/scale unity'.[74] An indisputable basic enthusiasm for Debussy's music is captured in phrases such as: 'A very rich harmonic palette, presented [. . .] in a natural, effortless manner'; there are also astute perceptions in identifying 'moments of stasis and movement, tension and release'.[75] Treatment of the first seven bars is shown in Example 7.4.

A conventional approach would view these bars as a sustained $V^{13/9}$ in D major, prolonged by the upper neighbour-note B♭, bars 8–9, and resolving onto the tonic at bar 14. Hints of mixture at the sixth and third degrees colour bars 1–3, with piquant pitch clusters emphasizing blueslike, rising appoggiaturas: B♭/B; F/F♯. This procedure is strengthened and balanced across bars 4–7 by descending chromatic gestures: G♯–G, A♯–A, E♯–E and finally D♯–D (bar 7), a Lydian inflection upon V. (The tritone, already present in bars 1–3, becomes a more audible melodic-harmonic element through bars 4, 6 and 7, with A♭[G♯]–D of the Lydian tonic mode continuing to feature across bars 8–9.) Significantly, the only pitch not made fluid in this manner is the leading note, C♯, prominent as the 'bass' of bars 1–2 ($c\sharp^1$), a middle-texture feature of bars 3–4 ($c\sharp^2$), and the uppermost pitch across bars 4–7 ($c\sharp^3$).

Early on, however, Russell perceives that 'the use of G♯ in bars 4 and 6 together with his [Debussy's] exploitation of the 9 T.O. using three-note Lydian Major Seventh Chords reveal[s] a much broader concept of key' than the traditional D major key signature would indicate.[76] (The designation '9 T.O.' indicates a construction extending through to the ninth pitch, working up mainly in fifth intervals from D, i.e. E♯.) The most salient point here, almost identically as for the Ravel, is the imagining or Bloomian rewriting of history such that it is Debussy who is subscribing ahistorically to the 9 T.O. notion, rather than the other way round.

Essentially, Russell concurs with the idea of an overall dominant prolongation – note his insightful annotation of ' . . . insinuated . . . ' in Example 7.4 – although, arguably, this stance is rather undermined by viewing $A^{7(9/13)}$ simultaneously as G Lydian starting on the second degree, seemingly at a higher level.[77] ('Aug.' in bar 1 refers to the raised fifth: A, i.e. G×, the resultant

---

[74] *Ibid.*, 198ff.   [75] *Ibid.*, 198.   [76] *Ibid.*, 199.   [77] *Ibid.*, 198–9.

Example 7.4 Russell (and Geha) analysis of Debussy, *Préludes* (Book II, No. VIII), 'Ondine' (bars 1–7; reproduced from Russell, *Lydian Chromatic Concept*, 199)

scale being almost synonymous with a wholetone collection on C♯.) Again, interestingly, Russell appears to afford a higher status to what might typically be seen as mere surface-level coloration. Take, for instance, the right-hand semiquaver figurations at bars 4, 6 and 7, yet it should be made clear that, in an accompanying note, he qualifies these 'Lydian major chords' on D, B and B♭ (see again Example 7.4) as 'absolutely passive'.[78] All activity is referenced to Lydian collections upon various degrees, with D Lydian Chromatic [LC] regarded as the main modal source, but, while this practice

---

[78] *Ibid.*, 199n. Russell's abbreviation 'PMG' here stands for Primary Modal Genre, with II indicating 'seventh chords' and I, 'major chords'.

Example 7.5 Russell (and Geha) analysis of Debussy, *Préludes* (Book II, No. VIII), 'Ondine' (bars 54–7; reproduced from Russell, *Lydian Chromatic Concept*, 203)

usefully emphasizes tritonal features, some of these features might be elucidated as well or better via wholetone or Locrian modality.[79] Beyond bar 7, the interpretation continues in a similar vein.

Curiously however, following the return of the D major key signature at the 'Mouvement' marking (bar 54), a localized E♭ [LC] scale has to be qualified as 'c minor blues', implying that one Lydian size does not quite fit all; see Example 7.5. In fact, the supporting discussion for this portion of 'Ondine' is more wide-ranging and engaging. An intriguing, plausible point is made: 'Bars 54 and 55 suggest that Debussy may have been influenced by Boogie Woogie'[80] (see similar observations in Chapter 3), followed by the qualification that Debussy died shortly before this style became popular in Chicago, and well before it was really promoted by the boogie-woogie and jazz pianist Pete(r) Johnson (1904–67) and others. Therefore, anticipating Brown's balancing in *Debussy Redux*, Russell surmises either that Debussy must have been receptive to generic 'jazz influences of this nature [...] in the early 1900s', or else he concedes the 'not so remote possibility that this short excerpt from "Ondine" might have influenced Boogie Woogie'. Immediately, however, he is anxious to counter that many jazz musicians influenced 'European modernists: Debussy, Ravel, Stravinsky, Milhaud, Messiaen, and others'. It is noteworthy that Russell's selection of modernist names comprises four out of five who were French, with Stravinsky too residing in France and eventually gaining French citizenship. To be fair-minded, it should be said that Russell gives a little in observing that jazz musicians were also influenced. Nevertheless, even in his recognition of exchange, the priorities are clear: 'The cross-pollination that occurred between the true innovators of both musical genres accounts for the

---

[79] Maximilian Hendler, 'Gedanken zum "Lydischen Konzept"', *Jazzforschung*, 16 (1984), 163–71, also makes this point about the Locrian mode.

[80] This and following quotations: Russell, *Lydian Chromatic Concept*, 203.

traditional respect Europeans still maintain for true jazz innovation and innovators.' Back in bar 54, the G pedal-point is appropriately noted, but an argument is presented that Debussy's introduction of E♭ (bar 56) 'thereby reveals that his frame of reference from bar 54 has all the while been the E♭ Lydian [LC] Scale'.

While the Lydian mode definitely has a presence in 'Ondine', I would argue that the modal repertory invoked is far more fluid and varied – embracing Lydian, Dorian, Phrygian, wholetone and octatonic.[81] As for that final conjuring trick: once more, the underlying point about meaning is that in this rewriting of musical history Debussy appears almost to have become subservient, in his wholehearted adherence, to Lydian Chromatic principles. If slightly less acute in its revisionism than was the case with Ravel, this reading of Debussy still seems very well served by reference to the main tenets of Bloom's theory.

Interpretation, implications and conclusion

To the so-called classical musician, this assimilation and manipulation of Debussy and Ravel may feel sacrilegious. As an extension, it may seem that the two composers have somehow been hijacked and that their music has been used for a purpose they were not in a position to approve – that the goal posts or boundaries have been forcibly moved. We should, however, recognize our likely hypocrisy since this was generally how French music and its modernist composers engaged with jazz, including Ravel in his 'Blues' of the Violin Sonata. (Indeed some might view my motivic analysis of Evans, in the next chapter, as analogous to Russell's activity.) We recall Ravel's advocating in 1928 of adoption of a given source within the act of creation, swiftly followed by 'stylization' and 'manipulation': a stance that also bears some comparison with Bloom's 'dialectic of revisionism' (*limitation, substitution, representation*) and 'revisionary ratio'.[82]

Where *Le Tombeau* itself is concerned, there is a tendency to overplay the extent to which Ravel's creation is a national act of homage, at worst 'bon enfant' (merely 'well behaved'), and thereby underplay its originality and significance. The work may yet have been more revisionary, modernist, international and influential as a neoclassical prototype than we

---

[81] See too Richard S. Parks, *The Music of Claude Debussy* (New Haven, CT and London: Yale University Press, 1989), 341n. For an analysis of the opening of *Prélude à l'Après-midi d'un faune* that tests out Russell's Lydian concept, see Vuk Kulenovic, 'The Lydian Concept', *Sonus: A Journal of Investigations into Global Musical Possibilities*, 14/1 (Fall 1993), 55–64.

[82] Bloom, *A Map of Misreading*, 84.

typically acknowledge. After all, the start of its composition in late summer 1914 substantially predated Satie's *Parade* (1916–17) and Stravinsky's *L'Histoire du soldat* (1917–18). The very fact that a jazz musician such as Russell was interested to invoke this piece of Ravel as part of his own wider quest, some fifteen years after the composer's death, is testimony to Ravel's continuing potency and relevance, even in his supposedly most traditional moments.

If we continue in this direction, there may be an alternative, more positive way to interpret this situation. Russell, just like Ravel, was engaging with a powerful foreign music, albeit that the positions are reversed. He too was perfectly entitled to make his artistic mark, especially as a pioneer African-American jazz theorist who surely had stronger reasons than many for needing to assert his position in the face of an overwhelming Western hegemony: interestingly, one who remained largely independent of the 'so-called freedom direction'.[83] If we return to Bloom's point that any 'Reading [. . .] if strong is always a misreading',[84] this is not of itself a negative comment: rather, there is considerable personal strength of an admirable nature evidenced by Russell's endeavour. Russell might thus be regarded as Bloom's 'strong reader, whose readings will matter to others as well as to himself' and who consequently has to face his revisionist 'dilemmas', in seeking 'to find his own original relation to truth [. . . and] to open received texts [including those of Ravel and Debussy] to his own sufferings, or what he wants to call the sufferings of history'.[85] In this way, Russell's role in canon reformation is usefully emphasised, with his effective raising of the status of jazz artwork and its processes in relation to those of the long-established classical canon.

We might choose to see his championing of a Lydian theory for jazz improvisation in an audacious spirit similar to that of Pieter C. van den Toorn's promotion of the octatonic perspective in Stravinsky.[86] And while it may yet be hard not to view his analyses of Debussy and Ravel as mainly self-serving, his summative remarks do suggest a more complex, ambivalent balancing act: 'with no single, cohesive, all-embracing theory of music, innovative composers like Ravel, Ellington, Varèse, Debussy, Ives, and Stravinsky were left to their own devices. Their music, full of order and discipline, broke all the rules of theory with daring and imagination.

---

[83] Russell quoted in Jones, 'Conversation with . . . George Russell', 67; see too Monson, 'Oh Freedom'.

[84] Bloom, *A Map of Misreading*, 3.   [85] *Ibid.*, 3–4.

[86] Pieter C. van den Toorn, *The Music of Igor Stravinsky* (New Haven, CT and London: Yale University Press, 1983).

Their [...] personal theories were the foundation of their individual genius and identity.'[87] Equally, we should acknowledge that, following his period in Europe and his reassociation with Schuller's Third Stream blend of classical music and jazz, Russell does discuss the term 'pan-stylistic' and argues for influence in a more even-handed manner: 'with regard to all the musics [jazz and non-jazz] that I consider vital, one thing is certain – they have all influenced each other. So Penderecki is influenced by Miles Davis, or influenced by jazz elements, you know. And jazz is influenced by Penderecki. They're all going the same way.'[88] It is also worth quoting an earlier comment, both honest and modest, which accompanied the recording of *New York New York* in 1959 that 'Composers Alban Berg, Béla Bartók, Igor Stravinsky, and Stefan Wolpe are just a few [...] who shaped my thinking.'[89]

Despite its inconsistencies and flaws, Russell's treatise still demonstrates, potentially, the benefits of rethinking old binary divides – for example, any sense of classical music versus jazz – in favour of shared attributes: in this case, his brand of Lydian modality. So, while dealing with conflict or dissonance can be unavoidable and sometimes necessary, reharmonizing in new consonant terms may offer a refreshing alternative, even if that common object is an augmented fourth/'flatted' fifth construct. In a sense, this was exactly what Schuller's notion of Third Stream music was striving to do and what, at least for a while, it achieved as jazz–classical fusion.

Future avenues of enquiry might include a wider interpretation of Lydian modality,[90] or simply modality per se, that could enable Russell's particular Lydian chromatic jazz theory (and practice) and early twentieth-century French music to coexist on a more equal footing. Elsewhere, the humble seventh chord – dominant or otherwise – could offer a most productive focus for dual, yet individuated, treatment across classical and jazz domains. One final suggestion would be to probe the half-diminished 'Tristan chord': F, B, D♯, G♯, from Wagner's *Tristan und Isolde* (see again Chapter 3) that is both the climax of the other 'Ondine': Ravel's opening movement of *Gaspard*

[87] Russell, *Lydian Chromatic Concept*, 223.
[88] Jones, 'Conversation with ... George Russell', 67.
[89] Russell, quoted by Burt Korall, in original liner notes to *New York, New York* (Impulse! IMPD-278, 1998).
[90] In my continuing analytical work on Ravel, Lydian constructs are proving relevant to a wider repertory than would first be apparent. In a different context, see too a substantial article that pursues this agenda: Brett Clement, 'Modal Tonicization in Rock: The Special Case of the Lydian Scale', *Gamut*, 6/1 (2013), 95–142.

de la nuit (1908),[91] and the likely inspirational first step for Coltrane's celebrated studio album *Giant Steps* (1960).[92] In this way, through exploring a genuine intersection or common ground between any two territories, we may succeed in removing – or at least making fluid – part of an unhelpful boundary.

[91] See Lloyd Whitesell's excellent, nuanced harmonic reading: 'Erotic Ambiguity in Ravel's Music', in Mawer (ed.), *Ravel Studies*, 74–91: 82–5.

[92] John Coltrane, *Giant Steps* (New York: Atlantic Records SD 1311, 1960; reissued Not Now Music NOT2CD391, 2011).

8 Bill Evans's modal jazz and French music reconfigured

At an anecdotal level, French concert music, especially of the twentieth century, is commonly understood to have played a role in Bill Evans's improvisational thinking in the later 1950s, as part of a larger eclectic tradition that extends back to Ellington, Beiderbecke and others.[1] But, equally, the relevance of this repertory to Evans as a classically trained musician has often been dismissed glibly as an unsurprising given, and so has rarely been probed in any scholarly, musical depth.[2] In this respect, at least, a situation that Chuck Israels described soon after Evans's death has changed relatively little: 'Few have gone deeper into his work to find the underlying principles.'[3] This complacency begs various questions: for instance, how significant a force was French music for Evans, in comparison, say, with Russian repertory? What roles might French music play in Evans's art? And, more particularly, in what ways might French music be reconfigured within his modal jazz?

---

[1] Earlier versions of this chapter were given at Leeds International Jazz Conference (25–26 March 2010) and at the Nordic Jazz Conference (Helsinki, 19–20 August 2010; *The Jazz Chameleon: The Refereed Proceedings of the 9th Nordic Jazz Conference*, 2011: http://iipc. utu.fi/jazzchameleon/). I am grateful for feedback from Paul Berliner, Benjamin Davies, John Elliott, Bruce Johnson, Robert Keller, Claire Levy, Janne Mäkelä, Brian Priestley, Tony Whyton, Justin and Katherine Williams.

[2] An increasing amount of material about Evans is posted on websites. While this is testimony to Evans's continuing popularity, it creates challenges in corroborating the status of, and sources for, much recycled information that lacks proper referencing. Dedicated, well-used sites include: The Bill Evans Webpages (www.billevanswebpages.com), which enables access to the *Letter from Evans* newsletters, edited by Win Hinkle, and Time Remembered: Bill Evans Jazz Pianist (www.billevans.nl/). The official Bill Evans Archives (www.billevans.org/), located in Los Angeles, California, also house much information, but are not open-access. In 2012, the usefully extensive resources of the Jazzinstitut Darmstadt were listed: www.jazzinstitut.de/Jazzindex/Evans_Bill.pdf.

[3] Chuck Israels, 'Bill Evans (1929–1980): A Musical Memoir', *The Musical Quarterly*, 71/2 (1985), 109–15: 109. Some exceptions to this rule are found in unpublished research, such as Paula Berardinelli, 'Bill Evans: His Contributions as a Jazz Pianist and an Analysis of His Musical Style' (PhD dissertation, New York University, 1992); or Philippe Fourquet, 'De l'impressionisme dans le jazz: Une étude de l'influence du langage musical français du début de la siècle sur les musiciens de jazz américains, de Bix Beiderbecke à Bill Evans' (Master's dissertation, Université de Paris IV [Sorbonne], 1993), which includes a significant portion on Evans (162–203).

The loci of Evans and French music appear to offer an ideal opportunity for detailed investigation of relations between musical types. Implicit are crossings and transformations of genre, culture, national identity and time frame, and at issue is the nature and mutability of music materials, or sometimes the constancy of materials in an altered context. Also implicit is the ubiquitous question of influence, situated within a wider, fluid notion of intertextuality as a web of multiple texts. While some relations may be explored historically, others may be pursued interpretatively, including ahistorically, as noted by Klein (Chapter 2). These relations range from intertextual parallels and potential intersections, through to specific eclecticisms, which may assimilate, adapt and individualize a given source – 'chameleon'-like. This latter type of linkage, utilizing quotation, modelling or allusion, is what I have referred to earlier as a source–product relationship. Again, it should be stressed that examining such eclectic processes holds no derogatory implication, but points up the fact that no musician flourishes in a vacuum, or in isolation from their sociocultural historical milieu.

As a French specialist, I am interested to explore the impact of pre-World War I and interwar French music in later settings, especially jazz, but I also want to offer some probing of the interplay between Evans and French music that has been lacking. Firstly, I wish to check out the general assumption of Evans's association with French music, and ascertain how extensive or close this association was. In support of the comparative study, I introduce ideas on eclecticism espoused by Evans, as well as those propounded by Ravel. Secondly, in two representative case studies on aspects of the album *Kind of Blue* and 'Peace Piece' from the late 1950s, I look to investigate these proposed relations, albeit on a small canvas. In doing so, I also wish to foreground the artistry of Evans.

Relations between Evans and classical (especially French) music

Evans was born in Plainfield, New Jersey in 1929 and died in New York in 1980. The combination of his parentage and schooling meant that he was exposed to a great variety of music. His mother, Mary Soroka, was of Ukrainian origin, and as his main biographer, the classical pianist Peter Pettinger points out, with some geographical extension: 'From these lands in the nineteenth century came two of the greatest pianist-composers of all time – the Hungarian Franz Liszt and the Pole Frédéric Chopin. It is fitting that Bill Evans, a poet of the piano – and once dubbed the Chopin of jazz – traces one side of his ancestry to this part of the world.'[4] This Russian–Eastern European connection helped to develop Evans's fondness, even as a child, for Stravinsky's *Petrushka*,[5] as well as for the music of Rachmaninoff, Aram Khachaturian and others.

As a young boy, Evans learnt to play the piano and violin, though his interest lay less in the instruments themselves, or their associated scales(!), than in the imaginative potential they unleashed: 'I've learned with feeling being the generating force. I've never approached the piano as a thing in itself but as a gateway to music.'[6] As Pettinger notes, this musical 'gateway' enabled Evans to access a diverse classical menu: 'sonatas by Mozart and Beethoven and works by Schumann, Rachmaninoff, Debussy, Ravel, Gershwin (the Piano Concerto in F), Villa-Lobos, Khachaturian, Milhaud, and others'.[7] Immediately, our attention is drawn to a broad palette of Western composers, from classical and romantic Austro-German figures through to a selection of Russian and French twentieth-century composers. The Russian–Ukrainian dimension is clearly important and thus the Evans–French connection is not in any sense exclusive (a similar situation pertains with Brubeck in Chapter 9).

The scope for rich crossings between classical music and jazz was developed further by Evans's higher-level study of music, including harmonic theory and composition, at Southeastern Louisiana College (whence he graduated in 1950) and later at Mannes School of Music in New York.[8] Subsequently, in 1956, Evans led the recording of *New Jazz Conceptions* and was taken on as the pianist in George Russell's *The Jazz Workshop*. He became a key thinker and performer in Miles Davis's sextet for *Kind of Blue* and enjoyed a most successful later period leading the Bill Evans Trio, initially with Scott LaFaro and Paul Motian, while also recording as a solo artist.

Interestingly, Evans sought to minimize any sense of opposition between musics, arguably downplaying the differences, favouring an inclusive approach that promoted commonalities, including those of pulse and beat: "To me there's not much difference between classical music and

---

[4] Pettinger, *Bill Evans*, 4. There is also Gerber's French biography *Bill Evans*, though its materials are largely drawn from Pettinger and Gene Lees.

[5] Wayne Enstice and Paul Rubin, *Jazz Spoken Here: Conversations with Twenty-Two Musicians* (Baton Rouge: Louisiana State University Press, 1992; New York: Da Capo Press, 1994), 136.

[6] Evans quoted by Gene Lees, 'The Poet: Bill Evans', in Gottlieb (ed.), *Reading Jazz*, 419–44: 426.

[7] Pettinger, *Bill Evans*, 16.

[8] Stan Britt, 'The River Stops Flowing', *Jazz Journal International*, 33/11 (1980), 15.

jazz. [. . .] If you get deep enough into any music, the language and fundamental principles are the same. [. . .] By trying to learn the language of
music I look to all kinds of music.'[9] This broad, eclectic underpinning along
the lines of Eliot will be borne in mind below.

Having set out this brief classical–jazz overview, it makes sense to pursue
Evans's specific relationship with French music in greater depth. In an
extensive, insightful article, Gene Lees, the respected Canadian jazz writer
(editor of *Down Beat* and good friend of Evans), observed that, in his
creative work, Evans 'brought to bear coloristic devices and voicings and
shadings from [a range of] post-Romantic composers, including Debussy,
Ravel, Poulenc, Scriabin, and maybe Alban Berg',[10] of varying Russian,
Austrian and French nationalities. In this way, Lees emphasizes the
French impressionists, Debussy and Ravel, while expanding the neoclassical
representation, with Poulenc joining Milhaud. He also enlarges the Russian
domain, with inclusion of the French-influenced composer Scriabin. More
recently, Barrett has concurred with Lees in observing 'Evans's classical tone
and impressionist voicings'.[11] Barham makes the point that Evans's own
recordings provide clear evidence of his formal and technical classical
engagement, particularly with 'French music of the late-nineteenth and
early twentieth centuries'.[12] This discography includes his 1960s recordings
of Satie's second 'Gymnopédie' on the album *Nirvana*, together with Fauré's
'Pavane' (plus a Bachian 'Valse', Chopin's 'Blue Interlude' and Scriabin's
'Prelude') on *Bill Evans Trio with Symphony Orchestra*. Meanwhile, the
composer-theorist Tymoczko views Evans as one 'whose chords and scales
relate to Debussy's in very clear ways', whilst also acting as a conduit in
transmitting Debussyesque techniques to a much later generation of tonal
composers;[13] thus, Tymoczko perceives intertextuality and an unconventional new lineage. So, albeit a generalized foundation, there is historiographic consensus among Evans's biographers and other writers that
French classical composers did constitute a significant force for him.

---

[9] Bill Evans talking to Frank Everett, from *Jazz Journal* (August 1968), quoted at www.
    billevans.nl/Classical.htm. For more on Evans's view of the relationship between classical
    music and jazz, see Felix Manskleid, 'Bill Evans Discusses the Jazz Scene', *Jazz Monthly*, 6/5
    (July 1960), 10–11: 10.
[10] Lees, 'The Poet: Bill Evans', 421. This invaluable source, frustratingly, lacks scholarly
    references.
[11] Barrett, '*Kind of Blue*', 186.
[12] Barham, 'Rhizomes and Plateaus', 187. Bill Evans and Herbie Mann (jazz flautist), *Nirvana*
    (New York: Atlantic Records SD 1426, 1962; released 1964); Bill Evans, *Bill Evans Trio with
    Symphony Orchestra* (Englewood Cliffs, NJ: Verve V6 8640, recorded 1965; released 1966).
[13] Tymoczko, *A Geometry of Music*, 352. His view is a very positive one, which includes a
    detailed study of Evans's version of Sonny Rollins's 'Oleo', from *Everybody Digs Bill Evans*.

Crucially, we find authorial support for upholding French music among various interviews that Evans himself gave. In one such interview of 1965, albeit with the Frenchman Jean-Louis Ginibre and so potentially partial,[14] Evans declared: 'I love impressionists. I love Debussy. He's one of my favourite composers [. . .] I don't know if I'm an impressionist or not.'[15] Around the same time, however, he substantiated this statement by explaining his subtle, quasi-impressionistic approach of 'shadow lettering', whereby 'you don't actually draw the letters, but rather the shadows of the letters, yet you see the letters and not the shadows'.[16] Similarly, where neoclassicists such as Les Six were concerned, Evans recounted: 'I remember first hearing some of Milhaud's polytonality and actually a piece that he may not think too much of – it was an early piece called *Suite provençale* [1936] – which opened me up to certain things.'[17] What then were these 'certain things' to which Evans was receptive: what was the appeal and role of this French music?

Building upon Lees's comments, I propose (and test out below) that it was particularly in early twentieth-century French repertory that Evans found an affinity of soundworld with his own improvisational priorities: lyricism and polyphonic lines; a rich harmonic palette of seventh and ninth chords with integral major/minor second clusters, which yet did not undermine melodic primacy; subtle textures and 'voicings' – a notion which encompasses registral spacing, chordal inversions and doublings, sometimes of the melody itself. In short, a vehicle for emotional expressivity.

In privileging lyricism and melody, I am not claiming their exclusivity to this relationship. Clearly, Evans's intricate right-hand melodies develop in part directly out of jazz pianistic traditions, especially those of 'Bud' Powell (1924–66), Nat 'King' Cole (1919–65) and Lennie Tristano (1919–78),[18] in turn influencing Hancock, Corea, Jarrett and Peterson's later ballads.[19] Similar left-hand voicings were used by Tatum and Peterson. Equally, some modal and timbral qualities of French music are shared with other modernist musics, especially Russian ones. Nonetheless, this French repertory, too, was still tonic-based, and for Evans: 'I think of all harmony as an

[14] On partiality, Barrett ('*Kind of Blue*', 185) notes an overstatement by Evans about spontaneity and performer freedom in *Kind of Blue*.

[15] Jean-Louis Ginibre, 'Il parle, le trio dont on parle', *Jazz Magazine*, 116 (March 1965), 28–33; reprinted and translated as 'Bill Evans: Time Remembered', *JazzTimes*, 27/1 (February 1997), 32–5, 38, 144–5.

[16] Evans quoted in Keith Knox, 'Bill Evans – An Introduction', *Jazz Monthly*, 12/8 (October 1966), 5–7: 6; originally from a conversation with John Mehegan, *Jazz* (January 1965).

[17] Evans quoted in Enstice and Rubin, *Jazz Spoken Here*, 136.

[18] See Nat Hentoff, 'Introducing Bill Evans', *Jazz Review*, 2/9 (October 1959), 26–8: 28; Manskleid, 'Bill Evans Discusses the Jazz Scene', 10; Israels, 'Bill Evans', 109–10.

[19] Britt, 'The River Stops Flowing', 15. See too Israels, 'Bill Evans', 115.

expansion from and return to the tonic'.[20] When asked by Lees, 'Why does a flat ninth work with a dominant chord?', Evans responded, knowingly, by invoking the concept of voiceleading: 'It has to do with counterpoint more than harmony. It's the ninth of the dominant moving through the flat ninth to become the fifth of the tonic.'[21]

In addition, crossing in and out of French-inflected classical repertory seemingly contributed to Evans's development of a subtle, distinctive piano tone. Lees asserts that, historically, 'He changed the tone character of jazz piano. [. . .] Bill brought into jazz the kind of tone appropriate to Debussy and Ravel and modern harmonic function [. . .] obvious in the classical world in the playing of Walter Gieseking and Emil Gilels.'[22] Pettinger meanwhile attests to Evans's 'thoroughly trained and exquisitely refined touch at the keyboard', including his attention to pedalling.[23] Most significant, such interchange appeared to stimulate Evans's creativity in his piano-centred role as 'one of the most imaginative, inventive, and adventurous improvisers the art has known'.[24] After all, every improvising musician needs some kind of background formulae – their inspired, stylistic hallmarks, as the eloquent writer Paul Berliner has pointed out.[25] Indeed in respect of *Kind of Blue*, Evans stresses the importance of such structures: 'As the [Japanese] painter needs his framework of parchment, the improvising musical group needs its framework in time. Miles Davis presents here frameworks which are exquisite in their simplicity and yet contain all that is necessary to stimulate performance with a sure reference to the primary conception.'[26]

Much has been made of comparing Evans and Chopin (as a nineteenth-century predecessor and naturalized French citizen). Pettinger's comments apart, consider for instance: 'The poetry of Bill's playing compels the comparison to Chopin, whose music, incidentally, Bill played exquisitely' (that quality reiterated), or 'the subtle linear aspect of Evans' harmony was Chopinesque'.[27] And this traditional comparison still proves fruitful. But what about an alternative comparison of the artistic personas and musical attributes of Evans and Ravel? At a superficial level, both espoused sartorial elegance, but also endured physical frailty. 'Bill was one of those elegantly coordinated people. His posture and his bespectacled mien made him seem almost fragile',[28] while Ravel was quite the dandy, cigarette in hand,

---

[20] Lees, 'The Poet: Bill Evans', 434.   [21] *Ibid.*   [22] *Ibid.*, 441.
[23] Pettinger, *Bill Evans*, 16.   [24] Lees, 'The Poet: Bill Evans', 442.
[25] Berliner, 'Introduction: Picking Notes Out of Thin Air?', in *Thinking in Jazz*, 1.
[26] Evans's liner notes for Miles Davis, *Kind of Blue* (New York: Columbia CL 1355, 1959).
[27] Lees, 'The Poet: Bill Evans', 420; Israels, 'Bill Evans', 110.
[28] Lees, 'The Poet: Bill Evans', 423.

but self-consciously slight. Politically, both were liberal in their views: Evans was 'passionately anti-racist' and Ravel too supported black perspectives, as demonstrated in his setting of *Chansons madécasses*.

For each (as for Chopin), the piano formed the focus of their artistic creation, the core of their being. For Evans, 'the piano, on which he could attack and sustain with crystal clarity, remained his one true love';[29] Ravel invariably composed at the piano and set about orchestration as a second stage. Both were much more comfortable with small-scale miniatures than with large-scale creations,[30] typically favouring subtle nuance over forceful dynamic. Melody was imperative, supported by luscious harmonies. For each, their creativity often involved a struggle: Evans counselled that 'My message to musicians who feel the same way is that they should keep at it, building block by block. The ultimate reward might be greater in the end even if they have to work longer and harder in the process.'[31] Both were experts on their heritage: Ravel on Couperin, Mozart and Felix Mendelssohn; Evans on Chopin and Ravel. Evans's interest in Ravel, and later in Lili Boulanger, was supported by his French friend Francis Paudras, who wrote about 'Ravel et le jazz'.[32] An earlier French article in *Jazz hot* of 1961 declared 'Bill Evans . . . or art for art's sake',[33] and the same philosophy held true for Ravel.

Both Evans and Ravel were intensely private, sensitive individuals for whom music offered a powerful nonverbal outlet for emotional expression.[34] In respect of Evans, Lees talked of 'Music [. . .] summoning shades of emotion for which we have no words,' while Stan Britt in his obituary tribute was drawn by 'a superbly understated depth of emotion'.[35] Again, we may find affinities in Eliot's description of a poetic ideal: 'The emotion in his poetry will be a very complex thing [. . .] to express feelings which are not in actual emotions at all'.[36] Similarly for Ravel, poetic, melancholic and

---

[29] Pettinger, *Bill Evans*, 11.   [30] Israels, 'Bill Evans', 114.

[31] Evans quoted from conversations with Brian Hennessey, 'Bill Evans: A Person I Knew', *Jazz Journal International*, 38/3 (March 1985), 8–11: 8.

[32] Francis Paudras, 'Ravel et le Jazz', *Musical*, 4 (June 1987), 36–51. The latter part of this article: 'Le Jazz et Ravel' (48ff.) outlines the fascination with Ravel felt by many jazzmen: Monk, Ellington, Strayhorn and Waller. Pertinent mention is made of Evans and Ravel (49): 'La reprise totale de l'esprit de Ravel dans l'œuvre du compositeur et pianiste Bill Evans a une importance que nous n'avons pas encore pleinement mesurée.' ('The total recall of the spirit of Ravel in the work of the composer and pianist Bill Evans has an importance that we haven't yet fully measured.')

[33] Demètre Ioakimidis, 'Bill Evans . . . ou l'art pour l'art', *Jazz hot*, 161 (January 1961), 14–17.

[34] See the fitting obituary tribute to Evans by Brian Case, 'The Quiet Innovator', *Melody Maker* (27 September 1980), 28.

[35] Lees, 'The Poet: Bill Evans', 420; Britt, 'The River Stops Flowing', 15.

[36] Eliot, 'Tradition and the Individual Talent', 41–2.

passionate expression could sometimes be overt and intense (*La Valse*), at other times concealed or suppressed (*Boléro*). Conversely, as avid readers of novels and poetry both men valued words: Evans favouring Thomas Hardy and William Blake; Ravel selecting Proust, Stéphane Mallarmé and Edgar Allan Poe. Lees said of Evans: 'His speech was low level, but he was highly literate and articulate.'[37] Likewise, Ravel crafted words in his correspondence, his scenarios for ballets and writings about music.

Ravel's own lecture on *Contemporary Music*, presented on his American tour in 1928, offers a set of artistic eclectic principles for relating classical music and jazz which may be inverted to test Evans's practice, as pursued in the case studies. Each eclectic artwork, whether it be composition or improvisation, for which a reliable source may be found 'adopts' (assimilates) some of that material as a starting point, then submits its find to 'minute stylization' – even 'manipulation', transforming it in a new setting that embraces both 'national characteristics' and 'individualities', so creating an original product (for main coverage see Chapter 5).[38] And for Evans, like Ravel, the notion of engagement with models was crucial. Relating to his most influential jazz sources, Evans mused: 'Nat was one of my favourite piano players and, I think, one of the most under-rated. I sat at the same piano and played the same keys as Nat King Cole. It was reverential.'[39] This is, however, in no sense a second-rate creativity.

In order to support the case studies which follow, the reader is advised to consult the relevant main recordings, scores and transcriptions detailed in footnotes at their first occurrence in the text.

Case study 1: Evans and French inspiration in *Kind of Blue* (1959)

This short case study serves to highlight a source–product relationship between part of the iconic album *Kind of Blue*[40] and Ravel's Left Hand Concerto,[41] which was introduced to Davis by the catalyst Evans.[42] In respect

---

[37] Lees, 'The Poet: Bill Evans', 423.

[38] Ravel advocated this approach in his own encounters with jazz: *Contemporary Music*, 140.

[39] Evans quoted in Hennessey, 'Bill Evans: A Person I Knew', 8.

[40] Miles Davis, *Kind of Blue* (New York: Columbia CL 1355, 1959; reissued Columbia/Legacy CK 64935, 1997).

[41] Maurice Ravel, *Concerto pour la main gauche* (Paris: Éditions Durand, 1931).

[42] See comments in Davis, *Miles: The Autobiography*: 'Bill brought a great knowledge of classical music, people like Rachmaninoff and Ravel' (216), and 'Besides Ravel and a whole lot of others, Bill Evans had turned me on to Aram Khachaturian' (220). See too Pettinger,

of this album, Davis explains in his no-nonsense autobiographical style that 'because we were into Ravel (especially his Concerto for the Left Hand and Orchestra) and Rachmaninoff (Concerto No. 4), all of that was up in there somewhere' and 'We were just leaning toward – like Ravel, playing a sound only with the white keys.'[43] Davis's wife, Frances Taylor, corroborates the idea of a daily listening diet which included Khachaturian, Ravel and Brahms.[44] Meanwhile, Ashley Kahn makes the point that, for all their differences of character, 'Both [Davis and Evans] were ardent fans of modern classical composers such as Rachmaninoff and the French impressionists. In their ears, jazz and classical were two streams feeding into the same river.'[45] So, in a sense, it is not important who introduced whom to what, except that Evans's role in 'Blue in Green', 'Flamenco Sketches' and the introduction of 'So What' in *Kind of Blue* has sometimes been eclipsed;[46] the significance here is the prominent position of Ravel.

Sure enough in the opening riff of 'All Blues',[47] played by Paul Chambers on bass, albeit swiftly and in a subdued fashion on the reissued 1959 recording, the opening contrabassoon figure from the Left Hand Concerto has seemingly been adopted and adapted: the jazz chameleon at work; see Example 8.1. After placing its initial G, the Davis/Evans riff explores the pitches D–E–D–F. Meanwhile, in a minor mode a tone higher on E, Ravel presents the pitches E–F♯–E–G, in a dotted rhythm, beginning on a semiquaver anacrusis; he then extends the figure upwards (for further detail, see Example 5.2). The upper reach of the Davis/Evans short phrase, F, is balanced by a descent to the lower G: D–E–D–G, and in fact this latter pattern matches a motive from the 'Blues' movement (bars 8–9) of Ravel's Violin Sonata: E♭–F–E♭–A♭. (Interestingly, these Ravel works are products of neoclassicism rather than impressionism.) Additionally, Evans's opening piano material comprises a simple tremolo oscillation, G–A, where another

Bill Evans, 56: 'he [Evans] went on to introduce Davis to the music of Khachaturian and Rachmaninoff (as well as Ravel)'.

[43] Davis, *Miles: The Autobiography*, 224–5; and Davis quoted in Ashley Kahn, *Kind of Blue: The Making of the Miles Davis Masterpiece* (London: Granta Books, 2000), 145. Reputedly, Davis kept a score of Ravel's concerto in his shirt pocket.

[44] Kahn, *Kind of Blue*, 74.   [45] *Ibid.*

[46] On Evans's role, see Charles Blancq, 'Bill Evans . . . A Remembrance', in David C. Olsen and Tom Roed (eds.), *The Artistry of Bill Evans*, with transcriptions by Pascal Wetzel (Miami, FL: CPP/Belwin, Warner Bros. Publications, 1989), 2; Kahn, *Kind of Blue*, 117–20, 112–13; Pettinger, *Bill Evans*, 82. Significantly, 'Blue in Green' also features on Evans's own album, *Portrait in Jazz*: Bill Evans Trio (New York: Riverside RLP 12 315, 1960).

[47] See Miles Davis, *Kind of Blue*, transcribed scores by Rob Du Boff, Mark Vinci, Mark Davis and Josh Davis (Milwaukee, WI: Hal Leonard, n.d. [*c*.2000]); their transcription is based on 'All Blues', take 1 (22 April 1959).

Example 8.1 Comparisons of the four-note motive
  (a) Davis/Evans, *Kind of Blue*, 'All Blues' riff
  (b) Ravel, Concerto for the Left Hand (opening)
  (c) Milhaud, *La Création du monde* (fugal subject)

Ravelian connection (this time, an impressionistic one) is implicit: 'A number of tunes started with brief atmospheric introductions, colored by delicate, pointillistic rippling. This was Evans the orchestrater [*sic*] at work, thinking perhaps of the *pianissimo* flutes, clarinets, and harps of dawn in Ravel's *Daphnis and Chloé*.'[48]

From an *esthesic* stance and extending a Tymoczko-like mapping, it is a moot point whether an initial similarity with the double bass motive that begins the fugal subject in Milhaud's *La Création* might be even greater (for extended treatment, see examples 4.4 and 4.5). After sounding the D tonic, Milhaud utilizes the same fragment: D–E–D–F(–D), and then extends the idea via the blues third: D–E–D–F♯/F–D; see Example 8.1c. In turn, as discussed in chapters 4 and 5, these figures relate closely to Gershwin's song 'The Man I Love' and *Rhapsody in Blue*. All partake of a kind of intertextual paradigm identified by the veteran critic Hodeir.[49] (This does not negate the Davis/Evans testimony, but serves to remind us that *esthesic* and *poietic* perspectives are not synonymous.) And so the cycle continues ... As Davis remarks, white-note (Dorian) modality has much to answer for,[50] while dotted or swung rhythms are another common feature.

Evans's affinity with Ravel is evident too in his extended solo, about two-thirds of the way through the extended 'All Blues' (c.8.26 in the reissued recording; rehearsal letter D, bars 1–10, in the Hal Leonard transcription),

[48] Pettinger, *Bill Evans*, 144. Pettinger's example is Evans's treatment of the love theme from the film *Spartacus* (1960), the score for which was composed by Alex North.
[49] Hodeir, *Jazz*, 254.   [50] Davis, *Miles: The Autobiography*, 225.

Example 8.2 Evans and Ravel: motivic and contour comparisons
(a) Evans's solo in 'All Blues' (*c.*8.30) and Ravel, Concerto in G, I (Fig. 4^{+2})
(b) Evans's solo in 'All Blues' (continued) and Ravel, Concerto for the Left Hand
(Fig. 9^{-3})

again with much white-note modality. As an equivalent activity to Larson's Schenkerian voiceleading, we may fruitfully adopt a motivic stance here. The start of Evans's melancholic melody in the Dorian on G: G, A, B♭, C, D, E, F, G, holds similarity, in its contour and motives a, b and c, with the piano solo in the first movement of Ravel's Concerto in G (Fig. 4^{+2}), as shown in Example 8.2a, where the Ravel is transposed from F♯ to G.[51] Evans's expressive figurations (x and y), plus emphases upon the minor third interval: G–B♭ (z), combined with flattened seventh (F), are reminiscent of the exquisite solo cantilena in the Left Hand Concerto (Fig. 9^{-3}, again transposed into G); see Example 8.2b. Additionally, both loci create a spacious quality. Evans's treatment favours longer note values and use of the upper register, while Ravel highlights the third and seventh degrees through metrical placement. Some pitch and contour similarities may simply be

---

[51] Maurice Ravel, *Concerto pour piano et orchestre* (Paris: Éditions Durand, 1932). According to John Szwed, *So What: The Life of Miles Davis* (New York: Random House, 2012), 161, Davis had been very taken by Arturo Benedetti Michelangeli's 1957 recording of Ravel's Concerto in G, introduced to him by Evans.

Example 8.3 Evans and Ravel: chordal-rhythmic patterning
  (a) Evans's solo in *Kind of Blue*, 'All Blues' (*c*.9.05)
  (b) Ravel, Concerto for the Left Hand (Fig. 4^{+3})

generic Dorian; others may result from a confluence of the musicians' pianism: idioms that lie well under the hands. But given the historically documented trace of the Left Hand Concerto, we might interpret Evans's approach as an effective borrowing and rereading of certain Ravelian traits.

Evans's block harmonies here, presented in second inversion: D–E–F in the tenor line, combined with long-short swung rhythms (at letter D), might be heard as an adaptation of the piano entry in the Left Hand Concerto (Fig. 4^{+3}), which features second-inversion triads mixed with seventh chords in dotted rhythm, as a variant of the contrabassoon figure. (Second-inversion block triads occur too in Ravel's *Valses nobles et sentimentales* (1911), in the second waltz (bar 25ff.), where the slow tempo, quiet dynamic and expressive qualities ('doux et expressif', 'un peu plus lent et rubato') are congruent with Evans's practice and his theory in privileging French impressionism.)[52] This similar chordal-rhythmic patterning is especially striking later on in Evans's solo (letter D^{+15}), which effectively amplifies Ravel's triads and sevenths as a series of ninth chords, repeated within a dotted rhythm: F, A, E, G; G, B, F, A; A, C, G, B; compare Example 8.3a and 8.3b. The faster tempo and greater sense of urgency in 'All Blues' is one important way in which Evans's eclectic response is 'individualized', or its Ravelian traits are reinflected.

More speculatively, but mindful of Evans's embrace of Debussy, might there be any connection between his first main solo in the peaceful, relaxed 'Blue in Green' and 'La Fille aux cheveux de lin', from the first book of *Préludes*? There are certainly strong parallels, with specific intersections from an *esthesic* or hermeneutic stance. Commonalities include the slow

---

[52] The liner notes for Jean-Yves Thibaudet, *Conversations with Bill Evans* (London: Decca 455 512-2, 1997) suggest that Evans knew and rated *Valses nobles*: 'New York's leading jazz radio station had a weekly show on which noted jazz musicians played and discussed a variety of recordings, and on one memorable occasion, the guest disc jockey was Bill Evans. Among other things, his playlist included Ravel's *Valses nobles et sentimentales*.'

Example 8.4 Evans and Debussy: contour comparisons
  (a) Evans (*Kind of Blue*), 'Blue in Green' (opening)
  (b) Evans's first main solo in 'Blue in Green' (*c*.1.45)
  (c) Debussy, *Préludes* (Book I, No. VIII), 'La Fille aux cheveux de lin' (bars 1–4)

tempo and spacious feel (note Debussy's markings of 'Très calme et douce-
ment expressif' and 'sans rigueur'), the wavelike ebb and flow whereby
the arpeggiated descent–ascent contours of the respective openings are
combined with a fondness for subdominant relations: Evans, in F (localized): I–IV; Dm: I^7–IV^{11}; Debussy, in G♭: IV–I. Nevertheless, yet still in
Debussyesque fashion, Evans's choice of voicings 'are not only rich in
fourths [...], but also make harmonic implications ambiguous'.[53] The
melodic similarities, privileging perfect fifths and varied seventh spans,
are shown in Example 8.4. Rhythmic common ground occurs with the
figuration: quaver, two semiquavers, quaver, especially evident in Evans's
ten-bar interlude (*c*.1.45 in the reissued recording; letter B of the Hal
Leonard transcription);[54] compare Example 8.4b and 8.4c. Overall, however, Evans's rhythmic identity is more diverse and his pitch palette more
chromatic, with a measured voiceleading ascent: D–D♯–E, than Debussy's
opening with its distinctly pentatonic leanings.[55]

[53] Barrett, '*Kind of Blue*', 191.
[54] Their transcription is based on 'Blue in Green', take 5 (2 March 1959).
[55] Debussyesque moments apart, some chord sequences are reminiscent of Gershwin or
      Porter songs, especially towards the end of 'Blue in Green'.

As a link into the second case study, a fundamental feature of 'Flamenco Sketches' is known to have been initiated by Evans, since it can be traced back to 'Peace Piece'. This non-French feature concerns the alternating bass chords C^{maj7} (C, E, G, B) and G^{11} (G, B, [D], F, A, C), which constitute a double borrowing: beyond revisiting his own work, Evans borrows this progression from Bernstein's 'Some Other Time' from the Broadway musical, *On the Town* (1944). Evans's long-term girlfriend, Peri Cousins Harper, remembered how he would cross or 'drift' from one locus to the next,[56] hence the fluidity and this interpolation. Similar testimony on his creative process is provided by Evans's son: 'he would practise some classics like Bach or Ravel, [...] as if to shake out the blues and traditional jazz and exercise his hands [...] But then, suddenly, he would burst into his own thing.' On the ensuing relationships, Evan Evans continues: 'Obviously he was hoping there'd be some correlation [...] that part of what he discovered artistically by playing would be brought in[to] his own music. A kind of osmosis.'[57] Effectively, Evans uses Bernstein's bass as one of his neutral frameworks to facilitate this elusive 'osmosis'. Along Metzer's lines, his quotation also implies a compliment to Bernstein, as an Eliot-like engagement with his heritage, so that here I would argue for a more substantive source–product relationship over the 'thoroughly rhizomatic' one identified by Barham.[58] Evans's improvisatory technique in 'Flamenco Sketches', where his spacious, syncopated arpeggio waves in G are used as a warm-up to more intricate moments, also recalls 'Peace Piece', where this same device cues a winding down of activity. Equally, under a banner of Spanishness,[59] 'Flamenco Sketches' and Ravel's *Boléro* share the marked Phrygian progression D♭–C, in a major modality on C.

Case study 2: Chopin, Messiaen and 'Peace Piece' (1958)

This main case study on Evans's improvisation 'Peace Piece'[60] serves to demonstrate a finely nuanced source–product relation with Chopin, plus a striking parallel with potential points of intersection in respect of the

---

[56] Pettinger, *Bill Evans*, 68. It was for Peri that he wrote 'Peri's Scope', on *Portrait in Jazz*.

[57] Evan Evans in interview (2000), cited in 'Bill Evans and Classical Music: Glenn Gould, Maurice Ravel': www.billevans.nl/Classical.htm.

[58] Barham, 'Rhizomes and Plateaus', 190. See too n. 61.

[59] Shortly afterwards, Davis produced *Sketches of Spain* (New York: Columbia CL 1480, 1960; reissued Columbia/Legacy CK 65142, 1997), with its rethinking in collaboration with Gil Evans of Joaquín Rodrigo, *Concierto de Aranjuez* and Manuel de Falla, 'Will o' the Wisp', from *El amor brujo*.

[60] Bill Evans, 'Peace Piece', *Everybody Digs Bill Evans* (New York: Riverside RLP 12 291, 1958). The main transcription referred to is that by Aikin, 'Bill Evans: *Peace Piece*. Transcription'. For full reference, see 'Analytical approaches' in Chapter 2, page 62.

modernist composer Messiaen. I shall critique and build on Pettinger's treatment of Evans's piece, and will relate *en passant* to Barham's more recent analysis.[61] Pettinger identifies Chopin's *Berceuse*, Op. 57 in D♭ major, composed in Paris during 1843–4, both as 'a piano piece that Evans knew well' and as a 'clear precursor' to 'Peace Piece' from *Everybody Digs Bill Evans* which is, he claims, 'precisely parallel'. (Similarly, Barham perceives structural connection with the *Berceuse*, while observing an affinity of patterning and sonority with Satie's *Trois gymnopédies* of 1888.)[62] He also questions: 'we know he [Evans] was a Scriabin enthusiast, but did he know Olivier Messiaen, whose *Catalogue d'oiseaux* [1956–8] for piano was just appearing?'[63] And although Pettinger responds with the throwaway line 'No matter', I want to test his propositions and examine the materials and relations in greater depth.

Pettinger describes the *Berceuse* as based upon 'a two-harmony left-hand ostinato which, like "Peace Piece", never varies until it makes a cadence at the end'. Although he is broadly correct since both pieces are based on a tonic–dominant oscillation, there are subtle bass-stave alterations in Chopin's second half of the bar, especially across bars 55–60, while Evans too creates small variations, again mostly in the latter half of the bar. For the basic comparative pattern, see Example 8.5a and 8.5b. (I have amended Aikin's transcription with the introduction of chordal tie markings and omission of a tonic seventh in bar 1.) The effect of Evans's ever-changing melody over the Bernstein bass[64] is to create new harmonic inflections, such as the expressive superimposition of A♭/A, creating simultaneous minor/major ninths, over G: that favoured V^9 construct alluded to earlier, G, B, D, F, A♭/A. Both musicians introduce their melody after several iterations of the ostinato: Evans does so after six bars and Chopin after two bars. (We might even propose a further reference and thus triangulation here: despite

---

[61] Pettinger, *Bill Evans*, 69; Barham, 'Rhizomes and Plateaus', 187–90. Curiously, Barham does not credit Pettinger's interpretation, which first identifies the potential modelling upon Chopin's *Berceuse*. For a complementary reading of French affinities in 'Peace Piece', see Ed Byrne's thorough analysis at http://freejazzinstitute.com. See too Israels's brief analysis: 'Bill Evans', 113, where he comments that the work 'owes more to Satie and Debussy than to Ravi Shankar'.

[62] Barham, 'Rhizomes and Plateaus', 187.

[63] Olivier Messiaen, *Catalogue d'oiseaux* (Paris: Alphonse Leduc, 1946); Pettinger, *Bill Evans*, 69.

[64] Barham also illustrates melodic correspondence between 'Peace Piece' and Evans's recording of Bernstein's 'Some Other Time', included in the 1991 Riverside CD reissue of *Everybody Digs* and 'thus revealing only then concrete evidence of the similarity between Evans's reading of the Bernstein song and its offshoot in "Peace Piece"': Barham, 'Rhizomes and Plateaus', 190.

Example 8.5 Evans and Chopin: tonic–dominant oscillation
  (a) Evans/Bernstein (*Everybody Digs Bill Evans*), 'Peace Piece' (bars 1–2)
  (b) Chopin, *Berceuse*, Op. 57 (bars 1–2)

metrical differences, the sounding of the left-hand bass pattern followed by the expressive right-hand cantilena may set up intertextual association with the opening of the slow movement of Ravel's Concerto in G, noted in relation to 'All Blues'.)

For Pettinger, in the *Berceuse*, 'The right-hand line starts simply, each succeeding two- or four-bar section introducing a fresh decorative idea.' What he does not say is that this is because Chopin's piece is a formal theme and variations. Evans also enjoys frequent variation, often working in two-bar melodic breaths joined as eight-bar spans (the length of his main 'head' melody), although his conception is somewhat freer. Indeed, the riff or ostinato apart, Evans actually felt his piece to be 'completely free form'.[65] There is one really similar melodic gesture, however, which is hard to hear other than as a reference by Evans to Chopin: the reiterated Gs preceded by upper grace notes seemingly on F♯ (bars 66–7 of Aikin's transcription; recording *c*.5.25–5.30), as a remaking of Chopin's reiterated A♭s preceded by grace notes at the octave, across bars 15–18 of the *Berceuse*; see Example 8.6a and 8.6b. Evans's version with major seventh, dissonant descents (F♯–G) might be perceived, in a Bloomian sense of historical misreading, as a poignant rewriting of Chopin's octaves.[66] Pettinger too suggests that, in making his way through 'Peace Piece', Evans 'may well have been spiritually and formally conscious of Chopin's work'.[67]

---

[65] Hentoff, 'Introducing Bill Evans', 28.
[66] We might also hear close correspondences with Ravel's *Valses nobles*, II, bar 25ff., mentioned earlier, the top line of which features reiterated Cs preceded by grace notes on the same pitch. On a larger scale, Evans's decision to conclude each side of his *Everybody Digs* LP with an 'Epilogue' creates another commonality with *Valses nobles*.
[67] Pettinger, *Bill Evans*, 69.

Example 8.6 Similar melodic gestures
 (a) Evans, *Everybody Digs Bill Evans*, 'Peace Piece' (bars 66–9)
 (b) Chopin, *Berceuse*, Op. 57 (bars 15–18)
 (c) Messiaen, *Catalogue d'oiseaux* (p. 4), 'Le Chocard des alpes'

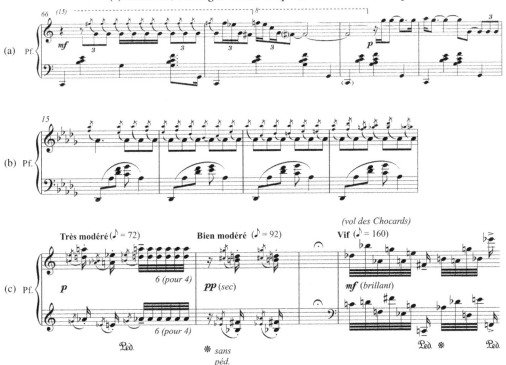

Despite minor differences, the extent of parity here – the slow tempo; sense of striving for calm; basic I–V ostinato; continual variation often in two-bar units; upper piano register; intricate passagework comprising scales, arpeggiation and trills; coda with beautifully controlled rhythmic augmentation; sustained chords with a final *diminuendo* to nothing – means that, rather than Chopin's lullaby being just a 'precursor', we might view it as a conceptual-formal model for Evans's eclectic response. Such modelling would not be an isolated phenomenon on at least two counts. Where the *Berceuse* is concerned, Brahms's much discussed *Romanze*, Op. 118, No. 5, precedes 'Peace Piece' in an allusive relationship that at times entails actual appropriation: Korsyn regards Chopin's *Berceuse* as Brahms's 'central precursor-text'.[68] Where Evans is concerned, as Lees has commented: 'The pattern of chords in eighth notes in "Young and Foolish" [also] on *Everybody Digs*, for example, recalls the

[68] Korsyn, 'Towards a New Poetics', 18ff.

Chopin E-minor Prelude.'[69] But the relationship between 'Young and Foolish' and Chopin's Prelude is more sonically overt than that between 'Peace Piece' and the *Berceuse*, where, notwithstanding a borrowed formula, sophisticated development has ensued, including the creation of a wholly new context.

As a pertinent aside, Pettinger's observation that 'in performance [. . . the *Berceuse*] should sound like a written-out improvisation', enables us to take another step, as an instance of Klein's 'historical reversal'.[70] While Evans doubtless gained from Chopin, in the light of Evans's improvisation and now turning the tables, we are better able to appreciate that, in addition to his conventional composer status, Chopin too was an improviser.[71] His ever more virtuosic variations – replete with arpeggiated, scalic and chromatic figuration – inhabit that elusive realm between composition and quasi-spontaneous, improvised performance. And, as Barham has remarked, such processes extend well beyond this one piece: 'the idea of increasingly complex melodic variations in the right hand [is] characteristic of Chopin in general'.[72]

As a second layer of our analysis, in relating 'Peace Piece' to *Catalogue d'oiseaux*, Pettinger perceives 'much birdsong incorporated around the apex of the Evans arch, where the bitonal texture scintillates in the manner of the French master'.[73] (Barham, too, notes 'harmonic sonorities and birdsong imitations of the type used by Messiaen', comparing Evans's intricate melodic figuration with Messiaen's earlier *Réveil des oiseaux*, for piano and orchestra of 1953.)[74] This is a fair assessment, but it would be foolish to force any argument for direct influence, while the linkage between Messiaen and birdsong itself connotes a further layer of intertextuality.

Strictly speaking, Evans's improvisation would be better regarded as bimodal, occasionally polymodal, rather than bitonal. Although the bass functions in an unequivocal C major (subscribing to Evans's tonal priorities, mentioned earlier), the melodic line invokes a much wider, fluid modality

---

[69] Lees, 'The Poet: Bill Evans', 420–1.   [70] Klein, *Intertextuality*, 4.

[71] On *The Universal Mind of Bill Evans*, directed by Louis Cavrell (New York: Rhapsody Films 9015, 1966; EFORFilms 2869016, 2004), Bill Evans talks to his brother Harry about the relationship between composition and improvisation, commenting that for many years notation was the only way to preserve an interpretation, so subjugating improvisation. See too his comments in Manskleid, 'Bill Evans Discusses the Jazz Scene', 10–11.

[72] Barham, 'Rhizomes and Plateaus', 187.   [73] Pettinger, *Bill Evans*, 69.

[74] Barham, 'Rhizomes and Plateaus', 187. He also finds jazz similarities in Messiaen's 'Joie et clarté' from *Les Corps glorieux*, as part of his case for a rhizomatic network (190–2). In my terms, this would simply constitute a wider intertextuality, explored hermeneutically from a listener stance.

with sharpened tendencies. We may reference Ionian, Lydian, wholetone, chromatic and blues-inflected collections, evidenced for instance by the E/D♯ and A♯/B inflections across bars 60–5 (Aikin's transcription). In terms of modal balance, for Keith Knox writing in *Jazz Monthly*, the 'harmonies [feel] much closer to Debussy than to the blues, due to the interesting use of a whole tone scale, but the important aspect is the overall sense of completeness'.[75] In the first half of the piece (bars 20–3, 30–4 of Aikin's transcription), I suggest that it is melodic amplification via consecutive fifths, more associated with pentatonicism, which creates Debussyesque oriental sonorities, but that later there are fleeting wholetone fragments: B, C♯, D♯, E♯ (bar 47); D♭, E♭, F, G, A (bars 48–9); G, A, B, C♯, D♯ (bar 58); and further pentatonic constructs: G, A, C, D (bars 53–4). Certainly, in the middle and towards the end of 'Peace Piece', Evans's palette is more piquantly dissonant than is his typical practice. Intriguingly, however, amid bell-like, percussive, crystalline and cascading textures – effects that might loosely be termed impressionistic – those trills, grace notes and reiterated pitches highlighted apropos Chopin are still relevant.

As an interpretative act, we may hear translated equivalents of decorated repeated notes from *Catalogue d'oiseaux*. One instance concerns a reiterated demisemiquaver sextuplet construct: A♭, D, A, preceded by grace notes, in the opening piece from the first book entitled 'Le Chocard des alpes' (The Alpine Chough, p. 4, bar 1); see Example 8.6c. A particular parallel may be drawn between Evans's improvisation and Messiaen's second number, 'Le Loriot' (The Golden Oriole): they share a relaxed tempo, alternations between songful bursts and sustained pitches, and contrasts of dynamic. (Alternating tempos and characterizations are also demonstrated by Messiaen's eighth piece, in the fifth book, 'L'Alouette calandrelle': The Short-toed Lark.) Like Evans, Messiaen enjoys upper registral extremity, incorporating many *8va*, even two-octave, designations: florid evocation of the wren involves trills ('Le Loriot', p. 2, bar 1). Meanwhile, evocation of the song thrush foregrounds intricate major sevenths and minor ninths: for example, B♭–A and E♭–E ('Le Loriot', p. 3, bars 4–10),[76] both comparable with intervallic features of Evans's improvisation: for example, E♭–E; D♯–D and F♯–G (bars 60–6, Aikin's transcription). Evans's piece concludes with open fifths in the bass (see description below), while Messiaen enjoys open-fifth textures across 'Le Loriot'. Moreover, Messiaen's third piece of the first book, 'Le Merle bleu' (Blue Rock Thrush) features a final 'Très lent', marked 'souvenir du Merle

---

[75] Knox, 'Bill Evans – An Introduction', 6.

[76] Major sevenths: D–E♭ and B♭–A, also feature prominently in Messiaen's evocation of the nightingale in the ninth piece (fifth book), 'La Bouscarle', 15.

bleu' ('Le Merle bleu', p. 24, bar 11), which has a similarly expansive feel to the coda of 'Peace Piece', each also using quartal harmonies.[77]

Of course there are salient differences between the loci: which is not to make a value judgement; rather, each creator is an individual. The works exist on very different scales: 'Peace Piece' is a one-off improvised mini-ature (*c*.6.43 in duration), strictly speaking, 'two-off' since the second take was used;[78] *Catalogue d'oiseaux* is an extensive multivolume collection. Messiaen's textures, sometimes extending to three staves, are busier and more complex than those of Evans, which are notably spacious. A stronger notion of melody and accompaniment is preserved in Evans, whose practice is, ironically, more in the classical tradition: Evans main-tains his Bernstein bass quotation, while Messiaen extends his bass register to match the treble. Finally, there is a literalism to *Catalogue d'oiseaux*, which is specific – almost scientific – to the bird being evoked; by contrast, Evans's conception is much freer and in that sense more imaginative.

In fact, in its internalizing rather than externalizing and in its spiritual dimension, there is an intertextual affinity between Evans's approach and that of Messiaen's compatriot André Jolivet (1905–74). The final four bars of 'Peace Piece' find a harmonic-spatial counterpart in the conclu-sion (bars 34–5) of Jolivet's forward-looking 'La Princesse de Bali' from *Mana* (1935); see Example 8.7. Both endings balance an arpeggiated gesture that descends from treble to bass by an ascent featuring bell-like sonorities, which both follows on from and finishes with a pause. Evans's last two bars have a quartal emphasis: G, C, F; A, C, E; A, D, G, before a final fifth-based construct: C–G[–D], the sound then fading away.[79] Jolivet's has greater tritonal content, his final bar marked 'comme un gong très grave', with pitches enunciated from a very low B♭, through G, E♯–B♯, F♯.

Conclusion

There is little doubt about the relevance of French music to Evans (arguably as a force of comparable stature to Russian music), evidenced by a brief

---

[77] Other instances of quartal bass activity in *Catalogue d'oiseaux* include: 'Le Merle bleu', 15 (comprising a mix of quartal and quintal constructs); 'La Bouscarle', 15 (quartal and tritonal constructs); and the tenth piece (sixth book) 'Le Merle de roche', 11–12.

[78] See Hentoff, 'Introducing Bill Evans', 28, and Pettinger, *Bill Evans*, 69. Information from Orrin Keepnews, Evans's producer for the Riverside Records recordings.

[79] As discussed in Chapter 2, there are some inaccuracies in Aikin's transcription, the final page of which is reproduced in Pettinger, *Bill Evans*, 70.

Example 8.7 Evans and Jolivet: comparison of endings
(a) Evans, *Everybody Digs Bill Evans*, 'Peace Piece' (bars 73–6)
(b) Jolivet, *Mana*, 'La Princesse de Bali' (bars 34–5)

survey of biographical literature, supported by Evans's own views and coupled by explorations of his practice in the analyses. In pursuing the role of French music in Evans's improvisatory art, I have emphatically not been interested in some kind of contest. If one were ever tempted, Lees's words would offer a salutary caveat:

> In jazz [...] you are listening to individual expression. You may listen to a Frenchman for what his philosophy of life contributes to your own; to an American Indian or an Australian aborigine [...] for the insight he offers. But you are not going to get the same thing from all of them, nor should one want to. Therefore, to compare them on some sort of competitive scale is foolish, and meaningless. You accept them for what they are.[80]

But, while we fully respect artistic individuality, it is still defined partly by reference to some 'other', involving a complex equation of comparison and contrast. As Eliot attested, 'No poet, no artist of any art, has his complete meaning alone.'[81] When asked about influences upon him, Evans himself

---

[80] Lees, 'The Poet: Bill Evans', 441.   [81] Eliot, 'Tradition and the Individual Talent', 37.

responded, 'There are so many. You hear musicians all your life. [...] all musical experience enters into you.'[82]

I conclude that sympathetic probing of the cultural and genre-based crossings between Evans and French music does serve to reveal an ornate network of connections – Klein's 'dense web of intertextual relationships',[83] which, in the given case studies, foregrounds Ravel, Chopin, Debussy, Messiaen and Jolivet. (In these loci there is less evidence of the specific impressionism to which Evans alluded, though looser impressionistic effects are apparent.) In response to the main question about how French music is reconfigured in Evans's art, the evidence confirms two ways of similar prevalence and importance: firstly, *esthesic* parallels and intersections between texts; secondly, identifiable eclecticisms that may involve quotation and modelling.[84] The relationship between 'Peace Piece' and Messiaen's *Catalogue d'oiseaux* (or between 'Blue in Green' and Debussy's Prelude No. VIII) illustrates the former category, including hermeneutic points of inter-section, especially harmonic ones. Examples of the latter source–product category, supported by sufficient documentation and involving implicit reconfiguring, even transforming, of material, include Ravel's Left Hand Concerto–*Kind of Blue* and Chopin's *Berceuse*–'Peace Piece'.

Arguably, the linkage between the Davis/Evans 'All Blues' and the Left Hand Concerto (Case study 1) involves a double source–product relation since Ravel's opening contrabassoon figure very likely emerged from early jazz in the first place.[85] Notwithstanding various caveats, we may reasonably interpret this as a limited 'chain of influence'.[86] This incipient circularity of jazz–(French-)classical–jazz anticipates a relationship between Milhaud and Brubeck. 'Peace Piece' (Case study 2) furthers this idea via a creative triangulation: Evans, Chopin and Bernstein; plus Messiaen and Jolivet.

Some relations are clear-cut, or closed, while others are more ambiguous, or open-ended. For example, was Evans actually influenced by Messiaen at some level? Although the composition of *Catalogue d'oiseaux* (only

---

[82] Hentoff, 'Introducing Bill Evans', 28.   [83] Klein, *Intertextuality*, 4.

[84] Reminiscing on this special connection, Keepnews went so far as to say that 'It's like having Ravel, Debussy and Satie coming back through Bill'; quoted at www.billevans.nl/Classical.htm.

[85] Evans's association with Ravel's Left Hand Concerto took on a particular poignancy in the early 1960s when his heroin addiction left his right arm temporarily paralysed, as a latter-day Paul Wittgenstein. Other pianists came to the Vanguard jazz club in New York's Greenwich Village out of curiosity to hear how Evans managed to fulfil his week of engagements convincingly, playing entirely with his strong left hand. See Pettinger, *Bill Evans*, 145.

[86] Klein, *Intertextuality*, 4.

published in 1964) was absolutely contemporary with the creation of 'Peace Piece', as an adventurous musician Evans may well have heard earlier works by Messiaen that presaged the sounds of birdsong. It is hard to imagine he would be unfamiliar with the *Quatuor pour la fin du Temps* (1940–1), including its 'Liturgie de cristal' and 'Abîme des oiseaux'. He might conceivably have known of later works for solo piano and orchestra: *Réveil des oiseaux*, or *Oiseaux exotiques* (1955–6). (Equally, there could be a more complex triangulation here: after all, Evans went on to create his own version of 'Ornithology' (1946) by Charlie 'Bird' Parker and Benny Harris.)[87] It is unlikely that we will find firm evidence to support or refute this possibility. As another more open-ended matter, we may recall the idea of Chopin's *Berceuse*, as a model for 'Peace Piece', itself remaining open to reinterpretation, ahistorically, as improvisation in the light of Evans's work.

Methodologically, the flexible approach advocated in Ravel's *Contemporary Music* has proved applicable to Evans's eclecticism: those loci with an identifiable source have encompassed 'adoption', 'stylization' and varying amounts of colourful reinflection, through to transformation, in their new artistic settings.[88] Other places where this approach might be conducive include 'Waltz for Debby' from *New Jazz Conceptions*, as well as 'Peri's Scope' and 'Autumn Leaves' from *Portrait in Jazz*.

Generally, I would concur with Israels who maintained that 'Nothing sounded pasted on or [overtly] eclectic; ideas filtered through him and emerged with deep conviction; he rarely did anything superficial [...] everything was synthesized into an integrated style.'[89] Despite being a quotation, Evan's use of Bernstein's bass feels integral, organic rather than interpolated from outside. 'Integration' is perhaps a good way of understanding Evans's idea about there not being much difference between classical music and jazz. Indeed Barrett talks in such terms about the interracial partnership in *Kind of Blue*, where 'The restrained mixing of styles [...] points to the aspirations of the integrationist movement.'[90] Although Bloomian thinking, focusing on a misreading of history, has been of limited hermeneutic applicability,[91] Evans's overall approach subscribes much more comfortably to an inclusive, generous embrace of one's cultural history, as advocated by Eliot.[92] While reinterpreting classical sources

---

[87] Bill Evans, 'Ornithology', on *The Solo Sessions*, 2 vols. (Milestone MCD 9170 and 9195-2, 1963), vol. II.

[88] Ravel, *Contemporary Music*, 140.   [89] Israels, 'Bill Evans', 110–11.

[90] Barrett, *'Kind of Blue'*, 186; see too 195, 196.

[91] Bloom, 'Introduction: A Meditation upon Misreading', *A Map of Misreading*, 3–6.

[92] Eliot, 'Tradition and the Individual Talent', 37: 'His significance, his appreciation is the appreciation of his relation to the dead poets and artists.'

with an American jazz accent, at one level, Evans is paying homage to French music.

Equally, French repertory has been shown to act as a significant modal (melodic-harmonic) and textural catalyst, especially in Evans's most intro-verted moments such as 'Peace Piece'. The case studies apart, we may also note Evans's involvement as pianist in June 1958, with Davis and Coltrane, in the album *Legrand Jazz* (1959): Legrand's early French–jazz crossover experiment in orchestrating jazz standards. A longer-term interest in French music is supported by his later recording, albeit as a commercial activity, of arrangements of Fauré and Chopin for the Bill Evans Trio with symphonic accompaniment.[93] Having heard Evans play, the acclaimed concert pianist Arturo Benedetti Michelangeli reputedly commented that 'Bill Evans would be an ideal interpreter of the music of Gabriel Fauré'.[94]

Such association with the French classics has likely raised the cachet of Evans's creative work in Europe, probably widening his appeal here,[95] if not in the United States where he had to contend with being white and often regarded as effeminate.[96] Certainly, for Brian Hennessey, reminiscing on this period, Evans's 'inclusion of compositions from Bach to Chopin widened his potential audience'.[97] We may witness the beautifully finessed, yet curiously literal, performances of Evans's improvisations by the renowned French classical pianist Jean-Yves Thibaudet. Thibaudet recorded 'Peace Piece' on his album *Conversations with Bill Evans* (1997), the title of which makes affectionate allusion to Evans's *Conversations with Myself*.[98] Meanwhile, Evans's French friend the jazz pianist Bernard Maury (1943–2005) set up the Bill Evans Piano Academy in Paris,[99] declaring that 'Modern jazz musicians owe him an enormous debt. In the world of

[93] See n. 12. In fact, Evans credited his namesake Gil Evans for the initial idea behind the Chopin track: Hennessey, 'Bill Evans: A Person I Knew', 11.

[94] Quoted from the website Time Remembered (www.billevans.nl/); source unknown. For another perspective on Evans and Fauré, see n. 101.

[95] In allusion to Ravel's *Le Tombeau*, the French poet and critic Jacques Réda wrote a balancing tribute, *Tombeau de Bill Evans*, with one poem in this collection entitled 'Peace Piece'. Information from www.billevans.nl/Classical.htm.

[96] See Davis's testimony: 'Many blacks felt that [. . .] I should have a black piano player [. . . Evans] was too delicate': Davis, *Miles: The Autobiography*, 221.

[97] Hennessey, 'Bill Evans: A Person I Knew', 11.

[98] Jean-Yves Thibaudet, *Conversations with Bill Evans* (London: Decca 455 512-2, 1997); Bill Evans, *Conversations with Myself* (New York: Verve V6 8526, 1963). Evans's exper-imental solo album was distinctive and controversial in its overdubbing of three separate piano tracks for each song. It was, nonetheless, very well reviewed in *Down Beat* in 1963 and earned Evans a Grammy Award in 1964.

[99] Bill Evans Piano Academy at 13, rue de Tlemcen, 75020 Paris. See http://bill-evans.net/index.html.

jazz he's also a direct descendant of the French school of Fauré, Ravel, Debussy, Lili Boulanger and Henri Dutilleux.'[100]

Tellingly, Evans's exquisite modal jazz has the power to bridge falsely separated domains. He enables relatively old French music to live on and accrue new relevance as one special inspiration, reconfigured and recoloured – chameleonlike – in a postwar world.[101]

---

[100] Quoted from the website Time Remembered (www.billevans.nl/); original reference: 'Isabelle Leymarie Talks to Bernard Maury', *UNESCO Courier* (December 1996).

[101] Among the many possible French-related composers, Chopin and Ravel seem to have proved the strongest catalysts for Evans. As Pettinger (*Bill Evans*, 168) remarks about classical arrangements: 'Some composers survive "treatment" better than others. The works of J. S. Bach, for instance, will withstand a good deal of rough and tumble. [...] On the other hand, Gabriel Fauré's short orchestral piece *Pavane* fares less well – there is such a quiet perfection about this French master's music that it seems a sacrilege to tamper with any detail.' Ravel's output, however, seems to have been sufficiently substantial to withstand allusion and rethinking within Evans's creative mix.

9 Milhaud and Brubeck: French classical teacher and American jazz student

This final chapter concerns itself with a double relationship: while offering a distinctive nuance on French classical–jazz interactions, it superimposes an intriguing interplay of composition teacher–student. Up to a point, it complements the two preceding case studies which involved, at least implicitly, a teacher–pupil relationship between George Russell and Bill Evans. Here, balancing the treatment in Chapter 4 (and sharing that reciprocal spirit of Brown's *Debussy Redux*), part of the focus returns to Milhaud, but with a marked difference. Highly successful as a jazz-inspired composer in Paris during the interwar years, Milhaud also enjoyed a postwar existence as a European Jewish émigré in the United States. This change of circumstance enables a close study of his teacher–student relationship with David Warren Brubeck, who would emerge as one of the most significant figures in West Coast jazz of the 1950s and beyond.[1] Brubeck's very existence as a creative artist was founded on 'cultural exchange' between European music and the developmental needs of jazz itself, an idea promoted by the German researcher Ilse Storb.[2] This versatile concept extended to interactions between jazz and African, South American and Eurasian musics: Turkish, Japanese and so on. As Brubeck himself clarified: 'As a musician I feel free to explore the whole area of my musical heritage – from African drum batteries to Couperin, Bach, Jelly Roll, Stravinsky, or Charlie Parker.'[3] From

---

[1] I am very grateful to Darius Brubeck (Brubeck's eldest son) for his feedback on this chapter and for our stimulating meeting at the Brubeck Institute (12 November 2013). On Brubeck and his family of musicians, see the Brubeck Music Official Website: www. brubeckmusic.com/ and The Brubeck Institute, University of the Pacific: www.pacific. edu/Community/Centers-Clinics-and-Institutes/Brubeck-Institute.html. See too the Brubeck Collection (www.pacific.edu/Library/Find/Holt-Atherton-Special-Collections/Brubeck-Collection.html), which houses a rich repository of Brubeck's manuscripts, published music, commercial and personal recordings and other documentation (photographs, programmes, correspondence and interviews), supported by a good Finding Aid.

[2] Ilse Storb and Klaus-Gotthard Fischer, *Dave Brubeck: Improvisations and Compositions – The Idea of Cultural Exchange*, trans. Bert Thompson (New York: Peter Lang Publishing, 1994), 151ff. Storb has undertaken valuable historical research about Brubeck, though the music analysis is fairly rudimentary and descriptive. Frustratingly, this book has no index, which limits its accessibility and usefulness.

[3] Brubeck, 'Jazz Perspective', 206. This philosophy of the mixed heritage and artistic status of jazz is also expressed eloquently in Dave Brubeck, 'Jazz's Evolvement as Art Form', *Down Beat*, 17/1 and 17/2 (27 January 1950), 12, 15.

a critical perspective, we may perceive an Eliot-like holistic hold, or Klein's intertextual webs, with strong candidacy for cultural hybridity. So classical–jazz interplay is practically a given, with Bach as a staple; what matters, therefore, is the nature of a specifically French–jazz relationship and, in particular, one with Milhaud.

The first objective is to assess historically the impact of Milhaud's compositional teaching upon Brubeck: part of a dynamic pedagogical practice that nurtured would-be eminent jazz- or popular-based composers and those working in a classical tradition: Burt Bacharach (b. 1928), Steve Reich (b. 1936), David del Tredici (b. 1937) and William Bolcom (b. 1938). The second objective is to assess the relations, analytically and interpretatively, across selected music by both composers. Building upon initial comparative work by Storb,[4] I want to investigate and test Ted Gioia's claim that 'Even the classical influences from Milhaud and others, played up by the media when Brubeck later achieved a mass audience, were only marginal influences. A comparison of Milhaud's supposedly jazz-inflected works with his student's actual jazz work reveals, underneath the superficial borrowings, a world of difference.'[5]

A notable focus for both objectives is provided by the crucial concepts of polytonality[6] and polyrhythm.[7] While the conceptual detail is pursued below, polytonality may be defined as involving superimposed triads of differing tonalities (a polychordal harmonic emphasis), and/or combined horizontal lines composed in different keys (a linear perspective); sometimes, there is also ambiguity between bitonality and strict polytonality

---

[4] Ilse Storb, '"The Duke Meets Darius Milhaud and Arnold Schönberg" (Dave Brubeck and His Teachers)', *Jazzforschung*, 28 (1996), 63–75. Other contemporaneous research includes John Salmon, 'What Brubeck Got from Milhaud', *American Music Teacher* (February–March 1992), 26–9, 76; see too John Salmon, 'The Classical Side of Dave Brubeck', *American Music Teacher* (February–March 2001), 23–8. The relationship was noted earlier in the French press; see an article in the Brubeck Collection, Series 1-E-General Clippings: 'Brubeck et Milhaud', *Le Provençal* (17 April 1984).

[5] Ted Gioia, 'Dave Brubeck and Modern Jazz in San Francisco' (chapter 4), in his *West Coast Jazz: Modern Jazz in California, 1945–1960* (New York and Oxford: Oxford University Press, 1992), 60–85: 73.

[6] Extensive worthwhile research on Brubeck's polytonality and its linkage to Milhaud has been undertaken by Mark McFarland, 'Dave Brubeck and Polytonal Jazz', *Jazz Perspectives*, 3/2 (2009), 153–76. In turn, McFarland relates to my previous work on Milhaud's polytonality (Mawer, *Darius Milhaud*), for instance, by invoking set theory.

[7] Brubeck's 'polyrhythmia' is related to aspects of modernity as cultural, critical history in Andy Birtwistle, 'Marking Time and Sounding Difference: Brubeck, Temporality and Modernity', *Popular Music*, 29/3 (2010), 351–71.

(three or more simultaneous tonalities).[8] Similarly, there is interpretative flexibility regarding polyrhythm and polymetre,[9] and, potentially, the constant usage of an irregular metre.

The interrelationships here are complex and appear to exist across a spectrum from loose association to tight correlation, as they did in a different setting for Evans. The basic premise is that – as a minimal relationship – polytonality and polyrhythm, together with other shared attributes, exist as important forces for Milhaud and Brubeck independently, effectively working in parallel, even though Milhaud's experience predates that of Brubeck. In several instances, however, a much more precise and maximal relationship may be established in two ways. With sufficient documentary evidence, a plausible argument may be made for direct cause–effect as a result of teacher–student interaction. It is worth bearing in mind Brubeck's lighthearted, but revealing, remark about the nature of Milhaud's influence: 'if someone had mentioned Darius Milhaud using two tonalities, on the job that night *I'd* be using two tonalities'.[10] Alternatively, a hermeneutic argument may be made for a measure of polytonal or polyrhythmic intersection as a result of close compositional comparison.

In practice, matters frequently involve a much finer nuancing: ambiguities fuelled by multiple perceptions, personal positionings (of Milhaud, Brubeck, commentators and listeners, ourselves included) and the passage of time itself. As elsewhere, a challenge in creating this study has been how best to structure discussion of these interactions – incorporating autobiographical commentaries, plus varied critique – to maintain reciprocity and balance, while avoiding troublesome duplication or becoming tied in knots.

Milhaud and Mills College

Milhaud's association with Mills College, Oakland, California from 1940 onwards defined a period when, suddenly, he was separated from his

---

[8] See Darius Milhaud, 'Polytonalité et atonalité', *La Revue musicale*, 4 (February 1923), 29–44, where both approaches are illustrated. Milhaud's theory section demonstrates chordal superimposition (36–7); his examples of compositional practice, especially his own, are much more contrapuntal (39). Bitonality is also embraced (32–3), including reference to *Petrushka*. For many, the whole notion of polytonality remains highly contradictory and, in Schenkerian terms, an impossibility.

[9] Milhaud's highly rhythmic *L'Homme et son désir* includes percussive passages that are technically polymetric, as well as polyrhythmic. For conducting simplicity, however, they are barred in 4/4, with accents added to the independent rhythmic ostinati to retain the intended polymetric effect.

[10] Brubeck quoted in Ralph J. Gleason, 'Dave Brubeck Remembers: "They Said I Was Too Far Out"', *Down Beat* 25/16 (8 August 1957), 17–19: 18. (Original italics.)

beloved France, exiled as a consequence of Nazism and World War II. Beyond 1947, in a surprisingly systematic fashion, he alternated his new life with his old Parisian one, on a yearly basis. In his resilient way, he sought to embrace his new environment, as evidenced by his *Opus Americanum No. 2* and by his composing of other American-themed works like *Kentuckiana* in 1948, albeit that Mediterranean lyricism and other European hallmarks still underpinned his writing. Similarly, he approached the compositional teaching opportunities afforded to him at Mills with the same responsibility and commitment as he did those at the Paris Conservatoire. Engagement with young composers and the wider community was a far more important part of his artistic persona than it was, say, for Ravel. Indeed returning to Mills in 1948, 'Teaching and work began at once.'[11]

For Mills, which had offered him a faculty position, Milhaud's presence was a significant coup, as he was 'one of France's most celebrated musical figures in the 1930s';[12] it too was in uncharted territories, reassessing its values and practices after World War II. As an institution set up for women, which had flourished under the inspired Presidency of Aurelia Reinhart and Lynn White, it first admitted male ex-servicemen graduate students in 1946, so complying with the GI Bill of Rights. In his autobiography *My Happy Life* (*Ma vie heureuse*), Milhaud devotes space to describing the culture and curriculum of Mills, relevant to assessing his teacher–student relationship with Brubeck.

Milhaud is very taken by the rich vegetation of this warm temperate climate, yet this paradise is contrasted by the appalling European reality: 'our hearts remained attached to our native shores, and our thoughts were ever with those who had to live in the midst of the tragedy that had engulfed our world'.[13] He senses the unique character of American colleges: 'little islands, set apart in time and space' that are culturally well provided for and self-sufficient, and is struck by the liberal arts philosophy that encompasses music for the very young, performance opportunities in bands, orchestras and choirs, and the notion of music appreciation.

According to Milhaud, the enlightened four-year BA curriculum included harmony (Bach chorales, through to extended variations), counterpoint in up to four parts, and orchestration.[14] It also embraced music history, of genres such as the symphony and chamber music, with a full year's study of

---

[11] Milhaud, *My Happy Life*, 222. Information on Milhaud's later life may also be gleaned from Paul Collaer, *Darius Milhaud*, ed. and Eng. trans. Jane Hohfeld Galante (San Francisco, CA: San Francisco Press, 1988).

[12] Fred M. Hall, *It's About Time: The Dave Brubeck Story* (Fayetteville, AR: University of Arkansas Press, 1996), 32.

[13] This and following quotation: Milhaud, *My Happy Life*, 205.   [14] *Ibid.*

Bach; practical skills included score reading, conducting, orchestral or choral participation, plus a solo recital. 'Finally, they are allowed to compose and study, in absolute liberty, every possible form of musical expression': this last statement is most telling. Milhaud's comments about postgraduate provision provide a direct foundation for Brubeck's experience: the master's course offered 'the study of fugue form, the composition of a large-scale work, or a thesis on some musical subject'.[15] He mentions the six-week cultural summer school at Mills which, in progressive and possibly unique fashion, brought in French writer-artists via its Maison française. Although American interest in French culture tumbled following the collapse of France in 1940, just a year later the perspicacious director Reinhart engaged figures of the stature of the artist Léger and the novelist and biographer André Maurois (1885–1967), as well as Milhaud and his wife Madeleine.[16]

In addition to describing Mills's Music curriculum, Milhaud discusses the American women students, who constituted the majority of the cohort and who were, from his educational experience, a more unusual phenomenon. These observations are, however, still pertinent to the Milhaud–Brubeck relationship for what they tell us about his priorities and approach. Milhaud admires the natural ability of many of these students but, arguably, their positive psychological makeup and cultural conditioning impresses him more: 'They are self-confident, and free from all complexes and inhibitions. They do not look upon composition as something solemn or momentous, but rather as a subject like any other.'[17] They are not fazed by being asked to compose to a brief and this, Milhaud implies, contributes to their rapid progress. He relates to a form of best practice which, while detailed and informative, maintains student confidence (a crucial issue to which we shall return): 'Another teacher, Marguerite Prall, has the secret of opening up before her pupils the whole vast field of musical knowledge without filling them with dismay.' In such references, his appreciation of collegial relations and communication skills is also clear.

Although Milhaud's main critique is of his female students, he adds that he has had several ex-soldiers studying with him. Explaining how these students are prepared for his classes via their briefing in advanced harmony and associated matters by 'young composer-teachers', he introduces Brubeck's brother, Howard Brubeck (1916–93). Following Pete Rugolo (1915–2011), Howard was the second male student to pursue graduate study with Milhaud in 1940, then remaining as his assistant. Milhaud is understandably proud that both Howard and his previous assistant Charles Jones were asked by Pierre Monteux to conduct their music with the San

---

[15] *Ibid.*, 206.   [16] *Ibid.*, 207.   [17] This and following quotations: *ibid.*, 206.

Francisco Symphony Orchestra. And later in his memoirs, apropos a short film entitled *A Visit to Darius Milhaud* (1954),[18] he refers warmly to his former male students. In one episode he was asked for his views on teaching; another features 'a surprise "jam-session" arranged by my old students Dick Collins [trumpet], Jack Weeks [trombone, bass], William Smith [clarinet], Dave [van] Kriedt [tenor saxophone] and Dave Brubeck, most of whom have become well known in the world of jazz'.[19]

Brubeck's experiences prior to Mills College

Although Brubeck came late to formal study, he was brought up in a very musical household on a Californian cattle ranch. His mother was a classically trained pianist-teacher of Russian descent and both his brothers were musical: Henry (1909–86), the eldest son, was a drummer with the hugely respected Gil Evans (1912–88); meanwhile Howard, the middle son, was as an organist-composer associated for a period with Palomar College.[20] As Fred Hall points out, 'Music was a constant at home, with piano recitals and chamber music and choir practice. Mostly classics or light classics were played on the wind-up phonograph when Dave was young: Sousa marches, some opera, and, rarely, lighter fare.'[21] Those classics would likely have involved French repertory,[22] and crucially, as Brubeck himself suggested: 'my brother [Howard], being a student of Milhaud, must have told me about polyrhythms and polytonality'.[23]

This family introduction was combined with early jazz influences of Waller, Tatum and a host of others: 'In Dave's easy-swing, locked-hands performances, however, there were traces of Billy Kyle, pianist with John Kirby and later Louis Armstrong, and Milt Buckner, famed for his work with Lionel Hampton.'[24] But among the most powerful forces were those of the pianist 'Count' Basie (1904–84) and the incomparable pianist-composer

---

[18] A copy of this film (dated 1955) is preserved in the Brubeck Collection (Series 5: Video and Film, Box 1: 1937–1961).

[19] Milhaud, *My Happy Life*, 230. Milhaud was also interviewed with his students Bolcom and Betty Bonds on KPFA-FM, Berkeley, in 1961 (copy in Brubeck Collection: Subseries 4: Interviews and Other Spoken Word Materials, Box 1.1). These students appear in the jacket photograph.

[20] Gleason, 'Dave Brubeck Remembers', 17.   [21] Hall, *It's About Time*, 10.

[22] See Ilse Storb, 'An Interview with Dave Brubeck [25 April 1980]', *Jazzforschung*, 16 (1984), 143–60: 143. Bach and the émigré Chopin are seen as part of the mix, together with Debussy.

[23] Ted Panken, 'An Interview with Dave Brubeck, July 23, 2007': http://tedpanken.word press.com/2011/08/11/an-interview-with-dave-brubeck-july-23-2007/.

[24] Hall, *It's About Time*, 11.

Ellington, for whom Brubeck later wrote his popular tribute, 'The Duke' (see below). Accordingly, the piano was the focus of Brubeck's activity, and in this capacity he played in band gigs: early repertory tended to comprise reworkings of tunes by Sammy Kaye, or Guy Lombardo, coupled with Dixieland-style renditions of *Tiger Rag* or Euday Bowman's *Twelfth Street Rag*.[25]

Brubeck's ranching background, via his father's profession, was very important to his whole outlook; he had intended to train as a vet to return to the ranch and originally enrolled in 1938 at the College of the Pacific in Stockton, California, for this purpose.[26] Only later did he change to major in Music, then finding serious challenges in music reading caused by a kind of dyslexia and having to brook his father's assessment of an early concert as 'The damndest bunch of noise I ever heard.'[27] Ironically, although the college held little regard for Brubeck as a Music undergraduate, it later awarded him an honorary doctorate[28] and now houses his Brubeck Collection.

Employing a certain poetic licence, Hall relates Brubeck's predisposition for polyrhythm to his ranching heritage: 'Polyrhythms countered the gait of his horse while herding cattle. Indian and Spanish rhythms and melodies were still heard in a part of California where Spanish land grants and a dwindling population of Native Americans had a century before given way to seekers of gold.'[29] Nevertheless, this stance is founded on Brubeck's own account of a curious occurrence when on horseback: 'I started thinking polyrhythmically against the noise of the horse's feet.'[30] The substantive point here is to avoid the dangers of over-reading, or essentializing: the presence of polyrhythm in Brubeck does not instantly connote the exclusive influence of Milhaud; equally, Brubeck was as or more exposed to Spanish and Native American sounds as to those of France.

Brubeck enlisted for army service in 1942 and was stationed in Europe, including France, from 1944: usefully, during these later years of World War II, he managed to acquire further band experience. Despite being shaken by misgivings about his early jazz harmonies, expressed by no less a figure than Stan Kenton,[31] he began to realize that music was his passion and mission. Having met Milhaud before enlisting, on his discharge in 1946

[25] *Ibid.*, 12.

[26] Richard Wang and Barry Kernfeld, 'Dave [David Warren] Brubeck', in Kernfeld (ed.), *The New Grove Dictionary of Jazz*, vol. I, 329–31: 329.

[27] Quoted in Ralph J. Gleason, 'Brubeck', *Down Beat*, 24/15 (25 July 1957), 13–14: 14.

[28] Hall, *It's About Time*, 18.   [29] *Ibid.*, 10.   [30] Storb, 'An Interview', 154.

[31] Gleason, 'Dave Brubeck Remembers', 18–19.

Brubeck returned to California for more academic study, 'determined to get his still-evolving, polytonal, polyrhythm but not-bop music accepted in the jazz community and to make it a part of the American musical mainstream'.[32]

Teacher–student interactions

Apart from Milhaud's account of his teaching at Mills, a notable proportion of what can be gleaned of his interaction with Brubeck, including his personal and interpersonal qualities, comes from his student, and we should, therefore, not lose sight of this positioning and potential for bias, or folklore across the years. Milhaud seems to have been firm yet non-judgemental, encouraging and keen to build his pupils' confidence through promoting their self-worth and independence.[33] Brubeck, in turn, is revealed as a strong-minded, motivated and imaginative student who had immense talent; according to his fellow student Smith, 'He played chords you wouldn't believe. It was astounding. His harmonic sense was so far advanced, it was shocking.'[34] Conversely, he is shown as one who weathered his frustrations well. His limitations in reading and notating music were the cause of a refrain from Milhaud: 'Very good, Boo-Boo, but not at all what you have written.'[35] Implicit here and elsewhere is the fundamental importance of a positive, healthy psychology to secure teacher–learner partnerships.

Brubeck's lessons began officially in autumn 1946, setting up a long-term association: 'I was in Milhaud's classes off and on for years'.[36] Beyond this formal study, Milhaud acted as a private tutor and remained a supportive mentor, even friend, until his death in 1974.[37] As one of a group of returning servicemen musicians admitted to Milhaud's composition class, Brubeck entered an upbeat creative scene at Mills concerned to establish 'music's new meanings for a postwar world'.[38]

---

[32] Hall, *It's About Time*, 31.

[33] This impression was confirmed in discussion (12 November 2013) with Darius Brubeck, and by his note on 'What Brubeck Learned from Milhaud', in a programme for *Music by Darius Milhaud and Dave Brubeck*, Mills Music Now 2013–14 (27 September 2013).

[34] Hall, *It's About Time*, 33.

[35] Dave Brubeck, liner notes, *Reminiscences of the Cattle Country*, quoted in Storb and Fischer, *Dave Brubeck*, 28.

[36] Storb, 'An Interview', 146.

[37] The Brubeck Collection includes personal correspondence with Milhaud as late as 1971 (Series 1-C- Personal Correspondence & Fan mail, Box 3: 1968–77) and, with Madeleine Milhaud, through to 1999.

[38] Hall, *It's About Time*, 32.

Europe (France) or America; classical or jazz?

As a representative in exile of French and wider European music, Milhaud disillusioned Brubeck early on of any aspirations to develop as a traditional classical composer: 'he told me that I could never become a typical composer from a European point of view'.[39] At one level, this might seem a harsh, negative assessment and one likely to demotivate, but Brubeck was already in his later twenties and still could not read music fluently. There was, therefore, a compelling honesty in Milhaud's engagement with his pupil, and an avoidance of the common pedagogical problem of imitation – seeking simply to create a student in his own image. Incidentally, this was absolutely contrary to Brubeck's recounted experience of Schoenberg as a teacher: 'I can tell you why you should write the way I want you to write'.[40]

Conversely, and much more positively, Milhaud's priority was to give Brubeck and his other students the space to be themselves and establish their identities. As Storb has observed, it was part of his *métier* to establish his students' sociomusical and cultural milieu,[41] and hence Brubeck's reporting that Milhaud said to his apprentice composers: 'You have to think about your own musical background – of your own country.'[42] Indeed, according to Brubeck, Milhaud went so far as to tell him that he should not worry about not becoming a classical European-style composer: 'You represent America. You are in a much better position, because you don't have this European background.'[43] Implicit, perhaps, from Milhaud's perspective is the burden of a Bloomian 'anxiety of influence' explored elsewhere in this book.

Although Milhaud's experience of early jazz and its meanings in 1920s Harlem was quite different from the post-1945 phenomenon, it was his continuing pro-jazz sympathies that appealed to students like Smith or Brubeck. In latching on to this shared interest, Milhaud ensured the relevance of his classes to those who worked outside the classical canon. In fact, he went further in upholding the value of jazz, insisting 'that he [Brubeck] not give up the freedom jazz offers as music and life style'.[44] Thus Milhaud's pedagogical far-sightedness is demonstrated: his philosophy was well ahead

---

[39] Storb, 'An Interview', 146. Nonetheless, his composerly credentials were well recognized in a jazz context, evidenced by articles such as Leonard Feather, 'Dave Brubeck, Composer', *Down Beat*, 33/13 (30 June 1966), 18–20.

[40] Interview with Brubeck (25–26 April 1980), quoted in Storb and Fischer, *Dave Brubeck*, 4.

[41] Storb, 'An Interview', 146.

[42] Brubeck interview for 'Our Sunday Visitor', quoted in Storb, 'An Interview', 146.

[43] Storb, 'An Interview', 147.

[44] Storb and Fischer, *Dave Brubeck*, 28. As a related matter, Milhaud and Brubeck shared 'a lifelong hatred of racism': Gene Lees, *Cats of Any Color: Jazz Black and White* (New York and Oxford: Oxford University Press, 1995), 57.

of that of most conservatoires in not merely permitting, but positively endorsing, the serious pursuit of jazz.[45]

Performance and compositional techniques

While crucial to all would-be composers, the role of performance in Milhaud's pedagogical toolbox follows on directly from his privileging of jazz. In those early classes, Milhaud enquired, 'How many jazz musicians are here?', and after Brubeck and others had identified themselves, he responded, 'From now on, all of your compositions should be written for this instrumentation [jazz ensemble].'[46] When the products proved worthwhile, he would urge their performance in assemblies at Mills, for which a brief signature opener called 'Curtain Music' was created in 6/4 metre.[47] In the short term, this strategy made technical study much more enjoyable, purposeful and real, no doubt also raising standards. The longer-term significance is that this insistence on performance was largely responsible for creating the early Dave Brubeck Quartet – in other words catalysing a major part of Brubeck's professional identity in leading jazz ensembles, firstly his Trio and then the Quartet. The five players already mentioned were supplemented by the legendary alto saxophonist Paul Desmond and others. As a corollary of performance, Milhaud emphasized concertizing and, as Brubeck recalls, it was his composition teacher who 'asked us to play a benefit concert at Mills College, and that was our first concert with the Octet'.[48] In a nice inversion or layering, Brubeck, as a jazzman of the later 1940s drawing on a classical heritage, reorchestrated for his Octet sections of Milhaud's *La Création du monde*, as a jazz-inspired pinnacle of the 1920s, though the piece was not actually performed by the group.[49]

Compositional techniques were founded on principles of musicianship, developed through assignments in harmony, counterpoint, fugue and orchestration that were also deemed suitable as material for subsequent performance. As noted above, Milhaud initially sent his pupils to Brubeck's brother for such foundational training which focused on Bach chorales in the Riemenschneider edition.[50] Interestingly, this study was supplemented by a harmony text written by André Gedalge (Milhaud's own teacher at the Conservatoire) and analytical texts by Walter Piston (himself taught

---

[45] See Storb, 'An Interview', 154.   [46] *Ibid.*, 146.
[47] Hall, *It's About Time*, 34, 36. This item begins the four-CD compilation Dave Brubeck, *Time Signatures: A Career Retrospective* (Columbia/AllMusic C4K52945, 1992).
[48] Storb, 'An Interview', 146.   [49] Hall, *It's About Time*, 33.
[50] See Storb, 'An Interview', 153.

by Nadia Boulanger), who in turn referenced Schenker's voiceleading approach.[51]

More specifically, Milhaud was the polytonalist *par excellence*, and irrespective of whether Brubeck's brand predated his studies with Milhaud (if not those of his brother) it was surely nurtured by them. As Brubeck attested, his teacher 'lived absolutely in polytonality'.[52] But even before venturing into multi-key relations, Brubeck was strongly affected by Milhaud's approach to a single key: without a tonal centre, both composer and listeners lose the marvels of modulation. 'They can't get anywhere, if they have never been anywhere.' As for a polytonal curriculum, it appears that Milhaud used his seminal article-cum-manifesto 'Polytonalité et atonalité' as a resource for his graduate students,[53] presumably in its American edition.[54] Without explaining its full contents,[55] we can emphasize that its approach is systematic and logical, yet it does not lose sight of the non-intellectual, emotional contribution: feeling.[56] It extends from mapping all two-key triadic combinations in root position and inversions, in major and minor inflections, to an equivalent charting of three keys. The second part of the article is presented as its antithesis: atonality; several of Milhaud's more experimental pieces do explore a free, chromatic use of serial procedures, but are generally still founded on extended modal centres. As a less formal possible catalyst, in an interview with Ted Panken Brubeck recalled seeing a noticeboard at Mills upon which was posted an article about Milhaud where 'he's talking about playing in two or three keys at the same time. So I don't know how this [polytonal enquiry] started to happen, but it did.'[57]

To a greater extent, polyrhythmic procedures seem to have been an incipient hallmark of Brubeck's style by the time of his studies with Milhaud.[58] While disentangling exactly what came from where is nigh on

---

[51] Information from Storb and Fischer, *Dave Brubeck*, 5.

[52] This and the following quotation are from Storb, 'An Interview', 145. Darius Brubeck ('What Brubeck Learned from Milhaud') confirms 'polytonal harmony' as 'the main lesson'.

[53] McFarland, 'Dave Brubeck and Polytonal Jazz', 155. Information from Katherine Warne, a former composition student of Milhaud.

[54] Darius Milhaud, 'Polytonality and Atonality', *Pro Musica Quarterly*, 2 (October 1924), n.p.

[55] See Mawer, *Darius Milhaud*, 19–26.   [56] Storb, 'An Interview', 148.

[57] Panken, 'An Interview with Dave Brubeck'. This may be a vagueness created by the passage of time; by contrast, McFarland has asserted that Brubeck would have had a copy of the article before starting his graduate studies: McFarland, 'Dave Brubeck and Polytonal Jazz', 156; see too 175n. Whatever the precise truth, the evidence of Brubeck's having studied the article is readily discernible in his music.

[58] Hall, *It's About Time*, 32–3.

impossible, we can argue for strongly paralleled priorities which suggest that Milhaud was an ideal teacher – a suggestion supported by the sheer warmth of Brubeck's recollections. It would be foolish to assert a direct cause–effect relationship (complicated by Howard's contact with Milhaud and by Brubeck's own meeting before he enlisted that likely predisposed him in certain directions), yet it would be equally naïve to claim the development of Brubeck's polyrhythmic skills as unrelated to Milhaud's intervention. This is especially so since, as Andy Birtwistle has pointed out, Brubeck's early identification with polyrhythm, while distancing him from contemporary jazz critics and some jazz musicians, was closely aligned with a broader cultural modernism.[59] It is harder to ascertain exactly how polyrhythm was taught beyond experimentation with small-scale compositions and reference to Milhaud's own practice.

Finally, we should return to those crucial personal qualities that underpin any meaningful, long-term relationship. From the start, Brubeck seems to have been convinced of a potential special bond with someone who was prepared to go further to meet him: 'If I survived the war, I knew the first thing I was going to do was go study with him [Milhaud] because he understood me.'[60] Even among supportive teachers that he had experienced at the College of the Pacific, Brubeck clearly viewed Milhaud as exceptional: 'Milhaud was by far the *most* encouraging'. It was the latter's reassurance that supported him through the ongoing struggle of trying to notate the music in his head. Hall offers an apt summary of this pedagogical experience: 'Studying with Milhaud was a combination of private lessons and group sessions that left an indelible mark on Dave Brubeck's music and his heart.'[61] The nature of that musical mark cues the second half of this chapter.

Relations between the music and approaches of Brubeck and Milhaud

On the one hand, Brubeck's creative output comprises numerous short self-contained jazz pieces ('songs'), which are collected and recorded across several albums: effectively jazz standards that could be further reinterpreted and improvised upon by Brubeck or others. Within this repertory are important original compositions or conceptions, including 'The Duke';[62]

---

[59] Birtwistle, 'Marking Time and Sounding Difference', 353–5.
[60] This and the following Brubeck comments are quoted in Hall, *It's About Time*, 33.
[61] *Ibid.*
[62] *Jazz: Red Hot and Cool* (Columbia CL 699, 1955). See too *Dave Brubeck Interchanges '54*: Dave Brubeck, Paul Desmond, Bob Bates, Joe Dodge (Columbia/Legacy CK 47032 [CD], 1991).

'Three to Get Ready' and 'Blue Rondo à la Turk';[63] 'Unsquare Dance', 'It's a Raggy Waltz' and 'Bluette';[64] as well as the most famous tune that Brubeck never wrote: Desmond's 'Take Five' (*Time Out*, 1959).[65] Such pieces are distinct from arrangements of existing standards like *St. Louis Blues*, 'Take the "A" Train', 'Ol' Man River', 'Tea for Two' and so on.

On the other hand, there is a lesser-known repertory, generally later in date, of serious larger-scale compositions. The majority are religious choral works that set New Testament texts: the oratorio *The Light in the Wilderness* (1968), with its exhortation to 'Love Your Enemies'; and several cantatas, including *The Gates of Justice* (1969), with its section urging 'Open the Gates'. There are at least two ballet scores: the nicely entitled *Points on Jazz* (1961) and *Glances* (1983); additionally, we find smaller-scale serious items and lighter numbers, which have the feel of compositional exercises.[66] Some of these, for example 'The Chickens and The Ducklings', form part of Brubeck's first compositional exploration, *Reminiscences of the Cattle Country* (1946), and emanate from the period of his study with Milhaud.[67]

Our main concern is with Brubeck's jazz compositions and recorded improvisations, but the choral repertory, if more conventional, is mentioned *en passant*. This latter Christian repertory, revealing Brubeck's deeply held convictions about social justice, finds a counterpart in Milhaud's Jewish-inspired works, some of which are overtly liturgical such as the *Service sacré* (1947). According to John Salmon, Brubeck recalled hearing Milhaud's

---

[63] *Time Out*: Dave Brubeck, Paul Desmond, Eugene Wright, Joe Morello (Columbia CL 1397, 1959; see also Columbia Jazz Masterpieces: CK 40627 and Columbia/Legacy CK 65122 [CD]). On this pivotal year, see again the excellent essay by Darius Brubeck, '1959: The Beginning of Beyond', 177–201.

[64] *Time Further Out: Miró Reflections*: Dave Brubeck, Paul Desmond, Eugene Wright, Joe Morello (Columbia CS 8490, 1961). For a neat compilation of original pieces, see *Dave Brubeck: The Very Best* (Columbia/Sony Jazz 499694-2, 2000).

[65] Brubeck's association with this tune nevertheless continues. See Luke Jennings, 'From Orwell to Brubeck' [dance review], *The Observer* (6 May 2012), on a 2012 production by Birmingham Royal Ballet: 'The evening's final work was BRB director David Bintley's *Take Five*, set to well-known pieces by Dave Brubeck. This hits the spot immediately.' On a French connection, however: 'If this entertaining piece has a shortcoming it's Jean-Marc Puissant's costumes for the women; the Peter Pan collars looks more staid than cute, and the mid-thigh length abbreviates the dancers' legs.'

[66] Various score excerpts are reproduced in Ilse Storb, 'Dave Brubeck, Komponist und Pianist', *Jazzforschung*, 13 (1981), 9–44, and Storb and Fischer, *Dave Brubeck*.

[67] Storb and Fischer, *Dave Brubeck*, 28. See too 'Composition Exercises, c. 1946 [pencil]' and 'Darius Milhaud Lessons, 1946–1947 [pencil & ink notes w/ musical examples]' (Brubeck Collection, 3A.1.3 and 1.4).

grand opera *Christophe Colomb* (1928) during his studies,[68] an experience that may potentially have encouraged his own choral quest.[69] Equally, Brubeck is likely to have been inspired to some extent in his ballet writing by Milhaud's successful exemplars, including *L'Homme et son désir* and *La Création*; some comparisons are given below but, even at a surface level, *Points on Jazz* and *La Création* (in its *Suite de concert* version) share three movement titles: 'Prelude', 'Fugue' and 'Scherzo'. Although our focus is on exploring Milhaud's impact as a teacher-cum-theorist or source, Brubeck, as a pianist (somewhat analogous to Evans's position), is also intrigued by Debussy,[70] Stravinsky,[71] Bartók, Shostakovich (1906–71)[72] and Jean Langlais (1907–91).[73] In other words, whilst undeniably being very important, the Milhaud relationship is by no means exclusive.

'The Duke Meets Darius Milhaud' (1955)

Before returning to polytonality and polyrhythm from a compositional stance, a useful way in is created via Brubeck's celebrated early piece 'The Duke'.[74] According to Storb, this tribute work originally held an extended title: 'The Duke meets Darius Milhaud and Arnold Schoenberg'[75] and so offers historical evidence of Brubeck's crediting of Milhaud's role. In time, the title was shortened, not least because any inclusion of Schoenberg

---

[68] Salmon, 'What Brubeck Got from Milhaud', 27. Personal contact between Salmon and Brubeck (22 March 1991).

[69] Nonetheless, Brubeck's choral contribution can be viewed independently. A tribute concert on 6 October 1985, 'Dave Brubeck Salutes Darius Milhaud' (which included Brubeck's *Pange Lingua Variations* of 1983), evinced slightly provocative reviews by Donald Rosenberg, 'Brubeck Choral Effort Outshines Teacher Milhaud', *Akron* [Ohio] *Beacon Journal* (7 October, 1985), and Robert Finn, 'Jazz Fans at JCU [John Carroll University] Wait out Milhaud for Pure Brubeck', *Cleveland Plain Dealer* (8 October 1985). (Brubeck Collection: 1-E-Clippings 5a.6: Reviews, 1985.)

[70] Storb and Fischer, *Dave Brubeck*, 84–8.

[71] See McFarland, 'Dave Brubeck and Polytonal Jazz', 171–5.

[72] According to Darius Brubeck (personal conversation, 12 November 2013), his father was very taken by the intensity and style of Shostakovich's music and acquired many scores.

[73] Langlais's 'Point d'orgue' from *Vingt-quatre pièces* (1934–9) was among materials in Brubeck's library (source: Brubeck Collection: 3C.2.12).

[74] 'The Duke' was later arranged by Gil Evans and appears in this version on Davis's *Miles Ahead* (New York: Columbia CL 1041, 1957; reissued Columbia/Legacy CK 65121, 1997). Brubeck's more extended composition features on *Dave Brubeck: The Very Best* (New York: Columbia/Sony Jazz 499694-2, 2000).

[75] Storb and Fischer, *Dave Brubeck*, 79, 87, 154. Storb's source is a personal interview with Brubeck in New York (7 July 1972).

Example 9.1 Brubeck, *Jazz: Red Hot and Cool*, 'The Duke' (bars 1–6)

was obviously more diplomatic than deeply felt.[76] Connection with all three figures may be discerned in the music, but Ellington, who was 'my biggest influence among composers of jazz and arrangers',[77] takes precedence as the single dedicatee of 'The Duke' in its published transcription.[78] It is marked 'With a relaxed beat' and set in cut-common time, and Brubeck has commented that he was reminiscing over an early Ellington piece whose title had, fortuitously perhaps, temporarily eluded him; undoubtedly he evokes most successfully 'the essence of the romantic, chromatic, and witty Ellington persona';[79] see Example 9.1.

The opening pitch material may also be related to Milhaud and Schoenberg though it is important to note that the pianistic treatment, with its grace notes, triplets, offbeat starts and syncopations, is already developing a clear Brubeck signature. Curiously Schoenbergian is a quasi-serial melodic bass line that still maintains a clear pitch-centre on C, supported by an anacrusic dominant pick-up (F♯, G). Across the first two bars, Brubeck introduces eight pitches of a full chromatic scale, with the first two repeated: F♯, G, C, E, F, (F♯), (G), A, A♯, B. The remaining four pitches are then supplied, usually in prominent positions: D (bar 4, beat 1); A♭ (decorative); E♭ (bar 5, beat 1) and D♭ (bar 5, beat 3), again in combination with previously heard pitches. The phrase concludes back upon C at bar 6 (beat 1). Interestingly,

---

[76] McFarland suggests that Schoenberg's name was added as a lighthearted afterthought once someone had pointed out the similarities: 166n.

[77] Storb, 'An Interview', 149.

[78] See Dave Brubeck, *Brubeck Plays Brubeck: Original Themes and Improvised Variations for Solo Piano*, transcribed by Frank Metis, 2 vols. (Delaware, PA: Shawnee Press Inc., 1956).

[79] Hall, *It's About Time*, 58–9, 11.

this fully chromatic writing, within a larger modal framework, is a trait of Milhaud's young experimental voice (see 'La Lieuse' from *Machines agricoles* of 1919, discussed below). Aside from this chromatic ploy, the bass line embodies a wonderful eclectic fusion. It is a swung walking bass, with much stepwise ascending motion, which also enjoys bold falling fifth progressions that have a distinctly Bachian feel, especially when followed by ascending fourths in a cycle of fifths gesture: G–C (bar 1); B–E (bars 2–3); B♭–E♭, A♭–D♭, G–C (bars 4–6). A first-time bar, on a dominant construct, to cue a repetition of the eight-bar section adds to this neoclassical sense, which may perhaps link to Milhaud's neoclassical example and pedagogy, though Brubeck surely also appreciated Bach at first hand.

A closer connection to Milhaud lies in the opening polychords. Above the quasi-serial bass is featured a chain of descending polytonal triads (bars 1–2): e, d, C, a, G, e, C. While this is not strict polytonality, it is the form in which Brubeck most frequently uses it. The practice may be interpreted variously: as a small-scale succession of polytriads; as a bitonal progression of diverse triads over a bass founded on C; thirdly, as essentially monotonal since, with the exception of their grace notes, the selected triads are all diatonic in C anyway. A similar gesture occurs across bars 3–4: G, G, a, F, while the remainder of bars 4–8 tends toward quartal components, which might link to Milhaud and Bartók. Our kneejerk reaction to quartal harmonies is to credit Bartók, but Milhaud too references quartal and quintal sonorities in 'Polytonalité et atonalité'[80] and in turn is influenced by his overlooked compatriot Charles Koechlin (1867–1950).

The music that follows the second-time bar (bars 10–13) surely derives from Milhaud's practice, offering a tight source–product relationship; see Example 9.2. This writing is in overt chordal blocks, rather than the initial inverted melody beneath triads. Across each loosely sequential two-bar phrase (bars 10–11, 12–13), Brubeck presents strong contrary motion between a stepwise minim descent in the bass and tripletized swung ascent in the treble, completed by a final small descent. The bass yields a succession of predominantly major triads: F–E–D–C (bars 10–11); b♭–A♭–G–f (bars 12–13). Above, the treble provides a more even blend of major and minor triads, supplemented by occasional seventh or diminished sonorities: e–F, G–a, b–C, C^7 (bars 10–11); f–g diminished, a♭–b♭, c–D♭, d^7 (bars 12–13). Salmon has pertinently compared these bars and the final five bars of Milhaud's miniature opera *L'Enlèvement d'Europe* (1927);[81] meanwhile Mark McFarland offers a set-theoretic and 'dissonance weight'

---

[80] Example 17 in Milhaud, 'Polytonalité et atonalité', 38.
[81] Salmon, 'What Brubeck Got from Milhaud', 28.

Example 9.2 Brubeck, *Jazz: Red Hot and Cool*, 'The Duke' (bars 10–13)

interpretation of these and successive bars.[82] Similar comparison may be made with the rest of Milhaud's trilogy, including the final section of *La Délivrance de Thésée* (bars 165–77) and various moments of *L'Abandon d'Ariane*: the ascending two-bar phrases (bars 100–3); the contrary motion, with triplets above (bars 249–53); or the ensuing portion (bar 255ff.) that begins with an identical spread triad of F major in the bass, plus minor triad above.[83] Alternatively, we might reference *Scaramouche*, 'one of Brubeck's favorite compositions by the French composer',[84] where the second piano (bar 5) features a chromatic descending bass line in octaves: F–E–Eb–D, with offbeat (second-inversion) major triads ascending in the right hand: E–F–F#–G.

Furthermore, we can relate the passage directly to Milhaud's theory in 'Polytonalité et atonalité', albeit that, strictly, we are still dealing with a series of bitonal superimpositions. In his second example, Milhaud details and numbers all the resultant possibilities from combining two triads: C plus Db (I), through to C plus B (XI).[85] As his third example, he presents the different major–minor combinations that may pertain to any two keys: major–major (A), minor–minor (B), major–minor (C), and minor–major (D).[86] Brubeck's practice may thus be illuminated through Milhaud's terms of reference, as shown in Table 9.1.

What this comparison usefully points up is that, although Brubeck is working within Milhaud's theory, he is applying it to serve his own jazz needs, with clear sonic choices emerging. In combining his bass and treble

[82] McFarland, 'Dave Brubeck and Polytonal Jazz', 166–7. Curiously, he does not really discuss the findings.

[83] Darius Milhaud, *L'Abandon d'Ariane* (Vienna: Universal Edition, 1928).

[84] McFarland, 'Dave Brubeck and Polytonal Jazz', 155–6. *Scaramouche* is used to illustrate Milhaud's polytonal principles, including the 'partitioning of polytonal keys by register' (156), a trait also employed by Brubeck. Equally, Brubeck had in his library a score of Milhaud's *Le Bal martiniquais* of 1944–5 (Brubeck Collection: 3C.3.6).

[85] Milhaud, 'Polytonalité et atonalité', 32; for more discussion, see Mawer, *Darius Milhaud*.

[86] Milhaud, 'Polytonalité et atonalité', 33.

Table 9.1 *Brubeck, Jazz: Red Hot and Cool, 'The Duke' (bars 10–13), related to Milhaud, 'Polytonalité et atonalité'*

Bars	10	(bt3)	11	(bt3)	12	(bt3)	13	(bt3)
Treble	e – F	G – a	b – C	C^{maj7}	f – g dim.	a♭ – b♭	c – D♭	d^7
Bass	F	E	D	C	b♭	A♭	G	$f^{(4-3)}$
Ex. 2	XI –	III V	IX X	–	VII IX	– II	V VI	IX
Ex. 3	C A	A C	C A	A	B B	C C	C A	B

triads, Brubeck favours here Milhaud's interval class IX (three occurrences): a euphonious major sixth. Next in frequency is interval class V: a perfect fourth – thus another quartal dimension. Brubeck's preferences of modal inflection are even more clear-cut and suit well his jazz context: we find six occurrences of manner C, five of A, three of B and none of D. In other words, Brubeck strongly favours major triads in the bass, upon which may be layered either minor or major triads. This combinative policy creates for his jazz richly extended major chords with added sevenths, ninths and blues inflections: a major third, melded with a poignant, or piquant, minor third above. For example, in downplaying any simultaneous bitonality, we may argue that bar 10 beat 3 yields in practice a single, composite E/e^7 chord from the bass: E, B, G♯/G, B, D; the roughly analogous bar 12 beat 3 produces an A♭/a♭ chord. Occasionally, Brubeck contrasts with a minor–minor combination, but he does not place a minor triad beneath a major one, which would tend to negate his instinctively acoustic-based approach that privileges the bass. This opening (and a later recurrence of chordal writing) provides the firmest evidence of Milhaud precedent-cum-tribute in 'The Duke' – a piece that extends to *c*.6.30 and contrasts several episodes, including a saxophone solo for Desmond.

Polytonality

Brubeck's gradual growth from his studies with Milhaud through to independence may be measured, firstly, via polytonality and wider pitch relations across a selection of pieces. A compositional piano exercise, 'The Chickens and the Ducklings' (1946), demonstrates a small-scale testing of Milhaud's polytonal theories and Brubeck's own early metrical enquiries (see below). A left-hand part in C 'major' (bars 1–5) is contrasted by a right-hand part in G Dorian: G, A, B♭, C, D, E, F, G (bars 1–2) then inflected to G major (bars 3–5); see Example 9.3. The strands unite briefly in E♭ major (bars 6–7) before bifurcating into C below and E♭ above (bars 8–18). Bar 18 presents the two triads as in Milhaud's article,[87] with the wider-spread bass triad: C, G, E, plus the close-position triad above: E♭, G, B♭. The interval between the tonalities is Milhaud's own favoured third relation: III, with the main modal combinative reference being to his manner 'A'.

Brubeck's *Points on Jazz*,[88] a Third Stream-type enterprise commissioned by the American Ballet Theater and scored for two pianos (orchestrated

---

[87] *Ibid.*, 32.

[88] Excerpts from the 'Fugue' and 'Chorale' are reproduced by Storb, 'Dave Brubeck, Komponist und Pianist', 24, 25.

Example 9.3 Brubeck, *Reminiscences of the Cattle Country*, 'The Chickens and the Ducklings' (bars 1–7)

by Howard),[89] also illustrates pitch procedures that may in part be derived from Milhaud loci. The double-piano texture again brings to mind *Scaramouche*, as a dance-related suite for two pianos. A slow four-part 'Chorale' (VI) in common metre can be referenced to Milhaud's modal combination (though it is actually monotonal): the first piano part adopts a C minor key signature, beneath which the second (bass) part operates in C major. Thus this usage is congruent with the major–minor combinative manner C favoured in 'The Duke'. A balancing 'Fugue' (IV) in regular cut-common time, marked 'Moderately fast in a swinging style', experiments most effectively with a fully fledged four-voice technique (Example 9.4a). Within C minor, Brubeck explores a highly chromatic fugal subject based on his Polish-inspired *Dziekuje* theme:[90] G–G♭, A♭–F, A(–F), E♭–D–C–B(–C) (bars 1–3), leading into Countersubject 1 which begins: B♭(–A♭–G–A♭), with pitches 11 (D♭) and 12 (E) supplied shortly after (bars 4, 6–7). As with 'The Duke', this is a free quasi-serialism involving pitch repetition which, in its intervallic contours and pitch structure, might be compared fruitfully with Milhaud's second canonic subject in 'La Lieuse' from *Machines agricoles* (Fig. 10). Its angular pitch sequence runs as follows:

[89] Leonard Feather, 'Dave Brubeck, Composer', *Down Beat*, 33/13 (30 June 1966), 18–20: 19.
[90] The theme, meaning 'Thank you' in Polish, was Brubeck's response to the warm reception that the Dave Brubeck Quartet received in Poland. Storb explains that 'after a visit to the Chopin museum [...] the piece developed into a lyrical jazz version with suggestions of Chopin'. Storb and Fischer, *Dave Brubeck*, 105. Chopinesque style is especially evident in the opening 'Prelude', 'Scherzo' and 'Waltz'.

Example 9.4 Imitative counterpoint in Brubeck and Milhaud
  (a) Brubeck, *Points on Jazz*, 'Fugue' (bars 1–6, reduced score)
  (b) Milhaud, *Machines agricoles*, 'La Lieuse' (bars 20–2, reduced score)

Example 9.5 Brubeck, *Time Further Out: Miró Reflections*, 'Bluette' (bars 1–6)

Slow waltz ♩ = 100

B♭m⁷   E♭m⁷   A♭⁺⁷ B♭m⁷   E♭⁷

Pf.

p expressively

E♭–D–E, B♭–A, G–F♯, F(–A), C, with the remaining C♯, B and G♯ supplied in the ensuing bar (Example 9.4b). Like Milhaud, who first employs the double bass and works his way upwards incrementally by instrument and register, Brubeck starts with the lowest voice (the bass of piano 2) and ascends with each new entry. This jazz-inspired fugal writing may also invite comparison with the bluesy 'Fugue' from *La Création*, where again the voices ascend from an initial double bass entry, with a 'polytonal' countersubject that quotes from *St. Louis Blues* (see Example 4.5).[91] In turn, both composers look back to Bach.

Brubeck's mature improvisatory jazz pieces dating from around 1960 tend towards the monotonal, finding their interest and originality through harmonic-melodic and, increasingly, metric-rhythmic means. In the aptly named slow waltz, 'Bluette', distinctiveness is achieved through rich seventh (ninth and eleventh) harmonies, mere hints of Ravel(?), and a melodic blues expression that operate in a melancholic B♭ minor; see Example 9.5. The contemporaneous 'Blue Rondo' (Example 9.6b) enjoys tracing small pitch inflections against a fixed ostinato background, with bold pedal points on F (major) and then A (minor, bar 9), on the principle – convincingly delivered here – that less pitch is more. A similar principle directs 'Unsquare Dance' with its ostinati and usage of an Aeolian-type mode on A. Meanwhile, 'Three to Get Ready' brings in its C-based pitch material successively rather than simultaneously, through layered improvisations or variations (Example 9.6a). 'Love Your Enemies' from *The Light in the Wilderness* maintains Brubeck's predilection for ostinato and pedal points together with quartal components, for instance, in the alternation: D, G, C; E♭, A♭, D♭ (bars 8–11). A note accompanying the opening portion of this

---

[91] Polytonal rethinking of *St. Louis Blues* offers a neat Milhaud–Brubeck link since Brubeck famously played this standard bitonally in E and G majors (left and right hands) with his Quartet at Carnegie Hall in 1963, to the surprise of his fellow players. See liner notes for *The Dave Brubeck Quartet at Carnegie Hall* (COL CL2036 [1963]).

movement states that 'the [louder] 3/4 measures should be sung with harshness and stridence [*sic*], while the answering 4/4 measures are softer, smoother, and more peaceful in character'. Hermeneutically, we might perceive echoes of Milhaud's pronouncement about the benefits of polytonality: 'the use of polytonality adds more subtlety and sweetness to pianissimos, and more stridency and sonorous force to fortissimos'.[92] This discussion of alternating, contrasting metres cues the next topic.

Polyrhythm

The second vehicle of polyrhythm, mixing rhythmic-metric matters, helps to secure the gauging of relationship with Milhaud and exhibits inevitably a little overlap with music discussed apropos polytonality. Background historical referents are Milhaud's extraordinary polyrhythmic ballet *L'Homme* and his *La Création*, which were influenced, like so much twentieth-century music, by the immensely powerful rhythmic drive of Stravinsky's *Le Sacre du printemps*. Polyrhythm is also crucially the main means by which Brubeck, in the company of Desmond (as creator of 'Take Five' and 'Eleven Four'),[93] establishes his artistic independence in jazz via his so-called 'Time Experiments' from 1954 onwards,[94] and for which he rightly maintains a measure of independent access via the environmental rhythms of horse-riding and ranching.

Back with our early locus, 'The Chickens and The Ducklings', Brubeck's interest in polymetric flexibility is manifested as succession rather than simultaneity; see again Example 9.3. Metric variation allows the intake of a breath at the close of a second two-bar phrase of 2/4 metre. Brubeck incorporates an extra 1/4 bar (bar 5), creating space to rejoin the polytonal strands into E♭ (9/8, at bar 6); similarly, he builds in a 'poco rit.' (6/8, at bar 7) to frame a reprise of the initial 2/4 metre and pitch identity (bars 8–18). The simple rhythms combine note-against-note and two-notes-against-one. Milhaud's writing also sets out successive polymetre to accommodate turns of phrasing, such as in the ebullient Concerto for Percussion and

---

[92] See Milhaud, 'Polytonalité et atonalité', 38: 'l'emploi de la polytonalité ajoute aux pianissimi plus de subtilité et de douceur et aux fortissimi plus d'âpreté et de force sonore'. This passage is discussed in Mawer, *Darius Milhaud*, 22.

[93] See Storb and Fischer, *Dave Brubeck*, 69, for an excerpt from 'Eleven Four' (subdivided into 3 + 2 + 3 + 3).

[94] *Ibid.*, 55–7, 177. Brubeck was not totally alone: Roach experimented with irregular metres in jazz around the same time. Nor was it a simple matter of the focus shifting completely from polytonality to polyrhythm. McFarland argues for a continuing relevance of polytonality, as polychordal textures, to some of Brubeck's later works, including the aptly titled *Tonalpoly* (2003) for piano.

Small Orchestra (1929–30), which displays an opening sequence of 4/4, 5/4 (two bars), 3/4 (two bars), 4/4 and so on.[95] Back in Brubeck, this principle of metric flexibility to expand phrases is resumed in 'Three to Get Ready'. An initial set of four three-bar phrases in 3/4 metre (bars 1–12) is expanded in the '1st Improvisation' (bar 13ff.) via an alternating pattern of 3/4 metre (two bars) plus 4/4 (two bars); see Example 9.6a. (Highly contrasted sections of 3/4 and 4/4 metre were identified earlier as a feature of 'Love Your Enemies'.) The notion of three is projected simultaneously across several parameters: 3/4 metre, three-crotchet and three-quaver groupings, three-bar phrases, and pitch intervals of a third. Meanwhile, the lively 'Blue Rondo' (Example 9.6b), with its 9/8 metre subdivided as accented 2 + 2 + 2 + 3, creates stronger connection with Bartók than with Milhaud, specifically with the fifth of *Six Dances in Bulgarian Rhythm*,[96] which employs the same metric division at a similar 'Allegro molto' tempo. In fact, Brubeck's patterning was likely inspired by a Turkish *aksak* rhythm.[97]

The final locus, 'Unsquare Dance',[98] enables further hermeneutic enquiry into the artistic association of Brubeck and Milhaud. Conceived in a 'Moderately fast' 7/4 metre, subdivided as 2 + 2 + 3, this dance was performed by Brubeck and his Quartet. As recorded by Columbia, it begins with a six-bar vamping supplied by the piano bass and (optional) hand-clapping that, as a combined pattern, sounds all seven beats. The piano supplies the main punctuation on 1, 3 and 5, while hand-clapping counters on the offbeats: 2, 4, 6 and 7. Interestingly, such hand-clapping foreshadows a well-known later work by another of Milhaud's illustrious students: Reich's *Clapping Music* (1972) for two players. Both instances may be linked to an early, highly innovative occurrence in Milhaud's *Deux poèmes tupis* (1918).[99] These remarkable unpublished songs, 'Caïné' and 'Catiti', for women's voices and hand-clapping, were settings of texts of the Tupi people indigenous to Brazil and Paraguay. Given his own highly probable Native American heritage on his father's side,[100] Brubeck would surely have been fascinated by Milhaud's undertaking. We might also venture that, beyond his description of it as 'Deceitfully simple, it refuses to be squared,'[101] Brubeck's 'Unsquare Dance' could be regarded as offering a

---

[95] Darius Milhaud, *Concerto pour batterie et petit orchestre* (Vienna: Universal Edition, 1966).

[96] See Béla Bartók, *Mikrokosmos VI* (London and Paris: Boosey & Hawkes, 1940).

[97] Storb, '"The Duke Meets Darius Milhaud and Arnold Schönberg" (Dave Brubeck and His Teachers)', 71.

[98] See score reproduced in Storb, 'Dave Brubeck, Komponist und Pianist', 30–1.

[99] Mawer, *Darius Milhaud*, 115.

[100] See, for instance, Lees, *Cats of Any Color*, 42: 'there was Modoc Indian in the line as well'.

[101] Brubeck, liner notes, *Time Further Out*. See n. 64.

Example 9.6 Brubeck's polymetric and polyrhythmic play
(a) *Time Out*, 'Three to Get Ready' (bars 13–17)
(b) *Time Out*, 'Blue Rondo à la Turk' (bars 1–4)

Native American-inflected remaking of an archetypal American genre. (Ironically, perhaps, it also references the well-known early nineteenth-century American folksong 'Turkey in the Straw', which often received blacked-up rendition.)

The bass plus hand-clapping continues as a harmonic-rhythmic framework (a compressed blues form), over which is layered a predominantly treble riff (bars 7–12), loosely echoing the bass but with a decorative diminution of grace notes and quavers. Full melodic-rhythmic identity (further diminution) only crystallizes in the next iteration (bars 13–18); see Example 9.7a. In the ensuing section (Figs. A–B of the score arrangement; bar 19ff.) a third percussive rhythmic element joins the established interlocking mechanism: drum sticks sounded on the side of a bass drum, resulting in a simultaneous polyrhythm. This stick patterning is highly inventive and ever-varying, featuring offbeat accents, syncopations and rhythmic diminutions, so that each bar is just slightly different, thereby creating a secondary successive polyrhythm, shown in Example 9.7b.

From an interpretative stance, the ultimate comparison, maintaining the dance context and extending a Native American perspective (albeit in a very different cultural milieu), is with Milhaud's South American folklore-inspired *L'Homme*. Allusion could be made to several pertinent passages, but the most striking one is that created for Scene V, marked 'Un peu moins vif', where Milhaud evokes the following portion of Claudel's scenario:

> V. All the creatures of the forest that come to look at the sleeping Man.
> [They are] represented exclusively by rhythms and movements. No costumes.
> Male and female dancers in working clothes. Wild and furtive movements
> and all of a sudden extremely rapid and rushed. The night moth, the bird, the
> deer, the swarm of hostile things that one fends off, the leaf (a kiss on the cheek)
> etc. All this must not last for too long.[102]

To convey this tropical forest scene bursting with life and rhythmic sonority, Milhaud like Brubeck builds up his textures, from an initial six parts to an array of eighteen percussive lines, each pursuing an independent ostinato of one or two bars' length, and thus creating a most intricate simultaneous polyrhythm. In tandem, tempo is increased via 'Animez', to a final 'Vif'.[103] Clearly, Milhaud's is a serious large-scale entity, for orchestral forces; Brubeck's is of a lighter, smaller-scaled nature, initially for jazz quartet though later orchestrated. Nonetheless, both composers share a focus upon interlocking patterns, accents, syncopation, decorative diminution, and at least a semblance of improvisatory spontaneity (note Milhaud's 'Rep. ad libitum');[104] see Example 9.8.

So, while Brubeck's use of polyrhythm and long-term commitment to a series of broader 'Time Experiments' certainly demonstrate his growth into a mature, fully independent artist, pertinent hermeneutic connection may still be made between selected outputs of the two composers – their musics enjoy a special, almost collaborative, affinity.

---

[102] Darius Milhaud and Paul Claudel, *L'Homme et son désir* [piano reduction] (Vienna: Universal Edition, 1969), 25: 'V. Toutes les choses de la forêt qui viennent voir l'Homme endormi. Représentés uniquement par des rythmes et des mouvements. Pas de costumes. Danseurs et danseuses en costumes de travail. Mouvements sauvages et furtifs et tout-à-coup extrêmement rapides et précipités. Le papillon nocturne, l'oiseau, la biche, l'essaim des choses ennemies qu'on écarte, la feuille (un baiser sur la joue) etc. Tout cela ne doit pas durer trop longtemps.'

[103] Milhaud, *L'Homme*, 27 and 29, respectively.   [104] *Ibid.*, 29.

Example 9.7 Brubeck, *Time Further Out*, 'Unsquare Dance'
(a) Emergent thematic identity (bars 5–14)
(b) Polyrhythmic complex (bars 19–22)

(a)

(b)

Example 9.8 Milhaud, *L'Homme et son désir*, Scene V (bars 1–3, reduced score)

Conclusion

These historical and analytical findings support a spectrum of relationship between Milhaud and Brubeck from broad parallels through to specific, direct influence, not unexpected in an initial teacher–student relationship.[105] Moreover they strongly suggest that Milhaud's impact on Brubeck, exemplified by comparing jazz-related and other works plus underpinning theory, is greater than that acknowledged by Gioia. (Additionally, they provide a context for Brubeck's later affinity with Stravinsky.)[106] This is not in any way to undermine Brubeck's artistic

---

[105] Albeit often remarked upon, the depth of personal affection between the two is evidenced by Brubeck's eldest son being named Darius. As compositional inspiration, Brubeck kept on his wall a plaque given to him by Milhaud, comprising an image of the composer framed by quoted snippets from *La Création* (information from Richard Jeweler: personal correspondence, 17 October 2013).

[106] See McFarland, 'Dave Brubeck and Polytonal Jazz', 173–4, where a good case is made for comparing Brubeck's 'Overture' from his ballet *Glances* with Stravinsky's 'Marche du soldat' from *L'Histoire du soldat*, a work mentioned apropos Satie in Chapter 3 of this book (pages 88–9).

status and indisputable originality in his development of (and his moving beyond) modal jazz. Rather, it shows how distinctive artistic forces may come together powerfully and fruitfully to generate further cross-cultural enhancement.

Brubeck will be remembered as the jazz musician who, together with Desmond, succeeded in bringing much-needed innovation into jazz from the mid 1950s onwards via polytonality – often bitonality or extended tonality – and especially polyrhythm. He has largely realized his stated intention: 'For twenty years my aim has been to use more polytonality and polyrhythms in jazz.'[107] But, as Carl Jefferson, the owner of Concord Jazz Records, noted perceptively, with his profound interest in cultural crossover: 'Dave's music sort of transcended jazz. The wonderful thing he did, he got a lot of people to cross over from whatever they were musically into – what they thought was jazz – and they liked it.'[108] Having entered Brubeck's life during his formative years, Milhaud functioned as the single most important catalyst to this end. As with Evans and French music, the association with Milhaud may also have invested Brubeck's art with a certain intellectual cachet.[109]

But this was no one-way relationship: from Milhaud's stance, the successful teaching of jazz musicians such as Brubeck furthered his legacy, enlarging his sphere of influence beyond twentieth-century French modernism. This legacy surely gained from Brubeck's generosity, with his participation in 'An Evening in Memory of Darius Milhaud' presented at Mills in spring 1976, and 'The Milhaud Connection' given in San Francisco in spring 1993, which featured works by various Milhaud pupils.[110] (Even so, Brubeck's phenomenal public profile is of a very different order.) As Brubeck himself has attested: 'This is the way my great teacher, Darius Milhaud, approached his students; from his classroom have come electronic composers, twelve-tone serialists, romantic modern composers, jazz arrangers: music of all styles based on his solid musical foundation, but not a mirror image of Darius Milhaud.'[111] There is however a fitting balance, reciprocity and perhaps irony, that Milhaud, as a classical musician who had a serious early love affair with jazz, should teach Brubeck, as a jazz musician, the necessary tenets of classical compositional training. As

---

[107] Liner notes, *Dave Brubeck Quartet at Carnegie Hall*: quoted in Storb and Fischer, *Dave Brubeck*, 45.

[108] Quoted in Hall, *It's About Time*, 40.

[109] This view is supported by Birtwistle, 'Marking Time and Sounding Difference', 355.

[110] See concert programmes dated 23 April 1976 and 16 February 1993 (Brubeck Collection, 1-F-Concert Programs 5.2: 1976 and 1-F.17.1: January – March 1993, respectively).

[111] Brubeck quoted in Hall, *It's About Time*, 144. (Frustratingly, no source is given.)

Salmon put it, nicely, if provocatively: 'Brubeck wishes to join the pantheon of great, western composers, even as Milhaud seeks to escape them.'[112] On the larger scale, such chains of relationship may be extended – potentially almost infinitely – since Milhaud's own fascination with polytonality (and quartal harmony) leads back down a French line to Koechlin. And beyond this strict French boundary, in respect of polytonality and polyrhythm the young Stravinsky is again looking on.

Supported by our investigations, Brubeck, even more so than Milhaud, does present as that rare tightrope act of a balanced hybridity. He evinces an Eliot-like cultural embrace of musics past and present, jazz and classical, endorsing a musical equivalent of a 'conception of poetry as a living whole of all the poetry that has ever been written'.[113] Thus we conclude the most targeted composer-on-composer relations explored in this book, which yet implicate a far wider, rich intertextual network. But at the centre is the inimitable Brubeck, as the only featured musician-composer who, at the time of writing in spring 2012, was still a living legend.[114]

---

[112] Salmon, 'What Brubeck Got from Milhaud', 28. See too Feather, 'Dave Brubeck, Composer'.

[113] Eliot, 'Tradition and the Individual Talent', 39.

[114] Sadly, Brubeck died on 5 December 2012, a day before his ninety-second birthday. Among many tributes, a few may be highlighted: Daniel E. Slotnik, 'Dave Brubeck, Whose Distinctive Sound Gave Jazz New Pop, Dies at 91', *New York Times* (5 December 2012, online): 'Mr Brubeck's very personal musical language situated him far from the Bud Powell school of bebop rhythm and harmony; he relied more on chords, lots and lots of them, than on sizzling, hornlike right-hand lines.' Ivan Hewett, 'Dave Brubeck', *The Telegraph* (6 December 2012): 'Brubeck didn't have the réclame of some jazz musicians who lead tragic lives. He didn't do drugs or drink. What he had was endless curiosity combined with stubbornness. [...] he was a prophet of the current trend for bringing world music into jazz'. John Fordham, 'Dave Brubeck Obituary. American Jazz Pianist and Composer Who Annoyed the Purists by Finding Global Fame', *The Guardian* (5 December 2012): 'Brubeck's pieces are now recognised for the harmonically subtle, melodically devious and original works they are, and his most classically oriented works (such as the soft-winds Bach tribute Chorale) as triumphs in a treacherous territory in which short-changing jazz or dumbing-down symphonic composition is very hard to avoid. [...] Brubeck's real achievement was to blend European compositional ideas, very demanding rhythmic structures, jazz song-forms and improvisation in expressive and accessible ways.'

Select discography

This discography lists only the main recordings referenced in the text; it consists primarily of jazz recordings where the original LPs (or 78s) have been reissued as CDs, listed alphabetically by composer/artist and then chronologically by album. It does not include items already referenced in the Appendix of Chapter 6. No attempt has been made to achieve comprehensive coverage, or to ascertain the current availability of the listed materials.

Brubeck, Dave, *Jazz: Red Hot and Cool*: The Dave Brubeck Quartet (New York: Columbia CL 699, 1955).

Time Out: The Dave Brubeck Quartet – Dave Brubeck, Paul Desmond, Eugene Wright, Joe Morello (New York: Columbia CL 1397, 1959; reissued Columbia/Legacy CK 65122, 1997).

Time Further Out: Miró Reflections: The Dave Brubeck Quartet (New York: Columbia CS 8490, 1961).

Dave Brubeck Interchanges '54: Dave Brubeck, Paul Desmond, Bob Bates, Joe Dodge (Columbia/Legacy CK 47032, 1991).

Time Signatures: A Career Retrospective (Columbia/AllMusic C4K52945, 1992).

Dave Brubeck: The Very Best (New York: Columbia/Sony Jazz 499694-2, 2000).

Chaminade, Cécile, 'Pas des écharpes': Robert Hood Bowers (cond.), Columbia Symphony Orchestra (Columbia 1658-D, 1928).

Coltrane, John, *Giant Steps* (New York: Atlantic Records SD 1311, 1960; reissued Not Now Music NOT2CD391, 2011).

Impressions (New York and Englewood Cliffs, NJ: Impulse! Records A-42, 1963).

Davis, Miles, *Miles Ahead*: orchestra directed by Gil Evans (New York: Columbia CL 1041, 1957; reissued Columbia/Legacy CK 65121, 1997).

'Round About Midnight (New York: Columbia CL 949, 1957).

Milestones (New York: Columbia CL 1193, 1958; reissued Not Now Music NOT2CD339, 2010).

Kind of Blue (New York: Columbia CL 1355, 1959; reissued Columbia/Legacy CK 64935, 1997).

Sketches of Spain (New York: Columbia CL 1480, 1960; reissued Columbia/Legacy CK 65142, 1997).

Debussy, Claude, *Children's Corner*, on *Claude Debussy, Piano Music*: Roy Howat (pf.), 4 vols. (Tall Poppies TLP 165, 2004), vol. IV.

Children's Corner, Préludes, on *Debussy, Complete Works for Piano*: Jean-Efflam Bavouzet (pf.), 5 vols. (Colchester: Chandos Chan 10421, 2007), vols. I and III.

Ellington, Duke [Edward Kennedy], *Diminuendo in Blue/Blow by Blow,* on *Ella and Duke at the Côte d'Azur* (Verve: V6 4072-2, 1967; reissued Verve 539 030-2, 1997).

> *Mood Indigo, Black and Tan Fantasy,* on *Duke Ellington* ('Dejavu Gold Collection', Recording Arts AG: 5X042, 2007).

Evans, Bill, *New Jazz Conceptions:* Bill Evans, Teddy Kotick, Paul Motian (New York: Riverside RLP 12 223, 1956; reissued Not Now Music NOT2CD299, 2009).

> 'Young and Foolish', 'Peace Piece', 'Oleo', on *Everybody Digs Bill Evans:* Bill Evans, Sam Jones, Philly Joe Jones (New York: Riverside RLP 12 291, 1958; reissued Not Now Music NOT2CD299, 2009).

> 'Peri's Scope', 'Blue in Green', on *Portrait in Jazz:* Bill Evans Trio – Bill Evans, Scott LaFaro, Paul Motian (New York: Riverside RLP 12 315, 1960; reissued Riverside/Original Jazz Classics 20 088-2, n.d.).

> *Conversations with Myself:* Bill Evans (pf.), using three overdubbed tracks (New York: Verve V6 8526, 1963).

> 'Ornithology', on *The Solo Sessions,* 2 vols. (Milestone MCD 9170 & 9195-2, 1963), vol. II.

> 'Valse', 'Prelude', 'Pavane', 'Blue Interlude', on *Bill Evans Trio with Symphony Orchestra* (Englewood Cliffs, NJ: Verve V6 8640, 1966).

> *The Universal Mind of Bill Evans:* Bill Evans (pf.) talking to Harry Evans; directed by Louis Cavrell (New York: Rhapsody Films 9015, 1966; EFORFilms 2869016 [DVD], 2004).

> with Herbie Mann, 'Gymnopédie', on *Nirvana* (New York: Atlantic Records SD 1426, 1964).

Gershwin, George, 'Summertime', from *Porgy and Bess:* Mabel Mercer (voice), Cy Walter (pf.) (Liberty Music Shops L362, mx W 36-1, 1941); reissued on *'S Wonderful: Songs of George Gershwin – Original Recordings 1920–1949* (Naxos Nostalgia 8.120828, 2005).

Grappelli, Stéphane, 'I've Had My Moments': Stéphane Grappelli and His Hot Four (Paris: Decca P77538, F 6150, 1935); reissued on *Stéphane Grappelli,* 2 vols. (Naxos Jazz Legends 8.120688, 2003), vol. II: *Swing from Paris, Original Recordings 1935–1943.*

Handy, William C., *St. Louis Blues:* Louis Armstrong (tpt.) and His Orchestra, directed by Luis Russell (New York: OKeh 41350 [master W403495-B], 1929); reissued on *Great Original Performances 1923–1931* (Louisiana Red Hot Records RPCD 618, 1997).

Joplin, Scott, *Maple Leaf Rag, Magnetic Rag,* on *The Entertainer: The Very Best of Scott Joplin:* Joshua Rifkin (pf.) (New York: Nonesuch Records 7559 79449-2, 1996).

Legrand, Michel, *Legrand Jazz,* including 'Wild Man Blues', ''Round Midnight', 'The Jitterbug Waltz', 'Django', 'Nuages', 'In a Mist'; performers: Miles Davis, Bill Evans, John Coltrane, Michel Legrand and others (New York: Columbia CL 1250, 1958).

Milhaud, Darius, *La Création du monde, Saudades do Brazil:* Leonard Bernstein (cond.), Orchestre national de France (EMI/Angel Records 7 47845-2, 1978).

La Création du monde: John Harle (alto sax.), on *Simon Rattle, The Jazz Album*, Simon Rattle (cond.), London Sinfonietta (Hayes, Middlesex: EMI 7 47991-2, 1987).

Mingus, Charles, 'Goodbye Pork Pie Hat', on *Mingus Ah Um* (New York: Columbia 1959; reissued Columbia/Legacy CK 65512, 1998).

Parker, Charlie, 'Blues for Alice' (New York, 1951); reissued on *Charlie Parker: The Complete Savoy and Dial Studio Recordings (1944–1948)* (Savoy 92911-2, 2000).

Ravel, Maurice, *Sonate pour violon et piano*: Gérard Jarry (vn.), Georges Pludermacher (pf.), on *Maurice Ravel: Musique de chambre* (EMI 7243 5 69279-2 6, [recorded 1973] 1991).

Sonate pour violon et piano: Chantal Juillet (vn.), Pascal Rogé (pf.), on *3 Sonates pour violon* (London: Decca 448 612-2, 1996).

Reinhardt, Django, 'Nuages' (Paris: Swing, SW88 OSW146, 1940); reissued on *Django Reinhardt and Stéphane Grappelli, with the Quintet of the Hot Club of France* (Ultimate Collection, Not Now Music NOT2CD251, 2008).

'Echoes of France (*La Marseillaise*)' (London, 1946); reissued on *Intégrale Django Reinhardt, The Complete Django Reinhardt (1946–47)* (Paris: Frémeaux & Assoc. Fr B0000501BJ, 2004), vol. XIII.

Russell, George, *Cubana Be, Cubana Bop*: Dizzy Gillespie (tpt.) and His Orchestra (New York: Victor 20-3145, 1947).

A Bird in Igor's Yard: Buddy DeFranco (cl.) and His Orchestra (New York: Capitol M-11060, 1949); reissued on Lennie Tristano, Buddy DeFranco, *Crosscurrents* (Capitol Jazz Classics, 1972), vol. XIV.

Lydian M-1, on Teddy Charles, *The Teddy Charles Tentet* (New York: Atlantic Records LP 1229, 1956).

The Jazz Workshop: George Russell Smalltet (New York: RCA Victor LPM 1372, 1956).

All About Rosie, on *Brandeis Jazz Festival: Modern Jazz Concert* (Columbia WL 127, 1957); reissued on *The Birth of the Third Stream* (Columbia/Legacy CK 64929, 1996).

New York, New York: George Russell Orchestra (New York: Decca DL 7-9216 and Impulse! Records IMPD 278, 1959).

Ezz-thetics: George Russell Sextet (New York: Riverside RLP 9375, 1961).

Satie, Erik, *Orchestral Works (Parade, Trois gymnopédies, Mercure, Relâche)*: Jérôme Kaltenbach (cond.), Orchestre symphonique et lyrique de Nancy (Nancy: Naxos, 8-554279, 1997).

Schuller, Gunther (John Lewis and others), *Music for Brass* (Columbia CL 941, 1956); reissued on *The Birth of the Third Stream* (Columbia/Legacy CK 64929, 1996).

Transformation, on *Brandeis Jazz Festival: Modern Jazz Concert* (Columbia WL 127, 1957); reissued on *The Birth of the Third Stream* (Columbia/Legacy CK 64929, 1996).

Thibaudet, Jean-Yves, 'Peace Piece', on *Conversations with Bill Evans*: Jean-Yves Thibaudet (pf.) (London: Decca 455 512-2, 1997).

Select bibliography

Given the size of the combined fields of French music and jazz, this bibliography is inevitably selective; there is no intention to provide comprehensive coverage. It contains predominantly books and journal articles that are referenced in the text, both subject-based and more critical, or methodological. It includes some published transcriptions of jazz loci relevant to the case studies, but does not generally list e-sources or websites due to their more transient nature.

Abbate, Carolyn, *Unsung Voices: Opera and Musical Narrative in the Nineteenth Century* (Princeton University Press, 1988).
  'Outside Ravel's Tomb', *Journal of the American Musicological Society*, 52/3 (Fall 1999), 465–530.
Adorno, Theodor W., 'On Jazz [1936]', in *Essays on Music*, ed. Richard Leppert and Eng. trans. Susan H. Gillespie (Berkeley and Los Angeles, CA: University of California Press, 2002), 470–95.
Aikin, Jim, 'Bill Evans [transcriptions]', *Contemporary Keyboard*, 6/6 (June 1980), 44–55.
Ake, David, 'Learning Jazz, Teaching Jazz', in Mervyn Cooke and David Horn (eds.), *The Cambridge Companion to Jazz* (Cambridge University Press, 2002), 255–69.
Ansermet, Ernest, 'Sur un orchestre nègre', *La Revue romande*, no. 10 (15 October 1919), 10–13.
Arbey, Dominique, 'Poulenc et le jazz', *Les Cahiers de Francis Poulenc*, 3 (2011), 129–33.
Archer-Shaw, Petrine, *Negrophilia: Avant-Garde Paris and Black Culture in the 1920s* (London: Thames and Hudson, 2000).
Armstrong, Louis, *Satchmo: My Life in New Orleans* (New York: Prentice-Hall, 1954).
  'What Is Swing?', in Robert Walser (ed.), *Keeping Time: Readings in Jazz History* (New York: Oxford University Press, 1999), 73–6.
Baker, David N. (ed.), *New Perspectives on Jazz* (Washington DC: Smithsonian Institution Press, 1990).
Baker, David N., Lida Belt and Herman C. Hudson (eds.), *The Black Composer Speaks* (Metuchen, NJ and London: Scarecrow Press, 1978).
Bakhtin, Mikhail, *Problems of Dostoevsky's Poetics*, ed. and Eng. trans. Caryl Emerson (Minneapolis, MN: University of Minnesota Press, 1984).

Bakriges, Christopher George, 'African American Musical Avant-gardism', PhD dissertation (York University, 2001).

Barham, Jeremy, 'Rhizomes and Plateaus: Rethinking Jazz Historiography and the Jazz–"Classical" Relationship', *Jazz Research Journal*, 3/2 (2009), 171–202.

Barrett, Samuel, '*Kind of Blue* and the Economy of Modal Jazz', *Popular Music*, 25/2 (May 2006), 185–200.

Barthes, Roland, 'The Death of the Author', in *Image, Music, Text*, Eng. trans. Stephen Heath (London: Fontana Press, 1977), 142–8.

Bauer, Marion, 'L'Influence du jazz-band', *La Revue musicale*, 5 (1 April 1924), 31–6.

Bellman, Jonathan (ed.), *The Exotic in Western Music* (Boston, MA: Northeastern University Press, 1998).

Benjamin, Walter, 'L'Œuvre d'art à l'époque de sa reproduction mécanisée', French trans. Pierre Klossowski, in *Zeitschrift für Sozialforschung* (Paris: Félix Alcan, 1936), vol. V, 40–68.

Berardinelli, Paula, 'Bill Evans: His Contributions as a Jazz Pianist and an Analysis of His Musical Style' (PhD dissertation, New York University, 1992).

Berendt, Joachim E., *The Jazz Book: From Ragtime to Fusion and Beyond* (Westport, CT: Lawrence Hill, 1982).

Berlin, Edward A., *Ragtime: A Musical and Cultural History* (Berkeley and Los Angeles, CA: University of California Press, 1980).

   King of Ragtime: Scott Joplin and His Era (New York: Oxford University Press, 1994).

   'Ragtime', in Stanley Sadie (ed.), *The New Grove Dictionary of Music and Musicians*, 29 vols. (London: Macmillan, 2001), vol. XX, 755–9.

Berliner, Paul F., *Thinking in Jazz: The Infinite Art of Improvisation* (University of Chicago Press, 1994).

Berton, Ralph, *Remembering Bix: A Memoir of the Jazz Age* (New York: W. H. Allen Press, 1974; reprinted Da Capo Press, 2000).

Bhabha, Homi K., *The Location of Culture* (London: Routledge, 1994).

Birtwistle, Andy, 'Marking Time and Sounding Difference: Brubeck, Temporality and Modernity', *Popular Music*, 29/3 (2010), 351–71.

Bizet, René, 'Le Music-hall: *La Revue nègre*', *Candide* (8 October 1925), 8.

Blake, Jody, *Le Tumulte noir: Modernist Art and Popular Entertainment in Jazz-Age Paris, 1900–1930* (University Park, PA: Pennsylvania University Press, 1999).

Bloom, Harold, *The Anxiety of Influence: A Theory of Poetry* (New York: Oxford University Press, 1973).

   A Map of Misreading, revised edition (New York: Oxford University Press, 2003; orig. publ. 1975).

Born, Georgina, and David Hesmondhalgh (eds.), *Western Music and Its Others: Difference, Representation, and Appropriation in Music* (Berkeley and Los Angeles, CA: University of California Press, 2000).

Boulez, Pierre, 'Speaking, Playing, Singing', in *Orientations: Collected Writings*, ed. Jean-Jacques Nattiez and Eng. trans. Martin Cooper (Cambridge, MA: Harvard University Press, 1986), 330–43.

Bourdieu, Pierre, *Outline of a Theory of Practice*, Eng. trans. Richard Nice (Cambridge University Press, 1977).

Bowie, Andrew, 'Jazz', in J. P. E. Harper-Scott and Jim Samson (eds.), *An Introduction to Music Studies* (Cambridge University Press, 2009), 176–85.

Bowman, Wayne D., 'Music as Social and Political Force', in *Philosophical Perspectives on Music* (Oxford and New York: Oxford University Press, 1998), 304–55.

Britt, Stan, 'The River Stops Flowing', *Jazz Journal International*, 33/11 (1980), 15.

Brody, Elaine, *Paris: The Musical Kaleidoscope 1870–1925* (London: Robson Books, 1988).

Brooks, George Benson, 'George Russell', *Jazz Review*, 3/2 (February 1960), 38–9.

Brothers, Thomas (ed.), *Louis Armstrong in His Own Words: Selected Writings* (New York: Oxford University Press, 2001).

Brown, Matthew, *Debussy Redux: The Impact of His Music on Popular Culture* (Bloomington, IN: Indiana University Press, 2012).

Brubeck, Darius, '1959: The Beginning of Beyond', in Mervyn Cooke and David Horn (eds.), *The Cambridge Companion to Jazz* (Cambridge University Press, 2002), 177–201.

Brubeck, Dave, 'Jazz's Evolvement as Art Form', *Down Beat*, 17/1 and 17/2 (27 January 1950), 12, 15.

'Jazz Perspective [1951]', *Perspectives U.S.A.*, 15 (Spring 1956), 22–8; reprinted in David Meltzer (ed.), *Reading Jazz* (San Francisco, CA: Mercury House, 1993), 202–7.

Brubeck, Dave, Doug Ramsey and Juul Anthonissen, Liner notes for *Time Signatures: A Career Retrospective* (Columbia/AllMusic C4K52945, 1992).

Bruhn, Siglind, *Images and Ideas in Modern French Piano Music: The Extra-Musical Subtext in Piano Works by Ravel, Debussy, and Messiaen* (Hillsdale, NY: Pendragon Press, 1997).

Buckland, Sidney, and Myriam Chimènes (eds.), *Francis Poulenc: Music, Art and Literature* (Aldershot: Ashgate, 1999).

Butler, Christopher, *Early Modernism: Literature, Music and Painting in Europe 1900–1916* (Oxford: Clarendon Press, 1994).

Modernism: A Very Short Introduction (Oxford University Press, 2010).

Caddy, Davinia, 'Parisian Cake Walks', *19th-Century Music*, 30/3 (Spring 2007), 288–317.

Carew, Les, 'How Are the Mighty ··· ?' *Nostalgia*, 10/40 (October 1990), 19–21.

Case, Brian, 'The Quiet Innovator', *Melody Maker* (27 September 1980), 28.

Cerchiari, Luca, Laurent Cugny and Franz Kerschbaumer (eds.), *Eurojazzland: Jazz and European Sources, Dynamics, and Contexts* (Boston, MA: Northeastern University Press, 2012).

Cerulli, Dom, 'George Russell', *Down Beat*, 25/10 (29 May 1958), 15–16.

Chefdor, Monique, *Blaise Cendrars* (Boston, MA: Twayne, 1980).

Citron, Marcia J., *Cécile Chaminade: A Bio-Bibliography* (Westport, CT: Greenwood Press, 1988).

Clement, Brett, 'Modal Tonicization in Rock: The Special Case of the Lydian Scale', *Gamut*, 6/1 (2013), 95–142.

Cocteau, Jean, *Le Coq et l'arlequin* (Paris: Éditions de la Sirène, 1918); reprinted in *Œuvres complètes de Jean Cocteau*, 11 vols. (Paris: Marguerat, 1946–51), vol. IX (*Le Rappel à l'ordre*), 13–69; Eng. trans. as 'The Cock and the Harlequin', in *A Call to Order*, trans. Rollo H. Myers (New York: Haskell House, 1974).

     Portraits-souvenir, 1900–1914 (Paris: Grasset, 1935).

     Correspondance Jean Cocteau-Darius Milhaud, eds. Pierre Caizergues and Josiane Mas (Montpellier: Université Paul Valéry, 1992).

Cœuroy, André, and André Schaeffner, *Le Jazz* (Paris: Éditions Claude Aveline, 1926).

Collaer, Paul, *Darius Milhaud* (Paris and Geneva: Éditions Slatkine, 1982); ed. and Eng. trans. Jane Hohfeld Galante (San Francisco, CA: San Francisco Press, 1988).

Collier, James Lincoln, *Louis Armstrong: An American Genius* (New York: Oxford University Press, 1983).

Cook, Nicholas, 'Theorizing Musical Meaning', *Music Theory Spectrum*, 23/2 (Fall 2001), 170–95.

Cooke, Mervyn, *Jazz* (London: Thames and Hudson, 1998).

     'Jazz among the Classics, and the Case of Duke Ellington', in Mervyn Cooke and David Horn (eds.), *The Cambridge Companion to Jazz* (Cambridge University Press, 2002), 153–73.

Cotro, Vincent, Laurent Cugny and Philippe Gumplowicz (eds.), *La Catastrophe apprivoisée: Regards sur le jazz en France*, Jazz en France (Paris: Outre Mesure, 2013).

Cowley, John H., 'Don't Leave Me Here: Non-Commercial Blues: The Field Trips, 1924–60', in Lawrence Cohn (ed.), *Nothing But the Blues: The Music and the Musicians* (New York: Abbeville Press, 1993).

Curtis, Susan, *Dancing to a Black Man's Tune: A Life of Scott Joplin* (Columbia, MO: University of Missouri Press, 1994).

Dauer, Alfons Michael, 'Das Lydisch-Chromatische Tonsystem von George Russell und seine Anwendung', *Jazzforschung*, 14 (1982), 61–132.

Davis, Francis, *Jazz and Its Discontents: A Francis Davis Reader* (New York: Da Capo Press, 2004).

Davis, Miles, *Kind of Blue*, transcribed scores by Rob Du Boff, Mark Vinci, Mark Davis and Josh Davis (Milwaukee, WI: Hal-Leonard, n.d. [*c*.2000]).

Davis, Miles, with Quincy Troupe, *Miles: The Autobiography* (London: Macmillan, 1989).

Dawdy, Shannon Lee, *Building the Devil's Empire: French Colonial New Orleans* (University of Chicago Press, 2008).

Debussy, Claude, *Monsieur Croche et autres écrits*, ed. François Lesure (Paris: Gallimard, 1971).

     Letters, ed. François Lesure, Eng. trans. Roger Nichols (London: Faber and Faber, 1987).

Delage, Maurice, 'La Musique du jazz', *Revue Pleyel* (April 1926), 18–20.

Delaunay, Charles, *Hot Discography* (Paris: Hot Jazz, 1936).

Deleuze, Gilles, and Félix Guattari, *A Thousand Plateaus*, Eng. trans. Brian Massumi (London and New York: Continuum, 2004).

DeLong, Thomas A., *Pops: Paul Whiteman, King of Jazz* (Piscataway: New Century Publishers, 1983).

Derrida, Jacques, 'Différance', in *Margins of Philosophy*, Eng. trans. Alan Bass, (University of Chicago Press, 1982), 1–27.

  'The Other's Language: Jacques Derrida Interviews Ornette Coleman, 23 June 1997', Eng. trans. Timothy S. Murphy, *Genre*, 36 (Summer 2004), 319–29; originally published in *Les Inrockuptibles*, 115 (20 August–2 September 1997), 37–40, 43; reproduced at *Jazz Studies Online*: http://jazzstudiesonline.org/.

DeVoto, Mark, 'Harmony in the Chamber Music', in Deborah Mawer (ed.), *The Cambridge Companion to Ravel* (Cambridge University Press, 2000), 97–117.

Dickinson, Peter, *Marigold: The Music of Billy Mayerl* (Oxford and New York: Oxford University Press, 1999).

Drake, Jeremy, *The Operas of Darius Milhaud* (New York and London: Garland Press, 1989).

Dregni, Michael, *Gypsy Jazz: In Search of Django Reinhardt and the Soul of Gypsy Swing* (New York: Oxford University Press, 2008).

Druskin, Mikhail, *Igor Stravinsky: His Personality, Works and Views*, Eng. trans. Martin Cooper (Cambridge University Press, 1983).

Duchesneau, Michel, '*La Revue musicale* (1920–40) and the Founding of a Modern Music', in Zdravko Blažekovic and Barbara Dobbs Mackenzie (eds.), *Music's Intellectual History*, RILM Perspectives I (New York: Répertoire International de Littérature Musicale, 2009), 743–50.

Duhamel, Georges, *America the Menace: Scenes from the Life of the Future*, Eng. trans. Charles Miner Thompson (London: George Allen and Unwin, 1931).

Dunsby, Jonathan, 'Criteria of Correctness in Music Theory and Analysis', in Anthony Pople (ed.), *Theory, Analysis and Meaning in Music* (Cambridge University Press, 1994), 77–85.

Eliot, T. S., 'Tradition and the Individual Talent [1919]', *Selected Essays* (London: Faber, 1951), 13–22; reprinted in *Perspecta*, 19 (1982), 36–42.

  Selected Prose, ed. Frank Kermode (New York: Harcourt Brace, 1975).

Ellington, Edward Kennedy, 'Certainly It's Music!', *Listen*, IV/12 (October 1944), 5–6; reprinted in Mark Tucker (ed.), *The Duke Ellington Reader* (New York: Oxford University Press, 1993), 246–8.

  Music Is My Mistress (New York: Doubleday, 1973; reprinted Da Capo Press, 1976).

Enstice, Wayne, and Paul Rubin, *Jazz Spoken Here: Conversations with Twenty-Two Musicians* (Baton Rouge: Louisiana State University Press, 1992; New York: Da Capo Press, 1994).

Evans, Bill, Liner notes for Miles Davis, *Kind of Blue* (New York: Columbia CL 1355, 1959; reissued Columbia/Legacy CK 64935, 1997).

Evans, Philip R., and Linda K. Evans, *Bix: The Leon Bix Beiderbecke Story* (Bakersfield, CA: Prelike Press, 1998).

Fairweather, Digby, Ian Carr and Brian Priestley, *Jazz: The Essential Companion* (London: Grafton, 1987); revised as *Jazz: The Rough Guide*, second edition (London: Rough Guides, 2000).

Fauconnier, Gilles, and Mark Turner, *The Way We Think: Conceptual Blending and the Mind's Hidden Complexities* (New York: Basic Books, 2002).

Feather, Leonard, 'Dave Brubeck, Composer', *Down Beat*, 33/13 (30 June 1966), 18–20.

Forte, Allen, 'Pitch-Class Set Genera and the Origin of Modern Harmonic Species', *Journal of Music Theory*, 32 (1988), 187–270.

Fourquet, Philippe, 'De l'impressionisme dans le jazz: Une étude de l'influence du langage musical français du début de la siècle sur les musiciens de jazz américains, de Bix Beiderbecke à Bill Evans' (Master's dissertation, Université de Paris IV [Sorbonne], 1993).

Fréjaville, Gustave, 'L'Orchestre du Dr Moreau', *Débats* (9 June 1927), n.p.

Fry, Andy M., '"De la musique nègre au jazz français": African-American Music and Musicians in Interwar France' (D.Phil. dissertation, University of Oxford, 2003).

  'Re-thinking the *Revue nègre*: Black Musical Theatre in Interwar Paris', in Julie Brown (ed.), *Western Music and Race* (Cambridge University Press, 2007), 258–75.

  'Remembrance of Jazz Past: Sidney Bechet in France', in Jane F. Fulcher (ed.), *The Oxford Handbook of the New Cultural History of Music* (New York: Oxford University Press, 2011), 307–31.

  Paris Blues: African American Music and French Popular Culture 1920–1960 (University of Chicago Press, 2014).

Gabbard, Krin (ed.), *Jazz among the Discourses* (Durham, NC: Duke University Press, 1995).

Gates Jr, Henry Louis, *The Signifying Monkey: A Theory of African-American Literary Criticism* (New York: Oxford University Press, 1988).

Gavin, James, 'Homophobia in Jazz', *JazzTimes* (December 2001), n.p. (http://jazztimes.com/articles/20073-homophobia-in-jazz).

Gerber, Alain, *Bill Evans* (Paris: Librairie Arthème Fayard, 2001).

Gilbert, Steven, *The Music of Gershwin* (New Haven, CT and London: Yale University Press, 1995).

Ginibre, Jean-Louis, 'Il parle, le trio dont on parle', *Jazz Magazine*, 116 (March 1965), 28–33; reprinted and translated as 'Bill Evans: Time Remembered', *JazzTimes*, 27/1 (February 1997), 32–5, 38, 144–5.

Gioia, Ted, *The Imperfect Art: Reflections of Jazz and Modern Culture* (New York: Oxford University Press, 1988).

  West Coast Jazz: Modern Jazz in California, 1945–1960 (New York and Oxford: Oxford University Press, 1992).

Gleason, Ralph J., 'Brubeck', *Down Beat*, 24/15 (25 July 1957), 13–14, 54.

'David Brubeck Remembers: "They Said I Was Too Far Out"', *Down Beat*, 25/16 (8 August 1957), 17–19, 39.

Goffin, Robert, *Aux frontières du jazz*, second edition (Paris: Éditions du Sagittaire, 1932).

   Louis Armstrong, le roi du jazz (Paris: Pierre Seghers, 1947); Eng. trans. as *Horn of Plenty: The Story of Louis Armstrong*, trans. James F. Bezou (New York: Allen, Towne & Heath, 1947).

Gorbman, Claudia, *Unheard Melodies: Narrative Film Music* (Bloomington, IN: Indiana University Press, 1987).

Gordon, Max, *Live at the Village Vanguard* (New York: Da Capo Press, 1980).

Gottlieb, Robert (ed.), *Reading Jazz: A Gathering of Autobiography, Reportage, and Criticism from 1919 to Now* (University of Chicago Press, 1996; London: Bloomsbury, 1997).

Grant, Madison, *The Passing of a Great Race*, fourth edition (London and New York: G. Bell & Sons, 1921).

Gridley, Mark, *Jazz Styles: History and Analysis*, fourth edition (Englewood Cliffs, NJ: Prentice-Hall, 1994).

Griffiths, Paul, *Modern Music: A Concise History from Debussy to Boulez* (London: Thames and Hudson, 1986).

   Modern Music and After, third edition (New York: Oxford University Press, 2010).

Guerpin, Martin, 'Why Did Art Music Composers Pay Attention to "Jazz"? The Impact of "Jazz" on the French Musical Field, 1908–24', in Luca Cerchiari, Laurent Cugny and Franz Kerschbaumer (eds.), *Eurojazzland: Jazz and European Sources, Dynamics, and Contexts* (Boston, MA: Northeastern University Press, 2012), 47–80.

   'Bricktop, le jazz et la mondanité (1926–1936)', in Vincent Cotro, Laurent Cugny and Philippe Gumplowicz (eds.), *La Catastrophe apprivoisée: Regards sur le jazz en France*, Jazz en France (Paris: Outre Mesure, 2013), 33–55.

Gumplowicz, Philippe, 'Hugues Panassié 1930–1934: une cause et un système', in Cotro, Cugny and Gumplowicz (eds.), *La Catastrophe apprivoisée*, 113–19.

Häger, Bengt, *Ballets Suédois* (London: Thames and Hudson, 1990).

Hajdu, David, *Lush Life: A Biography of Billy Strayhorn* (New York: Farrar, Straus & Giroux, 1997).

Hall, Fred M., *It's About Time: The Dave Brubeck Story* (Fayetteville, AR: University of Arkansas Press, 1996).

Handy, W. C., *Father of the Blues: An Autobiography*, ed. Arna Bontemps (New York: Macmillan, 1941).

Haney, Lynn, *Naked at the Feast: A Biography of Josephine Baker* (London: Robson Books, 1981).

Hardie, Daniel, *Jazz Historiography: The Story of Jazz History Writing* (Bloomington, IN: iUniverse, 2013).

Harrison, Charles, *Primitivism, Cubism, Abstraction: The Early Twentieth Century* (New Haven and London: Yale University Press/Open University Press, 1993).

Harrison, Max, 'George Russell – Rational Anthems, Phase One', *The Wire*, 3 (Spring 1983), 30–1.

Haydon, Geoffrey Jennings, 'A Study of the Exchange of Influences between the Music of Early Twentieth-Century Parisian Composers and Ragtime, Blues, and Early Jazz', DMA dissertation (University of Texas at Austin, 1992).

Heining, Duncan, *George Russell: The Story of an American Composer* (Lanham, MD: Scarecrow Press, 2010).

Helgeland, Kirsten Joan, 'Jazz and the Classics: A Study of American Crossover Solo Piano Works from 1920 to 1935', PhD dissertation (University of Cincinnati, 1999).

Hendler, Maximilian, 'Gedanken zum "Lydischen Konzept"', *Jazzforschung*, 16 (1984), 163–71.

Hennessey, Brian, 'Bill Evans: A Person I Knew', *Jazz Journal International*, 38/3 (March 1985), 8–11; part 2 (October 1985), 11–13.

Hentoff, Nat, 'Introducing Bill Evans', *Jazz Review*, 2/9 (1959), 26–8.

Heyer, David J., 'Applying Schenkerian Theory to Mainstream Jazz: A Justification for an Orthodox Approach', *Music Theory Online*, 18/3 (September 2012): *Festschrift for Steve Larson* (http://mtosmt.org/issues/mto.12.18.3/mto.12.18.3.heyer.php).

Heyman, Barbara, 'Stravinsky and Ragtime', *The Musical Quarterly*, 68/4 (October 1982), 543–62.

Hindemith, Paul, *The Craft of Musical Composition*, 2 vols., fourth edition (Mainz and London: Schott, 1942), vol. I: *Theory*.

Hodeir, André, *Hommes et problèmes du jazz* (Paris: Portulan, 1954; reprinted Marseille: Parenthèses, 1996); Eng. trans. as *Jazz: Its Evolution and Essence*, trans. David Noakes (London: Jazz Book Club, 1958).

  'Perspective of Modern Jazz: Popularity or Recognition?', *Down Beat*, 26/17 (20 August 1959), 40–2.

Hoefer, George, 'The Magnificent Gypsy', *Down Beat*, 33/14 (14 July 1966), 21–2, 25.

Hoerée, Arthur, 'Le Jazz', *La Revue musicale*, 8 (1 October 1927), 213–41.

Horsham, Michael, *'20s & '30s Style* (London: Grange Books, 1994).

Howat, Roy, *The Art of French Piano Music: Debussy, Ravel, Fauré, Chabrier* (New Haven, CT and London: Yale University Press, 2009).

Huddleston, Sisley, *Back to Montparnasse: Glimpses of Broadway in Bohemia* (Philadelphia, PA and London: J. B. Lippincott, 1931).

Huret, Jules, *En Amérique – De New-York à la Nouvelle-Orléans* (Paris: Fasquelle, 1904).

Hyde, Martha, 'Neoclassic and Anachronistic Impulses in Twentieth-Century Music', *Music Theory Spectrum*, 18/2 (1996), 200–35.

Hylton, Jack, 'The British Touch', *Gramophone* (September 1927), 146.

  (in interview with Perceval Graves) 'Taking or Inflicting Pains', *Melody Maker and British Metronome* (May 1928), 513–14.

  'Over Hurdles – Into Ditches: What Bands Should Avoid and What's Wanted', *Melody Maker* (October 1929), 921.

'Naissance et vie du jazz', *Le Courrier musical et théâtral* (15 March 1932), n.p.

'The High Finance of Jazz', *Rhythm*, 13/136 (January 1939), 3–7.

Ioakimidis, Demètre, 'Bill Evans ⋯ ou l'art pour l'art', *Jazz hot*, 161 (January 1961), 14–17.

Israels, Chuck, 'Bill Evans (1929–1980): A Musical Memoir', *The Musical Quarterly*, 71/2 (1985), 109–15.

Ivry, Benjamin, *Maurice Ravel: A Life* (New York: Welcome Rain, 2000).

Jackson, Jeffrey H., 'Making Jazz French: The Reception of Jazz Music in Paris, 1927–1934', *French Historical Studies*, 25/1 (Winter 2002), 149–70.

Making Jazz French: Music and Modern Life in Interwar Paris (Durham, NC and London: Duke University Press, 2003).

James, Burnett, 'The Impressionism of Duke Ellington', *Jazz Monthly*, 3/8 (October 1957), 5–7.

Jarocinski, Stefan, *Debussy: Impressionism and Symbolism*, Eng. trans. Rollo Myers (London: Eulenberg Books, 1976).

Jeanneret, Albert, 'Le Nègre et le jazz', *La Revue musicale*, 8 (1 July 1927), 24–7.

Jeanquartier, André, 'Kritische Anmerkungen zum "Lydian Chromatic Concept"', *Jazzforschung*, 16 (1984), 9–41.

Jenkins, Todd S., *I Know What I Know: The Music of Charles Mingus* (Westport, CT and London: Praeger, 2006).

Jones, Olive, 'Conversation with ⋯ George Russell: A New Theory for Jazz', *Black Perspective in Music*, 2/1 (Spring 1974), 63–74.

Jordan, Matthew F., *Le Jazz: Jazz and French Cultural Identity* (Urbana, IL: University of Illinois Press, 2010).

Kahn, Ashley, *Kind of Blue: The Making of the Miles Davis Masterpiece* (London: Granta Books, 2000).

Keil, Charles, *Urban Blues* (University of Chicago Press, 1966; reprinted 1991).

Kelly, Barbara L., 'History and Homage', in Deborah Mawer (ed.), *The Cambridge Companion to Ravel* (Cambridge University Press, 2000), 7–26.

Tradition and Style in the Works of Darius Milhaud, 1912–1939 (Aldershot: Ashgate, 2003).

Music and Ultra-Modernism in France: A Fragile Consensus, 1913–1939 (Woodbridge: Boydell & Brewer, 2013).

Kernfeld, Barry, 'Improvisation', in *What to Listen for in Jazz* (New Haven, CT and London: Yale University Press, 1995), 119–58.

(ed.), *The New Grove Dictionary of Jazz*, second edition, 3 vols. (New York: Oxford University Press, 2002).

'Blues Progression', in Barry Kernfeld (ed.), *The New Grove Dictionary of Jazz*, second edition, 3 vols. (New York: Oxford University Press, 2002), vol. I, 255–6.

'Miles (Dewey, III), Davis', in Barry Kernfeld (ed.), *The New Grove Dictionary of Jazz*, second edition, 3 vols. (New York: Oxford University Press, 2002), vol. I, 573–7.

Kerschbaumer, Franz, 'Impressionistische Strukturen im Jazz', *Jazzforschung*, 31 (1999), 65–74.

Klein, Jean-Claude, and J. Barrie Jones, 'Borrowing, Syncretism, Hybridisation: The Parisian Revue of the 1920s', *Popular Music*, 5 (1985), 175–87.

Klein, Michael L., *Intertextuality* in *Western Art Music* (Bloomington, IN: Indiana University Press, 2005).

Knox, Keith, 'Bill Evans – An Introduction', *Jazz Monthly*, 12/8 (1966), 5–7.

Korsyn, Kevin, 'Towards a New Poetics of Musical Influence', *Music Analysis*, 10/1 (1991), 3–72.

Kramer, Lawrence, *Music as Cultural Practice, 1800–1900* (Berkeley and Los Angeles, CA: University of California Press, 1990).

   Classical Music and Postmodern Knowledge (Berkeley and Los Angeles, CA: University of California Press, 1995).

   'Powers of Blackness: Africanist Discourse in Modern Concert Music', *Black Music Research Journal*, 16/1 (Spring 1996), 53–70; reprinted as 'Powers of Blackness: Jazz and the Blues in Modern Concert Music', in *Musical Meaning: Toward a Critical History* (Berkeley and Los Angeles, CA: University of California Press, 2002), 194–215.

   'Chopin at the Funeral: Episodes in the History of Modern Death', *Journal of the American Musicological Society*, 54 (Spring 2001), 97–125.

   Opera and Modern Culture, Wagner and Strauss (Berkeley and Los Angeles, CA: University of California Press, 2004).

   Interpreting Music (Berkeley and Los Angeles, CA: University of California Press, 2010).

Kulenovic, Vuk, 'The Lydian Concept', *Sonus: A Journal of Investigations into Global Musical Possibilities*, 14/1 (Fall 1993), 55–64.

Lago, Manoel Aranha Correa do, 'Brazilian Sources in Milhaud's *Le Bœuf sur le toit*: A Discussion and a Musical Analysis', *Latin American Music Review*, 23/1 (Spring/Summer 2002), 1–59.

Lambert, Constant, *Music Ho!: A Study of Music in Decline* (London: Faber and Faber, 1934).

Lambert, G. E., 'Bix Beiderbecke', *Jazz Monthly*, 6/4 (June 1960), 7–8, 30.

Lane, Jeremy F., *Jazz and Machine-Age Imperialism: Music, 'Race,' and Intellectuals in France, 1918–45* (Ann Arbor, MI: University of Michigan Press, 2013).

Langham Smith, Richard (ed.), *Debussy Studies* (Cambridge University Press, 1997).

Langham Smith, Richard, and François Lesure (eds.), *Debussy on Music: The Critical Writings of the Great French Composer Claude Debussy* (London: Martin Secker & Warburg, 1977).

Larson, Steve, 'Schenkerian Analysis of Modern Jazz', PhD dissertation, 3 vols. (University of Michigan, 1987); publ. as *Analysing Jazz: A Schenkerian Approach*, Harmonologica, Studies in Music Theory, 15 (Hillsdale, NY: Pendragon Press, 2009).

   'Schenkerian Analysis of Modern Jazz: Questions about Method', *Music Theory Spectrum* 20/2 (1998), 209–41.

'Composition versus Improvisation?', *Journal of Music Theory*, 49/2 (2005), 241–75.

'Rhythmic Displacement in the Music of Bill Evans', in David Gagné and Poundie Burstein (eds.), *Structure and Meaning in Tonal Music: Festschrift in Honor of Carl Schachter* (Hillsdale, NY: Pendragon Press, 2006), 103–22.

Lees, Gene, 'The Poet: Bill Evans', in *Meet Me at Jim and Andy's: Jazz Musicians and Their World* (Oxford University Press, 1988); reprinted in Robert Gottlieb (ed.), *Reading Jazz: A Gathering of Autobiography, Reportage, and Criticism from 1919 to Now* (London: Bloomsbury, 1997), 419–44.

Cats of Any Color: Jazz, Black and White (New York and Oxford: Oxford University Press, 1995).

Léger, Fernand, 'The Invented Theater' (1924), in Henning Rischbieter (ed.), *Art and the Stage in the Twentieth Century*, Eng. trans. Michael Bullock (Greenwich, CT: New York Graphic Society, 1968), 97.

Leiris, Michel, *Journal 1922–1989* (Paris: Gallimard, 1992).

Leroi, Pierre, 'Jack Hylton à l'Opéra', *L'Édition musicale vivante*, 37 (February 1931), 12–13.

Levine, Lawrence W., *Highbrow/Lowbrow: The Emergence of Cultural Hierarchy in America* (Cambridge, MA: Harvard University Press, 1988).

Lewis, George E., 'Improvised Music after 1950: Afrological and Eurological Perspectives', *Black Music Research Journal*, 16/1 (1996), 92–122.

Lion, Jean-Pierre, *Bix: The Definitive Biography of a Jazz Legend* (New York: Continuum, 2005).

Little, Eric, 'Should Drummers Use Parts?', *Melody Maker and British Metronome* (March 1927), 263.

Locke, Ralph, *Musical Exoticism: Images and Reflections* (Cambridge University Press, 2011).

Logan, Pamela W., *Jack Hylton Presents* (London: British Film Institute (BFI) Publishing, 1995).

Long, Michael, *Beautiful Monsters: Imagining the Classic in Musical Media* (Berkeley and Los Angeles, CA: University of California Press, 2008).

Lucas, Leighton, 'Arranging on the Stand', *Melody Maker and British Metronome* (March 1927), 264.

'What I Hate in "Jazz"', *Melody Maker and British Metronome* (February 1928), 137–9.

Manskleid, Felix, 'Bill Evans Discusses the Jazz Scene', *Jazz Monthly*, 6/5 (July 1960), 10–11.

Mawer, Deborah, *Darius Milhaud: Modality and Structure in Music of the 1920s* (Aldershot: Scolar Press, 1997; reprinted 2000).

'Musical Objects and Machines', in Deborah Mawer (ed.), *The Cambridge Companion to Ravel* (Cambridge University Press, 2000), 47–67.

The Ballets of Maurice Ravel: Creation and Interpretation (Aldershot: Ashgate, 2006).

'"Parisomania"? Jack Hylton and the French Connection', *Journal of the Royal Musical Association*, 133/2 (November 2008), 270–317; French trans. as '"Parisomanie"? La French Connection de Jack Hylton', in Vincent Cotro, Laurent Cugny and Philippe Gumplowicz (eds.), *La Catastrophe apprivoisée: Regards sur le jazz en France*, Jazz en France (Paris: Outre Mesure, 2013), 67–99.

'Jazzing a Classic: Hylton and Stravinsky's *Mavra* at the Paris Opéra', *Twentieth-Century Music*, 6/2 (September 2009), 155–82.

'Crossing Borders II: Ravel's Theory and Practice of Jazz' and 'Appendix: Itinerary for Ravel's Tour', in Deborah Mawer (ed.), *Ravel Studies* (Cambridge University Press, 2010), 110–13, 114–37.

'French Music Reconfigured in the Modal Jazz of Bill Evans', in Janne Mäkelä (ed.), *The Jazz Chameleon: The Refereed Proceedings of the 9th Nordic Jazz Conference* (Helsinki: The Finnish Jazz and Pop Archive, 2011), 77–89; Portuguese trans. as 'A música francesa reconfigurada no jazz modal de Bill Evans', trans. Fausto Borém, *Per Musi*, 28 (2013), 7–14.

McCarthy, Albert J., *The Dance Band Era: The Dancing Decades from Ragtime to Swing, 1910–1950* (London: Studio Vista, 1971).

McClary, Susan, *Feminine Endings: Music, Gender, and Sexuality* (Minnesota, MN: University of Minnesota Press, 1991).

McFarland, Mark, 'Dave Brubeck and Polytonal Jazz', *Jazz Perspectives*, 3/2 (2009), 153–76.

'Schenker and the Tonal Jazz Repertory: A Response to Martin', *Music Theory Online*, 18/3 (September 2012): *Festschrift for Steve Larson* (http://mtosmt.org/issues/mto.12.18.3/mto.12.18.3.mcfarland.php).

McKinley, Ann, 'Debussy and American Minstrelsy', *The Black Perspective in Music*, 14/3 (1986), 249–58.

Mehegan, John, *Contemporary Piano Styles*, Jazz Improvisation IV (New York: Watson-Guptill Publications/Simon and Schuster, 1965).

Meister, Barbara, *Music Musique: French and American Piano Composition in the Jazz Age* (Bloomington, IN: Indiana University Press, 2006).

Meltzer, David (ed.), *Reading Jazz* (San Francisco, CA: Mercury House, 1993).

Mendl, Robert W. S., *The Appeal of Jazz* (London: P. Allen & Co., 1927).

Messiaen, Olivier, *Technique de mon langage musical*, 2 vols. (Paris: Alphonse Leduc, 1944).

Messing, Scott, *Neoclassicism in Music from the Genesis of the Concept through the Stravinsky/Schoenberg Polemic*, Studies in Musicology 101 (Ann Arbor, MI: UMI Research Press, 1988).

'Polemic as History: The Case of Neoclassicism', *Journal of Musicology*, 9/4 (Fall 1991), 481–97.

Metzer, David, *Quotation and Cultural Meaning in Twentieth-Century Music* (Cambridge University Press, 2003).

Meyer, Leonard B., 'Innovation, Choice, and the History of Music', *Critical Inquiry*, 9/3 (1980), 517–44.

Style and Music: Theory, History, and Ideology (University of Chicago Press, 1989; reprinted 1997).

Middleton, Richard, *Studying Popular Music* (Milton Keynes and Philadelphia, PA: Open University Press, 1990).

Milhaud, Darius, 'Polytonalité et atonalité', *La Revue musicale*, 4 (February 1923), 29–44; Eng. trans. as 'Polytonality and Atonality', *Pro Musica Quarterly*, 2 (October 1924), n.p.

'L'Évolution du jazz-band et la musique des nègres d'Amérique du nord', *Le Courrier musical*, 25/9 (1 May 1923), 163ff.; Eng. trans. as 'The Jazz Band and Negro Music', *Living Age*, 323 (October 1924), 169–73; reprinted in Milhaud, *Études* (Paris: Éditions Claude Aveline, 1927), 5–19.

'Les Ressources nouvelles de la musique (jazz-band et instruments mécaniques)', *L'Esprit nouveau*, 25 (July 1924), n.p.

'À propos du jazz', undated typescript (Basle: Paul Sacher Stiftung, Collection Darius Milhaud), 1–7; published in two parts in *L'Humanité* (3 August 1926), 5 and (4 August 1926), 5.

Ma vie heureuse (Paris: Pierre Belfond, 1974; reprinted 1987); orig. publ. as *Notes sans musique* (Paris: René Julliard, 1949); Eng. trans. as *My Happy Life: An Autobiography*, trans. Donald Evans, George Hall and Christopher Palmer (London and New York: Marion Boyars, 1995).

Mitchell, Jack, 'Nardis: Bill Evans Remembered', *The Wire*, 3 (1983), 22–3.

Monson, Ingrid, 'The Problem with White Hipness: Race, Gender, and Cultural Conceptions in Jazz Historical Discourse', *Journal of the American Musicological Society*, 48/3 (1995), 396–422.

'Oh Freedom: George Russell, John Coltrane, and Modal Jazz', in Bruno Nettl and Melinda Russell (eds.), *In the Course of Performance: Studies in the World of Musical Improvisation* (University of Chicago Press, 1998), 149–68.

Mouëllic, Gilles, *Jazz et cinéma* (Paris: Cahiers du cinéma, 2000).

Muret, Maurice, *Le Crépuscule des nations blanches* (Paris: Payot, 1925); Eng. trans. as *The Twilight of the White Races*, trans. Lida Touzalin (London: T. Fisher Unwin, 1926).

Murray, Edward, and Barry Kernfeld, 'Bill Evans (ii)', in Barry Kernfeld (ed.), *The New Grove Dictionary of Jazz*, second edition, 3 vols. (New York: Oxford University Press, 2002), vol. I, 723–6.

Narmour, Eugene, *The Analysis and Cognition of Basic Melodic Structures: The Implication-Realization Model* (University of Chicago Press, 1990).

Nattiez, Jean-Jacques, *Music and Discourse: Toward a Semiology of Music*, Eng. trans. Carolyn Abbate (Princeton University Press, 1990).

Nicholls, Tracey 'Dominant Positions: John Coltrane, Michel Foucault, and the Politics of Representation', *Critical Studies in Improvisation/Études critiques en improvisation*, 2/1 (2006), 1–13.

Nichols, Roger, 'Cock and Harlequin', *The Listener* (30 January 1986), 30.

The Harlequin Years: Music in Paris 1917–1929 (London: Thames and Hudson, 2002).

Ravel (New Haven, CT and London: Yale University Press, 2011).

Nott, James J., *Music for the People: Popular Music and Dance in Interwar Britain* (Oxford and New York: Oxford University Press, 2002).

Oliver, Paul, and Barry Kernfeld, 'Blues', in Barry Kernfeld (ed.), *The New Grove Dictionary of Jazz*, second edition, 3 vols. (London: Oxford University Press, 2002), vol. I, 247–55.

Oliver, Paul, Tony Russell, Robert M. W. Dixon, John Goodrich and Howard Rye, *Yonder Come the Blues* (Cambridge University Press, 2001).

Olsen, David C., and Tom Roed (eds.), *The Artistry of Bill Evans*, transcriptions by Pascal Wetzel, introduced by Charles Blancq (Miami, FL: CPP/Belwin/Warner Bros. Publications, 1989).

Orenstein, Arbie (ed.), *Maurice Ravel: Lettres, écrits, entretiens*, French trans. Dennis Collins (Paris: Flammarion, 1989); Eng. trans. as *A Ravel Reader: Correspondence, Articles, Interviews* (New York: Columbia University Press, 1990).

Orledge, Robert, 'Satie's Approach to Composition in His Later Years (1913–24)', *Proceedings of the Royal Musical Association*, 111 (1984–5), 155–79.

Satie the Composer (Cambridge University Press, 1990).

'Satie and America', *American Music*, 18/1 (Spring 2000), 78–102.

'Evocations of Exoticism', in Deborah Mawer (ed.), *The Cambridge Companion to Ravel* (Cambridge University Press, 2000), 27–46.

(ed.), *Satie Remembered* (London: Faber and Faber, 1995).

Oswald, John, 'Bettered by the Borrower: The Ethics of Musical Debt', in Christoph Cox and Daniel Warner (eds.), *Audio Culture: Readings in Modern Music* (New York: Continuum, 2004), 131–7.

Panassié, Hugues, 'Le Jazz "hot"', *L'Édition musicale vivante* (February 1930), 9–11.

'Le Jazz "hot"', *La Revue musicale*, 11 (June 1930), 481–94.

Le Jazz hot (Paris: Éditions R.-A. Corrêa, 1934); Eng. trans. as *Hot Jazz*, trans. Lyle and Eleanor Dowling (London; New York: Cassell & Co., 1936).

La Véritable Musique de jazz (Paris: Robert Laffont, 1946); Eng. trans. as *The Real Jazz*, trans. Anne Sorelle Williams (New York: Smith & Durrell, 1942).

La Musique de jazz et le swing (Paris: Éditions R.-A. Corrêa, 1943).

Louis Armstrong, Les Maîtres du jazz (Paris, 1947; Nouvelles Éditions Latines, 1969; Eng. trans. New York: Charles Scribner's Sons, 1971), vol. I.

'Taking Oneself Seriously', *Jazz Music*, 8/1 (January–February 1957), 15–20.

Parks, Richard S., *The Music of Claude Debussy* (New Haven, CT and London: Yale University Press, 1989).

Parsonage, Catherine, *The Evolution of Jazz in Britain, 1880–1935* (Aldershot: Ashgate, 2005).

Paudras, Francis, 'Ravel et le jazz', *Musical*, 4 (June 1987), 36–51.

Pekar, Harvey, 'Third Stream Jazz', *Jazz Monthly*, 8/10 (December 1962), 7–9.

Perchard, Tom, 'Tradition, Modernity and the Supernatural Swing: Re-reading "Primitivism" in Hugues Panassié's Writing on Jazz', *Popular Music*, 30/1 (2011), 25–45.

Peress, Maurice, *Dvořák to Duke Ellington: A Conductor Explores America's Music and Its African American Roots* (New York: Oxford University Press, 2004).

Perloff, Marjorie, *Unoriginal Genius: Poetry by Other Means in the New Century* (University of Chicago Press, 2012).

Perloff, Nancy, *Art and the Everyday: Popular Entertainment and the Circle of Erik Satie* (Oxford: Clarendon Press, 1993).

Perret, Carine, 'L'Adoption du jazz par Darius Milhaud et Maurice Ravel: l'esprit plus que la lettre', *Revue de musicologie*, 89/2 (2003), 311–47.

Pettinger, Peter, *Bill Evans: How My Heart Sings* (New Haven, CT and London: Yale University Press, 1998).

Porter, Lewis, 'The "Blues" Connotation in Ornette Coleman's Music – and Some General Thoughts on the Relationship of Blues to Jazz', *Annual Review of Jazz Studies*, 7 (1994–5), 75–99.

Potter, Caroline (ed.), *Erik Satie: Music, Art and Literature* (Aldershot: Ashgate, 2013).

Priestley, Brian, *Mingus: A Critical Biography* (New York: Da Capo Press, 1984).
  Chasin' The Bird: The Life and Legacy of Charlie Parker (Oxford and New York: Oxford University Press, 2007).

Puri, Michael J., 'Memory, Pastiche, and Aestheticism in Ravel and Proust', in Deborah Mawer (ed.), *Ravel Studies* (Cambridge University Press, 2010), 56–73.
  Ravel the Decadent: Memory, Sublimation, and Desire (New York: Oxford University Press, 2011).

Radano, Ronald M., *New Musical Figurations: Anthony Braxton's Cultural Critique* (University of Chicago Press, 1993).

Rasula, Jed, 'Jazz as Decal for the European Avant Garde', in Heike Raphael-Hernandez, *Blackening Europe: The African American Presence* (New York: Routledge, 2004), 13–34.

Ravel, Maurice, 'Take Jazz Seriously!', *Musical Digest*, 13/3 (March 1928), 49, 51.
  Contemporary Music, Rice Institute Pamphlet, 15/2 (April 1928), 131–45.

Reilly, Jack, *The Harmony of Bill Evans*, 2 vols. (Milwaukee, WI: Hal Leonard Corporation, 2010), vol. II.

Reisner, Robert G. (ed.), *Bird: The Legend of Charlie Parker* (New York: Da Capo Press, 1975).

Reynolds, Christine, '*Parade*: Ballet réaliste', in Caroline Potter (ed.), *Erik Satie: Music, Art and Literature* (Aldershot: Ashgate, 2013), 137–60.

Riley, John Howard, 'A Critical Examination of George Russell's Lydian Concept of Tonal Organization for Improvisation', MA dissertation (Indiana University, 1967).

Roberts, Paul, *Images: The Piano Music of Claude Debussy* (Portland, OR: Amadeus Press, 2001).

Robinson, J. Bradford, 'The Jazz Essays of Theodor Adorno: Some Thoughts on Jazz Reception in Weimar Germany', *Popular Music*, 13/1 (January 1994), 1–25.
  'Blue Note (i)', in Barry Kernfeld (ed.), *The New Grove Dictionary of Jazz*, second edition, 3 vols. (New York: Oxford University Press, 2002), vol. I, 245–6.

'Riff', in Barry Kernfeld (ed.), *The New Grove Dictionary of Jazz*, second edition, 3 vols. (New York: Oxford University Press, 2002), vol. III, 415–16.

Roddy, Joseph, 'Ravel in America', *High Fidelity Magazine* (March 1975), 58–63.

Rogers, M. Robert, 'Jazz Influence on French Music', *The Musical Quarterly*, 21/1 (January 1935), 53–68.

Roland-Manuel, (Alexis), 'Une esquisse autobiographique de Maurice Ravel [1928]', *La Revue musicale*, 19 (special issue, December 1938), 17–23.

'Des valses à *La Valse* (1911–1921)', in Colette, Maurice Delage [et al.], *Maurice Ravel par quelques-uns de ses familiers* (Paris: Éditions du tambourinaire, 1939), 141–51.

Rose, Phyllis, *Jazz Cleopatra* (London: Chatto & Windus, 1989).

Roy Jr, James G., Carman Moore and Barry Kernfeld, 'George (Allan) Russell', in Barry Kernfeld (ed.), *The New Grove Dictionary of Jazz*, second edition, 3 vols. (New York: Oxford University Press, 2002), vol. III, 474–5.

Russell, George, *Lydian Chromatic Concept of Tonal Organization*, fourth edition (Brookline, MA: Concept Publishing Company, 2001; orig. publ. 1953), vol. I: *The Art and Science of Tonal Gravity* [of two projected volumes].

Rust, Brian, and Sandy Forbes, *British Dance Bands on Record, 1911–45 and Supplement*, revised edition (Harrow: General Gramophone Publications, 1989).

Sachs, Maurice, *Au temps du bœuf sur le toit* (Paris: Éditions de la Nouvelle Revue critique, 1948).

Said, Edward W., *Orientalism* (New York: Pantheon, 1978).

Salmon, John, 'What Brubeck Got from Milhaud', *American Music Teacher* (February–March 1992), 26–9, 76.

'The Classical Side of Dave Brubeck', *American Music Teacher* (February–March 2001), 23–8.

Sargeant, Winthrop, *Jazz: Hot and Hybrid* (New York and London: Jazz Book Club Edition, 1938, enlarged edition 1959); revised and enlarged as *Jazz: A History* (New York: McGraw-Hill, 1964).

Satie, Erik, *The Writings of Erik Satie*, ed. Nigel E. Wilkins (London: Eulenburg Books, 1980).

A Mammal's Notebook: Collected Writings of Erik Satie, ed. Ornella Volta, Eng. trans. Antony Melville (London: Atlas Press, 1996).

Schaeffner, André, 'Le Jazz', *La Revue musicale*, 9 (1 November 1927), 72–6.

Schiff, David, *Gershwin: Rhapsody in Blue* (Cambridge University Press, 1997).

Schmidt, Carl B., *Entrancing Muse, A Documented Biography of Francis Poulenc* (Hillsdale, NY: Pendragon Press, 2001).

Schuller, Gunther, 'Sonny Rollins and the Challenge of Thematic Improvisation', *Jazz Review*, 1/1 (November 1958), 6–11.

Early Jazz: Its Roots and Musical Development (New York: Oxford University Press, 1968; reprinted 1986).

Musings: The Musical Worlds of Gunther Schuller (New York: Oxford University Press, 1986).

'The Influence of Jazz on the History and Development of Concert Music', in David N. Baker (ed.), *New Perspectives on Jazz* (Washington DC: Smithsonian Institution Press, 1990), 9–24.

'Jazz and Musical Exoticism', in Jonathan Bellman (ed.), *The Exotic in Western Music* (Boston, MA: Northeastern University Press, 1998), 283–91.

The Swing Era, The Development of Jazz, 1930–1945 (New York: Oxford University Press, 2001).

Gunther Schuller: A Life in Pursuit of Music and Beauty (Rochester, NY: University of Rochester Press, 2011).

Scott, Derek B., 'Music, Culture and Society: Changes in Perspective', in Derek B. Scott (ed.), *Music, Culture, and Society: A Reader* (Oxford University Press, 2000), 1–19.

From the Erotic to the Demonic: On Critical Musicology (New York: Oxford University Press, 2003).

Shack, William A., *Harlem in Montmartre* (Berkeley and Los Angeles, CA: University of California Press, 2001).

Shadwick, Keith, *Jazz: Legends of Style* (London: Quintet Publishing, 1998).

Bill Evans: Everything Happens to Me – A Musical Biography (San Francisco, CA: Backbeat Books, 2002).

Shipton, Alyn, *A New History of Jazz*, revised and updated edition (New York and London: Continuum, 2007).

Solie, Ruth A. (ed.), *Musicology and Difference: Gender and Sexuality in Music Scholarship* (Berkeley and Los Angeles, CA: University of California Press, 1993).

Sowerwine, Charles, *France since 1870: Culture, Society and the Making of the Republic*, second edition (Basingstoke and New York: Palgrave Macmillan, 2009).

Stein, Daniel, 'Negotiating Primitivist Modernisms: Louis Armstrong, Robert Goffin, and the Transatlantic Jazz Debate', *European Journal of American Studies* [online] 2 (2011), n.p. (http://ejas.revues.org/9395).

Stoddard, Lothrop, *The Rising Tide of Color against White-World Supremacy* (New York: Chapman & Hall, 1921).

Storb, Ilse, 'Dave Brubeck, Komponist und Pianist', *Jazzforschung*, 13 (1981), 9–44.

'An Interview with Dave Brubeck [25 April 1980]', *Jazzforschung*, 16 (1984), 143–60.

'"The Duke Meets Darius Milhaud and Arnold Schönberg" (Dave Brubeck and His Teachers)', *Jazzforschung*, 28 (1996), 63–75.

Storb, Ilse, and Klaus-Gotthard Fischer, *Dave Brubeck: Improvisationen und Kompositionen – Die Idee der kulturellen Wechselbeziehungen* (Frankfurt am Main: Peter Lang, 1991); Eng. trans. as *Dave Brubeck: Improvisations and Compositions – The Idea of Cultural Exchange*, trans. Bert Thompson (New York: Peter Lang Publishing, 1994).

Stovall, Tyler, *Paris noir: African Americans in the City of Light* (Boston, MA: Houghton Mifflin, 1996).

Straus, Joseph N., 'Stravinsky's Tonal Axis', *Journal of Music Theory*, 26 (1982), 261–90.

    Remaking the Past: Musical Modernism and the Influence of the Tonal Tradition (Cambridge, MA: Harvard University Press, 1990).

Stravinsky, Igor, *Chroniques de ma vie* (Paris: Denoël et Steel, 1935); Eng. trans. as *Chronicles of My Life* (London: Gollancz, 1936); republished as *An Autobiography* (London: Calder and Boyars, 1975).

Stravinsky, Igor, and Robert Craft, *Memories and Commentaries* (London: Faber and Faber, 1960; reprinted 2002).

    Dialogues and a Diary (Garden City, NY: Doubleday, 1963; Berkeley and Los Angeles, CA: University of California Press, 1982).

Stuart, Walter, Stan Applebaum and 'Bugs Bower', *Encyclopedia of Improvisation* (New York: Charles Colin, 1972).

Suddarth, Roscoe Seldon, 'French Stewardship of Jazz: The Case of France Musique and France Culture', MA dissertation (University of Maryland, College Park, 2008).

Szwed, John, *So What: The Life of Miles Davis* (New York: Random House, 2012).

Taruskin, Richard, 'Revising Revision', *Journal of the American Musicological Society*, 46/1 (1993), 114–38.

Thibaudet, Jean-Yves, Liner notes for *Conversations with Bill Evans* (London: Decca 455 512-2, 1997).

Tomlinson, Gary, 'Cultural Dialogics and Jazz: A White Historian Signifies', *Black Music Research Journal*, 11 (1991), 229–64; reprinted in Katherine Bergeron and Philip V. Bohlman (eds.), *Disciplining Music: Musicology and Its Canons* (University of Chicago Press, 1992), 64–94.

Tournès, Ludovic, *New Orleans sur Seine: Histoire du jazz en France* (Paris: Librairie Arthème Fayard, 1999).

Tucker, Mark (ed.), *The Duke Ellington Reader* (New York: Oxford University Press, 1993).

Tymoczko, Dmitri, *A Geometry of Music: Harmony and Counterpoint in the Extended Common Practice* (New York: Oxford University Press, 2011).

Ulanov, Barry, *Duke Ellington* (New York: Creative Age Press, 1946).

Vallas, Léon, *The Theories of Claude Debussy*, Eng. trans. Maire O'Brien (London: Oxford University Press, 1929).

van den Toorn, Pieter C., *The Music of Igor Stravinsky* (New Haven, CT and London: Yale University Press, 1983).

    'Neoclassicism Revised', in *Music, Politics, and the Academy* (Berkeley and Los Angeles, CA: University of California Press, 1995), 143–78.

Vautel, Clément, 'Le Jazz à l'Opéra', *Cyrano*, 350 (1 March 1931), 1.

Vedey, Julien, *Band Leaders* (London: Rockliff, 1950).

Volta, Ornella, *Erik Satie et la tradition populaire* (Paris: Fondation Satie, 1988).

Vuillermoz, Émile, *Musiques d'aujourd'hui* (Paris: Crès et cie, 1923).

Waldo, Terry, *This Is Ragtime* (New York: Da Capo Press, 1991; reprinted 2009).

Walser, Robert, 'Out of Notes: Signification, Interpretation, and the Problem of Miles Davis', *The Musical Quarterly*, 77/2 (1993), 343–65.

(ed.), *Keeping Time: Readings in Jazz History* (New York: Oxford University Press, 1999).

Walsh, Stephen, *The Music of Stravinsky* (Oxford: Clarendon Press, 1993).

Wang, Richard, and Barry Kernfeld, 'Dave [David Warren] Brubeck', in Barry Kernfeld (ed.), *The New Grove Dictionary of Jazz*, second edition, 3 vols. (New York: Oxford University Press, 2002), vol. I, 329–31.

Watkins, Glenn, *Pyramids at the Louvre: Music, Culture, and Collage from Stravinsky to the Postmodernists* (Cambridge, MA and London: Harvard University Press, 1994).

Whiteman, Paul, and Mary Margaret McBride, *Jazz* (New York: J. H. Sears, 1926).

Whitesell, Lloyd, 'Erotic Ambiguity in Ravel's Music', in Deborah Mawer (ed.), *Ravel Studies* (Cambridge University Press, 2010), 74–91.

Whiting, Steven Moore, *Satie the Bohemian: From Cabaret to Concert Hall* (Oxford University Press, 1999).

Whittall, Arnold, 'Hunting for Harmony' [review of Dmitri Tymoczko, *A Geometry of Music*], *Musical Times*, 152 (Winter 2011), 93–102.

Whyton, Tony, 'Europe and the New Jazz Studies', in Luca Cerchiari, Laurent Cugny and Franz Kerschbaumer (eds.), *Eurojazzland: Jazz and European Sources, Dynamics, and Contexts* (Boston, MA: Northeastern University Press, 2012), 366–80.

Wiéner, Jean, *Allegro Appassionato* (Paris: Pierre Belfond, 1978).

Williams, Katherine, 'Valuing Jazz: Cross-Cultural Comparisons of the Classical Influence in Jazz', PhD dissertation (University of Nottingham, 2012).

Williams, Martin T., *The Jazz Tradition*, second revised edition (Oxford University Press, 1993).

Wilmer, Valerie, 'Conversations with Bill Evans', *Jazzbeat*, 2/4 (March 1965), 4–5.

Woideck, Carl (ed.), *Charlie Parker: Six Decades of Commentary* (New York: Schirmer Books, 1998).

Woodley, Ronald, 'Style and Practice in the Early Recordings', in Deborah Mawer (ed.), *The Cambridge Companion to Ravel* (Cambridge University Press, 2000), 213–39.

Worton, Michael, and Judith Still (eds.), *Intertextuality: Theories and Practices* (Manchester and New York: Manchester University Press, 1990).

Wyatt, Robert, and John A. Johnson (eds.), *The Gershwin Reader* (New York: Oxford University Press, 2004).

Index

Abbate, Carolyn, 55, 205
Adorno, Theodor, 41–2
Aikin, Jim, 62
American Ballet Theater, 260
analysis
  approaches to, 61–6
  motivic analysis, 61–2, 80–4, 115, 118, 119,
      121–3, 127, 158, 226–9
  pitch-set class theory, 65, 198, 257
  voiceleading analysis, xv, 64–5, 117–22, 221,
      222, 226, 227, 229, 252
Ancien Régime, 204
Ansermet, Ernest, 40, 89
Antheil, George, 31
  Ballet mécanique, 114
  Jazz Symphony, A, 31
Apollinaire, Guillaume, 17, 90
Armstrong, Louis ('Satchmo'), 23, 108, 143
  St. Louis Blues, 96, 101, 108
  West End Blues, 83, 143
Arndt, Felix, 83
  Desecration Rag, 83
Arnold, Billy, 46, 102, 137–8
art nègre, 18, 74, 100
Astruc, Gabriel, 20
atonality, 252, 257
Auric, Georges, 31–2
  Adieu New York!, 31–2, 102
avant-garde, 39, 45, 53, 75, 106, 113

Babbitt, Milton, 196
Bach, Johann Sebastian, 26, 67, 104, 115, 202,
      240
Bacharach, Burt, 243
Baker, Chet, 49–50
Baker, Josephine, 29, 75
Bakst, Léon, 99
Ballets russes, 18, 88
Ballets suédois, 113, 115, 203, 205
Baresel, Alfred, 41
Barham, Jeremy, 193
baroque, 61–2, 118, 120, 134, 204
Barrett, Samuel, 15
Barthes, Roland, 54
Bartók, Béla, 38, 257
  Contrasts, 38
  Six Dances in Bulgarian Rhythm, 265
Basie, William James 'Count', 247
Beatles, The
  'Help', 65
bebop, 34, 197

Bechet, Sidney, 23
Beethoven, Ludwig van, 50, 219
Beiderbecke, Bix, 25
  In a Mist, 25
Belle Époque, 16
Benjamin, Walter, 41–2
Berg, Alban, 215, 220
Berlin, Edward, 18
Berlin, Irving, 71
  Alexander's Ragtime Band, 143
  That Mysterious Rag, 90–5
Berliner, Paul, 222
Bernac, Pierre, 51
Bernstein, Leonard, 239
  On the Town 'Some Other Time', 230
Bertelin, Albert, 204
Bertin, Pierre, 106
big bands, 23–4, 27
Bill Evans Trio, 219
Bintley, David
  Take Five, 254
birdsong, 37, 52, 234, 239
Birtwistle, Andy, 253
Bizet, Georges, 166, 183
  Carmen, 180–2
  Petite Suite: Jeux d'enfants, 180
Bizet, René, 46–7
Black Swan records, 101
Blake, Eubie, 21
Bloom, Harold, 55, 58, 202–3, 209, 214
  Anxiety of Influence, The, 202
  Map of Misreading, A, 202–3
blue note, 32, 34, 117, 120
blues, 19–20, 31, 105, 141–2, 145
  blues scale, 61, 109–10, 118, 120, 121
  blues seventh, 121, 132, 154
  blues third, 85, 109–11, 117, 120, 152, 153,
      154
  twelve-bar blues form, 19, 34, 61, 117, 125–7,
      151–2
Bolcom, William, 243
Bolden, Charles 'Buddy', 22
boogie-woogie, 212
Börlin, Jean, 114, 133, 205
  Sculpture nègre, 114
Born, Georgina, 55
borrowing, 22, 57–60, 76, 92, 95, 146, 152,
      228, 230
Boulanger, Georges, 45
Boulanger, Lili, 223, 241
Boulanger, Nadia, 35

Made in the USA
Las Vegas, NV
08 July 2021

26105092R00177